the years on MOUNT OREAD

the years on

A REVISION
AND EXTENSION OF | *Across the Years on Mount Oread*

UNIVERSITY OF KANSAS PRESS ⨠ LAWRENCE ⨠ 1955

MOUNT OREAD

by **ROBERT TAFT**

Professor of Chemistry
University of Kansas

author of

Photography and the American Scene

Artists and Illustrators of the Old West

378.781
T/12

PRINTED IN THE U.S.A.

BY THE UNIVERSITY OF KANSAS PRESS

LAWRENCE, KANSAS

TO MY SON BOB, OF THE CLASS OF 1944,
AND TO ALL MY OTHER STUDENTS OF THIRTY YEARS
WHO HAVE PATIENTLY—OR IMPATIENTLY—
BORNE WITH ME IN BAILEY LABORATORY
THIS VOLUME IS INSCRIBED WITH AFFECTION AND RESPECT.

Preface

THIS EDITION of the history of the University of Kansas, like its immediate predecessor, makes no claim as a formal evaluation or complete account of the many aspects of University life. Possessing neither the intelligence nor the superior craftsmanship which a professional historian has recently pointed out are necessary for the writing of university histories, I have attempted to give the main facts in the evolution of the University in a more or less connected fashion. I have made extensive use of contemporary account, of anecdote, and especially of picture, a use which it is hoped will add some measure of lighter touch to an otherwise dry and labored story. To my mind the contemporary accounts and pictures also throw a very considerable, and at times quite different, light upon the tedious and heavy recital of narrated events.

Much of the earlier portion of this book remains essentially the same as in its predecessor published in 1941. Wording has been changed here and there, some corrections have been made, some additional material has been added, and the notes have been expanded somewhat. Sections 75-82 are entirely new, bringing the account up-to-date as of the present year.

I am indebted for valuable aid in this edition to my research assistant, Kermit R. Sewell; to Miss Mildred Clodfelter, assistant alumni secretary; to Mr. Raymond Nichols, executive secretary of the University; to Professor Clyde K. Hyder, editor of the University of Kansas Press; to Mr. Fred S. Montgomery of the Bureau of Visual Instruction; and to my friend, John H. Nelson. Mr. Robert Vosper, director of the University Libraries, has kindly placed at my disposal many facilities in Watson Library during this revision and extension of the University history.

ROBERT TAFT

Watson Library, May 25, 1954

Preface to the First Edition

IN THE PAGES which follow, I have attempted to describe for its former students, alumni, faculty, and friends some of the main facts in the growth of the University of Kansas from 1866 to 1941. Origins and beginnings have purposely been given prominence, not only because of the human interest that inevitably attaches to origins, but also because a knowledge of beginnings furnishes the most effective measuring stick for determining growth and change. I realize, of course, that most of the measurement will have to be done by the reader from his personal knowledge, for no one knows better than I how incomplete is my story; but in the time and space available I have attempted to trace briefly and informally a variety of aspects in the development of the University. I have likewise used frequent contemporary quotation and picture in the attempt to re-create the atmosphere of past years—something which seems to me most necessary in securing an intelligent understanding of our bygone life. A book following these methods, it is also hoped, will prove of wider interest than would a simple catalog or recital of events. The history of the University does indeed include an intensely stirring adventure in democratic education—an adventure that deserves something more than mere chronicle.

Fortunately, many of the omissions from these pages can be supplied by the reader. Using this book as a framework, if he will also use memory and imagination, the reader may create for himself a far more complete "history" than could be covered in a volume many times the size of the present one.

The sources upon which the content of this book is based have been cited in the notes after Section 75, although not all my notes have been there included. In addition to the primary purpose of authenticating my facts, however, I have given enough, I believe, to serve as a key to any one who may attempt a more extended history of the University. The research in locating this material has been extensive but not exhaustive; and I do not doubt that future investigation will show flaws in my work. However, if in reading this tale, you find that your recollection of specific events does not agree with my account, please remember that I have secured my information from contemporary published sources. It is possible, of course, that the original published account may be incorrect; whenever possible, however, supplementary and corroborative information has been sought, when the matter seemed important.

The reader will find, in the use of this book, no table of contents; but the titles of sections have been included in the index. One further point should be kept in mind in the use of the present volume. I have occasionally called attention to enrollment figures of the University as the years passed. These figures, unless otherwise stated, refer to the total student enrollment, and not to the number on the campus at any one time; the figures used have been taken directly from contemporary catalogs.

I am indebted to a great number of former students and friends of the University for the use of photographs,—to so many, in fact, that it would be impossible to enumerate them all here. Only a small number of the photographs submitted could be used, but even those not directly used in this volume have been of help in dating and understanding those actually employed. Since all could not be mentioned, it has seemed just to me that no acknowledgement should be made to those whose photographs were actually used. I trust that if an individual recognizes one of his own photographs in these pages, the recognition, with the general acknowledgement, will be return in part for the indebtedness of the University to each of the contributors.

A number of friends have given so generously of their time and talents that acknowledgement in person must be made. My sincere thanks are therefore expressed to Victor Kalin, of the class of 1942, who drew, from rather unsatisfactory photographs, the portraits of the first faculty and of Chancellors Fraser and Marvin; to Robert Sudlow, of the class of 1942, who drew the sketch of Mount Oread reproduced opposite page 1; to Professor T. D. Jones of the Department of Design and to Betty Ann Leasure, of the class of 1941, who designed the attractive book cover; to Charles M. Baker, Librarian of the University, who provided me with special facilities in Watson Library for my work; to Barbara and Catherine Owen, who typed and re-typed these pages; to Oren Bingham, University photographer, who was of real aid in the preparation of illustrations. The aid of the staff of the Kansas State Historical Society in supplying certain illustrations and source material is also gratefully acknowledged. I am especially indebted to Thomas C. Ryther, Superintendent of the Bureau of Printing, for his extensive work in the publication of this volume; to Raymond F. Nichols for his help in reading proofs; and to Professors U. G. Mitchell, F. E. Melvin, and Rose Morgan, and Miss Cora Dolbee, who read and criticized this book in manuscript form. Miss Maud Smelser, of Watson Library, has also read the manuscript and, in addition, has been of inestimable help in locating sources and material. All have contributed materially to the reliability and readability of these pages.

The responsibility for opinions expressed, for selection of material herein included, for the research back of it, and for any errors of commission or omission is, however, chargeable to me alone.   ROBERT TAFT

Watson Library, May 1, 1941

Why mourn the young flame laughing in
    the wood
With tears upon the ashes? I could laugh
All night remembering, forgetting half
The happy times before the world was old.
Do you remember, friends—?

—John G. Neihardt,
The Song of the Messiah, 1935.

Mount Oread eighty-seven years ago! The western slope of Mount Oread, looking south, is here shown in a photograph taken in 1867—probably from a point just east of the Stadium. The Campanile now occupies a site high up on the rise above the right end of the fence in the foreground; Green Hall and Bailey Laboratory eventually appeared on the skyline near the center of the picture.

1. Mount Oread

TO YOU who view Mount Oread through the bright and enchanting haze of memory, this prologue will not be necessary. To others not so fortunate, it should be pointed out that Mount Oread, lying in the state of Kansas some thirty miles distant from her eastern border, is, like Kansas itself, not only a physical reality but a state of mind, a remembrance of the happy golden days of youth.

As I write these lines on a late autumn afternoon, the whistle blows and classes are over. The air is filled with the noise of many moving feet, of calls and shrill voices, and of clamorous cars, whose range of pitch indicates wide latitude in date of vintage. Next year, and the year after, and for years to come, the places of the students will be taken by others, who, in action if not in dress, will not differ greatly from those of the present. We who teach will also be replaced by our successors, but Mount Oread and the University will steadfastly remain, a lofty and sturdy beacon in an ever changing world.

Mount Oread has not always been this busy spot of youth and learning. Its history extends into the dim reaches of the geologic past, but the written records lie almost solely in the past one hundred years and of course are part and parcel of the thrilling tale of all eastern Kansas. This section of Kansas is no flat and level plain, but rather it is a series of rolling hills and sharp ridges, the valleys between having been patiently carved by its many streams. The older streams have made broad valleys, leaving an upland rising usually from the stream floor with gently ascending slopes, but occasionally sharp bluffs have been formed where the hard limestone has resisted the advances of the restless, turbulent water.

Two of these streams, the Kaw (or the Kansas River, to be polite) and the Wakarusa are responsible for Mount Oread. Coming together at a moderate angle they have left wide valleys behind them, but encountering hard strata, they have formed a ridge dividing the two valleys, which in places rises abruptly several hundred feet above the floor below. This ridge, for some miles, runs roughly east and west, but near its eastern extremity, turns sharply north and forms a promontory only half a mile or so from the Kaw. From this promontory there is obtained a sweeping view of both valleys. "As far as the eye can reach," wrote a traveler of over a century ago as he stood on such a point, "he sees nothing but a beautiful green carpet, save here and there a cluster of trees; he hears nothing but the feathered songsters of the air, and *feels* nothing but a solemn awe in view of this infinite display of creative power."

Even before the day of the traveler, on this height stood many a Kanza warrior viewing a land that was literally the happy hunting ground. From this promontory, Monchonsia, chief of the Kanza tribe, may have viewed the great flood of 1844, which transformed the region into a vast inland sea. As the waters receded and time passed by, Monchonsia could also have seen from this same headland a growing number of caravans bound for the Shining Mountains, and for the oceans beyond, caravans whose predecessors for a quarter of a century had gradually deepened the ruts of the famous Oregon Trail. As still more years passed, the intermittent caravans had swelled to the proportions of a tremendous and continuous procession that stretched its dusty way from the Missouri River to the Pacific Ocean. For, beginning in 1849, there plodded up the southern slope of Mount Oread a vast emigration bound for the golden land of California. One branch of the great California and Oregon Trail thus passed over the very ground which is now part of the University campus, and many a campfire gleamed on summer nights from the crest where now throngs of students tread.

Even after 1849 the emigration continued and numerous were the travelers who cast envious eyes on the fertile valleys below, once they had gained Mount Oread's height. But the land was reserved for its original inhabitants "as long as the grass should grow and the water should run." Water stopped running and grass ceased to grow in a few short years as far as the politicians in Washington were concerned; for, in 1854, the land was removed from the red man's domain and given to the white man.

Among the first to settle the new territory was a band of New Englanders who, on the first day of August, 1854, camped on this same promontory and found the land beneath them good and their journey at an end. Thus was Lawrence born and the promontory named, for this pioneer band called the ridge "Mount Oread" the self-same day; "Mount Oread" from Oread Institute in a far-off town in Massachusetts, which, like the present University, occupied a commanding site overlooking its town.

Few were the months after the original settlement was made before the strife of territorial days began. The shrilling screams of hatred, urged to greater and greater fury by the fanatics on both sides, in time reached crescendo, and "bloody Kansas" with its woes became the cry of orators throughout the land.

2. Organizing the University

The first meeting of the Board of Regents of the Kansas State University met in the Council Rooms of the city of Lawrence, Kansas, Tuesday, March 21st, A.D. 1865, at nine o'clock A.M.

After an informal discussion and careful examination of the general interests of the University, its funds and necessities, together with the Statute creating the same, the Board of Regents [decided] to effect a permanent Organization by the election of the following Officers to hold such positions till the next Annual Meeting on the 1st Wednesday of December A.D. 1865.

Rev. R. W. Oliver of the Prot. Episcopal Church was elected Chancellor. Rev. G. W. Paddock of the M. E. Church was elected permanent Secretary. G. W. Deitzler was elected Treasurer.

—From the *Official Journal* (manuscript).

WITH ALL THE excitement and feverish activity of territorial days, schools were not forgotten. In fact, from the very first settlement of Kansas in 1854, efforts were made to provide an education for the children, as many of the early home-seekers were New Englanders, and were, in still greater numbers, emigrants from the Ohio valley, where free schools were already established and favored. It is not surprising then that even under pioneer and frontier conditions, schools were almost immediately organized. John Speer, for example, editor of the *Kansas Tribune,* who pioneered in the settlement of Lawrence, wrote: "Before we had a house—we mean a house which could be called a dwelling— a free school was started. . . . Its walls were of prairie sod, cut up about twelve inches square and laid down flat, 'breaking joints' as is done in ordinary stone work, thus making a wall twelve inches thick. The wall was about five feet high. On the wall stood rafters of round cottonwood poles with cross strips nailed on the rafters, also of saplings. The roof was covered with a thatch-work of prairie hay, the very longest that could be cut on bottom land. This was a free school."

It is not surprising that, under these crude conditions, results were far from satisfactory. In the rapidly growing pioneer communities, adequately trained teachers were difficult to obtain and more difficult to retain once they had been found. Even

nine years after the first settlement of Kansas, the report of the State Superintendent of Public Instruction concerning Douglas County (the second most populous county) reads: ". . . the smaller children sit listless and idle in their seats or try to amuse themselves as best they may, by playing sly tricks on their nearest neighbor. A majority of our teachers seem to have no genius for setting them at work. In many of the districts, the school houses have been so ill-arranged, and the seats so inconvenient, and the scholars so mixed up, that perfect order is well-nigh impossible, and whispering has prevailed to too great an extent. As fast as good school houses are built, and convenient seats provided, this evil will in a great measure cease." Although teachers for elementary schools lacked genius, and conditions— including "whispering"—were not all that might be desired, a start had been made, and what is equally important, the results had been criticized.

Not only had plans for elementary schools been initiated in the early history of territorial Kansas, but optimistic and far-sighted leaders were considering the possibilities of higher education. The first two territorial legislatures granted no less than twelve charters to collegiate institutions, the majority of which rejoiced in the title of "university." That none of these materialized did not deter succeeding legislatures from granting many other charters of like character.

Lawrence was one of the leaders in this movement toward higher education. One of the first charters granted in 1855 incorporated a "University of Kansas Territory" in Douglas County and a year later, the Kansas correspondent of the *New York Tribune* described a plan for a university at Lawrence devised by a group of interested men who met on Christmas Day, 1856. The aid of friends "East and North" and of the government was to be solicited. One of the avowed reasons—possibly the principal one—for initiating the venture stated that "an institution of learning in Kansas would invite a very desirable class of immigrants for settlement." A university in 1857 would have had little patronage if we can judge by the enrollment when the University actually opened in 1866. Nevertheless the aid of the Presbyterian Church and other friends "East and North" actually led to some definite steps in locating a college in Lawrence in 1859, when the foundation, at least, of a building was constructed on Mount Oread.

The direct establishment of the University of Kansas was a matter primarily of state history rather than of territorial history, however. The constitution under which Kansas was admitted as a state in 1861 provided for a state university, but did not fix its actual location. During the early years of statehood, the selection of the university site, and the location of several other institutions, was a matter of considerable logrolling among the politicians of the state. In 1861, both houses of the legislature passed a bill placing the university at Manhattan, but Governor Robinson, a resident of Lawrence, promptly vetoed it. Again

The above advertisement is reproduced from the *Junction City Union*, September 1, 1866.

in 1863, a heated contest arose between Lawrence and Emporia in their efforts to secure the university. Local feeling was considerably aroused and fervid orations and many promises were delivered in the Legislature, Lawrence eventually winning by one vote in the House when the final decision was reached. The bill locating the "University of Kansas" at Lawrence passed the Senate with-

Lawrence, 1859. This illustration is reproduced from an original wash drawing in the possession of the Kansas State Historical Society. Unfortunately it is of unknown origin. The drawing was also reproduced lithographically about 1860, but the events depicted took place in 1859. The stone in the foreground, near the brow of the hill, was used for the construction of the foundation of Lawrence University, the proposed Presbyterian institution. Looking north, one may see the Eldridge House, the largest building in Lawrence of 1859. A little to the observer's left, at the foot of the hill, is the Unitarian Church, for many years a landmark in the town.

out contest, and on February 20, 1863, became law after being signed by Governor Carney.

No immediate steps were even then taken toward the formation of the University. The following summer (August, 1863), Lawrence underwent the terror of death and destruction by Quantrill and his followers, and the resources of the town were largely directed toward its rebuilding and in doing its part in the War between the States. By the following spring, life had taken on a more normal aspect, and interest in the University revived. The Legislature in Topeka passed the act organizing the University, which Governor Carney approved on March 1, 1864.

The organic law stated that "the object of the University shall be to provide the inhabitants of this State with the means of acquiring a thorough knowledge of the various branches of literature, science and the arts," gave the government of the University to a Board of Regents, and directed them to proceed with the erection of suitable buildings when sufficient funds for the purpose were "on hand and provided for." As the Legislature made no appropriation for this purpose, University plans were still further delayed while contributions of land and money were solicited from the city of Lawrence and from all other available sources. Twenty thousand dollars, largely obtained from Quantrill relief funds, the need for which had disappeared, and a site of land were eventually obtained.

Utilizing the foundation of the college building started by the Presbyterians several years earlier, active work on the construction of the University was begun in the fall of 1865 and continued in 1866. By the summer of 1866 the building was nearly complete, occupying a site on the brow of Mount Oread. The Board of Regents met in Lawrence in July of 1866, inspected the building, elected a faculty, set the opening date for September 12, 1866, and authorized advertising for the University in the newspapers of the state.

3. Kansas of 1866

Immigration continues unabated. Hundreds of strange faces show themselves daily on our streets, and they grow more numerous as the trains arrive each day. Kansas is fast settling up with the very best material. During the past week more than twenty families, with their horses and wagons, furniture, bedding, cattle, etc., have passed through here, intending to locate in Osage, Morris and Chase counties. This state of things is not confined alone to the Kaw Valley. ——*Topeka Weekly Leader*, May 31, 1866.

ON THAT long-distant September day when the University first opened, the state of Kansas was but five years old. It had less than one-tenth of its present population and its citizens had settled very largely in the eastern third of the state. If Kansas of 1866 was largely eastern Kansas, it was also a Kansas expanding rapidly to the westward. The close of the Civil War in 1865 brought home-seekers to the state in thousands. To accommodate this horde and to stimulate the growth of its numbers to still higher levels, the first railroad across the state was rapidly being built. At the time the University opened, however, tracks had been laid but little past Man-

Kansas of the sixties: Topeka—looking north on Kansas Avenue. The large stone building on the left was the Tefft House, located at Seventh Street and Kansas Avenue.

Looking south on Massachusetts Street, Lawrence. The photograph is almost contemporary with the opening of the University, as it was taken in 1867, four years after Quantrill's raid. The Eldridge Hotel is the first building on the right. The tower in the distance belonged to the Methodist Church, which then occupied the site now occupied by the Masonic Temple. Several weeks before the photograph was made, the city fathers had passed an ordinance prohibiting the running of cattle on town streets!

hattan, and the country beyond Salina was still Indian and buffalo country. The sod house and dugout were the homes of many of these home-seekers, not only on the farms but even in the towns. A traveler writing in the *Topeka Leader* for September 6, 1866, just six days before the University opened, reports on a visit to Salina: "Owing to the scarcity of lumber—a scarcity growing out of the want of mills more than the lack of timber—a great many of the settlers live in caves excavated on the banks of the river and covered with earth; these earthen roofs are very popular hereaway and I was surprised to find the quarters at Fort Ellsworth covered with them."

It was a time of rapid development. Home-seeking, land speculation, railroad building, both actual and imaginary, bridge building, sawmill construction, and freighting by ox teams across the plains of Kansas to Santa Fe and Denver, were all pursued with vigor and intense activity. Indian troubles were increasing as the railroad advanced west, but the severe Indian wars were matters of the future in 1866.

Leavenworth was the metropolis of the state, with a population of 14,000. Lawrence was the second city of the state with an actual population of 6,000 but claiming more than 10,000 inhabitants. Topeka, the capital city, had difficulty in finding 4,000 names for its census records.

Educationally, too, the state was making progress by 1866. The first of the state schools to be established was Kansas Agricultural College at Manhattan. The Morrill Land Grant Act, providing for the aid of colleges giving instruction in agriculture and mechanical arts became a federal law in 1862, and our young state eagerly accepted the support thus offered. As Manhattan had been

5

disappointed in her efforts to secure the state university, the Legislature awarded her the agricultural college, especially after the trustees of Bluemont Central College—established chiefly through the efforts of the Methodist Church in 1860—offered to deed the state 120 acres of land and the college building as a location for the new state school. Kansas State began its service to the state on September 2, 1863, with a symmetrically proportioned enrollment of "twenty-six males and twenty-six females."

To compensate Emporia for her loss of the University, the Legislature established the Emporia State Normal School, which opened February 15, 1865, under severe handicaps. The town of Emporia at that time had not more than 500 inhabitants and its only connection with the outside world was a tri-weekly stage to Lawrence. School was begun with one teacher and eighteen students in the upstairs room of the village schoolhouse. Seats borrowed from a church were its only furniture, and its library consisted of an unabridged dictionary and a Bible, both of which belonged to the teacher, Lyman B. Kellogg.

The churches, too, had established a number of colleges by 1866. Baker University (Methodist) and Highland University (Presbyterian) were both chartered in 1858. Baker began its first classes on November 22, 1858, and has uninterruptedly continued its course to this day. Ottawa University (Baptist) was chartered in 1865, as was the Lane University (United Brethren) at Lecompton. The following year, Lincoln College (Congregational) was organized and began instruction in January, 1866. Two years later its name was changed to Washburn College.

Mention should also be made of the schools established by the Jesuit fathers at St. Mary's, and by the Benedictines at Atchison. A mission school, which later became St. Mary's College, was started in 1848 for the Pottawatomies. Incidentally, it should be remarked that this Jesuit mission school played a far more important part in the early agricultural development of the state than most people realize. The work of the Benedictines, originating in 1857, resulted eventually in the formation of St. Benedict's College in 1868.

Without exception, all Kansas colleges and universities in existence by 1866 had as their principal work the training of preparatory students. The towns and the state had not yet provided high schools, and the burden of preparation for college fell entirely on the so-called colleges and universities of state and church. Baker University, it is true, had graduated her first college class in June, 1866, a class of three; but over three-fourths of her enrollment at that time consisted of primary and academy students. Kansas was not yet ready for real colleges.

Kansas of the sixties: A Kansas home on the western frontier in the days when the University was established. The ranch was located on Clear Creek, a few miles east of the present town of Ellsworth. Note the grass growing in the sod roof and the tame young elk.

4. Opening the University

Lawrence, September 12, 1866

The dedication services of the State University drew a large concourse of the elite of Lawrence and visitors together at two o'clock this afternoon. Doctors, lawyers, clergymen, editors, ladies, with a large company of the musical fraternity assembled in the University Building to participate in and enjoy the interesting ceremony of the occasion. The executive committee made all necessary arrangements for the comfortable entertainment of the company and greeted them with an excellent program. The Rev. Mr. Oliver, chancellor, occupied the chair, and the band discoursed sweet music. —*Leavenworth Conservative*, September 15, 1866.

THE OPENING services having thus passed off so pleasantly and auspiciously, the real work of the University was begun. The three faculty members took stock of their students and found forty-nine on hand. The number of students increased in a few days to fifty-five, twenty-six ladies and twenty-nine gentlemen of whom forty-nine were from Douglas County. Evidently the newspaper advertising over the state was of little immediate value. What was still more discouraging was the fact that not one of the fifty-five students was ready for college work—all were preparatory students. The "University" was thus, in its initial venture, an academy, of necessity adapting itself to its times and circumstances.

There are two compensating factors, however, in addition to the fundamental one that the venture was actually launched and on its way. One of these factors doubtless was not discernible at the time and in fact did not make its effects known for many years. It was this: the University of Kansas was the first state university in the Great Plains region[1] and as the years went by was the first to establish its reputation, thus not only attracting an appreciable number of out-of-state students, but also setting a standard for a wide region.

The second factor was known and appreciated

[1]The University of Nebraska began its active career in 1871; the University of Colorado in 1876; the universities of the remaining Plains States (Texas, the Dakotas, Oklahoma, New Mexico, and Wyoming) did not become actualities until after 1880.

at the time. The Wyandotte Constitution of 1859, under which Kansas was admitted as a state, declared: "The legislature in providing for the formation and regulation of schools, shall make no distinction between the rights of males and females." The state schools of Kansas, of necessity, therefore, had to admit women as well as men, a principle almost revolutionary in its day. The framers of the legislative act establishing the University were more cautious, perhaps more skeptical, concerning coeducation, for one section of the act reads: "There shall be two branches of the university, viz: a male and a female branch. The female branch may be taught exclusively by women, and buildings for that branch shall be entirely separate from the buildings of the male branch." Fortunately, and of necessity, this provision was never put into practice. Funds were hard enough to secure for one branch, to say nothing of two.

Coeducation, however, was receiving trial outside of Kansas. Oberlin had begun its practice in 1833. The first state university to adopt it was, curiously enough, the University of the State of Deseret—later the University of Utah—to which women, as well as men, were admitted by its founder, the copiously bewived Brigham Young,

The University in 1867 (extreme left on the horizon) showing, in some detail, the whole east slope of Mount Oread and the town of Lawrence to the right. The observer is looking north from a point just east of present Battenfeld Hall; the stone house in the foreground is now a remodeled professorial residence just west of the Rowlands Bookstore on Fourteenth Street. Note that not a tree shows on the entire slope.

7

when it first opened in 1850. Six years later the University of Iowa began with the same provision, and the third state university to adopt the practice was the University of Kansas. Coeducation, then, was still in the experimental stage in 1866 and educators were asking, "Have young ladies the mental vigor and health to maintain a fair standing with men?"

The Kansas venture with coeducation, however, was looked forward to with confidence. Judge S. O. Thacher, who delivered the main address on the opening day, called specific attention to it. Said he: "As it is a provision of the constitution that in the School System of the State the same rights and privileges shall be accorded to both sexes, it follows the widest avenues to female education will be afforded in the State University. It may be deemed an experiment, but it is one whose result is certain. Wherever the barriers

of female education have been removed, good, and not evil, has been the result. It seems to be a well-recognized truth that the real advancement of man, his highest development, is in the ratio of the opportunities for culture given both sexes."

Good and not evil was the verdict of a visitor to the University in the first year of its existence. Josiah Copley, a reporter for the *Pittsburgh Gazette,* on a trip through Kansas in the spring of 1867, stopped at Lawrence and, observing University of Kansas students at work, wrote his newspaper:

"This institution [the University] places both sexes, so far as education is concerned, on an equality. Toward each other their deportment was that of well-trained brothers and sisters in the home circle. Kansas is sufficiently civilized to mingle the sexes in the higher schools without danger of folly or impropriety."

5. The First Faculty

The people of Kansas may be reminded that it is quite unnecessary to send their children abroad to obtain superior culture.—*Kansas Tribune,* July 21, 1866, upon announcing the election of the first University faculty.

THE STAFF of the University, according to its first catalog, consisted of three professors, a lecturer on hygiene, and a janitor. Just how extensive a canvass was made for available men on the first teaching force is not now known. It seems probable that no great search was made. Colleges and universities were increasing rapidly in numbers and size in the period 1861 to 1867, and it was with difficulty that properly qualified teachers were obtained. A school on the edge of the frontier had to resort to very young men with little experience, or to older men who desired a

The University of Kansas when it was one year old. Reproduced from a photograph by Alexander Gardner of Washington through the courtesy of the Missouri Historical Society, St. Louis. The view looks north toward the Kansas River, which, because of the long focal length of the lens employed in making the photograph, appears unduly close to the Hill. It was of this building that the State Superintendent of Public Instruction of 1866 wrote, "It is the most beautiful school building yet erected in the State."

Frank H. Snow, aged 26. Mrs. Cordley, wife of the Congregational minister of Lawrence, laughed when she met Snow and, turning to her husband, remarked, "Professor Snow doesn't look old enough to be a professor."

Elial J. Rice, Acting President of the Faculty; although forty-four years of age when elected to the first University faculty, his colleagues thought he was "about fifty." Rice, never a robust man, died in Colorado in 1872.

David H. Robinson, aged 29. Professors Snow and Robinson roomed together the first year at Mrs. Weld's; the two were known as "Mrs. Weld's little professor [Snow] and big professor."

change of locality in search of health or improvement of fortunes. In this latter class was Elial J. Rice, a graduate of Madison University in Indiana, and a teacher in the Evansville Public School. In search of health, and hearing of the new school in Kansas, he visited Lawrence early in the summer of 1866 and applied for a position on the faculty. D. H. Robinson, a young man of twenty-nine and a graduate of Rochester (N.Y.) University who was teaching in the Leavenworth Public School in 1865, also applied.

The Board of Regents met on July 19, 1866, and elected both of these men to the new faculty, Rice to the "chair of Belles Lettres and Mental and Moral Philosophy" and Robinson to the "chair of Languages." Also elected at this time was F. H. Snow, a friend of Governor Robinson and a young man of twenty-six who had been graduated from Williams College and from the Andover Theological Seminary. Snow, although trained primarily in the ancient languages and theology, was appointed to the "chair of Mathematics and the Natural Sciences." The Board of Regents was very careful in their selection of the faculty to make sure that no two were from the same church—all were from different denominations. Whether a faculty candidate

could preach may have had considerable weight with the Regents, too, for preaching was part of the duty of a University faculty man, as is apparent from frequent reports in the Lawrence press in the early years of the University.

Rice, being the oldest of the three newly elected teachers, both from the point of age and of experience, was made acting president of the faculty. The organic law under which the University operated, called for a University chancellor; the origin of this provision is itself of considerable interest. The Legislature of 1864 had instructed Charles Chadwick of Lawrence to draw up a bill organizing a university. Chadwick, being at a loss as to the procedure to be followed, looked up the charter of the leading state university of the day, the University of Michigan. Michigan by that time had a history of nearly thirty years and was enrolling yearly over a thousand students. Since it had achieved a very considerable distinction and was regarded with respect by all educational institutions, Chadwick soon decided that his troubles were over. Taking the original Michigan charter, Chadwick drew up one for the University of Kansas that did not greatly differ from it save in one respect—which we shall mention shortly. The Michigan charter called for a

9

governing body, the Board of Regents, appointed by the Governor, with several ex-officio members. The Kansas charter corresponded. The Michigan charter stated the objectives of the University. The Kansas charter repeated the same objectives. The Michigan charter called for a chancellor as the chairman of its Board of Regents. So did the Kansas charter, and it is for that reason that we have a chancellor. Curiously enough, the University of Michigan never had one. Michigan's charter in turn had been based largely on a model of English and Prussian universities—largely Prussian. The English universities had chancellors as their heads, so the title of Chancellor crept into the charter, but he was only mentioned as the chairman of the governing body. Just what other duties the chancellor should have, was not clear to the Michigan Regents when they met, and the election of a chancellor was postponed indefinitely. Several years later the matter was brought up and after considerable discussion it was decided that the title of chancellor was one "totally unsuited to democratic simplicity," and no chancellor was ever elected.

At Kansas, too, there seemed to be at first no very clear idea as to what a chancellor should do. The Rev. R. W. Oliver, the Episcopal rector in Lawrence, had been elected by the Regents as its chairman; and he was therefore, by law, the Chancellor of the University. He had no salary at first, but shortly after the University opened, his duties were enlarged. In addition to presiding at Board meetings he was also to serve as the finan-cial agent of the University; and for these combined duties he received five hundred dollars yearly "payable quarterly."

The original chancellor, then, had no direct connection with the faculty, for its acting head was President Rice. Rice, together with the other two faculty members, drew up the first curriculum and, with the opening of school, all performed their respective teaching duties. In December, 1866, Rice made his first report to the State Superintendent of Public Instruction, writing, in part: "Michigan University has been adopted as our model, save our basis is broader, consequently making the structure more difficult to rear, but of more value to Society when completed."

The broader basis to which Rice referred was the fact that Kansas was coeducational while Michigan was not, and did not so become until 1870. It was this difference which formed the most important exception in the transformation of the Michigan charter into the Kansas charter.

Of the original faculty of three, Snow and Robinson were to devote the remainder of their lives to the formation and development of the University of Kansas. Snow became its Chancellor in 1890; and in the year 1892-93, Robinson became the first dean of the School of Arts—later known as the College of Liberal Arts and Sciences. Rice left at the end of the school year 1866-67 to become president of the neighboring school, Baker University.

6. John Fraser

Lawrence, June 20, 1867

The annual examination of the classes in the State University commenced yesterday at 9 A.M. There was a respectable attendance of visitors from abroad, as well as citizens of Lawrence. The examination was most creditable to both teachers and students, evincing a thoroughness commensurate with the occasion. The beginners in Latin, in particular, exhibited a proficiency which reflects great credit upon their teacher.—The evening of the first day was rendered very entertaining by a grand temperance rally—in which Senator Pomeroy participated. Revs. Fisher, Cordley, Dearborn and Bodwell, fell in line handsomely, and fired some well directed shots.—*Leavenworth Daily Conservative,* June 21, 1867.

THE FIRST Chancellor of the University, in the sense of president of the faculty, was John Fraser, to whom we shall always owe a debt of real gratitude. Shortly after Rice left in 1867, Chancellor Oliver became dean of an Episcopal seminary at Nebraska City; and the University was thus left without either a chancellor or a president. An inspiration to combine these positions occurred to the Regents, as the combined positions (and salaries) would enable them to se-cure a man of greater attainments and reputation than would otherwise be possible. As a result, General Fraser visited Lawrence by invitation on December 4, 1867, and was elected to office the same day.

At the time of Fraser's election, the University was still a preparatory school, having only two college students in its total enrollment of 105. Further, it was a local institution; for nearly 90 per cent of its students came either from Lawrence or from the surrounding towns of Douglas County. When Fraser left in the fall of 1874, over one-fourth of its 259 students from thirty Kansas counties were of collegiate grade, and the impetus had been given which soon transformed an academy into a real college. These advances were primarily due to Fraser's zeal and enthusiasm in securing for the University a building adequate to the needs of a collegiate institution—in fact,

John Fraser, after a photograph made in 1874. A former student wrote of Chancellor Fraser: "In stature he was below the medium; but his sturdy, closely knit frame was impelled by a spirit extraordinarily active, earnest, and courageous."

far larger and more commodious than was necessary at the time of its first occupancy. But the care exercised in introducing the most modern features in its construction, as well as the fact that it was heralded as the largest university hall in the country, was responsible for arousing the interest and pride of the state as a whole in its University. In this enterprise, as one well-known Kansan wrote, Fraser was "entitled to a greater degree of credit than any and all others for his remarkable achievement which, however burdensome it may have been to the city of Lawrence, advanced the interests and standing of the University at least ten years."

The man responsible for this achievement was forty years old when elected to the chancellorship. A native of Scotland, he was educated at the Universities of Edinburgh and Aberdeen, from the last of which he was graduated in 1844 with highest honors in mathematics. After graduation, he taught for some time in the Bermudas and then came to this country. In 1855, he became professor of mathematics and astronomy in Jefferson College, Philadelphia. At Jefferson College he proved to be an able, interesting, and popular teacher. So popular was he that when he enlisted in the Union army at the outbreak of the Civil War, a whole company of students enlisted with him and were placed under his command in the 104th Pennsylvania Volunteers. Fraser saw much active service, taking part in the Battles of Chancellorsville, Gettysburg, the Wilderness, and Appomattox. He was twice wounded and once captured, exchanged, and returned to service. Near the close of the war, he was promoted to the rank of brevet brigadier-general for gallant conduct in battle. At the end of the war, Fraser was elected to the presidency of the Agricultural College of Pennsylvania at Bellefonte; and from there he came to the University of Kansas.

Fraser, although elected late in the fall of 1867, did not begin his active career at the University until the following summer, delivering his inaugural address on June 18, 1868. The man who faced his audience on that day was a short, trim, and stocky individual, with a heavy head of black hair, and wore, as was the custom of the day, a long beard. Restless and energetic in manner, he possessed a remarkably rich and musical voice that he could use on occasion with persuasive eloquence. "One of the most attractive talkers I ever listened to," wrote Professor Snow to a friend when he first met Fraser.

The students found in him a ready friend who, though an exacting and logical teacher, relieved the tedium of many a classroom hour by his lively Scotch wit, which on some occasions could be turned into fiery bursts of temper.

Of enthusiastic and optimistic temperament, he threw himself with all his vigor into the work of the school, and early set his heart on securing for the University a new, large, and well-equipped building. Times were hard in the late sixties; but so insistent was Fraser on realizing his ends, that with all the persuasiveness he could command, he presented his plan to the citizens of Lawrence, asking them to vote $100,000 in bonds for the purpose. Considering the time and circumstance—a

11

town of less than 8,000 and money scarce—the sum seems preposterously large, but so eloquent and convincing was Fraser's appeal that he carried all before him. The bonds were voted early in 1870, and the work of construction was begun.

With so exuberant and dynamic a personality, it is little wonder that friction with his fellow faculty members eventually occurred. Criticism of some of Fraser's methods brought a fiery response from the Chancellor and a general row ensued. As a result, Fraser offered his resignation in the spring of 1874. Fraser continued to serve as Chancellor, however, until his successor, James Marvin, was selected.

After Fraser's withdrawal from the University, he ran for the position of State Superintendent of Public Instruction, and was elected in the fall of 1874. He served two years in this position with notable success but failed in his stand for re-election. He died on June 4, 1878, shortly after beginning a professorship in Western University (now the University of Pittsburgh).

On June 9, 1897, by action of the Board of Regents, the building for which Fraser was largely responsible was named Fraser Hall, a fitting, if tardy, tribute to the gallant little Scotchman, whose years at the University were short but whose influence is long.

7. University Hall

From the careful scrutiny which they have made, the committee have carried away with them the impression that the new university building, even in its present condition, shows great results for the money expended upon it, and that when finished and furnished at a total cost of $150,000, it will not only be one of the cheapest of the public buildings in the state, but one of which the people of the commonwealth may well be proud.

In conclusion, the committee are unanimously of the opinion that the University of Kansas is a credit to the state, and worthy of the fostering care of the Legislature.
Feb. 13, 1873.

Respectfully submitted,
Legislative Visiting Committee,
M. M. Murdock, Chairman, Senate Committee
I. S. Kalloch, Chairman, House Committee

GENERAL Fraser's arrival in 1868 infused new life into the University. The enrollment increased, new teachers were added, and the number of courses and the catalog expanded. In the fall of 1869, over 150 students registered, seventeen of whom were of college grade. The eleven classrooms of the University were becoming crowded and, as the growth showed promise of continuing, General Fraser began his campaign for a more adequate building.

The bill locating the University at Lawrence

A closer view of University Hall. Note the boarded windows and the hitching rack in front of the building.

had required that a campus of forty acres be furnished by interested citizens. The necessary land was secured and approved by the commissioners selected by Governor Carney, but when actual construction of the original University building was begun, the site selected was thought to be too far from town. Further, the foundations of the school started by the Presbyterians were available, much nearer to town, and their use afforded a considerable saving in construction. The foundations were therefore utilized and about eight acres which surrounded them also became the property of the University.

As soon as Lawrence had voted bonds for the construction of a new building in 1870, the question of its site was considered. It was soon decided that the eight acres containing the original University building would not be adequate for still further expansion, and the new building was located on the forty acres originally provided for the University. Chancellor Fraser went East at his own expense to examine the most modern university buildings then in use. On his return he reported that "about eighty of the best buildings of the large universities had been examined to decide upon size and best arrangement of rooms, also for the best plans of warming and ventilating."

Utilizing Fraser's findings, plans for the building were drawn up by J. G. Haskell, and construction was started. By February, 1871, the building was nearly enclosed, and by fall of 1872, parts of the building were in use. By this time the need for a new building had become all too apparent. The original building—known as North College after the completion of the new building—was filled to overflowing, the overflow classes being held in the basement of the Unitarian Church. For a time the two buildings were simply called "the Old Building" and "the New Building"; but in 1877 the new building was officially named University Hall—to be changed twenty years later to Fraser Hall—but even the uncompleted building had a public opening on December 2, 1872, shortly after it was first put into service. From the main address, given by Chancellor Fraser, the following illuminating sentences may be quoted:

"Now by the grace of God, we have a building nearly completed that has not its peer in the whole land. This building was not erected by the princely aid of a nobleman or millionaire, but it is the work of the people, the toiling thousands of our blood-bought Kansas. We accept it as a token of their liberality. The people have reason to rejoice with the faculty at what has been accomplished, but they cannot yet fully understand its importance."

At the conclusion of the address visitors were shown through the new building. Student guides took particular care to point out that time signals were communicated to all classrooms from a standard clock by electricity, that the gas jets in the lecture hall could all be ignited the instant they were turned on by electricity, that the principle of panoptic curves[1] had been used in several of the lecture rooms, that the building was heated and ventilated with steam, and that the electric wires and pipes for conducting oxygen and hydrogen from gas reservoirs to the laboratory rooms were concealed in the walls.

The obvious pride in these arrangements may appear trivial and childish to us at present. Some, indeed, did not work very long, but all had a real

[1]For the benefit of University graduates—and fellow faculty members—the application of "the principle of panoptic curves" resulted in a floor gradually rising to higher level as the distance from the lecturer's desk became greater. Each sitter was thus a few inches higher than the one in front of him, enabling all in the room "to see everything on the lecturer's table."

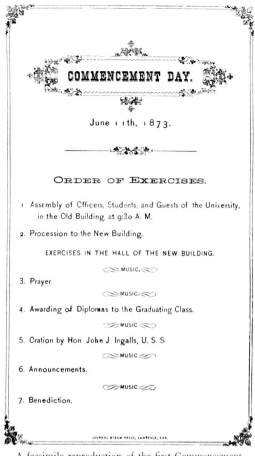

A facsimile reproduction of the first Commencement program.

significance. Here was an institution, itself but six years old, in a community but little past the frontier stage and on the edge of "the great American desert," adopting and adapting to its use the most modern developments of the science of that day. For, in 1872, be it recalled, the present machine age itself was no more than in its infancy. Nothing could show more clearly the progressive spirit and the earnest desire of these University pioneers to provide the children of Kansas the best that could then be had.

And the state responded. Scarcely an issue of the Lawrence papers appeared during the time that the building was in process of erection in which mention is not made of some out-of-town visitors who came to see the marvel. Editors from neighboring towns were among the most frequent of this group; and one of their number, the editor of the *Fort Scott Monitor*, summarized the opinion of the day: "The whole building is itself a textbook."

The earliest known photograph of University (Fraser) Hall, made shortly after its opening in 1872. The photograph was taken from near the present location of Blake Hall; the view looks northwest.

8. The First Commencement

The opening of the Commencement exercises took place Sunday evening, at the new hall of the University. Notwithstanding the very threatening aspect of the sky, a large audience assembled. The services commenced at precisely eight o'clock with the hymn "Before Jehovah's Awful Throne." Then followed Chancellor Fraser's introductory remarks.—*Daily Kansas Tribune*, June 10, 1873.

THE JUNE following the first use of University Hall saw the first Commencement. A college without a Commencement would lack one of its most colorful and remembered occasions. In fact, without a Commencement, many students would argue that there might as well be no college at all. In any case, it must have been with genuine satisfaction that Professors Robinson and Snow, the only two remaining members of the faculty of 1866, saw four of their students go through the ceremonies of graduation on June 11, 1873.

The ceremonies were planned with care, their form corresponding to the traditions established by eastern schools. There were a baccalaureate sermon, a Class Day, a Commencement procession and oration, the conferring of degrees, and last—but by no means least—a banquet.

Most of the exercises were held in the chapel of the new building, but one must remember, in forming a picture of the events, that the chapel was unfinished,—not even plastered. There was no balcony; a rough, temporary stage had been erected at the south end of the hall, and the audiences were seated on long, wooden, backless benches. These handicaps were all overlooked in the light of the happy fact that this was the first Commencement, the first of a long series of similar events yet to come.

The first baccalaureate sermon was preached by the Rev. Richard Cordley of the Plymouth Congregational Church. Mr. Cordley's discourse was a criticism of "the modern spirit," a spirit which manifested itself in an eagerness for immediate position, for immediate wealth and office without the willingness to undergo the compensating toil and preparation which should fitly precede the attainment of such ends:

This haste to be rich—this impatience for promotion—this eagerness for results, is the peril of the age. It is called a fast age. We hurry everything. We try to hurry the steps of nature; but as she likes to take her time, this makes trouble. Boys are hurried into manhood, when they ought to remain in Jericho till their beards are grown. This is why so many fail of the promise of their youth. They are pushed forward before they are mature.

The Flower that bursts before its time
    Will fade before its full.

We carry this into education. We have short cuts to science. "Latin in six short lessons"; "mathematics made easy." We cross the ocean in ten days; why not go through college in ten months?

Senator John J. Ingalls; a sketch reproduced by permission of Mrs. D. W. Collins, of Oklahoma City, from *Ingalls of Kansas* by William E. Connelley.

If the reference to Jericho and beards were deleted, we could almost imagine that these were the words of a present-day sermon, but they have a strangely unfamiliar sound coming from an era we are prone to believe belonged to a world of slower tempo, a world of a more leisurely life.

* * * *

Class Day began on Tuesday morning, June 10, and continued all day. Chancellor Fraser presided at the opening meeting and explained the nature of the various exercises, also telling the audience of a thousand that faculty and students had joined together to defray the expenses of the day. The members of the class were brought forward; and three of them, Flora Richardson, Ralph Collins, and L. D. L. Tosh gave orations. The fourth member of the class, Murray Harris, had been excused by the faculty from the preparation of an essay or oration. Chancellor Fraser stated, however, that Harris, the University's first engineering graduate, had, in lieu of an oration, prepared drawings and models of a bridge, which were on the stage.

The afternoon of Class Day was given over to the formal ceremony of the planting of a vine. The band, the classes of the University, the graduating class, and the faculty marched in procession to the place of planting. Murray Harris then stated that though the University grounds presented a bare and uninviting appearance, the planting of the vine by the class of '73 marked the first step in their ornamentation.

At the evening program, the seniors were formally presented to the audience, their biographies were recited, and one of the number, Flora Richardson, passed on their responsibilities as seniors to the junior class, who were present on the stage.

The final day arrived at last; "the weather delightful, the skies clear and the breeze fresh and invigorating." At ten o'clock the crowd assembled on the brow of the hill now south of the Spooner-Thayer Museum, although it had been the original intention to start the procession from North College. A procession by twos was formed, the band taking the lead, then followed in order "the students, the graduating class, the Faculty, the Regents, town, county and State officers, United States officers, chancellor and orator." The band struck up a march and the procession started off. On arriving at the main entrance, ranks were opened, and the assembly waited while Chancellor Fraser and Senator Ingalls passed into the building, the rest of the audience then following.

Chancellor Fraser opened the Commencement program by a very brief talk and awarded the diplomas, the first one going to Murray Harris. The band then played and was followed by the orator of the occasion, the representative of Kansas in the United States Senate, John J. Ingalls. Senator Ingalls, although he had but begun his career in the Senate, already had a nation-wide reputation as an orator; and according to the state press, his Commencement oration added to his reputation. Although the whole is too long to repeat here, the opening paragraph will help to preserve some of the flavor of this historic event in University annals. Rising slowly and walking to the rostrum, Ingalls paused, a tall, thin wraith of a man; then began. Utilizing scarcely a gesture, he achieved his hold on the audience by his eloquent and magic words and marvelous voice.

Mr. Chancellor, Ladies and Gentlemen:
The first time I stood upon this consecrated eminence, I looked southward and eastward down the enchanted valleys of the Wakarusa and the Kaw, through the vacant embrasures of a rude fortification that frowned with incongruous menace above the pastoral landscape for whose tranquil and diversified beauty, nature has no rival, art has no synonym. Clustered along its base, and mirrored in the sluggish stream, were the humble homes of those new Pilgrim Fathers of the West, impelled by
"The unconquerable mind

And freedom's holy flame"—
to establish in solitude the germs of those institutions which in this brief interval have grown and expanded into a civilization that is one of the great wonders and marvels of the world; a civilization that would have been almost miraculous had its energies been expended in the material triumphs which have been achieved over the stubborn forces of nature, and the wild and wasteful wilderness; the railroads that have been builded, and the cities that have been strung like pearls along their iron cords; the streams that have been bridged, the commerce that has been nurtured; the vast areas that have been rendered productive; the industries that have been developed: but far more marvelous when considered in its connection with those higher attributes which today find their highest expression in the rites which we here perform, to commemorate the first annual Commencement of the University of Kansas. This is the State's consummate hour.

After Ingalls' speech, the audience retired to other rooms of University Hall. The committee in charge cleared the benches from the chapel, set up tables, and brought in the dinner for the occasion. "It was in reality a banquet—well worthy of the name. The tables seated two hundred and sixty and were covered and heaped up with everything the most fastidious could desire. It was a grand thing."

9. A New Chancellor

Ed. *Tribune*: Why can not University students, while passing to and from recitations desist from pulling flowers and taking fruit off the bushes and trees that lie near the walk in the yards of citizens? A keener sense of propriety manifested, on the part of a few, would be appreciated much more than the foregoing actions. A citizen. —*Daily Kansas Tribune*, June 6, 1874.

THE city of Lawrence, as is evident from the preceding pages, played an important part in the early development of the University. Not only were its citizens responsible in a large measure for the first two University buildings and for the acquisition of the campus; but, as the years passed and the number of students grew, they had need of a remarkable forbearance and patience. Flowers would disappear from a favorite garden in the dark of the night, a fence gate would bar one's progress as the front door was opened in the morning, a buggy would be found on the front porch, or a bell would mysteriously toll at an un-

earthly hour. Seldom, however, did the wrath of the householder as a result of these misdeeds rise to such heat that he had to explode in the print of the daily paper. When the explosion did occur, he was sure to get a reply from the University paper to the effect that the innocent had been accused. Undoubtedly a town boy had done the dirty work and the blame had been directed at the wrong party.

On the whole, however, if one can judge by an examination of the contemporary newspapers, there has been, save on two or three occasions, surprisingly little friction between town and

Massachusetts Street, Lawrence. This view was taken from the top of a building at the corner of Seventh and Massachusetts Streets, and looks southwest toward the University. The Eldridge House is the first building on the right. Wooden awnings had been tabooed by a city ordinance of 1872, but photographs as late as 1900 still show them firmly entrenched. In the original photograph, two trees can be seen growing through openings in the sidewalk in the right foreground.

gown; and city and University have grown and developed together with mutual understanding and profit.

That developments were taking place in Lawrence, as well as in the University, is evident from our photograph, which was probably made in the late seventies. A comparison of this view with the one shown on page 5 reveals at least one important change—car tracks, instead of cow tracks, now run the length of Massachusetts Street. Every town of the last century aspiring to be a city has felt the necessity of securing a street railway system as one of the essentials in reaching its aspiration, and Lawrence was no exception. After considerable discussion in the public press, a streetcar and its tracks were secured and the system officially opened in November, 1871. It ran the length of the business district on Massachusetts Street and then north across the bridge to the Kansas Pacific station. The first motive power employed was a family horse. Later the horse was replaced by a team of small but lively mules. During the early eighties, the rails were

extended south on Tennessee Street, coming to an end at Seventeenth Street, and for many years University students had car service only to the foot of Adams (Fourteenth) Street.

The commanding position of University Hall with respect to the town is also apparent in this early picture—a position made especially prominent because of the fact that trees and houses on the Hill were still few and far between.

In fact, this appearance of Lawrence and the University must have been the view which Chancellor Carpenter obtained when he arrived in Lawrence in the summer of 1874. Chancellor Fraser's resignation had caused the Regents to undertake a search for his successor. A number of applications and recommendations were secured; and one was so outstanding that on July 15, 1874, the Board elected this candidate to the chancellorship without ever having interviewed him. The newly elected Chancellor was Professor S. H. Carpenter of the University of Wisconsin. Carpenter, after his election, arrived in Lawrence in

17

midsummer. It was a summer when the thermometer daily rose to 100 degrees or higher, and, as most Kansans could guess, a severe drouth accompanied the torrid temperatures. In addition, newspaper writers were vainly seeking for the proper adjectives to describe the countless grasshoppers then prevalent—for 1874

The car that ran on the first street railway tracks in Lawrence.

was "the grasshopper year." Carpenter arrived in Lawrence on a hot summer day, the only clouds being those caused by the innumerable hosts of grasshoppers, took one look at the University perched on the bleak hill overlooking the town— and departed. As soon as he had returned to his home amid the cool Wisconsin lakes, he wrote the Board declining the chancellorship.

Several Lawrence members of the Board, however, had heard a sermon preached at the Methodist Church during this same summer by a visitor, Dr. James Marvin of Meadville, Pennsylvania. The members were evidently much impressed and were delighted when they found that Dr. Marvin was professor of mathematics at Allegheny College and a clergyman as well. When Chancellor Carpenter's declination was received, Dr. Marvin was elected to the position vacated by Chancellor Fraser and entered on his duties late in the fall of 1874.

10. Improving University Hall

Mr. Blair said [before the House of Representatives] there were plenty of men in Kansas who were as competent to fill the chancellor's position as the gentleman who now occupied it. If the present chancellor could not live on $2000, then let him go back east. Great God! We have thousands of people who live on $200 a year.—*Topeka Commonwealth*, February 26, 1875.

CHANCELLOR MARVIN was greatly distressed by the appearance of the campus when he arrived in the fall of 1874. "The new university grounds, beautifully located and ample in extent," he told the Legislature, "lie exposed as common pasture for stray cattle." The Hall itself was far from completed. The chapel and corridors were unfinished—not even plastered; many of the classrooms could not be used, and a number of windows were boarded up, pending completion of the building. The winter of 1874-75 was unusually severe and some of the classrooms in use had to be abandoned, it was so cold. The drouth and grasshopper infestation of the previous summer had lowered the resources of the state, and money was scarce. Faculty salaries were reduced and attendance diminished. It was a most discouraging period in the life of the University. Times did eventually improve, however; and with the combined efforts of townspeople, faculty, and Regents, a legislative appropriation of $15,000 was secured in 1876 for finishing the building.

Within a year, sixteen recitation rooms were finished, the chapel was completed, including the

balcony, and the appearance of the corridors was vastly improved. In fact, the building was practically finished, with the exception of the front entrance (on the east) which still remained a temporary frame structure. The completion of this work was celebrated by the official dedication and naming of University Hall on November 22, 1877. Governor Anthony was present and took part in the ceremony, but the principal address was given by Chancellor Marvin. "Builders, teachers, students pass under the influence of this building, and they, in turn, pass away; but the University stands through the coming ages, a fountain of truth and knowledge to the generations yet unborn," proclaimed Marvin in the course of his oration, a prophecy that three-quarters of a century has not refuted. Not only had the interior of University Hall been improved in appearance, but the outward appearance had been changed for the better, also. In 1877, hundreds of trees were set out by the Douglas County Horticultural Society, the grounds were graded, a stone retaining wall was placed along the north side of the campus, and a gate was added at the top of Adams Street, as the photograph shows.

The gates served a useful, as well as an ornamental purpose, too, for they kept out the cows that had worried Chancellor Marvin. Tending these gates during the day and closing them at night was a job that helped several boys through college, including two who were later to become faculty members, Olin Templin and Miles W. Sterling.

More trees were set out in the years that followed, the heavy planting that was placed in the ravine north of University Hall eventually becoming known as Marvin Grove. In the fall of 1879 the stone retaining wall was continued along the east side of the campus in front of University Hall and during the same school year, the permanent stone entrance to the building was built, and a separate smokestack appeared on the campus for the first time.

The University must have presented then a vastly improved appearance when visited by President Rutherford B. Hayes and his wife on September 27, 1879. University Hall had already been visited by the chief executive of the nation on a previous occasion. General Grant, with Mrs. Grant and their daughter, Nellie, had stopped in Lawrence in April, 1873, and had been driven up to inspect the new University building. Grant did not speak either at the University or in town, an omission which the local paper attributed to his "apprehension of giving offense to St. Louis and other little places in the East." President Hayes, however, spoke briefly in chapel after being taken with his wife to the top of the north cupola to see the wonderful view, a favorite method of entertaining visitors. It seems reasonable to suppose that the shortness of Hayes' speech was due to the exertion of his previous toil, for it is a long though worth-while climb to the top of the cupola.

Those of you who have made the climb will agree in spirit with the exuberant reporter who first described the scene when he saw it over eighty years ago, although you doubtless would restrict yourself to fewer words. For he wrote:

This excellent view, looking southwest, was taken about 1882. Adams Street occupies the foreground; in 1913, by action of the City Council, Adams Street became Fourteenth Street. Note the visitors on the north cupola. For many years, it was the custom to keep a "visitors' book." During the two years 1884-86, over eight thousand signed the book. Their addresses showed that they came from nearly every state in the Union and from many foreign countries. When this photograph is compared with the earlier ones of University Hall, it will be noticed that a stone portico had replaced the temporary frame entrance used in the earlier years. The portico was originally designed for a building at the State Insane Asylum at Osawatomie; because of a mistake of the stonecutters it could not be used there. Although not similar in design to University Hall, it was shipped to the University and "stuck" on the front of the building.

"There are scenes in the Rocky Mountains more wild, bold and striking, mountain countries in Europe more grandly rugged and more interesting as fastnesses which God made for the safety and preservation of brave peoples; but for the grandest, serenest, richest, most beautiful and inspiring country which the Creator has provided for a peaceful, refined, and well-equipped people to live and rest in, we never expect to see anything like the scene which the eye takes in as we stand on the dome of the 'light house' of Mount Oread."

11. Early Fraternity Life

Chancellor Marvin's Advice to Students

System and division of time are essential to success in school work. A time for everything and everything on time is the only rule whereby students may be saved. But whatever is done let a scrupulous regard for physical health and strength be paramount. Sleep enough, exercise enough, and by that means and that alone will you be enabled to study enough.—A teacher is valuable not as a turnkey or a police functionary but as a guide and assistant. Treat the professor as he should be treated and his envelope of unpleasantness will readily disappear.—Opening convocation, September 15, 1875.

FRATERNITIES have long played a part in the life of students at the University of Kansas. University Hall had scarcely been put into use before Beta Theta Pi established a chapter on January 9, 1873. The example of the Betas was followed soon by a group of girls who secured a charter for a chapter of I. C. Sorosis on April 1, 1873—an organization known after 1888 by its present name of Pi Beta Phi. A chapter of Phi Kappa Psi was installed on February 19, 1876, and during the eighties some half dozen additional fraternities made their appearance on the campus.

Much—probably most—of the social life of the students during the eighties was centered about these fraternities. The actual number of college students was small in this period and almost half and sometimes more of the college students belonged to one organization or the other. Other student organizations, as a result, were largely controlled by the Greeks.

However, it must be recalled that fraternity life in the eighties and early nineties was an entirely different affair from that of today. There were no chapter houses and, at first, not even meeting places. In 1877, the prevailing mode of fraternity life was set for many years for, the *Kansas Collegian* reports, "The Phi Kappa Psi fraternity has fitted up an elegant apartment for its own use in the third story of the First National Bank Building."

The practice thus established was continued for over fifteen years. Even as late as 1893 the *Courier* records in its University directory:

Beta Theta Pi—meets every Saturday evening on 4th floor of Opera House block.

Phi Kappa Psi—meets every Saturday evening on 3rd floor of Opera House block.

Phi Gamma Delta—meets every Saturday evening on 3rd floor of Eldridge House block.

Sigma Nu—meets every Saturday evening on 3rd floor of Eldridge House block.

Pi Beta Phi—meets every Saturday afternoon at the homes of members.

Kappa Alpha Theta—meets every Saturday afternoon at the homes of members.

Kappa Kappa Gamma—meets every Saturday afternoon in its hall, 2nd floor K.P. hall.

Sigma Chi—meets every Saturday evening on the 3rd floor of Opera House block.

Saturday evening in the upper floors of the Opera House block doubtless was no quiet retreat on occasion. In fact, at least once it was reported that the roof rose and fell, so great was the noise; as a result the city marshal appeared.

"Mamma, is this a picture of a Show or Something?" questioned little Harold in anxious voice. "No, child," responded his mother tenderly. "It is not a Show. It is a place where everybody did not have a show; at least the Sig—but you, Dear Child, are much too young. I will not tell you of it. It is a picture of a number of Jolly, Jolly Boys who belong to secret societies having a Pan Hellenic. At a Pan Hellenic they dress up in Queer, Odd Clothes, and have what old folks call a High Old Time. They drink Cider so hard that it will turn Steel, and yell lustily the While. I hope, Dear Child, you will Never, Ah, Never participate in one of these. You won't, will you, my Precious?" "Oh mamma," said Harold, as he pulled poor Pussy's tail.

Fraternity life as depicted in the *Helianthus* for 1889.

The Kansas Chapter of Phi Kappa Psi, March, 1880. Top row, left to right: Modine, Spangler, Sterling, Davidson, Ed E. Brown; second row: Little, Marvin, Gleed, Ed Brown, Hutchings; remaining, left to right, Stocks, Raymond, Meservey, Twitchell, Williams, Smith, Webster. The group includes a number who became nationally prominent in later life. Four were connected with the University for many years: Dean Marvin, Professors Sterling and Gleed, and Acting Chancellor Spangler.

The present system of chapter houses was initiated in 1894, Beta Theta Pi leasing the Da Lee property on Tennessee Street in the spring of that year for a period of three years. "This will be the first trial in the West," reports the *Courier,* "of regular chapter-house life in which the entire management of the house will be in the hands of the members. Should the experiment prove successful, other fraternities will no doubt follow the lead of Beta Theta Pi."

Three additional fraternities followed suit the next fall, but in 1899 Sigma Chi moved into the first chapter house especially built for the purpose, "a cozy little brick house provided with modern conveniences" located at 1024 Ohio Street. Comparatively modest fraternity houses were in use until, with the post-war boom of the twenties, fraternities, like everyone else, felt the need of bigger and better things.

Fraternity life, of course, like most other American institutions, has been the subject of much criticism and discussion. During the eighties, arguments for and against the fraternity life of that day appeared in the University papers, and the rights of Greeks and Barbarians were discussed at much length and sometimes with much heat. The argument has continued until comparatively modern times. In 1909 and 1913, particularly virulent attacks were made on "aping the idle rich on five cents a day," but the fraternities had their defenders; one well-known alumnus pointing out the commonly accepted opinion that "these organizations fill a place in our college life that, for the present, at least, can be filled in no other way."

With the passing years, fraternities and sororities, while still numbering many students on their rolls, do not play the important part that they did in the early life of the University. The growing complexity of modern university life, with its many activities, has doubtless been responsible for this change. At the present time, two-thirds of the student body are not members of any of the social organizations.

12. The Chemistry Building

Yesterday morning was the coldest in many years. Some say the coldest ever known in Kansas. Others, the oldest inhabitants, affirm that the historic winter of '56 was as cold, if not colder. Prof. Bailey, of the University, reports the thermometer at 26 below zero.—*Kansas Tribune,* January 6, 1884.

THE EARLY efforts of Kansas citizens to establish colleges was recognition of the need for a better way of life. Colleges were centers of culture, where libraries were established, where a native literature could be developed, where the arts of music and painting could be cultivated, and where "the mind could be broadened and the intellect developed." Thus it was hoped that establishment of colleges would relieve the rawness and harshness of pioneer life.

The frontier, however, produced a reciprocal effect on collegiate education. The people of the frontier were faced with the task of breaking a wilderness, of creating homes and towns, of building bridges across unbridged streams, and of laying rails across virgin plains. Those trained for these tasks were all too few, so that it is not surprising that a rapidly developing country should make its demands of college instruction.

College instruction, at the time the University opened, was, in general, rigidly prescribed. There was but one way by which "the mind could be broadened and the intellect developed," and that way consisted in a study of the classics, of philosophy, and of mathematics. To be sure, the sciences had begun to creep into the college curriculum of 1866, but only as a very minor element. The early Kansas colleges patterned their offerings at first after those of existing models, but made faint concession to the times by inclusion of a course in surveying. Even the Agricultural College, for instance, when it opened in 1863, had but two instructors of professorial rank, a "professor of mental and moral science and ancient language" and a "professor of mathematics and natural science."

The demand of the frontier was for more "practical" instruction on the immediate needs of the day, and it was this demand that was one of the major factors in the liberalizing of the college curriculum that took place in the last half of the past century. Starting slowly, the change developed a considerable velocity, resulting by 1900 in a really amazing transformation.

The beginnings of these changes as they affected the University are early discernible in its catalogs. The first catalog describes simply "a college course" which included such "practical" subjects as agricultural chemistry and "astronomy with the use of instruments," and by 1870 a

The University as it appeared shortly after the completion of Chemistry Hall in 1884. The photograph looks northwest and was taken on a spot between present Blake Hall and Watkins Hall. Note the stone retaining wall that passes in a horizontal line through the center of the picture.

course in civil and topographical engineering had been added. The University was thus adapting itself to the needs of its environment, an adaptation that no doubt played a large part in the growth of enrollment which led to the construction of University Hall.

University Hall itself provided most adequate space at first for the practical subjects. The early advertising of the University calls particular attention to the fact that the "the Departments of Chemistry, Physics, Natural Sciences, Mechanics, Engineering, and Drawing, will *each* have a suite of four rooms." Such expansion in the sciences had, of course, called for additional instructors. An instructor in chemistry, Dr. W. H. Saunders, a local physician, was added in 1868 and a chair of mathematics and engineering was added the following year. In 1871, F. E. Stimpson was employed to teach physics and chemistry in place of the part-time teacher, Dr. Saunders; and three years later G. E. Patrick relieved Stimpson. Patrick remained for ten years, the Chemistry Department showing marked growth, for not only were professional chemists developed, but mineralogy, metallurgy, and assaying were taught to many students who subsequently utilized their training all over the mining West.

This rising tide of chemical students soon overflowed the bounds of the original ample space in University Hall, and the demand was made for a new building. The request for a new building had, however, a more potent reason than the simple need for more space. The Chemistry Department, as Patrick pointed out to the Regents, being located in the low basement of University Hall, had no way of removing those odorous and injurious gases which it seems to be the necessary lot of the chemist to produce. "Further," said Patrick, "these gases frequently rise into the corridors and rooms above, occasioning great annoyance to those in the other classes, if not actual injury to health."

Such arguments prevailed with the Legislature, especially after they had sent a committee down to inspect the University and to sniff for themselves; and in 1883, an appropriation of $4,000 with permission to use an unexpended interest fund of $8,000 for this purpose was granted.

A site was selected some fifty feet southwest of University Hall for the new building, and construction was begun. By January, 1884, Professor E. H. S. Bailey, who had succeeded Professor Patrick in the fall of 1883, was able to move his departmental belongings and odors into the second of the present buildings of the University.

13. Student Journalism

Prof. Robinson of the chair of ancient languages in the University of Kansas has gone to Dodge City. This week the great Spanish bull fight takes place there, something never seen outside of Mexico on this continent. The professor doubtless goes in the interest of classical history—Taurus, the bull, is an historical character and the professor will doubtless learn much to enrich his scholarship and illustrate classical studies in his class room.—We can assure him he will find a most unique and peculiar city out on the plains at Dodge, and will meet with a brave, generous, hospitable and soundly Democratic people, though a little wayward and volatile in non-essential particularities.—*Kansas City Times,* July 2, 1884.

FACULTY members of 1884 had to watch their step—as they do now. Professor Robinson spent many years—always with a twinkle in his eye—explaining the notice above, especially after a local paper prepared an editorial "A Bad Example" calling attention to the professor's westward trip. Fortunately the celebrated bull fight at Dodge City was not successful in permanently introducing the Spanish "pastime" in this country; so University professors had no further occasion to be led astray from such a cause. What the new chancellor—for a new one had just appeared on the campus—thought of this faculty publicity has not been recorded. His thoughts, if expressed, might have made reading as interesting as that

describing the faculty member in search of new adventures.

Dr. Marvin had resigned in the summer of 1883 and shortly became the first superintendent of Haskell Institute, the federal Indian school established at Lawrence in 1884. The Regents had elected as his successor Dr. Joshua A. Lippincott of Carlisle, Pennsylvania. Evidently the Board had come not only to accept residency in Pennsylvania as one of the requirements for the chancellorship but to insist on ability as a mathematician as well. Fraser, Marvin, and Lippincott all had these essentials, for Lippincott was professor of mathematics at Dickinson College when

THE WEEKLY·UNIVERSITY COURIER.

PUBLISHED EVERY FRIDAY MORNING.   UNIVERSITY OF KANSAS.   SUBSCRIPTION FIFTY CENTS PER YEAR.

VOL. III.   LAWRENCE, KANSAS, OCTOBER 24, 1884.   No. 7.

LOCAL.

All quiet.

Elections over.

Orophilian settled.

And Oread subdued.

Hallowe'en is coming.

There are over fifty students in the musical department.

It is about time for the "annual '87 ball" to materialize.

Watch dogs grow more numerous as Hallowe'en approacheth.

Both literary societies have good programs for this afternoon.

The Sophomores have their regular annual meeting to-day at 2:30.

The medic students are petitioning for a subject. Cleveland will do.

When Business College boys meet University boys, then comes the—policeman.

The annual faculty reception will be next Friday evening, one week from this evening.

There were a large number of students at the Republican rally, and manifested great enthusiasm over Col. Martin.

There is but one "Independent Republican" in the University of Kansas. If Blaine is elected he will hold an indignation meeting.

Having received written requests from a great many "interested" students, we suppress Dr. Millard's statement, of which we spoke in our last issue.

Miss Thompson and Messrs. Bales and Franklin form the orchestra about which we have heard so much since its exceptionally fine performance in Oread last Friday.

The K. S. U. foot ball team has received a formal challenge from the Washburn team to play a game of foot ball. The challenge has been accepted and the game will be played Saturday, Nov. 1.

We will say to "Mulcahai" that his lengthy, pleasingly written rythmic production on "Frat Initiation" occasioned our president a great deal of amusement, and he may insist upon its appearance next week: too late this, however.

Mrs. Turpin, the lady who cooks for the "Hungry club on Ohio street," spread some damp matches on the garret floor to dry. They dried, and if they had not been discovered when they were, the hole would have been burnt much larger.

There was a little boy,
And his name was Grover.
When he was initiated,
He was initiated all over.

A canvass among the faculty as to presidential preference, showed a remarkable unanimity for Blaine and Logan. All but three were straight Republicans, and those will probably get down on the Republican side of the fence. Almost all are for Martin for governor, but a few are not yet decided as to which side will win.

Instead of speaking to vacant chairs, as heretofore, the Seniors are "posted" for Friday mornings, when each student is expected to be in his seat. Although it may be somewhat trying on "us," the Seniors, at least, ought to thank either Prof. Brownell or Providence for this novel arrangement.

Are we to suppose from the action of the recent joint meeting of literary societies and the faculty, that the seventh page of our next catalogue is to be blank? Then are we going to do away with the library also, and finally put up the building at auction? Is this a University or is it a country school?

The Oratorical Association met Tuesday and formed a permanent organization, with the following officers: President, E. F. Caldwell; vice president, J. D. McLaren; secretary, H. A. McLean; treasurer, W. Y. Morgan; executive committee, W. H. Johnson, T. F. Doran, S. M. Cook. At the meeting to-day the date of the local contest will be decided upon.

As we prophesied in our last number, the tariff debate in Oread drew a large house. Two men on the negative failed to respond, and W. Y. Morgan, of the affirmative, suddenly changed his opinions and aided Mr. Bennett on the negative. Crane did nobly, pouring forth many facts in the most glowing eloquence. Gilmore painted the free trade and "protection" pictures in a most touching manner. Bennett showed very clearly that all the affirmative said was not what it was represented to be. Morgan, after making a neat speech of about ten minutes, in which he quoted statistics from his own mind, arose and denied all he had stated. It is evident from the facts produced that there are two sides to this question.

A large concourse of people have been filling the millinery parlors of the Misses Mugler for the last 24 hours. The event is their grand opening for the year. They are open all day to-day, and every young lady of the University should call.

PERSONAL.

E. F. Stimpson is the new Beta.

E. F. Neil is a Phi Delta Theta.

Mr. Grover is a new Beta Kappa Chi.

W. H. Johnson was in Ottawa Saturday.

Ed W. Hamilton is in Chanute, Kansas.

W. Y. Morgan is wrestling with the ague.

Miss Mabel Gore will be with us in a few days.

Harry Smith came back from Atchison Monday.

G. F. Gaumer, '76, is U. S. consul at Yucatan.

Warren Berry is attending school in St. Louis.

Prof. Fulton visited the University this morning.

T. H. Rockwell's father called on him Tuesday.

Pliny L. Soper, '81, was in town one day this week.

Miss Lily Leiby was at the University this week.

Fred Bowersock visited in Wyandotte Sunday.

Robt. McAlpine was at home in Wyandotte Sunday.

G. W. Harrington don't bet on election any more.

J. F. Cress, of Morris County, visited his son last week.

Miss Mamie Hudson is expected down from Topeka to-day.

F. W. Barnes visited relatives in Leavenworth this week.

Ed. Franklin is a recent addition to Phi Delta Theta's rank.

'86 will gain a good man from '85 in the person of E. E. Brown.

Prof. J. W. Green went to Ottawa Thursday, on legal business.

J. D. Davis went to Ottawa to play against the Kansas City Unions.

Barry Hatch was visiting at home in Ft. Riley, the first part of the week.

Mr. Burr, secretary of the Y. M. C. A. went to Leavenworth this week.

Victor Linley has been sick this week, and unable to attend school.

Wm. Albach comes from the Lawrence High School to enter K. S. U.

Prof. L. W. Spring was sick yesterday and unable to teach classes.

Sullivan visited his girl, in Kansas City, Saturday and Sunday.

C. D. Hawkins is principal pedagogue in one of the Fort Scott schools.

Miss Cora Pierson writes from Boston that she is enjoying her studies immensely.

C. S. Metcalfe, no longer president of the COURIER company, is working at his trade.

B. C. Preston has made arrangements to stay in Kansas City Saturday and Sunday of each week.

B. T. Chace, a last year's student, thinks he will go to Ann Arbor next year.

Prof. MacDonald will have charge of the music in Y. M. C. A. hall next Sunday.

Mr. J. Grover will receive applications for membership in the Beta Kappa Chi.

Mr. Cummings was obliged to stay out of school several days, on account of an accident.

Frank Hutchings, the great student tourist. went down to southern Kansas Monday.

Templin is losing his grip on the mashing business. One by one the daisies fade.

Wm. Priestley has returned from a summer in Idaho, and is now an agriculturist near Baldwin.

W. H. Sears and wife have returned from Chillicothe, Ohio. and will spend the winter in Lawrence.

Prof. Canfield will speak to the Y. M. C. A's. next Sunday evening in the Congregational church.

Chas. L. Smith writes that he attended Mormon services at the tabernacle, Salt Lake City, last Sunday.

Chancellor Lippincott and wife went to Topeka Wednesday, to attend a banquet given by the new M. E. bishop.

J. R. Turner returns to the Senior laws. He had intended to attend Ann Arbor, but the attractions of K. S. U. were strongest.

John T. Harlow, the leader of the Orophilians in olden times, has been nominated by the Democrats of Wyandotte County, for county attorney.

B. K. Bruce went to Leavenworth with the "Cyclones" Tuesday, and seems to be taking a vacation. Happy over his victory in Orophilian last week, he is probably enjoying himself at home, in Brunswick, Mo., for a few days.

Prof. R. I. Fulton, president of the Kansas City School of Oratory, will organize classes in elocution at the Y. M. C. A. rooms Thursday afternoon and Friday. He is said to even excel as a teacher, his associate. Prof. Trueblood, of last year

A typical page from the *Courier* of the eighties. A few weeks before the above issue was published, the editors had announced, "Instead of being filled with insipid matter that might have been written a century ago the *Courier* will contain only the latest, breeziest, and most interesting matter concerning the University."

Chemistry Hall, as it appeared in the late nineties; the view looks south.

elected, and like his immediate predecessor, was also a clergyman.

For much of the information on the administrations of Marvin and of Lippincott, as well as on the life of the University in general during this period, we are indebted to the student press. The student press, however, in its earlier years, had a hectic history, in keeping with the tradition of Kansas journalism.

Kansas, from its territorial days, has never lacked its articulate exponents. It doubtless is a fact of considerable importance that the first Kansas institution to be established was a newspaper, whose press was set up under an elm on the site of Leavenworth before a house was to be seen. From that day to this, the press of Kansas has been one of the distinguishing characteristics of the state.

Independent, optimistic, aggressive, and vociferous, Kansas editors have now for nearly a century proclaimed in no uncertain terms the particular merits of their state, put their critics and opponents "under the harrow" with a delightful singleness of purpose, consoled its citizens in their unfortunate days, and rejoiced with them in their prosperity. If a new cause needed support, a Kansas editor could usually be found to espouse it.

With this background of editorial tradition, it is not difficult to understand the early days of newspaper journalism at the University. Begun early in the life of the University, the student press in its first thirty years shows a history characterized by many papers, by frequent controversy and strife between individuals or factions, and by frequent consolidations. Between the years 1874 to 1904 there appeared no less than fifteen distinct titles of weekly or monthly papers. In the school year 1878-79—with a student enrollment of only 400—three of these student

folios were being published, and in 1885-86, two papers with identical titles were issued!

The first student paper in this devious history of the University press, was the *Observer of Nature,* the first issue of which appeared on April 1, 1874. The *Observer* was essentially a publication of the Natural History Society, but its pages also contain a number of items of general University news. The *Observer* was followed in 1875 by the *Kansas Collegiate,* which was "devoted to general literature and University news." The *Collegiate* survived for four years and was then consolidated with a rival in the *Kansas Review.* The *Review,* a monthly magazine containing general articles written by faculty and students, also included considerable University and personal news. The *Review* had the longest life among early University student publications, but came eventually to an end in the spring of 1896.

The two student weeklies that had the longest lives in this early period were the *University Courier* (1882-1895) and the *Kansas University Weekly* (1895-1904). The *Courier,* beginning originally as a biweekly, reached its heights in the late eighties, but during the later part of its career eked out a precarious existence.

Fraternity control and conflict, the clash of personalities, and even, on one occasion, jealousies between literary societies, were responsible for the rise and fall of these student journals. Without exception, however, all were ardent supporters of the University, and many of the advances and improvements in the University can be traced to policies advocated by the student press. For the most part, the weeklies reflect the wit and exuberance of youth, to say nothing of its cockiness. The policy of one journal of the

University Hall occupies the center of this picture, but at the extreme right may be seen Snow Hall, still under construction. The photograph, looking southwest, was taken in the fall of 1885.

25

nineties can be taken as more or less typical of all: "The *Journal* reserves the right to reprimand the presumptuous and the erring; it not only reserves the right, but will use it whenever and wherever occasion requires its use." Like all good Kansas newspapers, the student journals were no respecters of persons; and even administrative or professorial rank was no insurance against the darts of outrageous reporters. Will Snow, for example, was added to the staff of the University in 1891 as secretary to his father, Chancellor Snow. The *Courier* in commenting on the neatness and dispatch with which young Snow accomplished his work added the pert and pertinent judgment: "Papa's pants will soon fit Willie."

The student journals from 1874 to 1904 served as the proving ground for many students who later became well-known in Kansas journalism; and if the scope of our attention be widened still further we would find on the editorial pages of student papers names of many persons who later achieved distinction in many other lines of endeavor.

14. Snow Hall of Natural History

We meet, today, to formally celebrate another step in the growth and progress of the State University—to dedicate this beautiful building, the home for all future time of the Department of Natural History. Very properly the building is to bear the name of the learned, devoted and enthusiastic teacher to whose energy, industry and zeal the State is indebted for treasures that are gathered within its walls. I discharge a very pleasant duty, gentlemen of the Board of Regents, when, in the name of the State, I commit to your keeping this stately edifice.—Governor John A. Martin at the dedication of Snow Hall, November 16, 1886.

THE ARRIVAL of the elder Agassiz at Harvard University in 1847 marked the beginning of a new era in the teaching of the natural sciences in this country. For Agassiz emphasized the direct study of nature and assembled enormous working collections of animals, insects, shells, and stones in the Harvard museum. If insects were to be studied, there were at hand all classes and varieties of insects to be actually examined and compared. The textbook was thus not the primary tool in the study of a natural object, but the object itself was to be studied by the aid of textbook. This method, commonplace at present, was revolutionary in its day; but was, nevertheless, rapidly adopted. Schools and colleges over the country formed collections of natural objects which, as they were collected, were stored in suitable cabinets. "Cabinet Collections" soon became recognized working tools of every collegiate institution. The University of Kansas almost immediately upon its organization adopted this "modern" method of teaching, for the second catalog of the institution (that for 1867-68) announced the formation of "Geological, Mineralogical and Zoological Cabinets" and invited friends "to send to these Cabinets such specimens as may add to their completeness and value."

Friends of the University did respond in generous measure, but the growth of the cabinets in the University was primarily due to its professor of natural science, Francis Huntington Snow. Interesting his students in collecting expeditions during the summer vacations, Snow with his students ranged far and wide over Kansas, Colorado, and the Southwest, and built his cabinets to sizable proportions. University Hall, in its plans and construction, provided ample space at first for the cabinets and the natural history rooms in

Collector F. H. Snow in the field. Taken in Colorado, August, 1889.

26

Snow Hall, about 1895. The photograph shows the east side and, at the right, the front of the building, which faced north. The picture is of additional interest because it shows the western limits of the campus at that time. The road made a circle in front of the building but went no further west.

the upper floors of the south wing. By 1877, the collections numbered some 40,000 specimens; but in five years, because of the indefatigable Snow, the collection contained 100,000 specimens. The difficulties of classifying, arranging, and making easily accessible this valuable teaching equipment, it can be seen, would grow with its size. Students, too, in growing numbers, during these same years flocked to the University, the attendance increasing from 359 in 1877 to 582 in the fall of 1883. Space for the growing Natural History Department, even with the removal of the Chemistry Department to its new quarters in 1884, became difficult to find. The Regents, to remedy the situation, decided in the fall of 1884 to ask the Legislature for an appropriation of $50,000 for a natural science building. The prospects were none too good at first for securing this fund, as only the year before it was with difficulty that the $12,000 used in the construction of the chemistry building had been obtained.

For a number of years, however, Snow had diligently pointed out to the citizens of the state the value of his work, especially in entomology; for, wrote Snow as early as 1878, "The extensive collections are of practical value to the agricul-

tural and horticultural interests of the state, as well as to the students of the University, in the determination of the names and the habits of our insects, friends and foes." Such a utilitarian argument must have won the day, for the Legislature voted to appropriate the requested funds in the spring of 1885.

The Regents, upon receiving notice of the appropriation, not only allowed Snow to choose the location of the new building but also paid the professor of natural history a well-deserved compliment in naming the building "Snow Hall of Natural History" before construction was complete.

Snow selected a site about 200 feet west of the center of University Hall—in front of present Watson Library—and the work of construction was started in the summer of 1885 and continued during the fall. The *University Courier* in its issue of October 2, 1885, commenting on the progress of construction, remarks: "As the Natural History building grows, Professor Snow's smile grows broader and broader."

The walls of the building were up as far as the second floor when wintry weather stopped construction until the following spring. The building was complete by the fall of 1886 and the official dedication took place on November 16, 1886.

For forty-four years Snow Hall served well its purpose on the campus. Through its halls trooped thousands of students, many of whom were destined for great achievement. In those forty-four years it housed many departments and provided for many and varied activities.

Despite Governor Martin's prediction of 1886, engineers noticed by 1912 that the building was becoming unsafe for use, and with the growth of the University, more efficiently planned quarters became desirable. It was not used after 1930, but was slowly demolished, the last traces of the historic building disappearing in 1934, and students since that day are unfamiliar with its appearance save as it appears in photographs.

15. Rock Chalk, Jay Hawk!

At this time [the territorial period] patriotism and larceny had not entirely coalesced, and upon the debatable frontier between these contending passions appeared a race of thrifty warriors, whose souls were rent with conflicting emotions at the thought of their bleeding country's wrongs and the available assets of Missouri. Their avowed object was the protection of the border. Their real design was indiscriminate plunder. They adopted the name of "Jayhawkers."—John James Ingalls, "The Last of the Jayhawkers."

ALMOST as old as Snow Hall is the most famous college yell in America. Not to mention this most famous yell—a claim that we ourselves are modestly willing to admit—would be an oversight for which we would never be forgiven. But its fame, spread now over the world, insures it a place in any history of the University, no matter how formal or informal it might be.

Although now used for athletic contests and student rallies, the Jayhawk yell had its origin over doughnuts and cider at a social gathering following a meeting of the University Science Club. In an exuberance of good feeling in those plain and simple days, some one proposed the need for a suitable yell for the society. Professor Bailey, of the Chemistry Department, took the matter under consideration, and being familiar with the history of the state, he proposed the words "Rah, Rah, Jay Hawk, K.S.U." at a meeting of the Club, on May 21, 1886. After trying it out a time or two, repeating the words three times, with staccato emphasis, the Club adopted it for themselves.

The word "jayhawk" or "jayhawker," it should be stated, has itself a history of its own. It was used in 1849—possibly there may have been a still earlier use—by a harrowed band of Fortyniners on their way to California, to denote a group on a desperate venture. It was used in territorial days in Kansas to designate groups of despoilers, bushwhackers, or members of the opposition, especially as a term of opprobrium for free-state men of southern Kansas. As the years went by, the term gained sanctity, and eventually Kansans called themselves Jayhawkers with unmistakable pride.

Dr. Bailey's use of the term in his original version of the year was simply an apt adaptation, then, of a good Kansas word. The yell in this form was used by the Science Club during the following school year (1886-87), for there are frequent allusions to "The Science Club yell" in the Courier. In this period an important additional contribution was made. Someone suggested— an idea doubtless originating from the supposed outcroppings of chalk strata on Mount Oread— that "Rock Chalk" be substituted for "Rah, Rah." Both the idea and the rhyming were eminently suitable and met with favor among the members of the Science Club, and it was not long after its first adoption that "Rock Chalk, Jay Hawk, K. U." was substituted for the original version. The yell has thus uniquely preserved Kansas tradition and Kansas geology, with both of which we are well supplied.

The acceptance of these distinctive words for University use was probably the result of agitation by the Courier; its adoption, however, is intimately tied up with early oratorical contests. The state collegiate oratorical contest in the spring of 1886 was held in Topeka, and the Courier inquired, "Why don't we adopt a yell before we go to Topeka?" No response was made, but the University sent a considerable delegation to Topeka, for the Capital reports: "They [college students] began to arrive on the noon train on the Santa Fe, and by evening, several hundred, including the students at Washburn, were in the city. The boys of the University came up in force. their delegation numbering over 145. Many of them wore plug hats and carried canes, and as they came marching up Fifth Street in a body, the scene was suggestive to many of college days gone by." The University boys at Topeka yelled with great enthusiasm, especially when Cyrus Crane, the University representative, won first place in the contest; but the yelling must have been disorganized, if spontaneous, for even after the contest the *Courier* was still asking, "Why don't we have a college yell?"

With this expressed desire for a school slogan, it was not surprising that the unique Science Club yell attracted the attention of the whole school, for the following year, when the time for the state oratorical contest again came around, we find the earliest printed version of the famous yell. At the end of a paragraph (February 4, 1887) which attempted to work up enthusiasm for the contest, appeared the words "Rock-Chock-Jay Hawk-K.U." The yell was still so new to the reporter that the significance of the second word was not realized! By the next fall, however, it was known to all as the property of the whole University, for the *Courier* on November 4, 1887, reads: "Every college of importance in this country has a college cry. In every town in which a college is situated, the midnight air resounds with the hideous yells of the student, symbolic of victory, defeat, or devilment. The students of the University of Kansas use their yell but little and it is only amidst great victory that Rock-chalk-Jay-Hawk, K-U-U-U floats through the midnight air reminding one of a band of Apache Indians."

By 1889, the form was changed to the rolling, drawn-out cadence repeated twice and followed by three staccato renditions that have made it famous the world around.

As the years went by and the yell became better known, speculations as to the actual nature of a

One of the first places to resound to the "Rock Chalk" was the Santa Fe station, shown above. Here, as student delegations arrived and left for oratorical contests, there was always college color and atmosphere. The photograph was made in January, 1886, four years after the station was built. It was taken in front of the building from the top of a boxcar on the tracks; the view looks northwest toward town.

jayhawk were advanced. Some credulous individuals actually suggested the theory that a jayhawk was a bird combining the propensities of a jay with those of a hawk, and had it appear as if the liaison thus effected would produce a creature with the quarrelsome nature of one and the predatory instincts of the other. Doubtless there are Kansans with such proclivities, but the idea thus inferred and referred to the jayhawk did not strike popular fancy, and most individuals were content to treat the animal as purely a creature of tradition. Artists began, as early as 1901, to depict their imagination of the bird, and through the years a variety of creatures have been pictured as *the* jayhawk.

16. The Law School

The Law Department now offers to those seeking knowledge in this "learned profession" all the advantages of home instruction. A two year Law Course is provided for those who are prepared to enter upon this study with a purpose to master the principles and willing to perform the labor necessary to become proficient in the profession.—University advertisement, *Kansas Review*, November, 1879.

ONE OF THE most beloved figures in University student life had already appeared on the campus before the Rock Chalk was first heard. James W. Green, affectionately known to many generations of students as "Uncle Jimmy Green," was the first of the many deans who have served the University. Green, a lawyer by training and profession, came to Lawrence in 1875 as a young man of thirty-three. Three years later, the Regents of the University invited Green to head the newly organized Department of Law which had long been contemplated but never realized. Green accepted, and on November 4, 1878, the same day he was elected county attorney, be-

The first Law class—one of eight members—was graduated from the University in 1880, so that the one pictured here with Dean Green and Professor Summerfield was the sixth to be graduated. The lone whiskerless graduate appears almost indecently clad in the presence of his hairy contemporaries.

gan the instruction of thirteen young men who had hopes of a legal career. The state provided no income for its Law Department at first, but Uncle Jimmy was permitted to collect twenty-five dollars from each hopeful aspirant to the bar. Green, of course, had to continue the practice of law as a means of livelihood, and did not devote all of his energies to the Law Department until after 1885. Nevertheless, he appears in the University catalog for the fall of 1879 as the "Dean" of the Law Department, the first dean of the present professional departments of the University.

Since Green could devote only a part of his time to instruction, the legal education of the embryo barristers was supplemented with lectures by local and visiting members of the profession and by a requirement, established by state law, of actual service in the office of a practicing lawyer. The *Courier,* during the eighties, described on one occasion the result of this requirement. If some instances recorded are the result of the fertile imagination of the reporter, they are, at least, within the bounds of possibility. The student reporter wrote as follows:

> It is one of the requirements of the Law Department that each member of the senior class, in order to graduate, must read law in the office of a regular practicing attorney, and Professor Green a few days since made a round-up to see if the boys were located, and found Roberts in the office of Harris and Harris with his feet on the desk reading Bill Nye's address to the Major. King was nursing his burnsides and cleaning spittoons for Spangler. Jacobs was polishing the stove in the office of Barker and Summerfield. Gilmore was swearing legal oaths at a refractory stove-pipe which he was vainly trying to put up in Judge Thacher's office. Wolley was dusting carpets for Alford. Fidler was scrubbing out for Riggs and Nevison. Peairs was sweeping down the cob-webs and reading Peck's Bad Boy in the office of Hugh Blair and Palmer was sawing wood and advising Patterson on points of domestic relations. The others we are still to hear from.

A room for legal instruction was provided for Dean Green in University Hall, but the Law Department was shuffled through many rooms and several buildings before it came eventually to Green Hall in September, 1905. In its earliest years the Law Department had a room on the first floor of University Hall, but as the Univer-

This remarkable interpretation of legal training appeared in the *Helianthus* for 1889. It headed the section entitled "The Department of Law."

sity grew, the demand for space grew with it. To provide additional space, North College was again pressed into service. In the summer of 1890, the building was remodeled and the Law School—the department had become a *school* of the University in 1889—had two fine recitation rooms, a library, and a cloak room on the first floor of Old North. Old North had been little used by the University since 1872 but had been used for some time by the state as a home for the feeble-minded. The feeble-minded were moved to Winfield and the Law School moved in! The students of the law appeared to be content with their new quarters, save for occasional discontented murmurings caused by the odors which arose from the janitor's kitchen in the basement below, until the fall of 1894, when they were again moved back to University Hall. Here they again had more commodious quarters, as a good deal of the engineering equipment had moved into Blake Hall, then in the process of erection.

The first of the school rivalries had begun with the removal of the Law School to Old North, but it was not the traditional one that we now know between the Engineers and the Lawyers. Rather it began between the Lawyers and the Collegians —that is, the students in the School of Arts. The rivalry never reached any high-water mark and was due no doubt to the considerable distance separating the Law School from the rest of the University. Occasional forays were made on both sides, but as the *Courier* remarked on the occasion of their first encounter: "The Laws are not spoiling for a fight nor are the Collegians pervaded by an overwhelming desire to become pugilists. The whole affair is a mere exhibition of class spirit and shows that the school on the hill is what it claims to be, a University."

17. The Engineers

The side walk on Mississippi Street to the University has been completed. Many of the students this year have in consequence engaged rooms in West Lawrence.—*Lawrence Weekly Tribune*, September 21, 1888.

LEST THE charge of partiality be made after describing the brief story of the Law School, the Engineers will be passed in review. The well-known rivalry between students of these schools is comparatively modern in origin and, if present indications are signs of the future, will likely soon be ancient history. The first reference found concerning disagreement between these adversaries relates an occurrence of May Day, 1900. During the night following May Day, the Engineers placed a huge boulder on the campus—it is said to have weighed 5,000 pounds—with the inscription "Eng. '01" on it. The Laws saw it the next morning and with true legal inquisitiveness wondered if there was anything beneath it. Displaying more engineering skill than one would have expected, the embryo members of the bar were able to turn it over, probably with the idea of rolling it down the hill. The Engineers, however, were able to restore it to its original position. Chancellor Snow evidently saw in the stone the possibility of a long-continued school struggle, for the *University Weekly* remarks: "Wednesday morning the Chancellor unthoughtedly hid a charge of dynamite under the stone, and it was in some unaccountable manner discharged. It is certainly to be regretted as the stone was very much admired by almost all the students."

The first struggle being a draw, we shall have to examine earlier history to see if either faction should feel that Providence had smiled with unusual favor on their own efforts. Here again matters are not as conclusive as either side might wish. Although the Law School can claim an earlier existence as a department and a school than can the Engineers, yet engineering was in the University long before law courses. Frederic W. Bardwell had been added to the faculty as early as 1869 as professor of mathematics and engineering, and the first class to be graduated in 1873, it will be recalled, contained a graduate in civil engineering, although he had received a Bachelor of Arts degree.

Engineering, however, was continued in the

Engineering students, 1886. The photograph was taken in front of Fraser Hall and includes about one-half of the total number of Engineering students enrolled that year. Why the remaining Engineers were not included is unknown; possibly there were not enough derby hats to go around. The individuals portrayed have been identified as follows: 1. Chapin, F. S.; 2. Henshaw, L. D.; 3. Springer, C. E.; 4. Savage, F. J.; 5. Davis, F. L.; 6. Dalton, B. J.; 7. Oakley, F.; 8. Williamson, P. A.; 9. Birbeck, R.; 10. McAlpinge, R. L.; 11. Sloan, A. L.; 12. Short, R. H.; 13. Professor Marvin; 14. Eames, E.; 15. Stimpson, E. F.

Summer Surveying Camp, Civil Engineers, 1897. Dean Marvin is the seated figure in the foreground.

"Department of Sciences, Literatures, and Arts," and engineering courses drew increasingly larger enrollments, until in 1878 an additional man was added, F. O. Marvin, son of Chancellor Marvin, who at that time became assistant professor of mathematics, physics, and civil engineering.

The work of instruction in the engineering courses was carried out solely in University Hall until 1887. In that year, however, Lucien I. Blake came to the University as professor of physics and astronomy, and a four-year course in electrical engineering was announced with Blake's coming. A new powerhouse, erected in the fall of

One of the advantages of a training in civil engineering, according to the *Cicala*, the annual for 1884.

1887, provided additional space for instruction in mechanics and practical electricity, but continued increases in enrollment taxed the capacity of the University to provide for its engineering students. Blake was an active worker in securing the interest of the state and, backed by Marvin, who made many off-the-campus surveys, eventually secured an appropriation for a physics building, in which many of the engineering courses could be given. Ground was broken for the new building in the summer of 1893, but it was not ready for occupancy until the fall of 1895. The completion of the building again aroused the interest and pride of the state, and comments of the press were numerous. The *Hutchinson News*, for instance, remarked: "The new engineering building at the State University will be dedicated this week. Kansas University is the only institution in the west where electrical engineering, the greatest of all sciences, can be thoroughly studied."[1]

Originally called simply the Physics Building or Engineering Building, it was not officially named Blake Hall until the spring of 1898.

Before Blake Hall was built, the engineering courses had been organized into the School of Engineering in 1891, with F. O. Marvin as its first dean. The new Engineering School started

---

[1] It should be mentioned, of course, that although Kansas was a pioneer in engineering education in the West, other schools had led the way. Rensselaer Polytechnic Institute established apparently the first engineering course in this country in 1833. Rensselaer was followed by other schools in introducing engineering curricula, notably the University of Michigan in 1851 and Cornell University in 1868.

its first year with an enrollment of nearly a hundred and maintained that level for some years. New features were introduced occasionally in the early years, notably the summer camp for civil engineers in 1894, an institution that was a regular part of their curriculum for many years.

The Collegians apparently looked down on these early Engineers as a rough and uncouth lot, and it is surprising that a rivalry did not spring up between these two sets of students as it had to some extent between Laws and Collegians. But the Engineers had little time for such frivolity. Their curriculum was heavy and prescribed, and their energies were bent on completing an education. But the bright and cheerful guardians of public manners and morals on the *Courier* staff

were fond of slipping in sly remarks, such as "Engineering students taking draughting are more gentlemanly this year than they have been for years. Instead of expectorating tobacco juice all over the floor, as formerly, they confine themselves to the registers."

The Engineers may have been addicted to the weed, but they made some important improvements on the campus. Among the chief of these was the installation of the first electric lighting system of the University, the work of installing the dynamo and wiring the main building being accomplished by the students in 1891, although the University had a few of the "new" lights by 1888.

18. The University of 1887

The U. S. Census for 1880 shows a hundred and thirty colleges and universities with libraries of over 10,000 volumes. Sixteen State Universities (including several in the south) have libraries of over 12,000. Kansas State University has 8,000! Comment is unnecessary.—*Lawrence Weekly Tribune*, October 7, 1887.

WITH professional students in engineering and law, the University had, by 1887, begun to take on the aspects of an institution worthy of its name. Nearly five hundred students were present on the campus, and of these two-thirds were of collegiate grade. Among those students who climbed Mount Oread to enroll on a warm September day of that year were a number who later achieved considerable distinction. Vernon Kellogg, a junior, Will White, a sophomore, Edwin Slosson, a freshman, and Herbert Hadley, a preparatory student, despite their later reputation, all mopped their brows and panted as they toiled up Adams Street. Their effort, if it has been any consolation to them or to their fellow sufferers, was a planned part of their training foreseen many years before. For one of the com-

missioners who had selected the site of the University, had written in 1863, shortly after the choice was made:

"One capital idea in connection with the location of the University—while the student is climbing the hill of science he must every day climb Mount Oread. This will constitute practical gymnastics, to develop and strengthen the lungs, digestion, and the locomotive powers! Here muscular power will be developed with brain power!"

This commentary will doubtless be read with mixed feelings by all those who, with effort, have ever had to climb the Hill. The University papers have always freely advised newcomers as to the proper procedure for conditioning oneself for the climb after an easy summer's vacation. One of the better bits of advice given by the *Courier* reads: "After the new student has climbed the hill half a dozen times he imagines that he has every complaint known to medical science. Witch hazel oil is good. This is no fake."

Easier approaches to the campus and easier methods of getting on the Hill were still far distant in 1887. A few of the more fortunate home boys rode ponies, and some of the girls drove the family horse and buggy to class, which made it still more difficult for the walkers, as every buggy that passed up Adams Street threw clouds of dust in its train. Progress and improvements were being made, however, as is shown by the

Football in front of Fraser Hall. About 1887.

34

The University of Kansas, fall, 1887. The view, looking south, shows in the foreground Robinson's Pasture (now Stadium Field); in the middle distance is a field of shocked corn, and behind the field may be seen the young trees of Marvin Grove. The three buildings are (left to right) University Hall, Chemistry Hall, and Snow Hall of Natural History.

following revealing account from the *Lawrence Tribune* in the summer of 1887.

Work at the University

A *Tribune* reporter upon visiting the University yesterday, found Dr. Lippincott hard at work in his office with his coat off and his sleeves rolled up, working away as though his life depended upon it. Upon turning and walking down the hall, he was attracted by the workmen in the new library in the north end of the building. Turning his steps in this direction he found the librarian, Miss Carrie M. Watson, directing a number of workmen in fitting up the rooms to be occupied. The library as it will now be arranged, will contain over three times the room formerly occupied by it in the south end. As has been stated in a previous issue, Prof. Miller's old lecture room will be fitted up and used as a reading room. Prof. Templin's old room is with the general library, while the large hall opening into it will be fitted up with shelves and alcoves for Congressional documents. Prof. P. J. Williams' old room will be used for the law library. Miss Watson is hard at work every day arranging the books which are now being classified after the system used in the best eastern libraries. Miss Watson informed the reporter that the library would be increased very much in value by a gift of 250 volumes of valuable books, together with

Professor F. H. Snow and a party of K.U. students on the top of Long's Peak, August 6, 1889. Top, Herbert Hadley; second row from top, Vernon Kellogg (left), Nell Franklin, Will Brewster; third row, Fred Funston, S. C. Brewster, Eva Fleming; fourth row, Professor Snow, Frank Craig; bottom row, Harry Riggs, E. C. Franklin.

a large number of Congressional books, which would be known as the Haskell Loan Library. By this gift Mrs. Haskell will win the gratitude of every student in attendance at the University in the future. Mrs. Haskell's generosity to the University is only equalled by that of her lamented husband, both of whom have aided the University in every possible way. Workmen were also engaged in putting in new cases in Prof. Nichols' lecture room. The Chemistry Building was next visited, where Prof. Bailey and Mr. E. C. Franklin were busily engaged as usual, making chemical analyses. Prof. Bailey was found hard at work on the celebrated Tennyson case, making an analysis of the kidneys of the deceased for arsenic. Mr. Franklin was just completing an analysis of the celebrated Geuda Springs mineral waters, there being seven springs, and he was just completing the seventh analysis. Upon visiting Snow Hall, Judge West, Prof. Snow's able assistant in Paleontology, was found busily engaged in arranging the large collection recently purchased of W. J. Parrish, in the interchangeable drawers recently placed there by McFarland and Son. Will Snow was found printing labels on a small hand press for the different specimens contained there, upon which he has been at work for over six months. The old boiler house was found to be nearly torn down, and a large number of men were found at work excavating for the new building, under the direction of Mr. Schneider. Mr. Crocker is very busy with a large force of men rearranging the steam pipes in the main building. Every one around the builders seems to be busily engaged, and numerous improvements are being made in every part of the building. Dr. Lippincott is working day and night in the interest of the University, and the prospects for the coming year are as favorable as could be desired.

A legislative appropriation during the preceding year had given the University funds for tearing down the original smokestack and replacing it with more adequate equipment necessitated by the increased demands of the two "new" buildings. The work was slow in getting under way, with the result that cold weather caught the University before the new heating plant was installed and many and bitter were the complaints of the students. "What will the people of the East think," moaned the *Courier*, "when they have heard that sunny Kansas was obliged to close her University on account of cold weather? Even now some of the rooms are so damp that a great number of students have taken severe colds from having to sit in them during the recitation hours." The boilers and smokestack were eventually placed and classroom comfort was at last regained. (The new boiler house was down over the Hill and southwest of University Hall. It is now used as a garage and storehouse.)

A view looking north from the top of Fraser, 1887. The road that weaves its way down the center of the picture is Mississippi Street; enclosed in the hedgerows on the left is Robinson's Pasture. Note "Old North" on the extreme right and the Kaw River in the distant background.

36

19. Y.M.C.A.

The meeting of the college branch of the Y.M.C.A. is likely to be held at the University the same evening but a little before the literary societies. This will give the boys a chance to attend both meetings the same evening and will surely result in benefit to the organization.—University Times, October 17, 1888.

IF 1887 SAW improvements in the University, 1888 saw still another. Electric lights reached the campus and because Room 11 of University Hall could be lighted every Friday night, even-

ing meetings of the Y.M.C.A. were made possible. Thus one of the oldest and most useful organizations on the campus began its career. For sixty years this group not only has deepened and aroused interest in the religious life of many students but has provided social activities, imparted and published University information, found jobs for jobless students, and given comfort and encouragement to many homesick students in their first few weeks away from home.

The origin of the Y.M.C.A. really dates back to 1882. In that year, the expanding program of the national organization arranged for a state meeting at Topeka. A number of University and town boys attended and returned so enthusiastic that on October 22, 1882, a local organization was formed. Thirteen University men were part of this group but had a separate organization of their own. The town and the University group worked together in securing clubrooms. Funds were solicited from business and University men, some six hundred dollars being raised. With this capital, rooms were rented over a down-town grocery store, and social parlors, reading rooms, and baths fitted up. The combined organizations

proved successful and for six years continued to serve University and town men alike.

As the University grew larger, the possibility of an entirely separate organization was discussed, but until the advent of electric lights in 1888 no steps were taken to make the division. The separation was decided upon, but the division of the organization weakened both branches. By the following school year, however, the University Y.M.C.A. was a flourishing organization of sixty-five members among the three hundred men of the school. In addition to the regular weekly meetings and socials of this year, a special committee was appointed "to become acquainted with the new students as soon as possible and aid them in procuring pleasant rooms and boarding places."

Through the nineties, the activities of the Y.M.C.A. gradually expanded, but University Hall continued to be its meeting place and it was officered solely by students. In the fall of 1899 the first professional secretary, Perry O. Hanson, was employed, and Y.M.C.A. rooms were fitted up in a near-by residence. Hanson stimulated still further activity of the organization, his first year at the University culminating in the first annual Y.M.C.A. banquet in April, 1900, at which Governor Stanley of Kansas and many other notables were present.

Hanson also interested the men of the Y.M.C.A. in the summer conferences at Lake Geneva, Wisconsin, and K.U. men attended these conferences annually until the organization of the Estes Park conference in 1907. Since that time many University men have taken advantage of the inspiration and recreation afforded by the Colorado camp.

The Y.M.C.A. at the present day is probably best known to the student body at large as one of the co-publishers[1] of the *K-Book*, that most handy almanac and calendar of the University and University events. The first of these K books appeared in the fall of 1891 as the *Student's Hand-Book* and was originated by the University Y.M.C.A. It was a pocket-sized book of some thirty pages, containing notes on the Y.M.C.A., a map of Lawrence, a partial calendar of University events, a list of the Protestant churches, addresses of University professors, blank note pages, and advertisements.

[1] The Y.W.C.A., another co-publisher of the K book, and the sister organization of the Y.M.C.A., was initially formed in 1885 but was not very active until after 1892, when a reorganization was effected.

The faculty-senior game of June, 1890. The game was played on the site now occupied by Liberty Memorial High School. The action portrayed shows Professor E. M. Hopkins driving out a two-bagger!

20. Baseball

The *Courier* will do what it can to encourage the organization of clubs in boating, foot-ball and base ball. If we cannot afford boat clubs just at present we can the base and foot-ball. Foot-ball teams can be organized in the several classes, "83" has already taken steps in that direction and will ere long have a very formidable team. That we have the material for one of the best base ball clubs in the State, no one can deny. This was tested last June at Oskaloosa between the K.S.U.'s and the Leavenworth Reds, the club which last fall took the championship of the State, the game resulting in our favor.—*University Courier,* September 8, 1882.

BY THE LATE eighties, student activities were beginning to undergo change. Not only was the Y.M.C.A. brought to the campus, but a growing demand was expressed in student papers for organized athletics and for the formation of intercollegiate leagues. It took considerable missionary work before those hopes were realized. For one thing, the faculty had to be converted. As early as 1882, Chancellor Marvin had written in his annual report:

"Under the guise of college athletics, arrangements are often made for public contests, attended, with all the costs of outfit, time and attention for special drill, excitement of the final occasion, followed by the reaction of both mind and body always consequent upon such efforts. At a time when youth should be forming habits of economy in time and money—when steadiness of purpose in making most of opportunities for mental culture consistent with physical health is most important—all such subversive arrangements are criminal."

Only sporadic efforts against such opposition were made by students, but almost from the first day of University history, baseball had been played. In fact, this oldest of college sports has two common bonds with the University. Both institutions were introduced to the state in 1866, and the boys of the University were among the first to play an organized game.

Although baseball has a history antedating the Civil War, it was not commonly played over the country until returning soldiers brought home knowledge of the game, learned in passing away many an idle camp hour. First attempts to organize baseball teams in Kansas occurred in the spring of 1866, and by fall of that year the Frontiers of Leavenworth, the Wyandottes, and the Hopes and the Antelopes of Kansas City had crossed bats.

The newly aroused interest in the sport led to the organization of two University teams. The organization of the teams was followed shortly by public announcement of a match game to be played Thanksgiving Day, 1866. J. C. Rankin, later a well-known druggist in Lawrence, was to pitch for one team, and James H. Lane, son of Senator Lane, for the other. The announcement reads:

"The university baseball club will play a match game of baseball this forenoon, on the ground in front of the Blakely house, near the park. The game will consist of nine innings: and if they are not all played before the time for the union meeting at the Methodist church the game will be stopped until immediately after the service when the remaining innings will be played. The public generally and the ladies especially are invited to be present and witness this most interesting and exciting American field sport."

Whether divine services interrupted the game or not is one of the unrecorded facts of history, but it is probable that the interruption occurred, for next day the team headed by Rankin is reported to have won, 57 to 39. It must be remembered, however, that the rules of that day favored the batter. There was, for instance, no such thing as base on balls, so that scores were frequently higher than that given above.

No record of matched play with outside teams has been found for the first school year (that of 1866-67), but in the fall of 1867 at least two out-side games were played by the University team, both with the Shawnees of Topeka, the University team losing the first game, 97 to 57, and winning the second.

There are sporadic records of University baseball games through the seventies, but baseball in this period was confined pretty largely to the campus as a class sport.

The first intercollegiate baseball game of which there is definite record is one played with Washburn College on April 18, 1880, and won by Washburn, 29 to 23. With the exception of 1881, there are records of matched play all through the eighties, many of which, however, were with non-collegiate teams. The baseball team in the earlier years was handicapped by the lack of a suitable playing ground. During the late eighties a field was used on South Massachusetts Street (the site of the present Liberty Memorial High School), but its use had to be divided in time with the town team. As the field was also some distance from the University, regular practice was seldom attempted.

The acquisition of McCook Field, and the organization of the Triangular League (Baker, Washburn, and K.U.) in 1891, led eventually to the establishment of baseball as a permanent sport on the campus.

21. The First Football Season

Although laboring under a number of disadvantages, from lack of time and want of proper coaching, the football team has already developed a number of good men and several match games will be played within a few days. Tomorrow the eleven will make its first appearance at Baker, and the result will be watched with interest. The elevens are all provided with good canvas suits with black stockings, caps and belts. The boys will leave on the Southern Kansas, at 10 a.m. tomorrow morning. It is hoped that a large number of students will accompany them and give the proper enthusiastic backing. The fare for the round trip will not be over 95c at the further and will probably be 65c.—The Weekly University Courier, November 21, 1890.

THE YEAR 1890 marks the first intercollegiate football game at the University. Faculty members were becoming more interested in the game, especially after younger faculty men from the East urged its introduction. It had, in fact, become recognized in many eastern colleges as a regular student activity by 1880 and several attempts had been made to introduce it at the University during the eighties. The *Kikkabe* of 1882, the University annual of that year, lists junior and sophomore football teams on a page devoted to football, and through the year the *Courier* had advocated the organization of a football team for intercollegiate competition; but the day of football had not yet arrived. Two years later a foot-ball team was formed and uniforms bought, but there seems to be no record of any competition, although the *Courier* reports that the season of 1884 "had witnessed no defeat for either" football or baseball teams. A challenge had been received from Washburn College and a date set for the game, but for some unstated reason it was never played.

The interest in football remained dormant after these initial ventures until the organization of an athletic association in December, 1889, which included the entire student body, the faculty, and other employees of the University. The association advocated intercollegiate athletics and the acquisition of suitable playing grounds for

40

football and baseball. The interest in athletics continued into the fall of 1890, resulting in the formation of a football team. The first notice of the team to appear in the press occurs in the *Lawrence Journal* for October 29, 1890, which reports: "A match game of football will be played on the ball ground Saturday afternoon between the University eleven and the picked eleven." Whether the "picked eleven" were town boys or a scrub team does not appear, but the game served as a practice one for a game with Baker University at Baldwin on November 12, 1890, which Baker won, 22 to 9. The *Journal* in commenting on the game states that this game was "the first appearance of the K.S.U. football club." Five days later on November 27, the team and "a number of students and professors" went to Kansas City to play the city Y.M.C.A.; a game which was also lost by the University by a score of 10 to 18.

The crowning event of that football year, however, was the final game of the season, and the first home game of which we have record. It was played on December 8th on the Massachusetts Street field. The K.U. team showed a marked reversal of form and gave Baker a real game. The introductory paragraphs from the long account of the game in the *Lawrence Journal* give some realization of the intense interest created by the new University sport.

A Brilliant Game
K.S.U. The Victor Despite the Decision against It.

Lawrence has seen enthusiastic crowds, it has seen the students go wild when Crane won the oratorical contest at Topeka and when the baseball club batted out a lost game from Washburn in the 9th inning, but never did anything approach the wild enthusiasm, the unrestrained demonstration, the wild outburst of yells from a thousand throats when Coleman was seen to break forth from a writhing, struggling mass and after a brilliant run score the touch down which won the game.

Five hundred University students burst over the ropes, rushed across the field, lifted Coleman on their shoulders and bore him off in triumph. It was the most brilliant, the most exciting contest that ever occurred on Kansas soil.

The cheers and noise from several hundred tin horns was deafening. But above all other sounds "Rock-Chalk-Jayhawk KU" could be heard strong and clear. The day was a perfect one, warm enough to make it comfortable for the spectators but cool enough to inspire the players to their best efforts. Baker had the largest delegation present in

The Baker-K.U. Game at Lawrence, December 8, 1890, played on the Massachusetts Street grounds. The referee, Professor Carruth, preserves the dignity of the profession in derby hat and frock coat. The unfortunate victim at the bottom of the pile apparently survived, as there is no record of any casualties!

the memory of the oldest student and every Baker man had a tin horn.

But, as the subtitle of the above account suggests, there was a fly in the ointment of success. The game has always been carried on the University records as a victory for K.U., 14 to 12. Baker, on the other hand, has claimed the game, 12 to 10. The divergent claims arose in this manner. On the beginning of the last play of the game (Baker leading, 12 to 10) Baker had the ball near the K.U. line and on a wedge play tried to force the ball over the goal line. The ball was fumbled, recovered by Coleman of K.U., who ran the length of the field for a K.U. touchdown, and, according to K.U., a victory, 14 to 12. Baker claimed that the touchdown should not be counted because the umpire had called time before Coleman got the ball. The umpire, then the responsible official, was none other than the unfortunate, but honest, Professor Carruth of K.U. His predicament is told by the *Journal* reporter:

Professor Carruth was umpire and had whistled for play to stop but had done so on the request of Peairs (K.U.), who had quit the game. Coleman was acting captain and any decision Professor Carruth made on the understanding that Peairs was captain he should have changed. This he refused to do and persisted in giving the game to Baker when it can only appear that he made his decision on a misunderstanding. Whatever process of reasoning Professor Carruth may adopt to justify his decision, whatever technicalities he may find to fortify him in his position, the game will always be claimed by the entire student body, and will always be remembered as a brilliant and fairly won victory.

The students regarded it as a victory, for that evening the first bonfire of conquest was kindled in Central Park on Massachusetts Street.

The following season of 1891 saw the Triangular League formed. A year later the Western Interstate University Football Association of Kansas, Iowa, Missouri, and Nebraska universities was organized. Since then the record of intercollegiate football at the University is continuous.

22. The Men's Glee Club

Mark this prediction that September 19, 1890 will become one of the most important dates in the history of K.S.U. for it marks the effort toward supplying an urgent and long felt need in our institution.
— *University Courier*, September 26, 1890.

THE IMPORTANT event referred to by the *Courier* was the initial meeting of the Men's Glee Club. New activities were evidently coming thick and fast as the gay nineties opened. The formation and organization of this new student enterprise was largely due to George B. Penny, who came to the University in the fall of 1890 as the dean of the School of Music. Penny pointed out to his prospective members that in forming a glee club not only would they receive some musical education, but the organization would be useful in leading the music at chapel. Probably the main inducement which he held out to the men was a holiday trip out over the state "to bring the University before the people."[1]

With this inducement held out enticingly before them, active work was begun with nearly forty boys; a president (G. H. Sears) and a business manager (G. O. Virtue) were elected, and a program arranged. After two months' work it was decided that a trial concert could be given and Mr. Virtue made the necessary arrangements for an initial appearance in the neighboring town of Eudora.

The trip was made in wagons, and "a glorious trip it was. A few more could have been crowded into the house but it was comfortable as it was. The program opened with Upidee, the words being written for the occasion. The beauty of the thing didn't seem to dawn on the natives. They grinned a little and someone clapped once, but soon recovered his self-control." But the audience was eventually thawed out, and many encores were required.

The concert at Eudora was followed by one at No. 6 Schoolhouse—to which the members walked. These two out-of-town appearances constituted the promised tour of the state. A home

---

[1]It also was Penny's intention to form a girls' glee club, and some steps were actually taken in the fall of 1890 with this object in mind. However, no permanent girls' organization appears to have been formed until the school year of 1904-5.

concert and a rendition of Gilbert and Sullivan's *Trial by Jury,* however, compensated the men for their hard work.

The following year an extensive tour of the state was actually made by the glee club, largely because of the bustle and energy of its manager, John A. Rush. Rush got out handbills and placards, secured reduced rates on the railroad, borrowed five hundred dollars from former Governor Robinson to finance the trip, arranged an itinerary including nine towns, and cut down on expenses by asking hospitable citizens in each of the towns to care for the boys in their homes.

The boys were received royally, and made an excellent impression for the University—and on quite a number of girls—but some apparently were considerably disconcerted when asked to say grace at their hosts' tables.

The returns from this trip incited Rush to still greater efforts the following year; and an elaborate program including twenty-seven towns—the farthest west being Colorado Springs—was arranged for the spring of 1893. Dress suits replaced the collegiate cap and gown worn the first two years, an innovation that was decidedly novel, for many of the boys had never seen a dress suit, much less worn one. The boys returned from this trip with still more glory and credit, marred unfortunately by claims, mistaken no doubt, of hotel managers along the way that towels and silverware could not be found after the Glee Club members had left.

No little share of the success of these early programs was due to the closing number. All the melody and fervor of youth, an irresistible combination, swept audiences off their feet as the men sang the words, adapted by Professor Penny in 1892 from the Cornell song:

> Far above the golden valley
>   Glorious to view,
> Stands our noble Alma Mater,
>   Towering toward the blue.

The combined Glee and Mandolin Clubs of 1890-91. Back row, left to right: C. P. Peabody, Dan Krehbiel, A. J. Eicholtz, S. C. Bloss, C. H. Sears, E. E. Keys, D. Parks, C. A. Chapman, J. H. Sawtell, S. R. Boyce; second row: J. M. Challiss, E. F. Stimson, C. O. Scheffer, Director Penny, G. O. Virtue, E. F. Engel, F. B. Allshouse, Adolph Krehbiel; bottom row: Paul Merrill, J. S. Weaver, E. V. D. Brown, Arthur H. and Fred D. Crowell.

43

23. An Outstanding Faculty

President Eliot said that our University had made more progress in twenty-five years than Harvard had in two centuries, and it is safe to say that K.S.U. has advanced more toward the standard of a real University in the last five years than it did in the twenty years previous. Our progress has almost been in a geometrical ratio. No one who examines our catalogue and visits our University can help but feel that we have here a great institution of learning. No more rudimentary instruction, no more narrow restriction to arbitrary courses. No more apologizing museums. Everything is on a high, a grand, and an advanced order.
—*The University Weekly Courier,* September 11, 1891.

THE WIDENING interests of students in Y.M.C.A., collegiate athletics, and glee clubs should not make us lose sight of the fact that the University possessed a faculty. In fact, by the early nineties, this necessary evil had itself grown to sizable proportions. The original faculty of three had increased to forty-five teachers and lecturers in 1892, and in this same interval the fifty-five preparatory students had become nearly a thousand students, all of whom were of collegiate grade. The lowest year of the three years' preparatory work had been dropped in 1883; and two years later the second preparatory year, with the exception of the language courses, was no longer offered. The effect of eliminating preparatory work had at first resulted in a decrease in total enrollment, as the number in these courses had always been large.

University friends and faculty, however, viewed these changes with satisfaction even if the number of students suffered a temporary decrease. Because of the large number of elementary students, the University had been frequently called the "Lawrence High School" in derision, a term that evidently hurt from its nearness to the truth. Chancellor Lippincott almost from his first day of office advocated the complete elimination of preparatory work, as such a step "will relegate to the preparatory high schools and academies the entire field of the secondary education, in which the State University, indeed, had no rights to be a competitor among them." But this complete abolition did not come until after Chancellor Lippincott had resigned in 1889. Professor Snow was appointed by the Regents to become president of the faculty after Chancellor

The faculty of 1892-93. Standing, left to right: Professors Arthur G. Canfield, Sayre, E. M. Hopkins, Miller, Robinson, Williston, Dunlap, Carruth, Blake, Templin, Bailey. Seated, left to right: Professors Hodder, Dyche, Wilcox, Snow, Blackmar, Penny, Marvin. Missing when the photograph was taken were Professors Anna Dunlap, Gleed, Newson, Haworth, George E. Hopkins, and Dean Green. In addition to the above names, the faculty list included eighteen instructors and assistants.

Chancellor Snow and his executive secretary, Vernon Kellogg, in the Chancellor's office, Fraser Hall. About 1891.

Lippincott left, and the following year Snow became Chancellor. Through legislative action, a reorganization of the University had been made possible when Chancellor Snow took office; and in 1891, all preparatory work was dropped, and the Department of Sciences, Literature, and Arts became at the same time the School of Arts and the School of Engineering.

The faculty, headed by Chancellor Snow, through some fortunate circumstances of chance and of design, was a group of remarkably able men. It contained scholars and teachers who made important contributions to many fields of learning, and whose influence has shaped and molded the University to this day. In the period of the nineties alone this faculty group published over four hundred books and research articles. Many of them, to be sure, were of academic interest only, but many were of immediate practical value to the state itself. The researches of Snow in particular were of especial interest to the state and did much to stimulate good-will toward the University among its citizens. A state that was particularly "bug conscious," because of the grasshopper infestations of 1866, the particularly severe one of 1874, and the chinch-bug invasion of the late eighties, welcomed any information on the types, life histories, and control of insects in general.

The University was fortunate not only in its faculty at this period but in its student body as well. The effect was probably mutual. A brilliant faculty attracted able students. Able students stimulated the faculty to still greater efforts, with a resulting increase in reputation of the University in its faculty and students. Playing an important part in this incentive to productive

Chancellor Snow on his bicycle; from the *Oread*, the annual for 1899, where it appears under the caption, "The Chancellor on the Downward Path."

45

scholarship were the local chapters of the honorary societies, Phi Beta Kappa and Sigma Xi, both of which were formed by members of this same remarkable faculty group. Eight members of the faculty organized a chapter of Phi Beta Kappa on April 2, 1890, and about three weeks later the Sigma Xi chapter was formed. These chapters were both the first to be organized west of the Mississippi River. As a result of all these activities in the period of the nineties, there were produced many individuals who subsequently achieved a world-wide reputation.

But with all their scholarly activities and their interest and concern in the reputation of the University, the faculty was a human and likable group. Snow, for instance, invariably rode a bicycle, and the tales of Snow and his bicycle are legion. Blake prided himself on being the best-dressed member of the faculty, and was the only one to have a personal valet. But the most human tale of all that could be told about the faculty of

this period concerns itself with Penny, of the School of Music—a tale that deals with the legendary and habitual absent-mindedness of the college professor.

Penny had decided to go to Europe during the summer's vacation. After seeing his family off to make summer visits, Penny returned home and made his preparations for his own trip. Packing his bags, he carried them out on the porch, then went to the stable and hitched up the family horse. Locking the door and taking his bags he drove off to the station. Arriving there he tied his horse to the hitching rack and entered the waiting room. The train came in and Penny, unconcerned and carefree, mounted the steps to the coach, leaving his horse firmly tied but completely forgotten. Kind friends, knowing Penny's habits, however, came to the rescue of the horse.[1]

[1]When I first heard this story, I treated it as apocryphal, but several members of the faculty of that day have labored with me with such solemn faces and earnest mien that I am ready to accept it as gospel truth.

24. McCook Field

At the meeting of the faculty Tuesday night it was decided that a list of the members of all organizations, such as glee, baseball and football clubs, that travel around representing the University of Kansas, must be submitted to the faculty and receive their sanction before such tours are made. After this measure goes into effect K.S.U. will be represented only by good students.—The *Weekly University Courier*, January 6, 1892.

THE GROWING interest in athletics, beginning with the revival of the Athletic Association in 1889, led to a demand for a suitable field for baseball, tennis, and football. The grounds on south Massachusetts were used in the early nineties from lack of anything better. But the grounds were far from the University and were frequented by young town toughs who occasionally

A view of McCook taken in the late nineties; looking north and a little west from high ground above the Field.

McCook Field; a game probably played in the fall of 1898. The view looks south toward the University buildings. Notice the row of buggies—with horses removed—in the foreground.

had to be driven off before practice or play could begin.

The Commencement speaker of 1890 was Colonel John James McCook, a prominent New York lawyer. McCook took a decided liking to the rapidly developing University and concluded to aid it in a substantial way. In company with Regent C. S. Gleed he visited the grounds on Massachusetts Street and saw there the Senior-Faculty baseball game. The idea occurred to McCook that a contribution for an athletic field would show his interest in the University in an effective way and before he left Lawrence the Athletic Association was given fifteen hundred dollars for this purpose, and subsequently he added another thousand.

The question of location of the field was agitated for over a year, some members of the Board desiring to purchase the Massachusetts Street place. But through the co-operation of former Governor Charles Robinson it was finally decided to secure twelve acres of "Robinson's Pasture" northwest of the University.

Grading the grounds was not started until the spring of 1892, but by August 1 of that year the *Courier* was able to report:

The grading has been finished on the field and by September it will be leveled and rolled

as smooth as a floor. A grand stand to seat 1,000 people is well under way, the framework being now up and the carpenters working every day; this is in the northwest corner and will be painted crimson. A board fence is being built around the graded part of the grounds. At the northeast corner will be the entrance, ticket office and dressing rooms. Hitching racks will be put inside the fence, a good walk made from the street to

A sketch drawn and dated by Professor Frank O. Marvin, the University's most gifted dean—a judgment that will become apparent when the drawing on page 55 is considered. The above view looks north from the stone entrance of Old Snow Hall.

47

Faculty and students, 1893. This photograph, posed for on the west side of Fraser, was taken by A. C. Atherton of Salina on Monday, February 13, 1893, "at 11:00 a.m."

the gate, and, in fact, everything pertaining to a first-class athletic field will be in shape when the University opens. Clerk Robert K. Moody is giving much attention to the work on the grounds.

The field was called McCook Field almost the day that grading began, although *Quivera* for 1893 states that there was a formal christening. The first football game on the new field was played with the University of Illinois on October 27, 1892, and was won, quite appropriately, by K.U., 26 to 4.

For nearly thirty years McCook Field served its purpose, additions being made to the bleachers as the popularity of football increased, but even continued additions failed to provide the necessary capacity as the fabulous twenties began. It was decided to build a stadium and on May 10, 1921, McCook Field ceased to exist as its fence and decaying bleachers were torn down by student help.

25. The Crimson and the Blue

The football team was ordered onto the athletic grounds at 5 o'clock this afternoon for the first practice of the season. The most stringent rules have been adopted regarding practice and members of the team are also forbidden to stay out late nights or use tobacco on pain of immediate dismissal.
—*Lawrence Journal*, September 10, 1892.

THE GROUP photograph shown here included all of the student body, the faculty, and the football team who were present on the Hill on a day in February of 1893. The football team, as can be seen, is the important feature of this photograph. The faculty were allowed to sit on the front row—doubtless as a simple matter of habit. But the eye is attracted by those magnificent white sweaters—which, although the black-and-white photograph does not show it, were adorned with a resplendent crimson K.

The football team of 1892 were entitled to be the center of all eyes, for they were champions —champions of the West. That these were truly prehistoric days is shown by the fact that Nebraska had been defeated![1] Not only was Nebraska defeated but so were Missouri, Iowa, Illinois, and the Denver Athletics, the champions of Colorado! Yes, indeed, the faculty should have taken a back seat in the picture.

The crimson K's adorning the sweaters, however, are the real cause of the present discussion, and not the successes of the boys wearing them, for in 1892 the school color was crimson, and not the crimson and blue of the present.

All through the eighties when there had been occasion to wear school colors, maize-yellow and sky blue had been used. (These colors had been adopted at the University of Michigan.) One account suggests that they had been the colors chosen by the first class to be graduated by the University of Kansas and had been continued in use since 1873.

Up to 1890 there had been little occasion to use any colors for the University. Intercollegiate athletic contests were virtually unknown, and at occasional oratorical contests University students had identified themselves by pinning ribbons of yellow and sky blue on their persons. With the rising interest in athletics beginning in the nineties, the question of suitable colors was agitated and was the object of special discussion in the fall of 1891. It was agreed that sky blue and corn yellow were too delicate and would soon become

"Champions of the West." The photograph was taken one day before practice in the fall of 1892 at McCook Field. Left to right: (standing) Hugh Means, F. A. Lutz, A. E. Huddleston, W. J. Coleman, Bert (Shorty) Hammill, W. A. Matteson, W. E. Higgins; (middle row) W. H. Kutz, M. B. Mendell, Wilbur Kinzie, Dean Foster; (front row) O. K. (Swede) Williamson, W. H. H. Piatt, A. R. Champlin, O. C. Hill, L. W. Springer. Two of the principal players were not present when the photograph was taken: A. W. Shepard and C. W. Dum.

---

[1]This statement needs some interpretation for readers of today. Defeats of Nebraska before 1941 (when the above statement was written) were rare. The present generation of students has come to regard a Nebraska defeat as a customary event.

soiled if used in football and baseball suits, and that it took too long to say "corn yellow and sky blue." What was desired was a single color, easily distinguished, bright, and flaming.

As there were not many colors that would meet with these requirements, crimson was soon advocated to replace the previous colors. As crimson was also the color of Harvard, I am inclined to think that this fact played a part in the final decision, especially as the student papers of this time were referring to K.U. as "the Harvard of the West." The athletic board decided on October 19, 1891, to adopt crimson as the official color for the football team. Not all students were satisfied with the new color; many wished to retain the old ones. "The blue," they pointed out, "may be taken to represent Kansas skies and the yellow, her harvest fields of ripened grain. . . . The combination is beautiful in itself as well as significant."

The *Courier* made the suggestion that at the next game (after the adoption of crimson by the athletic board) both the color suggestions be given a trial. "If you are a crimsonite buy a bolt of flannel or buy all the red ribbon in town. If you favor the yellow and the blue cause a scarcity in the supply of those ribbons."

The game for the trial of colors was the famous one between Missouri and Kansas at Kansas City—the one in which the first football "special" was used. The score—quite immaterial, to be sure, in our discussion of colors—was K.U. 22, Missouri 8. The *Courier* in reporting on the color question states: "The advantage of crimson as an *advertisement*[1] for K.S.U. over the corn yellow and sky blue is settled beyond all possibility of a doubt since our trip to Kansas City." The students quickly found that crimson had another advantage, too, as a color for "painting the town red" took on an added significance after a victory.

There seems to have been common agreement among the students that crimson would be satisfactory, and it was used for the football seasons of 1892 through 1895. Doubtless our color today would still be crimson alone, if some stray letter had not come to the University in which the statement was made that Kansas was *imitating* another institution in using this color for its heraldry. To students who had been brought up in the faith that "Kansas always leads, but never follows" the momentary aberration in which the custom of another institution had been imitated called for prompt action when once the enormity of the offense was realized. Turning their backs on the boast "the Harvard of the West" they were soon proclaiming with equal fervor, "We owe Harvard nothing," and the search was under way for something new in colors.

Colonel McCook was written to and he suggested crimson and black or crimson and blue. The question was agitated through the school year of 1895, and finally in May of 1896 the athletic board decided to adopt crimson and blue as the colors for athletic teams. The University papers, encouraged by the faculty, fell in line the next fall, and crimson and blue it has remained to this day.

---

[1]Italics mine.

26. Student Life in the Horse-and-Buggy Days

Theatres always have been moral pest houses since their origin in Greece, twenty-four hundred years ago. —Respectable people and respectable business flee from their proximity as from a pestilence.—Theatres can never be reformed. Attendance upon them is a useless expenditure of money and time, and gives support to a class of mountebanks and buffoons that render no equivalent to society for the money they receive.—From a sermon by the Rev. W. K. Marshall in Lawrence on February 9, 1873.

TO THE student of 1954, the world of sixty years ago is antiquity, a world inhabited by strange creatures wearing still stranger clothes and behaving in a silly and unaccountable manner. And it is true! The world of the eighteen nineties, although not far removed in time from the present day—at least not far as history goes— was a world without many of the features of today. No cars, no movies, no radios, no basketball, no intersectional football games, and electric lights still a novelty, to catalog but a few of the differences.

Even with all these physical differences, human nature was, and is, still the same. The student of sixty years ago, in addition to burning occasionally some midnight oil, "romped and fooled and loafed and loved and sorrowed and was happy on the Hill," as do students now.

Without the organized outlets of youthful spirits and enthusiasm of the present day, it is

A student room—about 1891. J. M. Challiss, of the class of '94, on the left; the other student has not been identified with certainty, but he was probably Charles H. Johnson. Note the elegant commode and the bureau, the pitcher and bowl, the stove, and the kerosene lamp. Notice, too, that the mirror bears the photographs of thirteen girls.

not surprising that the most celebrated student pranks in University history occurred during horse-and-buggy days. One of these, the skeleton episode, happened during the week of the first Commencement in 1873, when a human skeleton bearing the label P.R.E.X. in large letters was lowered through a hole in the unfinished ceiling of the chapel, and made to dance and cavort in mid-air, to the horror of many present, as the band of the Fifth U.S. Infantry, imported from Leavenworth, played a public concert. A second prank was the telegram hoax of 1880, which originated in the minds of two "scholars" who had hopes of a day's holiday through their machinations. Hiring a town boy, they caused a false telegram to be delivered to Chancellor Marvin informing him of the sudden death of the Rev. F. T. Ingalls, of Atchison, a most active and loyal regent of the University. Marvin departed immediately for the funeral, after leaving instructions that a memorial service be held in the University chapel next day. At a crowded chapel service next morning Professor Snow delivered a touching eulogy,[1] only to find out at the conclusion of the service that Regent Ingalls was still actively and indignantly alive. The two cul-

prits responsible for this fraud were suspended from their scholarly activities. Probably it is of no significance that both subsequently became lawyers. One returned and finished his career at the University, and thirty years later appeared on the chapel program with a discourse to the students on the way to succeed in life. Nothing was said, however, in the course of his remarks, about the use of telegrams.

Two years after the memorial service for Regent Ingalls, the faculty was blessed by the addition to its ranks of a young graduate of an eastern—very eastern—school, who arrived in Lawrence wearing a silk hat, the first ever seen in use on the University frontier. A committee of students was organized to initiate the young professor into western ways. On Sunday evening he was invited to attend divine services with several of the "committee." If we can judge by the sequel it was probably the first time that some of them had ever graced church doors. As soon as services were over, one by one the members of the committee made excuses for leaving the faculty man to his own devices, but the last departing member was thoughtful enough to offer a six-shooter, cautioning the newcomer on the tough town characters likely to be encountered. As the vic-

[1] The original manuscript is extant.

The boarding club that lost its cow! Even the name of the club reflects a different and more naïve age, for the members called it "Eta Bita Pi."

Club Cow, which departed this life, October 7th, A.D., 1894" was published in the *Student Journal*. The ode began:

> Our cow is dead! her cheerful bawl
> No more will echo through the hall.
> No more is bran mash her delight;
> She overate herself last night!
> The cream she furnished for our wheat
> Was rich and pure and always sweet.
> In fact there never was an hour
> When milk from this cow would turn sour.[2]

* * * *

The Bowersock Theatre, to mention still another interest of bygone days, was originally built in 1882, and after its completion stock shows, eminent actresses and actors on tour, and celebrities of the lecture platform furnished amusement for many generations of students—most of whom patronized the balcony. Trips to Topeka and Kansas City to see similar happenings or to attend the first of the intercollegiate oratorical contests helped occasionally to relieve the tedium of daily affairs.

Then, too, there was infrequent excitement caused by those students who strayed from the straight and narrow path. For many years the University catalog contained the single rule of conduct: *unexceptionable deportment and strict*

[2] A. W. Cunningham, '95, was the author of these lines.

tim showed some reluctance to accept the proffered weapon, the thoughtful student pulled back his own coat and disclosed a similar weapon hung from the conventional holster. The professor hesitatingly accepted the revolver and started home through Central Park from Massachusetts Street. He had not gone far before he heard the sound of many feet trampling through the tall grass and underbrush. A quavering "Who's there?" was followed by a shot which sent the silk hat spinning and caused its owner to start out on a different but a still more rapid trajectory in another direction. In fact, an eyewitness of the event, W. Y. Morgan, of the class of 1885 (later Regent Morgan) stated that there were two shots in rapid succession. The first shot had started the professor from Massachusetts Street and the second one found him on Tennessee. The experience cured the Easterner of any hankering for western ways, and he departed town next day—without his hat.

The record of student pranks, if a complete one could be made, would more than fill these pages. But not all the students' spare time was spent in thinking up such major ones as have been described, or in minor ones which may have embarked an unsuspecting freshman on a snipe hunt.

Fraternities and literary societies furnished a social life with programs, dinners, and dances. Boarding clubs, organized in the early eighties, were meeting places as well as eating places. Board varied with the years, both in price and quality. On some occasions it dropped as low as $1.50 a week; on others it rose to $2.00. When a boarding club for the football team was organized in 1893, the charge was $4.50 a week, but in most other places board could be had for $2.00!

That students' interests were still bucolic in those days as far as the affairs of boarding clubs went, is evident from the fact that an "Ode to the

When nighties were nighties and not bifurcated and gaudy imitations of men's attire. A Pi Phi rush party that stayed all night. Taken by *flashlight* in the fall of 1897. It was made just before retiring; some of the members stayed up all night to finish the photographs so that prints could be used for place cards at breakfast the next morning.

attention to University duties. At times, it must be admitted, exception was taken to some students' deportment. Some students *drank*. Yes, sir, out of a bottle, too. And they not only drank but played cards! Such offenses were not regarded lightly in the rigid days before 1900—nor are they yet—but in those days the University was having a hard enough time establishing its reputation, especially so since it was charged with being a Godless institution containing on its faculty an anarchist, an evolutionist, and free-trader.[3] With

these worries on their hands, the faculty was likely to view with a particularly jaundiced eye any student behavior that would further mire the name of the University. In 1891, sad to relate, such an event occurred. Seventeen of the boys were caught red-handed. Three were indefinitely suspended, two were placed on probation, and the remaining twelve trod their way with uneasy air awaiting faculty action. The affair, of course, found its way into the press, and many and varied were their accounts. The prize account and explanation of the event, however, goes to W. A. White, who by 1891 was a reporter on a Kansas City paper, and who wrote:

[3] The "anarchist" was Professor Carruth, who advocated municipal ownership of local water works; the "evolutionist" was Professor Snow, a scientist *and* at one time a Congregational minister; the "free-trader" was Professor J. H. Canfield, who advocated, with some insistence, the principle of free-trade, in a Republican state. When F. W. Blackmar joined the faculty in 1889, the following notice ran through the press of the state: "Frank W. Blackmar, of Johns Hopkins University, has been elected to the new chair of History and Sociology in the Kansas University. He is a protectionist."

A keen taste for the succulent brew of the jack pot, a hankering for the hectic glow of the flush and an appetite for the monster that annually destroys the youth of our land caused the disturbance. It is needless to say that the evil of cards and of liquor has been

The Class of 1895 in front of Snow Hall (Old Snow). Nearly sixty years have come and gone since this picture was taken and most of the class, no doubt, have by 1954 joined the great majority. They look very serious; maybe they were, but I'll venture the opinion they had as much fun—perhaps more— than members of the class of 1954.

53

effectively stamped out in the State University. They don't even play authors there now, and the sight of a long-necked catsup bottle fills them with a feeling of vague unrest. The music of the mandolin is muffled, the voice of the kazoo is hushed and the tin horn is silent. Tennessee Street is damp with briny tears; the long bars of the midnight lamp fall uncurtained in the trees, where but last night a choked and stealthy ray oozed out from a scene of revelry, the cadent gallop of the industrious "pony" chases its own echoes in the deserted thoroughfare. The great American bounce is king.

27. Music and the Arts

Don't Rile a Kansan!
Now I would like to say to the gentleman from New York [George W. Ray] in reply to what he said concerning me, that I would rather start out with a monkey for an ancestor, and coming down, make progress and be able to ask such a question as I have asked than to have started from a perfect pair in the Garden of Eden, and give such a foolish answer as the gentleman has given.
—Congressman Jerry Simpson of Kansas in the House of Representatives, March 11, 1892.

FEW WHO read these pages will recognize in the photograph on this page one of the buildings of the University. However, for the years from 1892 to 1898 it appeared by picture and by title in University publications as Music Hall. A music hall in Kansas in an era that elected "Sockless" Jerry Simpson of Kansas to the national legislature, an era which heard the fluent and effective Mary Lease exhort her farmer audiences "to raise less corn and more hell"? But music and the Populist age were not incompatible. In fact, the Populists themselves utilized the agency of music in achieving their power. Their creed, set to popular tunes, furnished an emotional appeal that doubtless produced many a political convert.

Music in the Populist age, music in the frontier age, music in any age of American life has had its place. Writers and speakers in recent years have been particularly inclined to speak slightingly of culture on the frontier, meaning presumably the lack of literature, of art, of music, of the social graces, and of the time to pursue these "ornamental" features of life. In a large measure this attitude is justified but in the case of music especially some modification of ideas is necessary.[1] To use illustrations that will return us to our main topic, however, it can be pointed out that the second catalog of the University (that of 1867-68) lists as one of its seven faculty members T. J. Cook, "Professor of Instrumental and Vocal Music." To be sure, the inclusion of Cook's

name was largely a matter of increasing the length of the faculty roll, as he received no salary nor were specific courses in music described in the catalog. Doubtless he gave private lessons to such University students as desired them, and the inclusion of his name on the faculty list gave him some prestige in securing students. But the fact that Cook's name occurs on the faculty list shows that there was interest in music. More surprising than Cook's case, however, is the fact that in 1870 music was a required part of the college curriculum. Freshmen were required to take a music course which included harmony, choral harmonization, choral composition, history and aesthetics of music, and philosophy of musical sounds! Further, the requirement was made not only of students in the classical course, but of stu-

University Music Hall of the nineties. The building was the "old" Methodist Church whose spire—lost in the intervening years—was apparent in the distance in the photograph of 1867 (page 5). It was located at the corner of Tenth and Massachusetts Streets, the site now occupied by the Masonic Temple. At the extreme right may be seen the Trinity Episcopal Church, since the late fifties a Lawrence landmark.

[1] I am laboring under no misapprehensions about the difficulties and rigors of western pioneer life. To say there was no art, however, is to ignore certain evident facts. The arts, particularly music, were the only relief for many pioneers from the harsh vicissitudes of daily life. In many an evening hour the toils and troubles of the day were forgotten in community band or chorus.

54

The School of Fine Arts, 1900. Although "Old North" was the *home* of Fine Arts, externally it belied its name in a manner scarcely conceivable even in the disordered mind of a futurist.

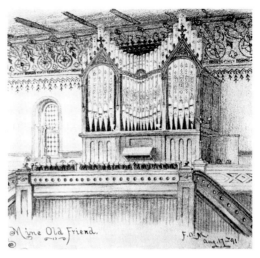

The organ in the Plymouth Congregational Church; from a pencil sketch by F. O. Marvin, of the School of Engineering. Marvin was not only an artist of talent but also the organist of the Plymouth Church for some years. This church (built in 1868) was, for many years, the leading student church. Before the installation of the organ in Fraser Chapel in 1898, the instrument pictured here was used for many of the University's musical functions.

dents in the scientific course and in the engineering course! Just how revolutionary this requirement was can be seen in the fact that music was not introduced even as *elective* in the curriculum of Harvard University until 1871.

The origin of this requirement — maintained for several years—I have not been able to trace. It smacks of Ben Franklin's famous outline of education that students should "be taught everything that is useful, and everything that is ornamental; but art is long and their time is short. It is therefore proposed that they learn those things which are likely to be most useful and most ornamental." Whether there was a close student of Franklin on the faculty or not, I do not know, but it is certain that the requirement is coincident with the appearance of the name of J. E. Bartlett on the faculty roll as instructor in vocal music and that it disappeared when Bartlett's name was dropped in 1874.

The year 1874-75 seems to have been a poor one for music, as not only does the requirement of music disappear, but there was no instructor of music listed in the catalog. Since that time, there has always been listed at least one instructor of music. Drawing, too, was early recognized in the University, appearing for the first time in the catalog of 1868, when John Folkmann was listed as "Instructor in the German Language and Literature, and Drawing." Folkmann was succeeded the next year by E. P. Leonard, "Professor of Modern Languages, Drawing and Painting."

A separate musical department appeared in 1877, but the most important development in the musical history of the University came in 1884 with the arrival of William MacDonald as the first dean of the department. MacDonald immediately established a curriculum leading to a music degree, formed a Department of Art the year after his arrival, and greatly stimulated interest in music in the University and in the state.

The Old Mill—long a Lawrence landmark. It was situated on the highest point of land at the west end of Ninth Street. In 1905 it was destroyed by fire. Not only was it a trysting place for student couples, but, in its shade, the class of 1892 practiced the first senior play! The photograph looks east toward the town.

MacDonald was succeeded in 1890 by Penny, whose intense and energetic efforts resulted in the formation of glee clubs, choruses, the acquisition of a fine organ for University Hall, and in many other musical activities. In the meantime, the Departments of Music and Art had become *schools* in 1889, the School of Music *and* Art in 1891, the School of Music and Painting in 1893, and eventually the School of Fine Arts in 1894.

Teaching in these various arts was at first conducted in rooms on the third floor of University Hall. When North College was remodeled in 1890, the Music School occupied the floor above the Law School, an arrangement which did not last long. Not that the Music Department complained, but the Laws were unable to stand the constant "racket and screeching"—the piano and voice practicing—and Music Hall on Massachusetts Street was rented. In 1898, the School of Fine Arts gained undisputed title to North College and remained here until 1917, when it was again moved to rented private property, this time on Tennessee Street. Its present location in Frank Strong Hall was acquired when the equipment of the school was moved in one night in the summer of 1919.

28. "Each in His Own Tongue"

Prof. W. H. Carruth, of Kansas University, is an ardent advocate of woman suffrage and is one of the hardest workers for the cause in the state. He says that the newspapers all over the state are coming out rapidly and strongly in favor of this issue.
—*Lawrence Journal* (reprinted in the *University Courier*, February 28, 1894).

THE FACULTY of the University in its eighty-odd years has published, collectively, a truly enormous volume of the printed word. Much of it has been of value, some as literature, some as contribution to our store of knowledge. Much of it, too, is buried so deep in forgotten tomes that it is doubtful if it will ever again be examined before the Day of Judgment.

Whatever the value, whatever the merit, whatever the lack of these qualities, no words penned by a faculty member of the University of Kansas, I venture to assert, have ever been more widely read, have ever been more profoundly felt, than the words of the simple lyric of four stanzas written by William Herbert Carruth, onetime professor of German language and literature in the University of Kansas.

If I may be pardoned a personal recollection, I would like to relate my first encounter with this poem, not because it is unduly important, but because I believe it is typical. I first read "Each in His Own Tongue" nearly forty years ago while a college student and before I knew anything about the University of Kansas or Carruth's connection with it. I was deeply moved by the words. I thought then that it was one of the most beautiful things I had ever read. Other students of my acquaintance thought as I did—and so, too, do students of the present generation. At least those do whom I have asked to read the poem and tell me what they thought about it. We—that is, college students in their formative years—are not, of course, competent critics of poetry. This poem, in the judgment of critics, may be real poetry or it may be no poem at all. But it matters not what the critics think, the poem is beloved of many and has had an influence out of all proportion to the few words that it contains.

The reason for this interest and affection can be explained in part by the era in which it achieved its greatest popularity, the first decade of the present century. In this decade the teachings of several generations of students in the theory of evolution were producing results that disturbed leaders of the church. Parents, and the public in general, were seriously concerned with the atheistic tendencies developed in the college student. It was this era, it will be recalled, that produced Haeckel's *The Riddle of the Universe*, written from the extreme point of view of the materialist. It is scarcely any wonder, then, that "Each in His Own Tongue," with its beauty of word and philosophical fusion of science and God, appealed to the moderates if not the Fundamentalists. The poem was published in a number of widely read magazines but still more extensively in the newspaper press, many times without crediting the author. It was translated into other tongues and even re-translated, in garbled form, back into English from an uncredited Russian version.

Actually, the poem was first published in 1895 and for several years was unnoticed. It was "discovered" several years later by the Reverend Edward Everett Hale, noted Unitarian clergyman, who asked Carruth's permission to reproduce it

56

in the *Christian Register*. Other papers followed suit and eventually it was used by one of the great agencies which supplied plate matter for thousands of small newspapers. Carruth republished it in 1908 in a collection of his poems, giving the book the same title as his best-known piece of verse.

"Each in His Own Tongue" was the inspiration of a single hour as Carruth and Chancellor Snow stood on one of Mount Oread's bluffs gazing out over the October beauty of the Kansas and Wakarusa valleys below them. Away to the east and north, the horizon hazily dissolved against a blue, blue sky—"the bluest sky in the world." In the intervening distance an infinite variety of greens and browns in orchard and hedge, in fields of corn and stubble, brightened by glimpses of shining river water, created an enchanting and magic scene. Both men stood speechless. Snow at last said briefly, "There is no season like the Kansas autumn." To which the other man slowly replied, "We can say nothing but 'God.'" As the two men turned homeward, Carruth remarked, "'God,' too, sums up evolution, Snow. You have wrestled long, I know, with its problems, but the one Word that is the source of the beauty of an autumn afternoon is also the explanation of the most difficult problem that you scientists have to face."

With these thoughts in their minds, the two parted upon reaching Snow's home; and Carruth walked on alone. As he walked, the poem gradually took form: "Some of us call it autumn . . . some call it evolution . . . others call it God." Thus was the simple and classic lyric born, inspired by the beauty visible from Mount Oread and by the presence of a friend.

Carruth was a native of Kansas, born during territorial days in 1859. He had attended Lawrence High School, herded the town cows after school hours, entered the University, and graduated in the class of 1880. Carruth not only was a student of languages but also was intensely interested in science, so his conversation with Snow on that inspiring autumn afternoon doubtless was not the first time that the problem of evolution had been discussed.

Upon graduation, Carruth became "instructor in German, French, and English" in the University of Kansas, where he continued to teach, save for leaves of absence for study abroad and at Harvard, until 1913, when he went to Leland Stanford University as professor of comparative literature. He died at his home in the California foothills on December 16, 1924.

The gentle splendor of "Each in His Own Tongue" has, in a large measure, almost obscured the light cast by Carruth's remaining poems. Yet there are many of these verses and a considerable number, according to the critics, are hardly less worthy than the best-known one. Nearly all are characterized by a deeply religious earnestness and "a simple and sincere workmanship." "Dreamers of Dreams," *"Hagen und Volker,"* "Under the Leaves" have all been singularized as verses of marked distinction. Each of these three, like the most noted of the Carruth poems, is short, the longest containing but six verses.

Appearing also in Carruth's collected volume of poems is one written for the University, "Life at K.S.U." Designed as a student song, its concluding stanza reveals Carruth's deep and abiding affection for his school and his native state:

"Each in His Own Tongue"—a manuscript version written by Carruth for a friend in 1912.

Earth's no vision rarer, not a landscape fairer
   Than each day before our eyes expands.
Kansas skies are bluer, Kansas hearts are
      truer
   Than the hearts and skies of other lands.
Then whate'er the weather, let us sing to-
      gether

Rock Chalk for the Crimson and the Blue;
Neither prince nor peasant lead a life so
      pleasant
   As the student's life at K.S.U.

Carruth, though a poet, dwelt in no ivory tower apart from the rest of the world. For example, he took an active part in town politics and was a councilman for a number of years. He ran for mayor on a reform ticket but was defeated because it was rumored that he would prevent the residents of North Lawrence from keeping pigs and chickens in their back yards! He took an even greater part in the life of the students. His connection with early K.U. football has already been mentioned and his upright and honest character can be inferred from that incident. It was no easy matter to make a decision which Carruth knew would be unpopular with his own students. Many years later Carruth wrote: ". . . the outcome of that game affected deeply my future standing in the University. From a founder of athletic culture I was shifted in the minds of the student body to an enemy of athletics, and no enemy could become a leader. Well, no matter now."

But Carruth underestimated his influence subsequent to the football game. His best friend gave a truer perspective when he wrote: "He did everything for his students; he got jobs for them; he invited them to his house; he mapped courses for them; he cheered them in their scholastic discouragements; he prodded them; he made them very uncomfortable sometimes; but all the while he lifted and inspired them; he lit candles in their souls."

William Herbert Carruth, from a photograph made about 1890.

29. Spooner Library

The library is [now] available more hours than heretofore. It was open from 9 A.M. to 1 P.M., from 1877 to 1885. Two hours in the afternoon were added in 1885. Then, in 1887, the hours were extended from 8 A.M. until chapel time, and from 9 A.M. to 6 P.M., except on Saturdays, when it was open from nine until twelve o'clock. It was decided, in 1888, to open the library Friday evenings from half past seven until ten o'clock.
   —Librarian Carrie M. Watson, 1891.

IN THE PICTURE at the bottom of the opposite page, even members of the class of 1954 will recognize some remaining landmarks. In the center of the picture Blake Hall appears. To the right of Blake is Fraser (still University Hall when the photograph was made); on the right side of Fraser can be seen two of the chimneys of Chemistry Hall; still farther to the right is Snow Hall—Old Snow Hall.

To the left of Blake is the Spooner-Thayer Museum, or, as it was known in 1896, Spooner Library. To the left of Spooner and down the hill is—or was—the Chancellor's Residence. Conspicuous by their absence to the modern student are the Union Building, Dyche Museum, Green Hall, and the paved drive along the crest of Mount Oread.

The buildings added to the campus skyline

since our view in 1887 had appeared in this order: the Chancellor's Residence—first used in December, 1893; Spooner Library, officially opened on October 10, 1894; and Blake Hall, dedicated in the fall of 1895.

Blake had been built with funds granted by the Legislature of 1893, and was the first building added to the campus by state funds since the completion of Snow Hall in 1886, for both the Chancellor's Residence and Spooner Library were built from funds bequeathed to the University by William B. Spooner, a resident of Boston and a great-uncle of Chancellor Snow.

Mr. Spooner had died in 1880, but so long and complicated had been his will that the executor of the estate was not able to transmit the actual bequest to the University until the fall of 1891. The legacy amounted to nearly $100,000, at that time the largest bequest ever made to a state university.

The use to which the legacy was to be put was not specified by Mr. Spooner, but suggestions were not long in coming. The *Courier* promptly requested that a portion be used to build a street-car system up Mount Oread. The Board of Regents, however, decided to use a portion of it for the construction of a suitable home for Mr. Snow during his lifetime, the building to be used subsequently as the home of following chancellors during their terms of office. Chancellor Snow was very desirous that a major portion of the bequest be used in the construction of a University library and to this desire the Board of Regents and the Legislature agreed.

Spooner Library—looking north—from a photograph made in 1894.

Work on both buildings was begun in the summer of 1893 and by November of that year the foundations of Spooner could be distinctly seen, the Chancellor's Residence was well on its way to completion, and the ground for the erection of Blake had been broken. The year 1893 was thus a busy one for the rapidly developing University; the development in the physical plant being reflected in the enrollment, which took a steep upswing in the early nineties. By the fall of 1896, when this picture was taken, the enrollment passed the 1,000 mark for the first time.

Such growth in physical plant and student body naturally attracted the attention of the state and of the nation. The completion of Spooner Library, in 1894, for example, was described not

The University of Kansas, 1896. This photograph of the campus was made from the top of the water tower (looking south). The paved walk coming north was fairly new when this photograph was taken. Notice the condition of Oread Avenue and the still poorer condition of Mississippi Street in the extreme right of the foreground. Notice also that the iron gates have disappeared (see page 19).

An unusual view of the University from the south; looking north. It was made at practically the same time as the preceding photograph. The buildings seen are the "new" power and heating plant (erected in 1887) on the left, then Snow Hall, Chemistry Hall, University Hall, and Blake Hall.

only in the state press but in such national magazines as *Harper's Weekly,* which stated:

> The architects, Messrs. Van Brunt and Howe of Boston and Kansas City, ignoring the old idea that a library is only a storage room or depository for books, erected a building simple in construction, convenient, adequate in its detail and thoroughly modern in design. . . . The reading room, commodious and well lighted, is modern in every detail, including reading-tables, deadened floors, lighted with incandescent electric lamps, furnished with alcoves for private study and at the east end of which is the librarian's office and catalogue rooms, equipped with the latest devices for the quick-handling of the 100,000 books[1] which is the capacity of the five-story fire-proof book stack that faces the east end of the entire structure.

[1] The capacity of Spooner may have been 100,000 volumes—and was—but in 1894 there were only some 20,000 books on the shelves. At that, it was the largest library in Kansas.

In troubled Kansas has grown up an educational centre where can be found culture and learning of the broadest type.

If national magazines commented so favorably, state editors were equally impressed. Even a farmers' paper, the *Topeka Mail,* was led to comment on the University: "The average Kansas man is not rolling in luxury. He lives plainly and stumps his toes on a good many rocks in his journey from the cradle to the grave. Hard seasons and low prices make him gray-headed before his time, while his wife and daughter are not, as a rule, clothed in purple and fine linen, but just the same this average Kansas man, who has hustled along through hot winds, and drouths, and chinch bugs and low prices, takes a pride in the fact that in the matter of general information Kansas stands very close to the head of the procession. As a rule, he doesn't growl much about his school tax, and down in the bottom of his heart he cherishes a hope that his boys and girls may go through the University."

30. The Spanish-American War

There has been considerable criticism of our country for non-interference in Cuban affairs. Some are inclined to blame the President for weakness. I do not criticize the actions of the government up to the present time. But now the time has come. The Spanish will have to leave the island, and the United States might as well assist them off.—Col. Fred Funston in a University lecture, March 4, 1898.

FOR A HALF century, from 1848 to 1898, the United States engaged in no war with foreign powers. On April 20, 1898, however, an ultima-

tum was delivered to Spain, and we then knew that the long record of peace with other nations was at an end. Volunteers were called for in the states, and Kansas was among the first to respond. On April 22, Governor John W. Leedy announced that Fred Funston, formerly a student at K.U., would be appointed colonel of the first regiment raised by Kansas.

Companies of volunteers were organized in various Kansas towns, and the National Guard was called out. Capt. A. G. Clarke, '97, was in command of the Lawrence unit of the Guard, which contained several University boys. On Tuesday, May 3, they paraded down Massachusetts Street, flag-bedecked and lined with citizens crying and cheering, turned down Winthrop Street to the Santa Fe station, and there boarded cars for the main encampment at Topeka.

Most of the University men, however, who enlisted for service, did not go to Topeka until the following week. The Sunday before they left, a special service was held in their honor in University Hall. The Hall was crowded and when the volunteers marched in, they were greeted with deafening cheers. In fact, patriotic enthusiasm was so intense that every speaker, including the minister who delivered the invocation, was greeted with tremendous applause.

The twenty-nine volunteers present at this service were all students enrolled in the University, whose intention it was to form a company of college students from Manhattan and Emporia. Most of the University men on their arrival at Topeka were assigned to companies in the 20th and 22nd Kansas regiments.

A farewell, as enthusiastic as that given Captain Clarke's company, was given the University volunteers who left for Topeka the following week. It was described by the *University Weekly*:

On Monday afternoon [May 9] the boys went to Topeka on the plug. They were escorted to the train by their fellow students, professors, and the Indian band. First came the band, then the student volunteers, and behind them professors and students headed by Chancellor Snow. There was besides a big crowd at the depot to see them off and as the boys reached the station they were heartily cheered.

While waiting for the train the volunteers were surrounded by their fellow college boys

University of Kansas Men in the Twentieth Kansas. This photograph of thirty-three men was made in front of a church in Caloocan, Philippine Islands, March, 1899. "The Kansas regiment contains more college men than any other in the Philippines," reads one contemporary account. The men in the front row have been identified (left to right): Lts. Hardy and Fry (standing), (seated) Capt. Glasgow, Capt. Buchan, Col. E. C. Little, Gen. Funston, Col. Metcalf, Capt. Adna G. Clarke, Capt. U. J. Watson, Lt. Simpson (standing).

61

and farewells were said. As the train whistled into the station the band struck up the Star Spangled Banner and a few minutes later amid the playing of the band and the giving of three hearty cheers by the crowd, another detachment, this time from the University, left Lawrence for Camp Leedy.

In addition to student volunteers, many former University students also enlisted, so that the total University representation in the armed forces of the United States for the Spanish War totaled nearly seventy-five men. Many of these men officered the several Kansas regiments, notably the 20th Kansas Volunteers, which achieved an especially wide reputation.

Assigned to duty in the Philippines, they saw active service in the war against the insurgents, and as the 20th Kansas went into action in the Philippine jungles their war cry was "Rock Chalk, Jayhawk!" There, too, the first University man to die in battle for his country laid down his life. The official roster reads: "Killed in action: First Lieutenant Alfred C. Alford,[1] before Caloocan, February 7, 1899; buried Lawrence, Kansas. Promoted to first lieutenant, September 5, 1898."

[1] Of the class of 1896.

31. Fowler Shops

The *Weekly* faculty advisory board consisting of Professors Hopkins, Sterling and O'Leary met with the *Weekly* board at noon today to try to outline the policy of the paper. The board is somewhat dissatisfied with the policy Mr. Seeds has been pursuing to what he considers some of the evils existing in the University. The main part of the discussion was upon this attitude toward some of the fraternities.
—*Lawrence Daily Journal*, October 24, 1898.

THE UNIVERSITY had been singularly fortunate up to March 22, 1898, in escaping any serious loss by fire, but on that date lightning struck the powerhouse. In the fire which followed, the heating plant and a good deal of the shop equipment used in the Engineering School were destroyed.

The misfortune hampered the work of the University for some time. The weather was still cold and no supplementary provision could immediately be made for heating the buildings. There is no cloud without its silver lining, and for the students the cloud was silvery indeed. They were given two weeks' vacation while the heating plant was made usable!

The Board of Regents had no funds for replacing the power plant, the Legislature was not in session, and Chancellor Snow was sorely pressed for a plan to repair the damage. After consulting with Governor Leedy and a committee of Lawrence citizens, it was decided to appeal for a loan which it was hoped could be refunded at the next meeting of the Legislature. Thirty thousand dollars was almost immediately subscribed in Lawrence and Kansas City, and the repair work on the heating plant started and was far enough advanced in two weeks to reopen school.

In the meanwhile, Professor Blake had a brilliant inspiration. One of his personal acquaint-

Upper—Blake Hall (center), Fraser Hall, and Fowler Shops (left). The photograph was made in 1899 or 1900 and looks northwest up the road that some people maintain was one of the approaches of the old Oregon Trail to the Hill.

Lower—Blake Hall, looking south; photograph made about 1899.

62

Fowler Shops, 1900, looking south from the Bailey Laboratory.

ances, a wealthy packer and rancher, George A. Fowler, of Kansas City, had once told him that young engineers should have greater opportunity to practice what they were taught before leaving school. Recalling this conversation, according to a story in the *Kansas City Star,* Blake made an appointment with Fowler, arrived in Kansas City at six o'clock the evening of his appointment, retold the conversation to Fowler, and returned to Lawrence on the seven o'clock train the same evening with a check for $18,000 from Fowler in his pocket. The sum was to be used for the construction of a shop building, provided the University used $20,000 of the public contribution to equip the building. The Regents most readily agreed to this proposal and hailed the gift with genuine rejoicing. "This unexpected gift is very gratifying," said Chancellor Snow. "It insures us a better building than we had hoped. The Regents would not have felt like putting up so complete a structure as this will be. In addition, it makes it easier towards securing a new chemistry building from the next legislature. Another feature of this matter which is very gratifying to us in the University is the liberty and spontaneity with which public-spirited citizens responded to our call for a loan. Not only from Lawrence, but from the two Kansas Citys, were subscriptions received. It showed friendliness and interest in the University and made us feel that if we had

had a hundred thousand dollar catastrophe instead of a thirty thousand dollar one, the needed aid would have been secured from half a dozen places."

A site for the new building was soon laid off "upon the upper plateau on the extreme southwest corner of the hill" and work was started during the summer. Mr. Fowler, in return for his generosity, was invited to deliver the Commencement address, but being a shy and retiring man, countered this proposal by giving the University an additional $3,000 for the shop building. This excellent result might well be called to the attention of all prospective Commencement speakers.

Work on Fowler Shops was begun in the summer of 1898, and by October 1 the walls of the first floor were up and the large iron smokestack, a characteristic feature of the University skyline for many years, was in place. Engineering students acquired a considerable fund of the practical experience desired by Fowler; for they were pressed into service in installing the new equipment and putting on the finishing touches. The building was first open to public inspection February 6, 1899.

The erection and completion of Fowler Shops— one of the best pieces of architecture on the campus according to a competent critic—was promptly reflected in the growth of the Univer-

63

sity. Departments of Mechanical and Mining Engineering were added in the spring of 1899, and the Engineering enrollment, nearly stationary for the eight preceding years, increased by 100 per cent in the following three years. The fire of 1898 was then a boon in disguise. Curiously enough, this building resulting from a fire has itself on two occasions been the object of disastrous fires; one in 1918 and the second in 1932.

The description given above of Fowler Shops may seem strange, or even in error, to the student of 1954, for the building we have designated as Fowler Shops is now the home of the William Allen White School of Journalism. The transformation was effected after the new Fowler Shops were constructed at the west end of the campus in 1949. "Old" Fowler was then remodeled, and the School of Journalism and the University of Kansas Press were able to hold open house in their new quarters on February 22, 1952.

32. Basketball

The University basket ball team went on its first extended trip Thursday, playing three games with Independence Thursday, Friday, and Saturday nights, and one with William Jewell College, Monday afternoon. The Kansans played good ball but were unable to stay with Independence [a city team, champions of Missouri and Kansas]. The William Jewell boys played a good game but not like Independence.
—*Kansas University Weekly,* April 8, 1899.

BASKETBALL was invented in 1891 by James Naismith of the Springfield Y.M.C.A. College as part of its research program in developing new games. In the fall of 1898, Naismith came to the University of Kansas as associate professor of physical training and chapel director. For forty-one years, his service to the University continued, interrupted only by leaves of absence for war work. It is safe to hazard the opinion that while there have been more important contributions to the world made by the members of the University faculty, none has touched more lives and brought greater interest to millions the world over than the invention of basketball by James Naismith. There is, then, more than an ordinary tie between the game of basketball and the University.

Although the game was not introduced into the University until after Naismith's arrival, its adoption had been suggested as early as 1896. In fact, in the East its adoption proceeded so rapidly that it can be said that a mania for it developed.

Naismith, on his arrival in Lawrence, outlined its short history, pointing out that unlike other games, it had not developed from simpler forms, but was the result of a deliberate effort to invent a game that would find a place in the season's sports between football and baseball, that could be played on any kind of ground, that would be interesting and easy to learn, and that would have none of the roughness of football.

Naismith's presence and active interest initiated the game at the University and in the state. Eight class and faculty teams were organized with the object of playing a schedule and developing material for a University team. The *University Weekly* in its issue of December 10, 1898, describes the interest aroused: "Every one who is at all interested in athletics is now talking basketball yet it does not stop here. Those who hitherto have manifested no interest in any sports of skill and strength seem now to be enthusiastic over the new game. It is talked at the club; it is discussed in the corridors; it is practiced and played in the gymnasium and on the campus. Even the professors have become actively interested in the game and are giving their time of recreation over to this pastime."

Massachusetts Street, looking north. The photograph was made in the same year that basketball was introduced in the University; Ninth Street runs east and west in the middle foreground.

64

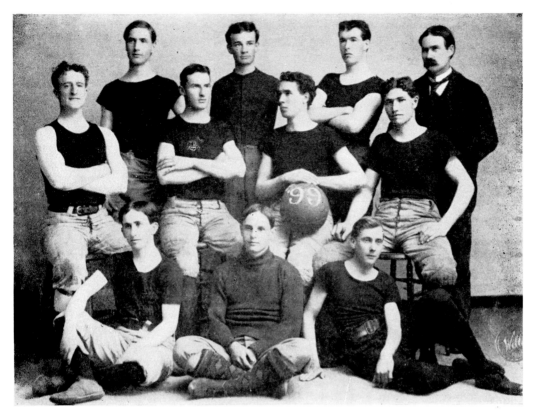

Basketball team of 1898-99. The first team consisted of: left to right (standing), Owens, Henderson, Walter Sutton, Dr. Naismith; (middle row) Avery, Emley, Will Sutton (captain), Hess; (in front) Rusell, Hoyt, Yahn. The team positions were named "forward," "center," and "back."

The gymnasium at this time was in the basement of Snow Hall and was woefully inadequate for any actual games. The skating-rink downtown (near the present Baptist Church), however, had a large floor and was rented on occasions for practice and for games.

After class games had developed some skill at the game, Naismith selected a varsity team and began scheduling games. The first game played was at Kansas City with the Y.M.C.A. team. Y.M.C.A. teams throughout the country had been quick to follow the lead of the Y.M.C.A. College, and its team was therefore a seasoned one; the Y.M.C.A. team won from K.U. by a score of 16 to 5.

K.U. had several very good excuses for not winning. It was the varsity's first game, while the Y.M.C.A. team was experienced and had, further, in its line-up a young man by the name of James concerning whom the *Weekly* wrote: "Jesse James, the man who has lately come into prominence by his alleged connection with the recent train robberies in Missouri, played a rough,

and at times, a very ungentlemanly game. He was cautioned and punished by the referees several times during the game." That the play of James must have had something to do with the score of this first game is shown by the fact that when the Y.M.C.A. team appeared in Lawrence later in the season for a return game, without the services of James, K. U. won, 17 to 14.[1]

The first home game was played at the rink February 10, 1899, with the Topeka Y.M.C.A. Score: "K.U. 31; Topeka 6. Attendance about 50." As far as the records show, no intercollegiate contests were played at home this year; the home season was cut short, however, by the burning of the rink in March. The first intercollegiate game abroad was played with William Jewell College on April 3, 1899, and was won by K.U., 19 to 3.

---

[1] Perhaps the *Weekly* account has misled the reader, as it did me. For a time I thought that K.U. really had a claim to the remarkable distinction of having played against *the* Jesse James but caution got the better of me and I looked up Mr. James' actual record. The celebrated Jesse James died—very suddenly—early one April day in 1882.

Maypole scrap of 1900. The fracas in 1900 took place in front of Fraser and, according to the *Weekly*, was "a battle royal." The freshman flag shown in the upper picture was brought down by a sophomore from the short-grass country who lassoed it. In the lower picture, note the senior girl with the mortarboard at the right and the ubiquitous small boy on the left. We also have positive proof, in this picture, that the passage of fifty-four years has produced no retrogression in the style of women's hats.

The following year practice was begun on outside courts west of Snow Hall. It was in this season that the first game with a neighboring state university took place. Nebraska was played at Lincoln on March 2, 1900. The score is not recorded in the *Weekly,* but it stated, "The little northerners tossed baskets so fast that our men lost count and did not linger to find the score after the game." The few home games were played in the local Y.M.C.A. gymnasium, a practice which was usually continued until Robinson Gymnasium was completed in 1907.

33. The Maypole Fight

May Day Contest
The Junior and Freshman colors waved over Mt. Oread all Tuesday morning.
All night long you could hear the different class yells as the boys were going up and down the hill making preparations for the next day. About two o'clock in the morning the pole was raised, with the Freshman colors, at the head of Adams street, near the entrance to the campus. The only excitement was caused by two of the Sophs and Seniors who were tied to the telegraph poles and left until morning.
The Freshman classes were the only classes disturbed by the conflict to any great extent, as the interest was not nearly so strong among the higher class men.
Nothing but good feeling and gentlemanly actions were shown all day save in the instance of the Senior who disgraced himself by slugging.—The *University Courier,* May 3, 1894.

ANOTHER event in the life of students of bygone generations, which had become well established by the time the first basketball team was formed, was the Maypole scrap. The first of these scraps occurred May 1, 1891. The junior men, during the preceding night, erected a pole forty feet high in front of University Hall bearing a banner marked with the figures '92. Two or three men were left to guard the flag, the remainder going home to catch up on lost sleep.

Other students in the University were amazed to find the flag on arriving for classes in the morning, and, as the event had just been initiated no organized opposition was at first apparent. Just after nine o'clock classes had started, the men on guard gave a distress call, and other members of the class of '92 rushed from the building to see the pole on the ground and their colors lying in the dust. Their guard they saw bound hand and foot; and a sophomore, with an axe, stood nonchalantly poised by the remaining stub of the pole.

The juniors, aided by the freshmen, attempted to regain their pole and banner, but the seniors came to the rescue of the sophomores and together they cut and burned the banner. Nothing daunted, the juniors and freshmen prepared two new flags and flung them to the breeze from the north dome of University Hall, where other classmen vainly stormed the heights in an attempt to destroy them. The battle raged for the whole day; and finally, as evening dusk was coming on, two daring sophomores scaled the domes from the outside and seized the flags, and the honors of the day rested with the class of '93.

This event apparently was the first to arouse the distinct class spirit that had long been known to Eastern schools,—for the *University Courier,* commenting on the fray, writes: "The enthusiastic class spirit which prevailed last Friday was something new for the University. We do not remember that classes have ever been quite so distinctly separate. The May-pole and the little axe did it all. It was a good thing and we all enjoyed it. It is just such episodes as those that make college life enjoyable and that will be the object of pleasant memories in the years to come."

The following year the juniors profited by the mistakes of their predecessors and mounted their colors on a stout iron pipe, with the result that when the hosts were joined in battle from nine o'clock in the morning until one o'clock of the next day, the colors remained in place.

The fighting was evidently more intense the second year, for an observant reporter records: "Many of the boys had the greater part of their clothing torn in shreds."

It was but natural that such a class fracas would engage the attention of the state press, and the disruption of the University classes for the day, the destruction of clothing, and the possibility of permanent injury to the participants were dwelt upon at length. But the event had captured the interest of the students to such an extent that it remained for nearly fifteen years an annual event.

As the University grew larger, class spirit engendered by the early Maypole scraps developed into a series of duels between freshmen and soph-

Maypole scrap of 1899. The photograph was taken from the top of Fraser and looks north. "Old North" may be seen in the distance, but still nearer is the water tower, on which may be deciphered many class numerals. From 1886 until 1931, the tower was a characteristic feature of the Hill landscape. Note, too, the hitching rack north of the crowd.

omores and was not confined to May Day alone.

Eventually, in the fall of 1904, the battle between freshmen and sophomores developed such ferocity that two freshmen were seriously injured. The faculty, particularly Chancellor Strong, became greatly concerned over the increasing brutality, and argued strenuously against the custom. Their arguments evidently bore fruit, for when May Day of 1905 came around, no class flag was flown. Instead a funeral

cortege paraded up Massachusetts Street preceded by a band. The procession wound its way up to Mount Oread, where the funeral oration was given and where a guard of honor fired a parting salute over the grave of the departed. "The remains" were the class of 1907 in effigy, and the mourners the class of 1908. The *Kansan* made the comment, "The funeral procession Monday probably meant the burying forever of the annual May-day scrap."

34. The *Jayhawker*

We will not vouch for a single word of truth in the '03 *Jayhawker*. Our aim has been to be entertaining, and I think you will agree that nothing is more entertaining than a cheerful harmless liar. Accidentally there may be some true statements herein, but you will find it the better plan to question everything.—THE EDITORS.

FOR MANY graduates, the most treasured possession of college days is the *Jayhawker*, the first volume of which appeared in 1901. Even before the *Jayhawker*, annuals had been published and altogether in these eighty-seven years, sixty-three yearbooks have been issued, ranging all the way from the original and smallest twenty-leaved pamphlet to lush volumes of half a thousand pages. *Hierophantes*, the first annual, was published in 1874 by members of the I. C. Sorosis and of Beta Theta Pi. It contained no illustra-

tions, save the two secret-society emblems, and was chiefly a catalog of faculty, classes, and organizations, including a baseball club. It did contain, however, an account of the first Commencement, and two sections in rhyme on "University Legends," from which we learn, among other things, that the first attempt to beautify the campus nearly resulted in failure:

Some "grads" set out a trumpet creeper
    small.
At first, ambitious, it essayed to climb:

But cattle nipped it in its youthful prime.
The more it grew the more they nipped the
    shoot.
Till now there's little left it but its root.

Despite this attempt to popularize the events of the year, the *Hierophantes* did not make ends meet, as far as outgo and income were concerned, and financial considerations evidently gave pause to students in succeeding years, for no annual appeared again until 1882, when the *Kansas Kikkabe* "was kicked into existence, named the *Kikkabe*, kicked by an able-bodied opposition, and after being kicked by midnight marauders, the first edition was kicked off at the rate of one hundred magazines daily." Like its predecessor, the *Kikkabe* catalogued faculty, classes, and organizations, but was and is unique in three ways: it is the first annual to contain illustrations; it contained the first history of University fraternities; and it was the first annual which was suppressed. The illustrations consisted of a photograph of the faculty—an actual photographic print and not a reproduction—and cartoons.

The attempted suppression of the *Kikkabe* arose from the fact that the first edition contained comments on members of the faculty, three of whom were offended by the published judgment of the editors. As Chancellor Marvin was one of the three, the "able-bodied opposition" mentioned by the editors had sufficient authority to call for

a revision of comments in the second edition. In the revised edition, the comments on the faculty are all quite favorable, and the faculty page bears the additional quotation:

> The love of praise, howe'er concealed by art
> Reigns more or less and glows in every heart.

Following the *Kikkabe* were the *Kansas Cyclone* of 1883; the *Cicala* of 1884; and the *Helianthus* of 1889,—the last containing the name of William Allen White as one of its editors and being further characterized as the first annual illustrated by halftone reproductions.

The most pretentious of the early annuals was the next yearbook, the *Quivera* of 1893, a goodly-sized volume of nearly two hundred pages. The ambitions of the editors, however, were not equalled by its sale, and the editorial board had the unpleasant, if not unusual, experience of "making up the difference." The pecuniary disaster involving the *Quivera* had an effect lasting for five years; for in 1894 no annual was published, and in 1895, 1896, and 1897 very small volumes cautiously appeared. The *Kwir Book* of 1896 set a pattern, however, that was used by all succeeding volumes; individual photographs of the seniors were reproduced.

Since 1895 there has been an unbroken series of annuals, but it was not until 1901 that the name

"The Hill in Winter." This cartoon should bring back vivid recollections to many. "Daddy" Haworth leads the procession down Fourteenth Street on an icy day. Drawn by T. W. Mayberry, of the class of 1901, the cartoon appeared in the first *Jayhawker*, 1901.

69

The portrayal of student characteristics was made by Henry Maloy, of the class of 1914, and appeared in the *Jayhawker* for 1912. Maloy was the student artist also responsible for our present pictured conception of the Jayhawker as a bird.

Jayhawker replaced the individual names of former years.

Increasing use of photographs in depicting the events of the school year becomes apparent at the turn of the century, but the stiff posed photograph was unrelieved until the *Jayhawker* of 1905 began publishing action pictures of football games and the 1907 issue made cautious use of snapshots.

By 1908 a standard book form had been achieved which was followed by succeeding classes with little change for a quarter of a century. Photographs of beauty queens, for some unknown reason without being so called, first appeared in 1915; juniors, rather than seniors, assumed charge of the *Jayhawker* in 1925; also, in the fabulous twenties the annual reached its greatest magnificence. Reproductions of paintings in color appeared and large portraits and photographs were used in profusion. This happy era ended abruptly in 1933, the *Jayhawker* decreasing in size from nearly five hundred pages in 1932 to slightly over three hundred in 1933— the depression was slow in reaching Kansas but it eventually got here. The present form, a four- or five-issue magazine, was inaugurated in 1934, patterned after the sophisticated style of the *New Yorker* and of *Vanity Fair*.

In addition to the primary purpose of serving as a memento of bright college days, the sixty-three volumes of University annuals are extremely valuable records for the historian. In their pages can be traced the changing styles of costume, of advertising, of manners and morals, of faculty face and form, and of college humor. Although much of the humor is topical, and in many cases a knowledge of the individuals concerned is necessary in order to understand the point, occasionally a volume contains real wit— both written and pictorial— that transcends time and place.

35. Bailey Chemical Laboratory

The new Chemistry building is almost ready for occupation. The builders are at work on it still and the greater number of rooms will be ready to use by the middle of this week. The building, just on the top of the knoll west and south of North Hollow, has been planned with the greatest care and knowledge of modern means of building and ventilation. Real work in classes began today, lessons were assigned, text books talked over and now earnest study is about to begin.—*Lawrence World,* September 10, 1900.

THE ORIGINAL chemistry building, in use by the end of 1883, was soon outgrown. Inside of five years, Professor Bailey in his report to the Regents pointed out the "vital" need for a new building or a suitable addition to the old one. Part of this need arose from the fact that the Department of Pharmacy was also housed in Chemistry Hall. Organized in 1885 with Lucius E. Sayre[1] as "Professor of Pharmacy," the department immediately found favor in providing professional training in a field with almost no western competition, and aided greatly in elevating a trade to the dignity of an educated profession.

Although the need for a new building became apparent from this double duty as early as 1888, insistent repetitions of the request for the next ten years had little effect on the Legislature. In 1896, Chancellor Snow made a particularly strong

---

[1]Sayre became Dean Sayre the following year.

appeal for a new building, pointing out that the freshman class in chemistry alone numbered two hundred students and had to be accommodated in quarters provided for only seventy-five students. Further, although two new rooms had been secured in Chemistry Hall by excavating a basement, they were so damp that the instructors who used the rooms "frequently suffered from malarial attacks on account of their unfavorable location."

The Legislature answered this touching appeal by reducing the University appropriations by $5,000. Nothing daunted, however, Chancellor Snow continued his requests for a new chemistry building; and finally in the early spring of 1899, the Legislature appropriated $55,000 for the construction of a new building.

The site of the proposed building became an immediate matter of discussion. Suitable locations on the crown of Mount Oread were becoming scarce on the original forty acres of the University property. Fowler Shops had been located as far to the southwest on the forty acres as topography would permit, the western end of the building being nearly on the west limit of the University campus. The west campus line at this time was marked by a tall hedge which ran north and south over the Hill;[2] near the top of the crest, it formed an arched gate leading to the wilderness still farther west.

It was finally decided to place the building "on the edge of the ravine northwest of Snow Hall and opposite Fowler Shops. It is necessary for it to be built at the edge of the hill in order to provide for the lighting of the basement. In order to practice economy and have more money to erect a large building, the building material will probably be the same as that of the Fowler Shops, being taken right out of the hill where the building is to stand." Professor Bailey and Colonel Haskell, the architect for the building, went east to examine "modern" chemistry buildings and on their return in May, 1899, work was commenced. By the fall of 1900, the Chemistry Department and the School of Pharmacy were able to move their belongings from Old Chemistry Hall— which then became Medical Hall—to the new building; but it was not officially dedicated until the Strong inaugural celebration in the fall of 1902.

An inquiring student reporter seeking for the School of Pharmacy after it had had time to accommodate itself to its new quarters wrote the result of his investigations for the *Jayhawker*: "The Pharmacy School occupies the east end of 'Bailey's Barn,' a building housing 7,200,000 square inches of floor space, and so constructed that every floor is a drum-head. The faintest noise in the base-

[2] The hedge, for the information of students who never saw it, followed a line later replaced by the streetcar line as it passed over the hill. The streetcar line, for the information of still later students, followed a north and south line between Strong Hall and Bailey Laboratory.

The "New" Chemistry Building. This photograph, taken about 1900, looks north and a little west from the tower of Fowler Shops. By action of the Board of Regents, the building was officially named Bailey Chemical Laboratory in 1938 in honor of Professor E. H. S. Bailey, for fifty years a member of the University staff.

Yes, indeed, it snows in Kansas even if few pictures in this volume show such scenes. Bailey Laboratory, looking northwest, 1912.

later (1906) Robert Kennedy Duncan arrived as professor of industrial chemistry, and developed the plan of industrial fellowships that led eventually to the formation of Mellon Institute of Industrial Research.

The importance of Duncan's work in Bailey Laboratory deserves more than mere mention. The stress that Duncan placed on industrial research with his arrival on the campus in 1906, really marks a milestone in the history of American industry. As I have pointed out elsewhere, there was virtually no chemical research in American industrial organizations at this time and the few chemists in American industry many times were treated little better than common laborers.

The efforts of Duncan were among the most important contributing factors in the tremendous development of chemical industry in the past fifty years. *Fortune* in the March, 1950, issue states that the chemical industry "must now be considered the premier industry of the United States." Although the growth of the chemical industry has been greatly increased in recent years, Duncan's insistence on the importance of research in industry, his ability to write and speak in a manner that drew the public attention, and his concern that the chemist receive a fair return for his knowledge, labor, and ability, played a leading and important role in these developments.

ment can be heard throughout the entire building. In the basement is the liquid air machine, and there is a 'hot air' machine on every other floor. There is also a smelter in the basement, and a 'squelcher' on every other floor."

With all its defects, including the squelchers, Bailey, in its fifty-four years of existence, was able to produce a lasting impression on many generations of students.

With its completion, the reputation of Chemistry 2 as "the white man's burden" grew, the liquid air plant and liquid air lectures begun in 1903 by E. C. Franklin, then professor of physical chemistry, achieved celebrity, and somewhat

36. Dyche Museum

The cinnamon bears that Prof. Dyche killed were perfect monsters of strength and ferocity. We had only been there [in camp on the west slope of the Spanish Peaks, Colorado] about a week when he killed the first one. A single shot from his . . . rifle dispatched him . . . . The professor can scarcely be excelled as a marksman. Soon after we reached Camp Bear Trail he scared up a herd of nine deer, and killed six of them before they could get out of his reach. . . . He made one lucky pull with his Sharps [rifle], sending a death bullet through three at once.—W. H. Brown in the *University Courier,* September 12, 1884.

THE FACULTY of the University of Kansas has had no more spectacular figure than Lewis Lindsay Dyche. Combining real ability with an unusual flair for showmanship, he brought attention and credit to the University, his efforts resulting eventually in a museum of natural history which, after Professor Dyche's death in 1915, was officially named "The Dyche Museum."

Dyche missed being a native-born Kansan by only three months, but with the exception of those three months, Kansas was his home for life. As a boy he ranged the Wakarusa Valley, hunting and

fishing its length in the days when it was still a happy hunting ground. He came to the University in 1877 as a preparatory student with no funds, camping the first few months of his University life on the site now occupied by Dyche Museum and supporting himself by hunting after school hours.

Coming under the enthusiastic influence of Professor Snow, he soon decided to devote himself to the study of natural history. He accompanied Snow on several of the early summer expeditions which secured many specimens for the rapidly growing University "cabinets." Upon graduation from the University, he was added to the teaching staff and by 1889 had achieved the title of "Professor of Anatomy and Physiology, Taxidermist and Curator of Mammals, Birds and Fishes."

Such magnificent titles were common in the college catalogs of those halcyon days, when the field of human knowledge was neither so broad nor so sharply differentiated as at the present day. It was by his display of mounted animals, however, that Dyche first drew national attention. As a result of numerous expeditions to the Rockies, he had collected many specimens of the larger mammals of the West. These he mounted, not in the stiff, formal position of ordinary museum exhibits, but rather in natural lifelike occupations against a convincingly real background of their natural habitat. Over one hundred of these animals prepared by Dyche were placed on exhibit in the Kansas Building of the Chicago World's Fair of 1893. Included in the exhibit was Comanche, the famous survivor of the Custer fight, a

Another view of Bailey Laboratory taken in 1906. The camera looks northeast from near the present site of Robinson Gymnasium and shows the western boundary hedgerow—severely trimmed—in the foreground.

specimen which Dyche had just finished in time for the Fair.

Dyche's display brought press comment from all over the United States, many claiming that the exhibit was the most remarkable to be seen

Dyche Museum, summer of 1902. This view, looking southwest, shows also the new Chemistry Building at the right. In the foreground, Oread Avenue is hedged in by a luxuriant growth of weeds. Dyche, like many of the University buildings, has suffered from insecure footings. It was closed in 1932 for repairs but was opened at Commencement, 1941, with an amazing display of natural history dioramas and panoramas that has still further enhanced its reputation as a notable museum.

No, you don't need to wipe your eyes! You saw it correctly the first time. These are the gargoyles used in decorating Dyche Museum in process of construction by the carvers, Joseph Robaldo Frazee and his son, Vitruvius. Two University students, Antonio Tommasini and Fred Pickett, stopped frequently to see the Frazees at work. They received a thrill never forgotten when Mr. Frazee allowed them to carve one of the figures. It is the feathered creature—said to be the original representation of the Jayhawk—with wings outspread that stands on a skull placed at the top of one of the four entrance columns of the Museum. Pickett, under Mr. Frazee's direction, carved half the Jayhawk and the skull, and Tommasini completed the work.

According to the *Kansan,* two girls passed by Dyche and noticed these unusual decorations. "What are they?" queried one. To which the second girl replied: "Oh, they are something like a sore throat, but I forget just what." The second girl, as might seem obvious to all who know her, was none other than the redoubtable Helen Rhoda Hoopes, then in her undergraduate days at the University.

at the Fair. A Chicago visitor, for example, wrote the *Topeka Capital*: "By reading the Chicago papers the past two weeks a person would almost be made to believe that there was but one state building in the World's Fair grounds, and that was the Kansas building. Since Prof. Dyche has arrived with the University exhibit, column after column has been devoted to a description of that exhibit. In fact, it has received so much notoriety that 'Kansas' has become the counting room and table talk of the city."

Chancellor Snow took this occasion to call the attention of the Legislature to Dyche's widely publicized work. "I also invite your consideration of the fact," wrote Snow, "that, when this collection of animals is returned from Chicago, the capacity of the natural history building will be taxed to its utmost extent to give it shelter. Indeed, the proper arrangement of this collection and a moderate provision for the continuation of Professor Dyche's work would seem to indicate the speedy necessity of a special building."

The Legislature, however, listened to the appeal of Blake for the more practical "electrical" building, and Dyche's display had to be stored where best it might in Snow Hall. Dyche continued to gain publicity, however, by a trip to Greenland for the relief of Perry, by accompanying Cook on one of his polar expeditions, by making several expeditions of his own, from all of which he obtained experiences which he utilized in lectures over the state and out of the state from coast to coast. So impressive became Dyche's record that the Legislature of 1897, in a wholesale reduction of faculty salaries, made a single exception in Dyche's case.

Utilizing Dyche's growing reputation, Chancellor Snow continued to ask for a natural history museum, and finally an appropriation of $75,000 was made in 1901. The *University Weekly* in its first issue of the fall of 1901 was able to record two changes on the campus: "Work has begun on the new museum building, a force of about twenty-five men being employed at present. The dirt excavated is being used to block up Mississippi Street[1] and the road angles off along the side of the slope reaching the top about where the Chemistry building stands. This will greatly facilitate the hauling of coal up the hill, as this has always been a steep climb, but the new road is a long gentle slope."

By the following fall, the building, although incomplete, was sufficiently near completion to house the inaugural program of Chancellor Strong.

[1] Previously, Mississippi Street had continued straight south, reaching the top of the hill near the present location of Green Hall.

37. The Inaugural of Frank Strong

Well, here we are again. In the gray dawn of a new epoch for K.U. the *Weekly* comes upon the scene revitalized and rejuvenated. With a new Chancellor and a new destiny, a new pulse of life fusing in every artery and vein, the University of Kansas is taking a long stride into the foreground and leaving the dead past to memory and dreams.—The *University Weekly,* Volume 11, September 12, 1902.

IN 1901, Chancellor Snow, buffeted by the successive blows of ill-health, the loss of a well-loved son, and the many cares of office, announced his intention of resigning. William C. Spangler,[1] long a powerful friend of the University, was appointed Acting Chancellor, while the Board of Regents undertook a canvass of eligible men to succeed Snow. After many sessions, President Frank Strong, of the University of Oregon, was asked to appear before the Board in April of 1902. Strong's affable manner, commanding stature, and glowing recommendations from many of the country's leading educators, won for him the approval of the Board and he was unanimously elected to the chancellorship on April 16, 1902. Immediately upon his election he was in-

terviewed by an enterprising reporter. "I like the Middle West," Strong told him, "especially the state of Kansas, and from what I have seen of Lawrence, I think I shall like the city as a home. It seems to me the possibilities of this school are great. Look at Nebraska with 2,500 students. I see no reason why we cannot have as many or even more in Kansas. We ought to draw heavily, not only from every county in Kansas, but from all contiguous states. My hobby is to organize. I want every alumnus to work with our university. The whole state must unite in building up the school." Further, in reply to a question on his attitude toward athletics, he replied. "I always encourage college sport of every kind and like to see live college spirit. I hope we can soon have a good gymnasium for our students."

[1] Spangler, '85, was also Acting Chancellor in 1889-90.

The inaugural procession forming on the steps of Fraser Hall, October 17, 1902. The figures on the first three steps are (left to right): Chancellor Snow, Governor Stanley of Kansas, President Hadley of Yale, Regent Potter, Chancellor Strong.

This statement brought an immediate and enthusiastic response from the student body. The night Strong was to return to Oregon a crowd gathered in front of the Eldridge Hotel, called for a speech, and obtained an immediate response. Strong was then placed in a borrowed hack, drawn through the city streets by the shouting students, and, accompanied by a bass drum and its energetic beater, was escorted to the train for his return trip.

In August, Chancellor Strong appeared for duty and immediately started work. When school opened in the fall, he found a student body of over 1,200 enrolled in seven different schools,[2] utilizing nine University buildings, and taught by a faculty of a few over seventy. The faculty, with the Regents, began plans for a formal inauguration of the new Chancellor and the dates of the events were set for October 16, 17, and 18 (1902).

Three days to inaugurate a Chancellor! The committee in charge evidently wanted ample time for a thorough job—and a gala occasion it was. Elaborately engraved invitations were sent to the colleges of the entire country. Even the

[2] The Graduate School—organized in 1896—and the Schools of Arts, Law, Pharmacy, Engineering, Fine Arts, and Medicine.

most sanguine were surprised at the response. Universities and colleges responded by the score. When the great day actually dawned, college presidents were as numerous on the University campus as brass buttons at a policemen's ball, ranging geographically all the way from President Benjamin Ide Wheeler of the University of California to President Arthur Hadley of Yale. It was without doubt "the greatest event in the educational history of the state," and served in a remarkable degree to focus the attention of the state on the University.

The inaugural ceremony began on the 15th with the dedication of the new Chemistry Building, Dr. Harvey Wiley of the U.S. Department of Agriculture giving the chief address.

The following day, the day of the inaugural proper, was "a blaze of color and a blare of noise at a very early hour." By nine o'clock, the marshals of the day were busy arranging visiting alumni and students in long rows forming a lane that extended from the front steps of Fraser to the entrance of unfinished Dyche Museum, which was used for the inaugural ceremonies. Through this lane, Governor Stanley of Kansas and Chancellor Strong led the procession of dignitaries and

Regent Hopkins delivering the charge to Chancellor Strong in Dyche Museum, October 17, 1902; from an original sketch drawn on the spot by H. Wood of the *Kansas City Star*. Artist Wood, incidentally, was the originator of the pioneer pictorial strip, "The Intellectual Pup."

invited guests, from Fraser Hall. The procession, bareheaded and—as one observant reporter noted —mostly bald-headed, wound slowly past the interested spectators.

The first floor of Dyche, still in the rough, was relieved by decorations of many school colors, banners, and emblems; a temporary platform had been erected; and seats had been provided for 2,500 spectators. Chairman Potter of the Board of Regents presided and introduced Governor Stanley and President Hadley, both of whom gave addresses. Regent Scott Hopkins then delivered the charge to Chancellor Strong, who replied with his inaugural address. The address, as is obvious from its reading, had been prepared with great care and called particular attention to the fact that the University "is created by the state. It is maintained in great part by general taxation. It must be, then, in a peculiar manner a servant of the commonwealth and must fulfill all the functions that such a relation requires. It ought to be the center of the intellectual life of the state. It should influence every department of life in the commonwealth, and must therefore keep itself in close touch with the great current of life in the state and out." This statement served as the keynote of Strong's entire administration, for when he retired from office eighteen years later, he himself felt that his most important contribution to the University and to the state had been the great increase in the scope and the usefulness of the University.

The conclusion of the inaugural ceremonies did not mark the end of the formal program, however. Four events were held in the afternoon and then in the evening a dinner was given to 1,115 guests, the main floor of Dyche again being called into service for the occasion. The dinner began at eight and was followed by no less than twenty-six after-dinner speakers! Still others were scheduled, but as a local paper pointed out, "Some speakers were forced to leave from weariness before their turn arrived."

38. The Flood

The students made a good showing Friday afternoon when President Roosevelt visited Lawrence. The old 'Rock Chalk, Jay Hawk, K.U.' could be heard above all the other shouting. Every one regrets that the President's schedule did not permit of his paying a visit to our University as he did to the University of Minnesota. But that being impossible, the next best thing was done and the students are to be congratulated on the rousing reception they gave the first man of the land.—*Kansas University Weekly*, May 2, 1903.

NO HISTORY of the University and its surroundings would be complete without mention of the flood of 1903. Of such magnitude was the event that it serves as a landmark—or watermark— from which happenings are dated. If you ask an old-timer when a given incident occurred, he will pause, reflect for a moment, and say, "Well, now, let me see. That happened *before* the flood." In fact if you will give the old-timer ample opportunity, you will soon be convinced that there was only one other flood in human history at all comparable to the flood of the Kaw in 1903.[1]

The valley of the Kaw and its tributaries was visited with heavy and continuous rains beginning about the middle of May. Although streams rose considerably, no great cause for alarm was noted in the lower valley until May 27, when the papers of Topeka and Lawrence indicated that the river was rising very rapidly.

At Lawrence, the Kaw began overflowing its banks on May 28, and the papers of May 29 report that the flood had assumed alarming proportions. Train service on the Union Pacific was completely abandoned, and on the Santa Fe service was with difficulty continued only to Kansas City and over the Ottawa branch to the south.

Even after the 29th the river continued to rise. The water works and gas works were inundated; the power company supplying the town with electricity was forced to suspend business, and Lawrence was nearly shut off from the outside world by rail and wire. The peak was reached on June 1, for the *Lawrence World* on June 2 consoled its readers: "Mark this date and event: On Monday, June 1, 1903, the Kaw river was ten miles wide just east of Lawrence. When you get to be the 'oldest inhabitant' this memorandum will come in mighty handy. The chances are no one will believe you."

The flood began to recede after June 1, leaving a scene of desolation and destruction. Homes had been carried away, bridges destroyed, livestock in large numbers drowned, growing crops wiped out, and lives of human beings ended.[2]

---

[1] "The Flood" was written in 1941. The flood of 1951 is described in section 80.

[2] Several lives were lost in Lawrence, but the death toll was much greater at Topeka and Kansas City.

Naturally, such a widespread calamity interrupted the even tenor of usual life. Coal oil lamps were brought out; water was carried from wells, or used cautiously from the reserve supply in the stand tower; especial precautions were taken against the appearance of disease; business, except at the grocery stores—which were worked overtime—came to a virtual standstill.

Naturally, too, these events were reflected in the life of the University. School was just ending. Students, who would ordinarily have gone home, were stranded in Lawrence with slim pocketbooks which became slimmer as additional days went by. Some students and faculty helped with the rescue work which went steadily on during the height of the flood, and the University light plant was called into service to supply hotels, restaurants, and public meeting places. The out-of-town students who were planning to attend the first summer school of the University were delayed in reaching Lawrence and some gave up the attempt altogether.

As the flood came at the close of the school year, it also interfered with the Commencement programs. In fact, it looked for a while as if an informal award of diplomas would be the only Commencement. But the flood had receded so far by Commencement Day, June 10, that for the most part the regularly laid plans were carried out. Some plans were changed and the usual out-of-town attendance failed to materialize, but the Commencement procession finally started on its way after waiting an hour and a half for the Commencement speaker, Judge David J. Brewer, of the United States Supreme Court and a former Kansan, whose train had been delayed by the great flood of 1903.

Above—The great flood of 1903. Looking north across the Kaw. Massachusetts Street is seen on the right; at the foot of the street may be seen the bridge with the north span gone.
Below—The flood waters at the Santa Fe Station.

39. The College of Liberal Arts and Sciences

The School of Arts [the College] has a teaching force of sixty-five—a greater number than the entire faculty of any other college in Kansas. It offers over three hundred courses including many courses in business in its higher relations in Journalism, Banking, Insurance, Mining, Manufacturing and Commerce. There are thirty-three departments.—Kansas University Weekly, December 17, 1903.

THE COLLEGE of Liberal Arts and Sciences, the largest of the many schools of the University, was officially named by the Board of Regents in 1904. Previous to this time it had been called the School of Arts and before 1891 it was simply a "department" of the University. The pattern of the work laid out by "the College" in prescribing a college education has, like the style in women's hats, changed its vogue with the passing years. Although the variations of collegiate education may not have been as violent—or as absurd—as those observable from year to year in women's headgear, they have been, nevertheless, quite pronounced. A college student graduated in 1885 with a Bachelor of Arts degree, for example, would have received a very different type of training from that given most students graduated with the same degree in 1900.

The transition from a rigidly prescribed college course to one which was largely elective and the return to one specifying a greater number of fixed requirements are of interest chiefly to the professional educator, but there are certain broad aspects of the local story which should be included even in an informal history. The original catalog of the University (1866) outlined a college course, similar to the typical courses of the day and including the classics, mathematics, and philosophy. Even this original course contained an option,[1] however. In the second semester of the junior year Greek *or* botany could be selected. As the student would have already taken, according to the outline, two years of college Greek before reaching his junior year, his classical education would doubtless not have been seriously impaired.

It has already been pointed out that the conditions of a frontier state necessitated more practical training than was afforded by the standard college course of the day. The faculty met this demand by offering sets of courses, the work of each set being as rigidly prescribed as was the original classical course. Students had, at least, the option of selecting which set of courses to pursue. In 1867 there was thus added a scientific course; in 1870 a civil engineering course; and in 1874 a course in chemistry and one in natural science; the last three professional courses and the scientific course were alike, however, in their first two years.[2]

All types of courses were also alike in requiring mathematics through analytics, and all required political economy and philosophy for their completion; but neither Greek nor Latin was required in the scientific courses. The mathematics requirement was the bitter pill for many, and long and dolorous were the student complaints, especially about analytics. "As the writer some day aspires to a place in the Christian ministry," wrote

[2] A modern language course was added in 1873.

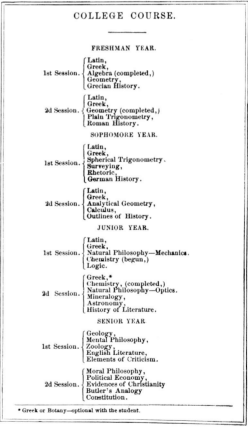

The Collegiate Curriculum of the University reproduced in facsimile from the catalog of 1866. The present catalog lists over 1,700 courses in schools of the University.

[1] There is also an amusing second option in our first catalog. Young ladies in the senior year of the preparatory year were permitted to take French in place of Greek "although it is earnestly recommended that all should pursue the Greek."

one complainer to the *Courier* in 1885, "it does not become evident to him why he should be required to take such a study, for the time necessary for its proper preparation is greater than that of any other study. . . . Then, too, its influence over the morals of a theological student is very bad. In the preparation of a lesson in analytics, the mind instead of dwelling upon pure and holy things, invariably passes to what might be termed very bad words. So the best thing that could be done would be to make analytics optional."

Whether the faculty took into account the morals of a theological student is not certain, although the same year that his plea was made, the requirement of analytics, in all save scientific courses, was changed to read "Analytical Geometry; or Zoology, and Laboratory Practice."

This change, however, was not the first made by the faculty in an attempt to liberalize the various curricula. In 1880, juniors and seniors in the general scientific and modern language courses (if they petitioned the faculty in writing) were permitted to *choose* two optional courses each semester from a rather limited group of studies, so that this year really marks the origin of the elective system in the University.

In 1887, although the work of the freshman-sophomore years was still prescribed in the several courses, the work of the junior-senior years was made still more flexible. In the last two years, a student was permitted to choose a major subject in any one of fifteen fields—the necessary work in each field being prescribed—and to choose two other subjects from selected lists of courses.

This plan of college education was followed with some minor variations until 1895, when the bars were let down further and junior and senior students were permitted to take anything they chose from the offerings of twenty departments, provided that a student did not take more than four courses under one instructor. The final step in the elective age was reached in 1903, when the only courses specifically required for graduation were rhetoric, hygiene, and physical education. Choice within several groups of studies had to be made by freshmen and sophomores, but most of this requirement could be satisfied if the student had had the required study in high school. It should be pointed out that even in this elective age, three years' work in Latin (or in German) was required for admission to the College.

The faculty permitted this idyllic condition—for the student—to continue until 1909, when the pendulum began swinging in the other direction. The faculty, rather than specifying individual courses, however, required limited selections from six groups of courses for freshmen and sophomores; and a major study, in some special field, was again required for juniors and seniors. Although modified, this system remains in effect today, circumscribed by a gradually increasing list of additional requirements.[3]

-----

[3] The dates 1903 and 1909 cited above are catalog dates for the changes stated. A transition period of at least a year was allowed in each instance before new requirements went into effect. It should also be noted that prior to 1903, junior and seniors were required to present two forensics or theses in each term in addition to their regular course work.

40. The *Kansan*

Even a Kansan Editor Had to Meet Requirements

Henry Clay Waters, who was editor of the *Kansan* in 1908-9, and who has for the last three months been city editor of the Lawrence *World*, is now making up his gym credits at the University, preparatory to taking a degree. During the four years he was a student of the University, Mr. Waters spent so much time poring over books in the sociological alcove at the Library that he could not quite find time to finish his gymnasium work. Now he is burning the midnight gas poring over physical culture studies.—The *Kansan*, March 10, 1910.

THE STORY of the development of the present University daily is also the story of the origin of the Department of Journalism. Both are of nearly the same age and the paths of their histories cross and recross each other. The title *University Kansan* was originally used by a paper that had a year's existence in 1889-90. Competition drove it from the field; and the name was not again used until fourteen years later, when

the *Semi-Weekly Kansan* made its appearance on September 17, 1904, the first University paper to appear more than once a week. The following year, the title became simply *The Kansan*, and this masthead was used until September, 1910, when the title became *The University Kansan*, the biweekly issue having changed to a triweekly in May, 1908.

A daily paper had, for fifteen years, been the

UNIVERSITY DAILY KANSAN

VOLUME IX. UNIVERSITY OF KANSAS, TUESDAY AFTERNOON, JANUARY 16, 1912. NUMBER 1.

THIS COMING EVENT CASTS SOME SHADOW

Cruel Truth Must Be Told If It Does Cause Heart-Burns

EXAMINATION SCHEDULE OUT.

Undergraduate Reign of Terror to Begin Week From Saturday And End Friday Following.

It's cruel and all that but it must be done. No matter if students are just back from a beautiful enforced holiday season, full of thoughts about coasting and skeeing and skating, it must be done. The truth must not be crushed to earth.

The schedule for examinations is out.

Horned hippogriffs and dreadful dinosaurs! Great globs of gloom! January 27 they begin, on a Saturday it is; Friday morning, February 2 they end.

Some gnashing and weeping of teeth will be forestalled, some, that is, if students of the College who find after studying the schedule that they have more than two examinations in one day will notify at once the Dean of the College.

Here is the list of events:

10:15 classes, Saturday morning, Jan. 27.

9:00 classes, Monday morning, Jan. 29.

1:30 classes, Tuesday morning, Jan. 30.

4:30 classes, Tuesday afternoon, Jan. 30.

11:15 classes, Wednesday morning, Jan. 31.

3:30 classes, Wednesday afternoon, Jan. 31.

8:00 classes, Thursday morning, Feb. 1.

2:30 classes, Friday morning, Feb. 2.

Three hour classes (and one hour classes meeting on Monday, Wednesday or Friday) will be examined from 8:00 to 10:00, if scheduled above for the morning; from 1:30 to 3:30, if scheduled above for the afternoon.

Two hour classes (and one hour classes meeting on Tuesday or Thursday) will be examined from 10:20 to 12:00, if scheduled above for the morning; from 3:50 to 5:30, if scheduled above for the afternoon.

Four and five hour classes, will be examined from 8:00 to 11:00, if scheduled above for the morning; from 1:30 to 4:30, if scheduled above for the afternoon

Laboratory classes are to be examined at the time corresponding in the schedule above to the first laboratory period or at the time corresponding to the lecture hours (when such an hour exists) at the discretion of the head of the department.

"BOIL DRINKING WATER FOR SAFETY," SAYS YOUNG

"Boil the drinking water," is the warning given out at the office of Prof. E. H. S. Bailey, head of the Chemistry department, this morning. The twenty-four ground wells from which the water supply is taken are insufficient and in order to meet the demand, it is necessary to pump the river water into the mains.

The river water is being sterilized with hypochlorite of calcium in such small quantities as to be harmless.

"They'll be tickled when they see who 'tis."

HIGH SCHOOL NEWS TO BE A FEATURE

Daily Kansan Will Have a Correspondent in Secondary Schools.

A department of high-school news will be one of the features of the Daily Kansan beginning next week. Correspondents have been secured in many of the high schools of the state and it is expected that most of the schools accredited by the University will be represented.

The Daily Kansan will go to all the high schools in the state. It will thus become the clearing house for general high-school news. It will keep the University informed on the important events at the sources from which come the great majority of its students.

In a few days announcement will be made of three cash prizes to be given to the school correspondents doing the best work.

TO SAVE ON LEMONS

Herbert S. Bailey,'02, Will Start Citric Acid Plant at Los Angeles, Cal

The United States government is taking steps to make citric acid from lemons and do away with the waste in the lemon industry at present. Herbert S. Bailey, '02, who is employed in the department of agriculture at Washington, has been sent to Los Angeles, Cal., to start a plant to make the acid. This will be the first plant of its kind in this country.

Bailey is spending a few days with his parents Professor and Mrs. E. H. S Bailey He is secretary of the Washington Chemical Association and secretary of the University of Kansas Club of Washington. Bailey will speak to the Engineering society tonight.

THE DUB.

A fine short story of a college man who "would have liked to make good but didn't have it in him."

Don't miss it in Wednesday's Daily Kansan.

Young to Make Address.

C. C. Young, of the department of state water analysis at the University, will speak at the Tenth Annual Convention of the Kansas State Bottlers' Association at Independence, Kas., January 17. Dr. S. J. Crumbine, also will give a talk on the purity of waters.

SENIORS PETITION AGAINST FINALS

Want Faculty to Exempt all "2" Students from Spring Exams.

The Seniors of the College are contemplating petitioning the faculty for a method of exempting them from the spring examinations. The method they advocate is that all seniors who have made a grade of "2" or better during the term's work should be exempt.

The principal argument advanced is that it will have the effect of raising the standard of the class recitations for the term and that, as a whole, better work will be done. Heretofore a scheme for giving examinations to seniors two or three weeks before the end of the spring term, in order that they might not come at a time when they were extremely busy, has been advanced. It is pointed out that this would not be feasible because the seniors would be very likely not to do much work after the quizzes had been given.

The doing away with the examinations has been successfully tried in other schools and the seniors assert that there is no reason why it would not be practical here. Chancellor Strong has already expressed the opinion that, as presented to him, he was entirely in favor of the plan.

Organize Scholarship Society.

Ten senior girls have organized an honorary society, "The Owl and Triangle," to give scholarship its proper place, to help some girls to study more, and to encourage others to take in more of the extra features of college life

The addition of several hundred names to the subscription list may cause some inconvenience in the routes. If you fail to get your Daily Kansan report to K. U. 25. The circulation department is trying to make prompt delivery of the paper; you can help out by reporting non-delivery.

IN GOOD OLD TIMES IT WENT BY RHYMES

Students Taught in Verse, but Some of It Limped Perceptibly

"Textbooks of fifty years ago," was the subject of a chapel talk Tuesday by Prof. U. G. Mitchell of the department of mathematics.

The speaker exhibited a copy of the "Illustrated Poetical Geography" by George Van Waters, published in 1863, to show one of the methods used. The pupils learned the poetry and sang it at the teacher. If the teacher asked a question about some island in the Atlantic the student would recite through about seventeen verses of "Islands" before he came to that particular one.

"There was one advantage in all this," said Professor Mitchell. "The teacher didn't have any trouble with pupils trying to bluff through a recitation. For instance if a professor asked, 'What are islands?' The pupil would rise and answer glibly,

"'Islands, upon all sides, the waves surround;
In rivers, lakes and seas, and oceans found.'

"Or if he wanted to know what the earth was, the very precocious pupil would say,

"'The earth is but a mighty ball profound,
Just five and twenty thousand miles around,
One fourth the surface of this globe is land,
Three fourths are water as you understand.'

"I can't imagine what the student thought the word 'profound' meant used in this respect, or why the poet should say 'Just five and twenty thousand miles around.' That distance is not correct by at least one hundred miles. Of course we might forgive him on the score of poetic license.

"The book is made up entirely of poetry, mostly concerning geography, but along towards the end in order to give good measure the poet branches off into arithmetic and here is where the height of his genius is given full sway It begins with the definition of 'addition.'

"'Addition is joining more numbers than one,
And putting together the whole sum,
Addition's the rule that learns us to count,
And the sum that's produced is called the amount.'

"So the work goes on through a number of pages. I look upon this book as a very valuable one because it shows the relic of the time when facts, and facts alone, were instilled into the student's mind, allowing the teacher or text book writer to do all the thinking for him."

At the University of Nebraska a trophy has been offered for the fraternity which has the highest scholarship standing each year.

ENTER CRAWFORD AND BROWN, JUNIORS, K. U. 1930.

Christmas day brought a son to the home of Prof. and Mrs. C. C Crawford, but he soon made himself at home and like the University Daily Kansan has come to stay. His name is George Ticknor.

Another future K. U. student arrived at Secretary E. E. Brown's house January 3. He has been christened Edward Benjamin. Mr. Brown was not quite certain as to the date of Edward, Jr.'s advent at K. U.

"Educational conditions change very much in a few years," he said smilingly.

RECITAL COURSE OPENS

Three More Entertainments to be Given This Winter.

The winter recital course under the auspices of the department of music of the University was opened last Tuesday evening with a piano recital by Myrtle Elvyn.

There will be three more recitals during the course. They are: January 25, joint recital, Walter Keeler, organist, William Willett, baritone; February 8, harp recital by Genevieve Smith; February 29, song recital by Ruth Standish Cady, assisted by Carl Preyer, pianist, and the University trio.

Addressed State Fair Meeting.

Charles Younggreen, a junior in the College, went to Topeka Tuesday evening to address a banquet given by the Kansas State Fair Association. Younggreen was the manager of concessions of the fair held at Topeka last fall. His speech was upon "Concessions that pay."

Were in Chicago During Holidays.

Prof. C. G. Dunlap, Prof. E. M. Hopkins, Prof. C. H. Gray of the English department, attended a meeting of the Modern Language Association at Chicago during the holidays. Those attending were guests of the University of Chicago and the Northwestern University.

KANSAS MAKING USE OF NEW HOSPITAL

Thirty-four County Cases Sent to Rosedale Since October 23.

Nineteen counties of Kansas have made use of the new hospital at Rosedale since it was opened by the University October 23, at which time the announcement was made that any county in the state could send cases to this state hospital upon proper certification by a physician in the county.

The range of disorders among the thirty-four county cases that have been treated at the hospital is wide from such comparatively common diseases as appendicitis, paralysis eczema, and hernia, to cases of more rare occurrence such as rabies, hysteria, morphinism, and pellagra.

Besides these county cases there have been 137 other cases treated at the hospital, and those on the staff have made dispensary visits to the number of 267.

The counties from which cases have thus far been received are: Shawnee, 1; Pratt, 1; Montgomery, 2; Washington, 1; Meade, 1; Leavenworth, 5; Lane, 1; Wyandotte, 4; Rooks, 1; Neosho, 1; Graham, 1; Miami, 1; Sedgwick, 2; Atchison, 1; Brown, 2; Grove, 1; Jackson, 1 Wilson, 1; Republic, 1.

MEDICS NOW LOCATED IN MUSEUM BUILDING

Moved Bag and Baggage During the Happy Holiday Season.

THEIR ROOMS TO JOURNALISTS

Where Daily Kansan Offices And New Printing Laboratory Are Being Installed

After a three weeks' fight with cold weather and other difficulties the School of Medicine and the department of journalism have finally been established in their new quarters. The doctors' now have their rooms in the north half of the museum basement, while the embryo newspaper men are located in the old Medic building, where they have installed their laboratory machinery, newspaper files, and editorial desks. Professor Thorpe, head of the department, has his office in the room formally occupied by Dean Sudler.

Those who have been wondering just why the Daily Kansan didn't come out on January 8 can secure a slight hint on the matter if they will interview the bunch of men who have worked night and day for the last twenty days to get things settled for business. The Los Angeles Times building never put up a more wrecked appearance than did the Medic building along about January sixth. The south-west wall of the basement had to be torn out to get the large new presses in. To insure a solid base for this heavy machinery the workmen planned to dig about three feet to bed rock which bedrock was peacefully resting under twelve feet of frozen earth. And that 40-mile blizzard wind singing through the hole in the wall.

Then the new monotype, which is a perfect beauty with twelve thousand complicated parts, slid blithly off of the moving van to warm up; it is still receiving treatment, in its corner of the Medic building.

The north side of the basement of the Museum has been partitioned off for the laboratory and offices of the anatomy classes. Here their equipment has been set up and they have the advantage of better light than in their former rooms.

DEAN TEMPLIN TO MEXICO

Will Visit Principal Cities And Universities of South.

Dean Olin Templin went on a trip to the city of Mexico the day after Christmas. He expected to be away six weeks. Prof. A. T. Walker has charge of his office during his absence.

This is the time in the year when Dean Templin takes his vacation instead of in the summer. He remains at the University during the summer months while the other officers in the administration are away. The Regents have formally approved the plan according to which Professor Templin will take a six week's vacation in the middle of the winter.

It has long been an ambition of Dean Templin's to visit the principal cities in old Mexico. He expects to spend considerable time at the University in the capital city. He expected to stop on the way to visit his orange ranch near League City, Texas.

SNOWBOUND, THEY ANSWER ROLL CALL BY TELEGRAPH

Three hundred miles from class and snowbound!

The sad story came today in the form of a telegram from Frank and Kail Carson, students in the University, who can not get back to school because the Santa Fe branch that runs down to Ashland, where the Carson boys live, has gone out of business until the plows get through.

Railroads seem to get colder at the extremities than anywhere else, and Ashland is at the extremity of the line that extends into Clark county near the southwest corner of the state.

There have been no trains down there for ten days.

The Carson boys looked up the track all day Monday.

Same Tuesday.

Same Wednesday.

Then they sent a telegram full of heartbreak, but breathing a faint hope that by the end of this week they would be delivered.

If the snow and the railroad should remain at loggerheads too long, the University Extension Division will be asked to take care of the absent ones through a correspondence course by telegraph, since there are no mails to Ashland. At the end of the semester Ralph Spotts, traveling representative for the Division, will carry the quiz to Ashland by a bold dash up the Cimmarron river on skates.

CLASS APPLIES ACID TEST TO POE'S COUGH THEORY

U-u-u-g-g-g-h-h-h!

Coughs long and coughs short. What was it, a contagion of winter colds, or a gasoline engine on a rampage? The noise proceeded from the journalism room. Wheezy coughs like the last protesting cry of the washer on an unprimed pump. Long coughs like the bold bad voice of a coast fog-horn.

Ugh, ugh, ugh! Perhaps a new yell for the department of journalism.

The trouble started from a question arising over a line consisting of fifteen printed "Ugh's" in sets of threes, which appeared in Edgar Allen Poe's "Cask of Amontillado" which the class in The Short story was studying. The members were in doubt as to just why the author wasted so much space with a line like that. Then some one suggested that it was natural to cough in three's, just as Poe had written them.

"No," remarked the professor "I believe I cough in one's." Then followed a short pathetic hack.

"I cough in three's," said one member of the class, agitating his bronchial tubes with sharp phlegmatic jerks.

"H'm, that's peculiar," puzzled the Prof. "Now let's all try it. All together.

Ugh, ugh, ugh—U-u-u-gh, Ugh, Ugh!

goal of the *Kansan* publishers, but it was not until January 16, 1912, that the first issue of the *University Daily Kansan* became a reality. To the *Kansan* and its numerous predecessors, we are indebted for a detailed and interesting account of past University life. It is the most important single source of information on University history.

Before the daily *Kansan* had arrived, the Department of Journalism had been organized, and eventually it assumed charge of the *Kansan* as a logical proving ground and laboratory for its students. Following Chancellor Strong's policy of increased service to the state, announced in his inaugural speech of 1902, the faculty planned courses in banking, business, insurance, domestic science, and journalism, which appeared for the first time in the University catalog of 1903-4. For the most part, these courses were selected groups of studies already being offered by the College of Liberal Arts and Sciences and involved, at first, no great additions to the teaching personnel of the faculty.

The course in journalism was thus made up from the fields of history, sociology, English, and law, to which was added a special course "Newspaper Writing," first taught by Professor E. M. Hopkins of the Department of English in the fall of 1903. The course as outlined was to be supplemented by lectures from outside editors and newspapermen and by some practical experience gained by the students as contributors to local, or home, newspapers.

At the time this original journalism course was proposed, University authorities, interested in its success, sent out a questionnaire to many editors asking their frank opinion of its merits. College training for a journalistic career was in its infancy, and the University evidently felt the need of moral support in taking such a pioneer step. This questionnaire brought instantaneous response, and discussion raged through the newspapers within the state and outside of it. A number of newspapermen agreed with an editor of the *Kansas City Star*: "You can't teach journalism by book. It is a trade, not a profession. The University can lay some of the groundwork, but it needs no special course." And Ed Howe, famed editor of the *Atchison Globe,* wrote: "The class of journalism at the State University will result in only one thing: making this world harder than ever for editors. When a young thing with long hair is graduated from this class, and returns home he will at once begin the writing of impossible articles for his home paper. When they

are refused, he will abuse the editor. He will discover that the editor never having been a member of the class of journalism, doesn't know enough to put a barrel right side up for catching rain. The editors of Kansas papers who encourage this piece of foolishness by giving lectures before the class, deserve the criticism they will some day get."

The majority of editors were in favor of the plan, however, and the cause continued to receive publicity and grew in favor. C. M. Harger, of the *Abilene Reflector* (later Regent Harger), was added to the staff in 1905 as "Director and Lecturer" in the journalism course but came to the campus only at scheduled intervals.

The *Kansan* management had undergone a reorganization shortly before Harger's appearance on the campus, and Professor Hopkins had made efforts to correlate the work of the two organizations. Prior to 1905, editors of the *Kansan* were elected by popular choice. In the reorganization, a *Kansan* Board was formed which selected its editors and reporters on a competitive basis. Although the requirement was not distinctly stated in the reorganization, candidates for places on the *Kansan* staff soon came from the class in journalism. To further consolidation, the Journalism "staff" and the *Kansan* shared a common office beginning in October, 1904.

The work of the journalists became still more practical when the *Kansan* began its actual publication[1] on the campus in 1906, utilizing the press of the *Graduate Magazine* set up in the basement of Fraser Hall. When Merle Thorpe arrived in 1911 as the first full-time director of journalism, the department and the *Kansan* had been removed to the basement of Medical Hall. Rights to the exclusive use of the building were not obtained until 1923, although Medical Hall was called the Journalism Building as early as 1913. The Journalism Building, vice Medical Hall, vice Chemistry Hall, remained in use until 1952, when new quarters were secured by the William Allen White School of Journalism which in 1944 had been established as the successor of the Journalism Department.

Students of the department first achieved remarkable publicity in 1908, when the editor of the *Lawrence Journal* allowed the University journalism class[2] to assume charge of the issue of

---

[1] Prior to September, 1906, the *Kansan* had been printed downtown.

[2] Aided by members of the Scoop Club, an organization of students who had, as their primary qualification, received real money for newspaper work.

April 25, 1908. Residents of Lawrence on that day received a shock that is still discussed; for upon reading the *Journal* they learned—at least many did—that liquor was sold in the supposedly dry town. The charge was made in both prose and verse, for among the students of that day was the celebrated Harry Kemp, known as the tramp poet. Kemp tells how the evidence was accumulated:

One night I went with several friends to see
The Bottoms and their gay activity.
First we went to a house of better style;
We drank some beer and lingered for a while.
Then forth we passed into the lowest place
In which a white man dared to show his
    face.
A little joint it was, unpapered, bare
Possessed of stove, a table and a chair.
But on inquiry careful, even here

A dusky woman furnished us with beer.
We killed a quart or so, and to a man
Our cheeks grew flushed, our tongues more
    glibly ran.
We then proceeded down the street, and
    came
Where reputation never had a name.
Here in a stuffy room, with finger snaps
And exhortations, Negro lads shot craps.
Nor did we tarry long, and even here
Between us three we killed another quart of
    beer.

Not only was the general charge made, but specific information where liquor could be bought was furnished. The result of this scoop was fully substantiated in the courts, so carefully had the embryo journalists done their work; and Lawrence had as thorough an overhauling as it has ever received.

41. Green Hall

"Uncle Jimmy" Green visited the Legislature last week. At Chapel Thursday morning he told the students about his work. He said his experience, though short, was sweet and he didn't want any more of it. What more could be expressed by added words? He ended with the remark that $50,000 had been granted by the legislature for a new law building. Then the future LL.B.'s let off steam and the whole student body was with them in spirit.—*University Weekly*, February 21, 1903.

YES, and the Engineers felt so thankful that the Laws were to have a new building that in the dark of the night they hauled a "small frame building" up the slopes of Mount Oread and placed it in front of Fraser. It bore suitable inscriptions,—"Green Hall," "The New Law Building," and "Gymnasium in the Basement."

The interior of "The New Law Building" had been filled with hay, and when the Laws saw it in the morning one of their number threw in a lighted match and another was hoisted to its roof where, wrapped in smoke, he delivered a dedicatory oration.

The authorities called out the janitor force and

Campus skyline, 1906. This view, looking east and a little south from the west end of the campus, shows the University buildings as they appeared after the completion of Green Hall. The buildings in view are (left to right): Spooner Library; Dyche Museum; Green Hall; Fraser Hall; Blake Hall (the pointed roof only is visible); Snow Hall; "new" Chemistry Building; and Fowler Shops.

Fraser, Green (center), and Dyche Museum. Although this view was made some ten years after the construction of Green Hall, it is included because it affords an unusual and pleasant picture of this portion of the campus. It was made from the top of one of the entrance posts to the Watkins property (now the Chancellor's residence). Note the lilac hedge in the foreground and the hitching rack in front of the hedge.

formed a bucket brigade and attempted to put out the fire. Laws and Engineers were now assembled in considerable numbers but on opposite sides of the "building." The Laws would give a heave and the building would go over on its side, but the Engineers would promptly replace it. The janitors felt that they were between three fires and withdrew from the scene of action, but it was not long before only smoke and ashes remained and the fracas subsided.

As the above account suggests, the possibility of a combined gymnasium and law building was considered. In fact, in the first plan proposed, the building was to be two and a half stories in height with a large basement; the gymnasium was to be in the basement, an auditorium on the main floor; and the Law School was to occupy the second floor.

A gymnasium had long been desired by the students and a request for a legislative appropriation had been submitted along with the request for the new law building; but only the last was granted. It was in the disappointment following the denial that the combined building was suggested. The inadequacy of such a plan led proponents of a combined building eventually to give up their scheme, and the site for a new *law* building was finally agreed upon, but the discussion caused delay in beginning the work of con-

struction until July, 1904. By September of the following year (1905), the *Kansan* was able to announce that "the School of Law of the University of Kansas is now occupying its new building. . . . Won't the law boys be lonesome in their new building—no pretty co-eds to linger with in the halls until Uncle Jimmy comes? Doubtless the feeling will not be confined to the boys alone."

Early in the fall a public meeting of the Law students was held, and it was voted to request the Regents to name the new building "Green Hall." The young lawyers were also concerned over the use of some of their rooms for "College" students. "This is our building," said their president, "and if we want to keep our furniture nice we must keep them out."

Both requests met approval. The Regents voted to call the building Green Hall, and the offending Arts classes were withdrawn from the sacred domain of law.

Green Hall was officially dedicated on November 3, 1905. The main address was given by Dean Green, who outlined the falling and rising fortunes of the Law School in the quarter of a century since its establishment in 1878. The student body had increased from its original thirteen members to nearly 150; nearly 700 students had been graduated, and the original faculty of one, who received no salary from the state, had been increased to four full-time members paid from University appropriations.

In addition to these changes, Dean Green was able to point out that legal standards of education had undergone a marked change. From an original requirement which practically amounted to the possession of the tuition fee of twenty-five dollars,[1] the requirement for admission had been

changed to specify a high school diploma; the length of the course had been increased from two to three years (in 1900); and in 1903 the Supreme Court of the state had been given supervision of the state bar examination, supplanting the previous bar examination, which, as one law journal expressed it, was "usually nothing more than a farce." The tide of increasing requirements still swept on, for, after 1943, admittance to the School of Law required a bachelor's degree.

[1] It was also the popular opinion that a good voice was an essential requirement in any aspirant for the legal profession.

42. Robinson Gymnasium

Commencement exercises on Wednesday morning will begin, as usual, at ten o'clock. Doors open at a quarter after nine. A part of the first floor will be reserved for ticket holders. Tickets will be given to alumni, in room 15, June 4; to seniors in the dean's office on Monday, June 3. The balance of the first floor and all of the balcony will be open to the public.—The *Kansan*, May 29, 1907.

THE Law School may have felt itself slighted as it was shuffled from building to building before the construction of Green Hall, but the path traversed by the University gymnasium is still more devious. Early athletics had consisted almost solely of baseball, rope pulls, class football, which resembled rugby football more than it did our modern game; and, beginning in the early eighties, the annual field and track meets held in the spring. Indoor exercise through inclement weather was out of the question for many years. In 1882, however, on the initiative of a few students, a room was fitted up in the basement of University Hall with dumbbells, Indian clubs, and a stand of parallel bars. Chancellor Marvin had consented to this innovation with consider-

able reluctance; but as the students were insistent, permission was granted. The floor of the gymnasium room was so hard and uneven that several loads of sawdust were spread over its surface. The students themselves raised a fund which paid for all expense incurred in providing for the new gymnasium, including the purchase of apparatus. There were, of course, no paid instructors to direct work, although some of the officers of the gymnasium association gave voluntary leadership. Interest subsided after the initial venture, but the gymnasium was revived again in 1891, when a room for a gymnasium was secured in the top of the north dome of Fraser. The venture was again paid for by the students and a fee was charged those who used it. The following

Robinson Gymnasium under construction, fall of 1906. The photograph was taken from an upper floor of the Chemistry Building and looks southwest. Note a portion of the western boundary hedge in the left foreground.

year, Chancellor Snow, pointing out the rising interest in football and other organized athletic sports, made the first faculty recommendation concerning a gymnasium to the Regents. "I would call your attention," he wrote, "to the urgent need of a well-equipped gymnasium, and a competent professor of physical culture, that all the students of the University may be provided with systematic physical training adopted to the peculiar needs of each individual. There are grave dangers attending the lack of regular bodily exercise, and dangers almost equally grave confront the youth who resorts to the more vigorous forms of muscular activity without intelligent guidance."

The "professors" of physical culture were added to the faculty in 1893; May Clark as the first woman instructor, and the Rev. Hector W. Cowan, the men's instructor and also the football coach. With the advent of the new regime, new gymnasium quarters were provided in the west half of Snow Hall basement. The gymnasium work expanded rapidly, especially after James Naismith's arrival in 1898; in 1899 a women's gymnasium was fitted up on the fourth floor of Blake Hall, and the entire basement of Snow was taken over by the men. Basketball practice was held in the basement of Snow, but even after the floor level was lowered there was only a fourteen-foot clearance between ceiling and floor. Even then an occasional intercollegiate game was played there when the downtown halls were not available.

"Physical culture" was added as a requirement for freshmen and sophomores in 1893 with the coming of the professors, and for the next forty years it was included in the programs of the students of most of the schools, including the largest one, the College of Liberal Arts.[1]

The swelling tide of students in the early nineteen hundreds taxed all the facilities of the University, including the gymnasiums. At each session of the Legislature Chancellor Strong was forced to ask the state for many new buildings. A particularly strong appeal resulted early in 1905 in a legislative appropriation of $100,000 for a new gymnasium, although the appeal had stressed the use of the building as an auditorium. Three sites were proposed for the new building: one north of Dyche Museum; a second near McCook Field; and a third west of Fowler on the south ridge of the Hill.

The last location was a decided innovation, as it was not on the original forty-acre campus of the University. Through the far-sighted efforts of several members of the Regents and faculty, however, a tract of fifty-one acres adjoining the campus on the west was secured late in the fall of 1904, from Frank B. Lawrence of Boston.[2]

With this addition to the campus, expansion of the University to the west was possible. The decision was made to erect the gymnasium in the new addition and to name it Robinson Gymnasium in honor of Governor and Mrs. Robinson. Construction was not begun until the spring of 1906 and was slow.

By May 17, 1907, however, the building was sufficiently complete to accommodate the junior prom; and a few weeks later the Commencement of 1907 was held within its walls.

[1] The College removed the requirement in 1933, but freshmen in the Engineering School and in the School of Fine Arts must still include physical education or military science in their courses. From 1924 to 1933 the famous swimming requirement appeared in the University catalogs. Students had to pass a swimming examination as one of the requirements for a college degree! Some students, I fear, received their degrees in this period under false pretenses. Many and varied were the schemes to "get by" the swimming examiner.

[2] The tract originally belonged to former Governor Robinson. Upon his death, the title passed to his widow, Mrs. Sara T. D. Robinson, who gave it to her nephew, Frank B. Lawrence. Mr. Lawrence offered to sell the land to the University for $10,000 and to will this sum, upon his death, back to the University. A counterproposal by the University of a $600 annuity for life was accepted. The first three years' annuity was paid as a lump sum on closing the transaction, but, before the three years had expired, Mr. Lawrence died. The University thus acquired this valuable addition to the campus for $1,800.

43. The School of Medicine

A communication from the Medical Society at Leavenworth was presented by Dr. Weaver, regent from Leavenworth "in reference to the establishment and organization of the Medical Department of the State University—that the Board of Regents recommend that the State Legislature appropriate the sum of $5,000.00 for the purchase of apparatus, fixtures and rent of building for such Medical Deparment."—Also that said Medical Department be temporarily located at Leavenworth.—Regents' Journal, July 18, 1866.

. . . after due consideration your committee [of three Regents] feel compelled to state that the establishment of any department of the University other than that of the Literary would be premature, inexpedient and fatal to the first great objects of a State University.—Regents' Journal, July 19, 1866.

THE charter of the University granted in 1864 provided for six departments of instruction including "the department of medicine." It was many years, however, before definite steps were taken to provide any interested citizens of the state with a medical education. The first announcement looking in this direction appears in the University catalog of 1879-80, which describes a preparatory medical course of a single year. Students who completed this year's preparatory work were advised that arrangements had been made with the Ohio Medical College at Cincinnati and the Rush Medical College of Chicago, which would permit them to enter the second year of the then standard three-year medical training.

Moreover, not only was the medical course then confined to three years' work but the standards of admission, judged from the modern point of view, were low. Although "a full collegiate course" before entrance to medical school was recommended by the University as desirable for the future M.D., actually it was possible to enroll in the medical course with less than three years of high school work.

That the preparatory medical training offered by the University aroused interest and attracted students is shown by the organization of a students' medical society in 1884. "For the present," records the *Courier*, "they are meeting in Dr. Punton's office. The doctor has kindly consented to hold quiz classes every week, and occasionally to lecture them on some subject of interest to the embryo 'Sawbones.' Rapid advancement is anticipated, for the doctor is a thoroughly practical man and one who has had a complete education, and possesses the faculty obtained only by hard continuous study,—that of easily and effectually transmitting his ideas. The members all show a great amount of enthusiasm, and it proves that a more thorough and complete course in medicine should be established in the University." That the new society was really in earnest is shown by

Eleanor Taylor Bell Memorial Hospital. Photograph taken March, 1906, before completion. Compare this photograph of the original Medical School "plant" with the one on page 180.

Three of the University's chancellors. This photograph, made on the campus in May, 1906, shows Chancellors Lippincott, Strong, and Snow. The occasion was a visit to the campus by Chancellor Lippincott, who had not seen the campus for seventeen years. When he left in 1889, there were but four buildings (not counting North College); in 1906, eleven buildings were in use and Robinson Gymnasium was under construction. It was the last visit of Chancellor Lippincott to the campus, for he died in December, 1906. Chancellor Snow died two years after the photograph was made, in September, 1908.

the fact that it petitioned the faculty for permission to secure a cadaver for dissection. Members of the faculty, with the exception of Professor Snow, were so horrified by this suggestion that their reaction nearly put the medical society out of existence.

After this refusal by the faculty, little was done to increase the scope of medical offerings until the question was agitated by the State Medical Association in 1888, which asked Chancellor Lippincott to discuss the question with them. Lippincott studied the matter with care and pointed out that the establishment of a complete medical curriculum was hampered by the lack of clinical facilities at Lawrence. Further, he was opposed to any division of the University plant. "To divide it," he said, "establishing one department in one place and another in another, is to weaken it, and to enormously increase the cost of its maintenance. Every true friend of the University of Kansas, every friend of higher education, will

87

resolutely oppose any measure looking to such dismemberment."

The question of division of University facilities was for a number of years a stumbling block in the way of providing more adequate medical training. Chancellor Snow, who followed Lippincott, was at first in complete agreement with the views advanced above. In his first report, Snow recommended the establishment of a complete medical course—and a dental course—with clinical facilities, at Lawrence but the recommendation was not adopted.

In 1894, the situation was altered by an offer by Dr. Simeon B. Bell of a gift of land at Rosedale (now incorporated as part of Kansas City, Kansas) for the location of a hospital which would be used to provide the necessary clinical facilities. Snow pointed out that if a medical course of four years[1] was adopted, the first two years could be spent at Lawrence and the last two at Rosedale.

The Board of Regents, however, took no action until 1899, when a School of Medicine offering but two years of a four-year course was organized with S. W. Williston as its first dean. Enrollment in the school was small and dwindled with the years, until after Chancellor Strong's arrival in 1902. Strong felt that Dr. Bell's offer, renewed and extended but still not utilized, was the answer to the problem of the Medical School. Starting to work, he effected with some difficulty

a merger of several independent medical schools in Kansas City. As a result of this merger, a four-year medical course, two years in Lawrence and the remaining two in Kansas City, was first begun in the fall of 1905.[2] The new school filled a decided need, if the number of students enrolled was any measure, for the number enrolled that fall was five times that of the preceding September. The *Kansan* was able to report the progress made by October, 1905: "Professor C. E. McClung, acting dean of the School of Medicine, was in Kansas City Saturday reviewing the work of the medical branch at that place, and is very highly pleased with conditions there as well as in the lower classes here. Professor McClung is confident that the University has laid the foundation of a great medical school, and the attendance in this, the first year, bears him out. There are ninety enrolled at Kansas City, and sixty in the school here."

Instruction in Kansas City was first given in the quarters formerly occupied by the College of Physicians and Surgeons, one of the merging schools, located in the Simpson block on Central Avenue; instructors were first selected almost entirely from local practicing physicians. The *Jayhawker* of 1906, for instance, devoted fourteen pages to the portraits (six to a page) of the medical faculty.

The work of constructing the Eleanor Taylor

---

[1] The lengthening of the standard medical course from three years to four occurred in the early nineties. Harvard, for example, adopted the four-year course in 1892.

[2] A training school for nurses was also included in the reorganization of 1905. The first class of nurses from this training school was graduated in 1909.

The Colorado game on McCook Field, October 27, 1906; won by K.U., 16 to 0. Note "Old North" on the skyline as you look east.

Bell Memorial Hospital was also begun in 1905. The hospital and a clinical laboratory, the latter erected from funds of the Bell gift, were first put into use in January, 1907.

The establishment of the Medical School led, in a few years, to an exciting and leading role played by Kansas and the University in the matter of public health. In 1911 Dr. S. J. Crumbine became dean of the Medical School as well as secretary of the State Board of Health, an office he had held since 1904. Led by Dr. Crumbine and his colleagues, extensive efforts were directed toward controlling typhoid, tuberculosis, and venereal disease. Public health education led to the abolishment of the common drinking cup and the roller towel as carriers of disease, to campaigns which used the cries "Swat the fly" and "Bat the rats"; all of which were notable steps in the history of preventive medicine. Although these efforts originated with Dr. Crumbine, he had the whole-hearted support of his colleagues at the Medical School as well as those on the Lawrence campus. In fact, in relating his experiences as a public health officer, Dr. Crumbine paid tribute in particular to Professor Marshall A. Barber, the first instructor of bacteriology in the University, who was himself later to achieve international fame in public health, and Professor W. C. Hoad of the School of Engineering for his pioneering studies of stream pollution and water purification.

44. Marvin and Haworth Halls

When Chancellor Frank Strong told the students that there was grave danger in the rapid social life that was led by many at the University, he simply added his influence to that of others who have long felt that way. The Chancellor spoke of the enormous amount of money expended by college fraternities and sororities during the nine months of the school year, the lack of interest in University affairs, and suggested that the remedy was with the members of the societies who he held were responsible for the condition. The annual expenses of the students' social life is said to foot the large sum of $10,000 annually.

—*Lawrence Daily Journal,* May 27, 1905.

BOOM times had arrived for the University by 1908. That year the enrollment passed the 2,000 mark for the first time, legislative appropriations for the year totaled nearly $400,000—a threefold increase in six years—and four buildings were in the process of erection. The Legislature of 1907 had granted funds for the erection of a new engineering building, engineering and power laboratories, a mining building, and a new service shop.

The engineering building was the first of these projects to be started, work being under way by the fall of 1907. The *Graduate Magazine* reports concerning the site selected: "The selection of a location for the new engineering building was a source of surprise to many who were not familiar with the reasons governing the choice. The building will be erected on the top of the Hill near the west limits of the campus and on a line directly west of Fraser Hall. The main buildings will be about as far from the gymnasium as the gymnasium is from Fraser. The purpose of the Board in choosing this site was to have room for a group of engineering buildings."

The westward march started by the building of Robinson Gymnasium was finished in almost one stride by the location of Marvin Hall. The building itself was completed by the fall of 1908 and could have been put into use, but there was no means of heating it. The old heating plant, taxed to its utmost by the erection of the Gymnasium, was inadequate; and Marvin Hall had to await the completion of an enlarged heating plant in the spring of 1909. In the meantime two units

Third Annual Engineers' Day Parade, 1913. Looking west, Bailey Chemical Laboratory in the background. The "exhibit" in the foreground was a "mulish automobile" but a Law student observed as it passed, "Well, well, well! They don't even know which end to hitch up." The second "exhibit" contains four students in top hats, the vehicle bearing the legend "Consulting Chemical Engineers."

of the Enginering Laboratory had been completed, and work on Haworth Hall started.

All buildings were in use by the opening of school in the fall of 1909 and were officially dedicated on February 25, 1910, the Regents having named Marvin Hall in honor of Dean F. O. Marvin and Haworth Hall after Professor Erasmus Haworth, the head of the Department of Geology.

The following year saw still another Engineering innovation—the first Engineers' Day was celebrated on March 31, 1911. A special chapel service for the Engineering students was held in the morning with speeches by visiting engineers. At noon, the big event of the day took place, a parade that made its way through the campus, down the Hill, up Massachusetts Street through the business district, and eventually ended at McCook Field. The University band led the way, followed by several automobiles carrying the Engineering faculty; then came floats prepared by the Electricals, Civils, Mechanicals, Miners, Municipals, and Chemicals. Included also was a scarecrow labeled "Delegate from the Law School," borne in a rickety wagon drawn by an emaciated mule.

At McCook Field, lunch was served, and athletic contests followed. The Miners had challenged the Mechanicals to a beer-drinking marathon; but the Mechanicals, after thinking it over, declined the challenge on the ground that it would be hopeless to compete with professionals. They did condescend to play the Miners a three-inning ball game, which the righteous Mechanicals won by a score of 1 to 0.

The great day was finished by a dance in Robinson Gymnasium attended by 250 couples. Shanty's five-piece orchestra furnished the music for the occasion, which lasted until midnight. Special decorations of illuminated emblems of the various classes had been prepared by the Electricals; and in the first of the three feature dances, all the lights except the colored ones from the emblems were turned off.

It was indeed a gala occasion, and the *Kansan* in commenting on it the next day encouraged its continuance with the editorial: "Our university has always lacked traditions. Other schools have days which are counted by the student body as the best of their school days. Kansas has never had these days and Engineers Day, established yesterday, is bound to become known as the initial attempt to establish traditions and customs that are to become an intrinsic part of our university life."

Marvin Hall and Engineering Laboratories. This photograph, looking west and a little south, was taken in November, 1908. In the foreground may be seen work on Haworth Hall, just begun. For a view of completed Haworth, see page 132.

90

The May Day Fete of 1908.

45. The May Fete

The sub-station of the Lawrence post office opened at the University Thursday. Stamps, registered letters, money orders, newspaper wrapping, special delivery stamps, and post cards may be obtained from the new office. It is located in the Registrar's Office.—The *Kansan,* April 18, 1908.

THE SUDDEN cessation of the Maypole scrap in 1905 left a vacant spot in the calendar of events, and faculty members concerned with student life and interests were troubled to find a satisfactory substitute. Finally in 1908, an event began which was annually observed for a number of years—the May fete. To be sure, the substitution of a May fete for a May fight was truly a remarkable change, but to Kansans accustomed to events which went from one extreme to another, it did not appear unduly incongruous. Of course, some alumni who were accustomed to the contests of the tough and brutal nineties sniffed quite audibly at the lady-like little Lord Fauntleroys who would tolerate such events as "Ring around the Rosy." But the public in general was convinced that the abolition of the traditional freshman-sophomore scrap was a real advance in college civilization. In fact, Chancellor Strong publicly stated: "Nothing has happened in the whole history of the institution that

has done so much to disarm criticism and beget confidence on the part of the state as that act of the student body." Fortunately the custom has never again been revived, but unfortunately the May fete is likewise an event of the past; so this photograph of the first May fete on May 23, 1908, is an important record of student life of a bygone generation.

To many who were present on the campus at that time, the picture will bring a flood of nostalgic memories. The white-gowned girls, gracefully winding the Maypoles on the pleasant lawn in front of Fraser and Blake, are bordered on the left by the famous lilac hedge. In the distance appears a glimpse of the beautiful Wakarusa valley.

But this picture is of greater significance than simply a record of the first May fete; for it is the first photograph we have showing automobiles on the campus! Thirteen of the vehicles drawn up about the spectacle are horse-drawn; four are automobiles. But there should have been five! The story of the automobile that didn't get in the picture is so interesting that it must be included. It was furnished by one of K.U.'s alumni[1] who read my story concerning this same picture in the *Graduate Magazine* for January, 1940, and who was kind enough to write me as follows: "Indeed your story and the picture of the May fete bring nostalgic memories and scores on about three counts with me. On that memorable date, a visitor to K.U. and a prospective student for the next fall semester, I got my first glimpse of K.U., saw my first May fete and had my first automobile ride. A fellow with a wheezy old open tonneau two-lunger offered to take four of us from Watkins National Bank corner to the University for a dollar. We made it out to Adams Street on Massachusetts and started up the hill. Somewhere between Tennessee and Ohio Streets the self-powered buggy coughed and died. Otherwise there might have been five automobiles in the picture. As I remember it we were late for the May fete; hence the extravagance of that ride. But I assure you I got a greater thrill out of it than any other ride I have ever taken. Up the hill we hurried, past the old Woodward house and Chancellor Strong's residence—then the sight of the pretty girls and smell of the lilacs and that glorious view out over the valley! Good Methodist that I was and with a girl that I liked pretty well at Washburn, I didn't even go to visit Washburn and Baker University as I had originally intended, but decided right then to go to K.U."

<hr>

[1] Dr. E. C. O'Roke of the class of 1912. .

The Lilac Hedge in its full glory, from a photograph made in 1912 or 1913.

A good many of us got our first automobile ride about this time, for while automobiles were increasing in number they were not yet the unnoticed feature of a street landscape that they are today. Indeed, just the week before the first May fete, thirty-five cars made an *endurance run* from Kansas City to Lawrence, a pilot car leaving Kansas City three hours before the run to mark the turns in the road by confetti!

This picture, then, marks also the beginning of another era. New problems of conduct were created, and educators grew increasingly alarmed about the moral menace of this rapidly increasing addition to modern civilization. But then, educators are always becoming alarmed about something. We seem to have survived the menace; or what is more probable, we have adjusted ourselves to it.

46. Student Government

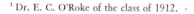

After three hours of heated wrangling last night over the form of organization for the Student Council the "committee of ten" finally split on the jagged rock of women's rights and as a result a majority and minority report will be presented to the mass meeting of students. The split was over whether the girls should be entitled to representatives in the Student Council.—The *Kansan*, May 7, 1908.

THE question of student control over student activities and conduct had been discussed many times in the early years of the nineteen hundreds, but no step toward some definite form of student government was made until nearly the close of the first decade. In the spring of 1909, the men of the University adopted a constitution specifying the election of a student council to make such rules and regulations as might be considered necessary. The election of the council took place on May 6, 1909, some 450 ballots being cast.

This event marks the beginning of formal student government in the University. Some two weeks later, the women adopted a somewhat similar constitution and held the first election of officers of the Women's Student Government Association, an election in which 370 women participated.

The Men's Council met for the first time on May 13 and made plans to include the Law and Pharmacy students, who, at first, refused to join the movement. The first action of the girls seems to have been a unanimous voice against "the pernicious mid-week date." As this step was made in the midst of the boating season, the *Kansan* called it "the high water mark for deeds requiring daring and cool courage." Whether their decision was actually lived up to, is, of course, another matter.

The active work of both associations began the following year, but the women apparently took more interest in their work than did the men. The *Kansan* reported, for instance, at the end of the first year's trial that "there is little doubt that the women have far outstripped the men at the University of Kansas." Remember, too, that this was before the day of woman suffrage. The women also led the men in another matter of government. They were the first to use the Australian ballot—the form in use at present—but at that time considered a very progressive method of election. Student government for both men and women, however, has had a checkered career at K.U., and an account of its ups and downs would nearly fill a volume. At least, it has given many embryo politicians a chance to practice and develop their persuasive powers, in addition to the very lasting benefits obtained from it.

The year 1909-10 was also memorable for several events of scholastic importance. The K Club was organized; freshman caps were decreed; a "revival" in elementary economics removed it from the list of snap courses; the University band and nightshirt parade had become "old" institutions; and fraternities and football were almost banned by the Regents.

Several of these activities deserve more than their simple cataloguing. Freshman caps, for instance, are still with us, but the custom of wearing them by decree had its origin in this period. Wearing class ribbons, green for freshmen, had been practiced almost from the beginning of University life; but it had been wholly voluntary, and the practice varied from year to year. Caps and mortarboards also had their sporadic appearances on the campus in the early years. In 1899, for instance, both men and women wore freshman caps. In 1908, however, the upperclassmen, at a mass meeting, decreed that freshmen should wear caps—blue caps with a colored button indicating the school. The freshmen rebelled, and as there was no means of enforcing the decree, but few wore them. The following year with the Men's Council in action, freshman caps were

The band at the Nebraska game, 1907. Band uniforms were first bought in 1906, and the following year J. C. McCanles was directing the destinies of the musicians.

an actuality for all. The enforcement of the custom since that day has varied with the activity of the Student Council, but it was a matter of some years before freshmen could be educated to the fact that the wearing of caps implied no mark of degradation.

The nightshirt parade of 1909 was the fifth annual one of its kind, and according to the *Kansan* was "a Hummer" with over seven hundred students in line. The first of these annual events was staged in the fall of 1905, the first year after class fights were abolished. Two hundred freshmen and sophomores paraded the streets of Lawrence in their nightshirts, visited the opera house, and finally, about twelve o'clock, wound up in front of Chancellor Strong's home. A few yells brought the Chancellor to the door, and the sophomore president explained to him "that both classes were there in a great peace jubilee."

"I am glad to see you clothed in the robes of peace," said the Chancellor. "I hope you have established a tradition that will take the place of the annual scrap. Wishing you good-night, I go again to my pleasant dreams."

"Everything was in accordance with the fitness of things," on this occasion, reports the *Kansan,* "for the Chancellor's habiliments were not different from those of his midnight callers."

The last two events of this memorable year we shall chronicle were the Regents' consideration of fraternities and of football. Fraternity life had been steadily going downhill since the inception of the chapter-house system, in the late nineties. Drinking and carousing were fairly familiar routine in some organizations, with the result that, scholastically, fraternity members were far down the scale. To emphasize this aspect of the matter, TNE, an organization of wastrels, made its reappearance on the campus in the winter of 1909-10, although it had been banned by faculty action three years earlier. The Regents formally outlawed TNE, but the fraternities themselves took the initiative with regard to improvement of scholarship; and as the result the general fraternity question was dropped by the Regents.

The abolition of football was almost an accomplished fact in the spring of 1910, the *Kan-*

From the *Jayhawker,* 1911.

san making the announcement at one time that rugby was to replace football in the fall of that year. The rising toll in football deaths over the country[1] and its evolution into a mass spectacle were attracting the attention of thoughtful educators. Two members of the Board of Regents moved that the game be abolished because "the game was dangerous, took too much of a student's time, developed brute instincts, and led to false ideals among students." The Chancellor was requested to bring the matter to the attention of the heads and governing boards of the other institutions in the Missouri Valley Conference. On April 19 a meeting of all the Valley schools was held in Kansas City, and the question of the abolition of football put to a vote. It was decided to retain the game, but three Kansas and two Missouri representatives voted against doing so. One aspect of the matter was alleviated to some extent in the following month when the National Rules Committee decided to make the forward pass "the most important play in the game."

[1] There had been only one death (in 1896) from football at the University since 1890.

47. Chapel Exercises in Fraser

Seats were assigned in chapel last Friday morning according to an entirely new plan. All the preparatory students are seated back of the middle aisle, and the collegians in front, being arranged in alphabetical order. Or in more familiar terms, the Faculty occupy the stage, the collegians take the dress circle, the pups go to the parquette, while visitors will probably enjoy the balcony. The boxes have been assigned to the ushers, and a late student may find himself "in a box," if he gets to wrenching on the chapel door knobs.

—University Courier, October 6, 1882.

CHAPEL was a daily part of the routine of University life for nearly fifty, out of the eighty odd, years of its existence. For many years the exercises had a twofold object, because, in addition to the primary purpose of providing a devotional period in the day's events, they also played an important part in the faculty's educational program. In the early years, *all* students were required to speak in chapel and were graded on their performance! Varied and wonderful must have been some of these exhibitions, for in many instances not only the performers but also the listeners were embarrassed. The *University Courier* carries frequent comments on the appearance and accomplishments of the student speakers, noting with particular glee the green and scared appearance of the freshmen as they appeared on the platform—which observations doubtless added no comfort to the freshmen whose turns were still to come. Flowers, in season,

were the reward of the abler ones, as at the conclusion of a pleasing oration, bouquets would be showered on the fortunate orator. The faculty, in time, put a stop to these accolades, since the bouquets, especially the heavier ones, would go astray and, quite accidentally of course, strike a faculty member. For some reason or other, the enjoyment of the audience seemed to increase as the ratio of faculty hits to student throws increased.

As the student body became larger, it became more and more difficult for all students to have their turns on the platform, and in 1892, speechmaking was required of only juniors and seniors; but even then, the number of students was greater than could be heard, so that college rhetoricals were soon abandoned altogether.

Up to 1904, chapel exercises were the first event of the school day and many students took advantage of the breathing spell offered by the chapel period for preparation of lessons, a practice

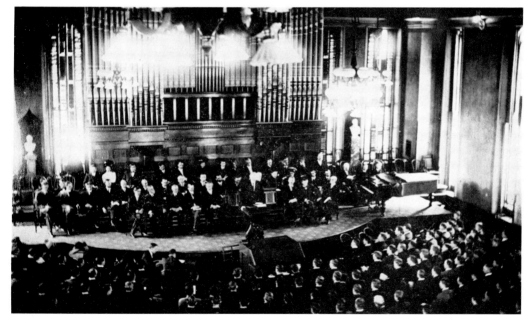

Chapel exercises in Fraser. The only photograph found showing an exercise in the Chapel. The occasion for this particular service was speeches by visiting celebrities at the dedication of Marvin and Haworth Halls, February 25, 1910. Chancellor Strong is presiding; many students of his day will recall his characteristic preface to the Lord's prayer: "After this manner therefore pray ye"; which was followed at the conclusion of the service by the curt but sonorous "You are dismissed."

95

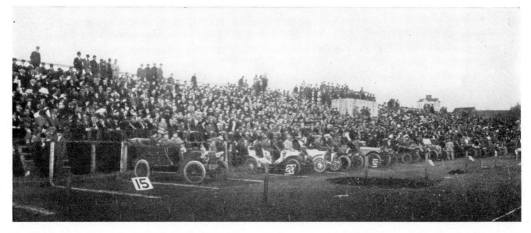

The Kansas-Iowa Game on McCook Field, 1909. The passing years are bringing changes. Compare this photograph with the one taken ten years earlier (page 47). Note "Old North" on the skyline at the right.

frowned upon by the faculty. On at least one occasion, Chancellor Lippincott caused consternation in the ranks of this wayward group by opening the devotional exercise with a long and fervent prayer for the students who found it necessary to study in chapel.

Attendance at chapel, for the longer part of its history, was voluntary, save, of course, for the unfortunate souls who happened to have the speaking assignment of the day. The chronological history of chapel exercise can be traced in the University catalogs. Up to 1872, all catalogs state, "Devotional exercises are held daily and every student is required to attend." The catalog of 1872-73—the first year that University Hall was used—modifies the statement somewhat by stating that "devotional exercises are held daily. Students who recite the first hour are required to attend." Beginning the next year, however, and continuing up to 1913 the University catalogs simply state, "Devotional exercises are held every morning," with no mention of compulsory attendance. In the year 1913-14 chapel exercises were held but twice each week, and the catalog for 1914-15 shows that chapel exercises had at last come to an end; for the brief statement is made, "Convocations are held occasionally."

Since chapel attendance was not compulsory, attendance varied markedly from year to year and even from day to day. On one occasion, after student rhetoricals had ceased, but three individuals were present: a faithful student in the audience, the faculty member whose turn it was to preside, and the song leader. The chapel exercise, however, was held. After Chancellor Strong's arrival in 1902, interest in chapel was greatly renewed and chapel attendance reached its high water mark in the early years of the Strong administration. Before this period, the student paper would occasionally express concern over the smallness of chapel attendance—possibly when other news was scarce. At one time during the middle eighties, the *Courier* pointed out that the small attendance at chapel was due to the poor attendance of faculty members, who, it reasonably could be assumed, were the models for student action. To remedy this situation, the *Courier* assumed the privilege of publishing the attendance of faculty members, recording the names individually and the number of times each member was absent or present. After continuing this practice for a month the editors were able to report with evident satisfaction, "The profs are coming to chapel better now."

48. Streetcars and Campus Improvements

The first streetcar of the Lawrence system to scale Mount Oread reached the summit at 2:30 o'clock this afternoon. The line is now completed to the loop at the gymnasium. The passengers on the first car up the hill were writers on the Lawrence newspapers. Several of them saw for the first time some of the University improvements which they have been enthusiastically working for and writing about.

—The *Kansan*, April 19, 1910.

SEVERAL generations of students have come and gone on the campus who never saw a Lawrence streetcar or rode one over the Hill; but for nearly a quarter of a century, streetcars were a familiar sight to students. Even in the days when horse-drawn cabs were the only wheeled method of reaching the hilltop, *electric* streetcars were fervently desired, and on one or two occasions had actually been discussed. The Board of Regents gave permission to an "Electric Railway Company" to skirt the campus as early as 1898, but the venture was apparently a promotion scheme that failed to materialize when funds were not forthcoming from Lawrence citizens.

Again, in 1903, an ambitious electric railway project was undertaken which had important consequences in the history of the University. The railway line as planned was to come south on Mississippi Street, turn west near the present stadium, turn south again, and then tunnel under Mount Oread near the present Marvin Hall. After emerging from the tunnel, the rails were to skirt southeast around the foot of Mount Oread, eventually circling back to town. Practically all the neighborhood through which the line would pass in the vicinity of the campus was then uninhabited wilderness. The backers of the scheme planned a real-estate development along their carline and set about securing options, including one to the western end of Mount Oread. University authorities became acquainted with the scheme at this stage of the game. Realizing that it would cut the University off from western expansion, they undertook negotiations with Frank B. Lawrence, as related elsewhere, that resulted in the acquisition of the western half of the present campus; and the railway project subsided.

The successful effort to secure an electric line came several years later. Downtown Lawrence secured "modern" streetcar service in the fall of 1909, and plans were made to extend the service to the Hill. A route was laid out that crossed the crest north and south between the Chemistry Building and the Gymnasium, and construction

Looking west past Robinson Gymnasium. Photograph made in the fall of 1910. Not only were the streetcars new but so was the lighting system when this photograph was made.

97

Massachusetts Street dressed up for Commencement, 1911. Looking north from Ninth Street. Note that even by 1911, we were still largely in the horse-and-buggy days.

was started. By late October, the line had been built as far as McCook Field, but winter held up further extension until the following spring. Finally, the first car reached the campus on April 9, 1910, and within a few weeks regular service was established and continued until streetcars were replaced by busses in the fall of 1933.

Other campus improvements became noticeable about the time that streetcars were introduced, one of which is also visible in the accompanying photograph: an improved system of lighting the campus at night. This sightly and useful addition was made in the summer of 1910. The most important campus improvement, however, is not visible in any photograph and although still in use, is almost unknown to the thousands of students who have tramped the campus walks from 1909 to the present day. For under their feet lies an extensive system of tunnels honeycombing the entire campus. Through these tunnels it is possible to pass to any building from any other. The purpose in building them was, of course, not to provide secret passageways—or bomb-proof shelters—but the more prosaic purpose of furnishing a system through which could be carried the heating mains, the water, gas, and sewage pipes, and the power lines necessary for all University buildings. The tunnels have added immeasurably to the sightliness of the campus and to the comfort and health of the students.

It is easy enough to write these words and to read them, but a more concrete measure of the utility of these tunnels as affecting student health, to consider but a single case, can be offered. Typhoid fever is at the present day almost a thing of the past; and, it might be remarked, the Uni-

versity played an important part in the eradication of this disease from the state and nation. Yet in the years preceding 1910 there were many, many cases reported among students and faculty, and fairly frequent deaths. Many of these cases were due to contaminated water and milk supplies. In 1906, for example, a member of the medical faculty at Lawrence severely scored the Lawrence Water Company for running untreated river water through its mains. The study of the pollution of soil and streams was still in its infancy, but the cause of pollution can be traced to such conditions as described by Chancellor Strong in his report for 1906: "The very critical situation of the University as to sewage calls for immediate attention. The Chemistry Building, Fowler Shops, Blake Hall, Medical Hall, and a part of Snow Hall have no sewer system, and the sewage is deposited on various parts of the campus, making a revolting spectacle, and being a menace to the health of the city and of the University. Unless provision is made at once, the new gymnasium will be in the same category. The other buildings of the University are also poorly provided for in the way of sewer facilities." As a result of this plain statement, funds were appropriated for the construction of a tunnel system. The few tunnels in existence at that time were enlarged and the network extended, especially in the summer of 1909. The extension of the tunnel lines made it possible to provide an adequate sewage system.

Mississippi Street (looking north) when streetcars first began their trips up the Hill.

98

Regatta on Potter Lake, Commencement, 1911.

49. Potter Lake

After the workmen have completed the spillway at the north end of Potter's Lake, a task upon which they are at present engaged, the lake will be ready for use. Recent rains and snow have partially filled the lake with water, but a pipe line is being constructed from the pumps on the hill to the lake so that water from the mains may be used to fill the lake. It will hold 4,000,000 gallons of water when completed and will cover an area of two acres.—The *University Kansan*, March 4, 1911.

PRIOR to 1911, the University had no adequate method of fire protection, although city mains supplied water to the campus. The reserve supply and the pressure of the city water were such that any serious fire on the Hill would have exhausted the city reserve within five minutes. With an increasingly large and valuable plant to protect against the hazard of fire, the Regents decided in the fall of 1910 to construct a lake that would serve primarily as a reservoir of needed water supply in case of fire.

The outline of the proposed lake was laid off in the ravine north of Marvin Hall. A sixty-foot dam was to cross the ravine and impound the drainage of the slopes in a lake some two acres in extent and some sixteen feet deep at the north end. Below the dam a powerful motor-driven pump was to be installed which could force an ample supply of water to any part of the campus.

Work of construction was started in the fall, and by March (1911) the dam and the pump house were complete. As the lake filled in the spring from snow and rains someone conceived the idea of having a regatta on its surface for Commencement. In order that the lake might be ready

by June, temporary water lines were connected with the city supply and the lake was rapidly filled. By this time the Board of Regents had officially named the body of water Potter Lake, in honor of State Senator T. M. Potter, a former member of the Board.

A regatta had, for several years, been a regular feature of the Commencement program; but previously it had been held on the Kaw River at the boating docks above the dam; so the decision to have it on Potter Lake was, after all, no great innovation.

The program took place on Monday, June 5, at two o'clock on "an exceedingly warm day"—a familiar enough report—in the presence of Mr. Potter himself, so the occasion had the aspect of a dedication. The band led off with a concert and there then followed swimming races, diving contests, canoe races, and water games. Sometime during the course of events, a whale was sighted. Just how a whale could appear so readily in a handmade, fresh-water lake does not seem to be a matter of record. A boat put out to capture the whale but was upset and the whale continued to disport himself—or herself—during

99

the remainder of the afternoon. Maybe it is still there; at least, no mention of its final disappearance was made.

From that day to this, Potter Lake has continued its existence on the campus as one of its beauty spots and as a source of health and pleasure both in summer and in winter—and of tragedy. The lake was not finished before it claimed its first victim. Toward the close of the school year in the spring of 1911, a group of Civil Engineers attended a party in Marvin Hall. Returning home late in the evening, they went by the lake and decided to take a swim. Carefree, they discarded all clothes and swam across the lake; and then, on the return trip, when about halfway across, one of them went down in twelve feet of water. Although the boys remaining made every effort to find their missing comrade, it was nearly an hour before his body could be found.

Death from drowning followed frequently in the succeeding years. In 1921, the *Kansan* reported that at least six students had lost their lives in the waters of Potter and urged adequate protection for bathers and swimmers. The possibilities of recreation for hot days of summer school, too, led, in the early twenties, to a more carefully planned use of the lake. In 1924, a diving tower and a pier, springboards, and dressing rooms for men and women were built and—most important

Upper: Swimming in Potter Lake.
Lower: *Skating*. Both photographs were taken in 1925.

of all—life guards were provided. Cementing the entire basin of the lake and making provision for properly disinfecting the water were even contemplated at one time, but after the completion of an adequate public pool in 1927, all improvements were abandoned and bathing in Potter Lake was forbidden by an official decree.

50. Frank Strong Hall

The unfinished wing [west] of the Administration Building is still in the embryo. Fifteen men were busy yesterday excavating for the foundation of the wing, the center foundation having been completed some time ago. Seven laborers were busy with horsedrawn scoops, following a plow which loosened the tough gumbo. Others were digging at the rocks with which the soil is filled and which greatly hinder the work of excavation.—*University Daily Kansan*, November 23, 1917.

FRANK Strong Hall, known until 1938 as the Administration Building—or still more briefly as "Ad"—was slow in taking its final form. Ground was originally broken for this building, one of the largest on the campus, in December, 1909, but it was not until January, 1924, that the finishing touches were finally applied.

During the early years of the nineteen hundreds, students increased so rapidly in numbers that despite the addition of the Chemistry Building, and of Green, Marvin, and Haworth Halls, space could hardly be found for the new students. The classes held in most of the new buildings had previously been held in Fraser Hall, yet

so swiftly did the enrollment increase that Fraser was more crowded after their completion than it was before. More classrooms and office space were greatly needed, and the Legislature was asked to provide a new building for this purpose. The request was granted by the Legislature of 1909, $50,000 being made available for this purpose in 1910 and $75,000 the following year. The building, as originally planned, was to be built with two wings and an elaborate central rotunda higher than the wings, but the original appropriation of $125,000 was used for the construction of the east wing only.

Excavation was begun at the site selected for the new building, west of the Chemistry Build-

100

Campus view, spring, 1913. Looking east, and a little north, toward Fraser.

Central Ad, under construction, 1918.

ing. Before much progress was made, it was decided to change the site somewhat, setting it farther north and west than originally planned. The change, a wise one, was made "because it was thought the new building would otherwise be too close to the road which runs in front of the gymnasium and engineering buildings. It was feared that the huge mass, over four hundred feet in length, would loom up near the road in such a way as to give the impression that the buildings were crowded together on the top of the hill."

Work progressed slowly on the wing through 1910 and 1911, and it was almost January of 1912 before the building was ready for occupation.

Late in the fall of 1911, several departments started to move in. Psychology laboratories occupied the basement floor; philosophy and mathematics classes were held on the first floor, history classes on the second, and the Department of Painting took over the third floor. For a number of years "East Ad" was used in this manner, standing up alone and looking—from the standpoint of the present— as if it needed some support on the west to hold it up properly. The Legislature of 1911 provided additional funds for the enlargement of the building, but they were sufficient to build only the foundations of the central section. The foundations were in place by 1913, but further construction was delayed for four years. In the fall of 1917, funds again being available, work on the west wing was begun; and this section of Strong Hall was in usable condi-

East Ad, 1913.

101

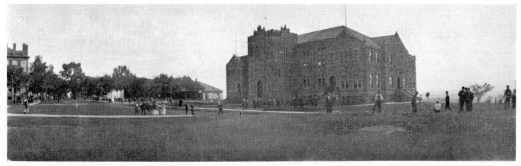

The west end of the campus about 1912. One looks east at Robinson Gymnasium on the right; Bailey Chemical Laboratory at the extreme left.

tion by Christmas of 1918. The central section was not completely finished for five years more, but finally, during the Christmas vacation of 1923, the administrative offices were moved from Fraser, where they had been housed since 1872, to their new quarters in Strong Hall, and the work of fifteen years was ended.

During the years of 1911 and 1912, which marked the first use of the Administration Building, several other changes in the life of the school took place which continue to affect the lives of students and faculty to this day. Examination week became part of school life; enrollment for college classes was first carried out in Robinson Gymnasium; and the whistle, which marks the end of each class hour, started its initial blasts. Truly remarkable changes! Previous to the spring of 1911, each instructor gave the examination in his course as he saw fit, usually during the last regular recitation periods. For the first time in May, 1911, an examination schedule was adopted by the faculty. You remember it, don't you? "Nine o'clock classes, five, four, and three hours, Thursday morning, 8:00 to 9:50," etc. As was to be expected, the students didn't accept the new method without a groan, but the faculty was adamant, and it still stays with us.

Enrollment in the Gymnasium for students in the College was accepted with enthusiasm when introduced for the first time in January, 1911;

Commencement, 1913. Faculty marching into Robinson Gymnasium for the final exercises of the week.

for previous to this time, in enrolling, the unfortunate student had to plod his weary way from building to building, and see each individual instructor before his enrollment was complete. The new method, necessitating the presence of instructors and advisers on the main floor of the Gymnasium, was a real relief to the student, as the process of enrollment, at best, is a tedious one. In the original plan, too, registration, preceding enrollment, took place at the same time, and as the student left the Gymnasium, the treasurer, seated near the door, relieved him of his fees.

And then the whistle! What an expression of relief comes over the student's face as it blows! I've watched students now for over thirty years

and the expressions never fail to materialize. Well, the sound of the whistle may be relief for faculty members, too.

Although used for many years to get students out of bed in the morning (7:45 A.M.) and to get them into bed at night (the curfew), it was not until March 25, 1912, at 9:50 A.M. that the class whistle on the powerhouse blew for the first time. "If the instructor isn't through when the whistle blows," stated Chancellor Strong in the announcement concerning the replacement of class bells by the whistle, "get up and go"—and since that day only faculty members who are hard of hearing have kept their classes after the whistle blows—or maybe you have a better explanation.

51. Commencement

If your life is sometimes stodgy, drab and commonplace, sometimes flat, stale and unprofitable, take up some work for the alma mater. You will find, with me, release of energy in the vital power of a great affection, and your deadline of forty will be faded superstition.—Thornton Cook, '93, Alumni Address, June, 1922.

DOWN the long line of years since 1873, Commencement Day—*the* Commencement Day—looms in the hearts and minds of University graduates as the brightest of all bright college days, the culmination of dreams come true, the never fading remembrance to be cherished—and renewed—through all of life.

In general features, Commencement exercises have not varied greatly since the first Commencement. There have always been a baccalaureate sermon, a Class-Day exercise, Commencement exercises proper, and lastly a celebrating dinner. As the years passed by and the number of graduates increased, reunion of alumni became a part of the annual event.

For many years, Commencement grew with the school by following the original plan, but in the spring of 1908 definite steps were taken to change the festivities of the week. The *Graduate Magazine* describes the changes:

> The old Commencement was an occasion marked by several interesting events, but each one isolated. It was a time for much individual enjoyment, but without much organized, visible manifestation of the spirit of festival. The new Commencement is developing the character of a continuous performance. The breathing spells and the time for quiet walks and the hours of sweet-sad reminiscences come before and after—except,

of course for the person who prefers to take himself off. The spirit of the week is becoming manifest not only in happy faces and hearty hand shakes—by no means modern inventions—but in gorgeous banners and gay umbrellas, in band music morning, noon, and night, in the big picnic and the class reunions, in the umbrella parade stretching almost from Marvin Grove to McCook Field, and the banner parade winding in and out among the buildings on the way from the east campus to the Robinson Gymnasium.

Yes, the gay class banners were new in 1908 and in addition to the series of carefully planned

Commencement, 1923. For one year, Commencement exercises were held in this tent near the Stadium. One year was enough. It was so hot that those who attended the fifty-first Commencement still shudder when they see this picture.

103

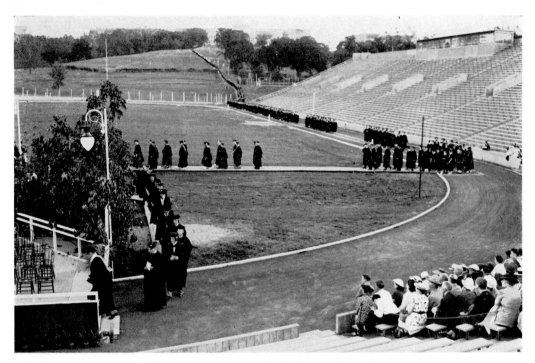

Commencement, 1938. Marching down the Hill into the Stadium. Although Commencement exercises have been planned for the Stadium since 1924, the evening exercises, now the custom, did not begin until the following year. Previously, they were always held in the morning, regardless of place and weather.

events, another new feature appeared for the first time that year—Chancellor Strong and Vice-President Carruth marched in cap and gown in the Commencement procession. As nearly as I can determine, the class of 1897 was the first to appear in collegiate caps and gowns at Commencement. The class of 1899 made an attempt to introduce the senior custom of wearing collegiate regalia through the school year. They appeared in body thus arrayed on several occasions, and some of the girls of the class wore the costumes more or less regularly on the campus. The same class also requested the faculty to wear academic robes at Commencement, but Chancellor Snow pointed out that "we [would] lay ourselves open to ridicule by the state. The majority of Kansans would have no sympathy for such a form." Succeeding senior classes, however, made repeated and pointed requests of the faculty to this effect for many years, but not until 1908 did their pleas fall on any save deaf ears. It was to take many more years of pleading to get the rest of the faculty into collegiate robes for the Commencement procession; not until after Chancellor Lindley arrived was the practice adopted—and then not without a struggle.

104

The year before "the new Commencement" went into effect, graduation exercises were held in Robinson Gymnasium, and for sixteen years the annual procession of faculty and graduates wound its way from Fraser down the University drive into the main entrance of Robinson for the awarding of diplomas.

The Gymnasium, too, was the scene for many years of the University dinner following the Commencement exercises; but the dinner from year to year has been held in many different places. The original dinner, it will be recalled, was held in Fraser Chapel, which was used for Commencement itself until the building of Robinson Gymnasium. But the dinner has been held in the basement of Snow—Old Snow—in the top floor of Spooner Library, in Dyche Museum, in a large tent pitched in front of Fraser, in Fowler Shops, then in the Gymnasium, and finally in 1929, after the completion of the Union Building, in its large ballroom.

For the graduate of recent years and for many spectators, no Commencement sight has been more impressive than the long line of graduates marching down over Mount Oread from Strong

Hall to the Stadium in the glory of a June evening. This striking feature was initiated in the Commencement of 1924, and has—weather permitting—been carried out annually since that day. Many and bitter have been the tears of the girl graduates who have been denied this privilege by the vagaries of the weather, and even the prosaic and matter-of-fact males must have felt some twinge of regret when the same favor was withheld.

52. The Theatre

Merely because the students at the play last night were calling for the usual rendition of Boola-Boola, ex-Congressman Bowersock appeared in the gallery with a squad of police and attempted to suppress the demonstration. After sizing up the situation, however, the minions of the law decided to lay hands on no one, as the "gods" numbered about 200 and showed a disposition to hold together.—The *Kansan*, October 24, 1908.

SINCE 1882, the Bowersock Theatre has amused, beguiled, and instructed, for better or worse, the students and faculty of the University. From 1882 until 1915, it was the Lawrence house of tragedy, drama, and comedy, and occasionally of burlesque. Many notable figures in the dramatic world appeared on its stage in this interval, and scarcely a week passed during "the season" when it was not visited by one or more traveling companies.

The gallery gods in these earlier days were chiefly students who, it must be stated in all honesty, did more than simply attend. Arriving early, they would take their seats in the heavens and announce in loud unison the names of University couples, faculty or students, as the later arrivals entered the parquet below them. Once the curtain went up, actors had to be on their mettle to give their best efforts. Any lagging or uncertainty in lines was sure to produce audible advice from the gallery, and stage directions were not always lacking when the performers were letter-perfect. Occasionally gallery conduct would become so bad that the management would remove the chief offenders, which always had the salutary effect of allowing the play to go on unhindered.

Attempts to emulate the stage professionals do not seem to have come to the serious attention of students until the Bowersock had been

"Oh, me! Oh, my!" but they are doing more than black that tiger's eye—they are burning him in front of Fraser! An annual custom for many years preceding the Missouri football game. The view here shown is of unusual interest as it was taken the day before the first homecoming on November 23, 1912. In addition, in the background at the right, may be seen the Watkins home under construction. In 1939, the Watkins home became the Chancellor's Residence.

Theatre advertisements or reviews from University papers, 1884-1916.

exhibiting its wares for some years. The first senior play was staged by the class of 1892 and was a burlesque on *Julius Caesar,* although the year before the Department of Music had presented *The Bohemian Girl* at the "Opera House." In 1898, a dramatic club was organized which, by 1906, was known as the Masque, in earlier years having occasionally been called by this name. From this time until 1914, dramatic organizations increased in such numbers as to cause administrative concern. As a result, all University plays were put under the general supervision of the Department of Public Speaking, which, in 1942, became the Department of Speech and Dramatic Arts.

Our brief story of the theatre, however, would be incomplete without some mention of the motion picture, the most popular amusement and recreation of the present day. Although the new theatre art was in its infancy in 1903, Lawrence had the distinction of possessing a motion picture house at that early date. Clair Patee and his wife, while in New York in the summer of 1903, were inveigled into buying from a young Frenchman "a funny-looking machine that could make pictures move." After trying to get established with the machine in New York, Mrs. Patee was called to Lawrence by the illness of her parents. Upon her arrival, she decided to rent a building on Massachusetts Street for the sole purpose of showing moving pictures. This period, it must be recalled, was even before nickelodeon days. In fact, it was only the year before (1902) that the first motion picture theatre of the country had been established, appropriately enough, in Los Angeles. The Patee, in existence today, was therefore a distinct innovation in amusement circles. It is surprising, therefore, that absolutely no mention of motion pictures occurs in the student papers from 1903 to 1905, either in comment, allusion, or advertisement. In fact, the first printed statement to appear concerning motion pictures was a Bowersock advertisement of the Britt-Nelson prize fight in the *Kansan* for October 18,

1905. The motion picture houses themselves did not commence to advertise until 1907, and then only occasionally. From 1903 to 1907, however, the motion picture industry had made tremendous strides—and enemies. The press, the church, and the legitimate theatre condemned motion picture houses as "hopelessly bad." Although the criticism was based largely on economic grounds, it had the effect of making attendance at one of the new theatres, if not immoral, at least an adventure open to criticism. Parents warned their children to stay away from these evil places, with the result that the attendance at the movies only increased. The lack of early motion picture advertising in the *Kansan* is at least understandable for this reason, and it was not until 1914 that advertisements of motion picture theatres appeared regularly in each issue. Part of the suspicion of the "jitney houses"[1] was lulled by the practice of benefit performances, first begun in 1912, when the Patee and the Aurora turned over their profits for an evening to a University dormitory fund then being solicited. That the tide was turning towards motion pictures can also be seen in the changing fortunes of the Bowersock. By the fall of 1914, the list of stage attractions offered was rapidly dwindling, and the following year the Bowersock announced the policy of motion pictures five nights a week, one night being reserved for such traveling stage companies as could be induced to stop. Several years later, even this policy was discontinued, and the transition of the Bowersock Theatre from an opera house to a motion picture was complete. Talking pictures at the Bowersock were introduced in March, 1929, and the following fall its name became the Dickinson Theatre. A few years more, and students will be as unfamiliar with the name Dickinson as they are now with "Bowersock," for in 1940 the Dickinson Theatre became the Jayhawker.

---

[1] A "jitney house," it should be explained to the modern student, was a motion picture theatre, because a jitney was a nickel, and a nickel was the price of admission.

53. Oread Training School

The neat-appearing bungalow (cost $6,000.00), that returning students notice the first thing just north of the Library is the new home of the Oread Training School. The Training School has been housed in Myers Hall for five years, but has outgrown its crowded quarters there.—*Daily Kansan,* September 13, 1915.

A *Kansan* reporter returning from a summer spent in working north with the wheat harvest of 1915 observed upon his return that seven of the faculty owned automobiles; that although "the weather was unusually hot for the time of year" it would be best to have an overcoat on the

Oread Training School; a photograph, looking west, taken in the spring of 1936; Spooner-Thayer Museum at the left.

hook besides one's palm beach suit; and lastly, that a new building had appeared on the campus north and east of Spooner Library. Although all of these observations are interesting commentaries on their time, we have only the space to pursue in greater detail the last one. The new building was the Oread Training High School, which had been built during the summer. Oread High was not itself a new institution at this time, however, as it had been first organized in the fall of 1911 and had had its classrooms in Myers Hall (built in 1906), a building erected through the agency of the Christian Church for Bible instruction. The School of Education had been formed in 1909 with the express purpose of giving professional training to prospective high school teachers and administrators, although previous to the organization of the new school such training had been provided by a Department of Pedagogy within the College of Liberal Arts. One of the first developments of the School of Education was to establish Oread High School (the title was changed to University High School in 1941) as a training school for observation and practice by prospective teachers. It served, in addition, as a high school which gave the usual training afforded by a secondary school. Large enrollments after World War II found University High School far too small for teaching-practice courses. As funds were not available for extensive addi-

tions to the building, University High was discontinued in the spring of 1950. In the months that followed, the building was remodeled and—through the generosity of Roy Roberts of Kansas City—it was pleasantly furnished for the use of the staff of the University of Kansas. Since 1951 it has been the Faculty Club.

Thus in 1911, the University returned to the practice of giving high school training, a practice from which it had tried so desperately to depart during the first quarter century of its existence. The objective of this practice had, by 1911, of course very materially altered. Originally the University had been forced to give preparatory work because of the inadequate training provided by the few public high schools of the state. In 1877, for example, there were only four high schools of the state whose work was regarded as satisfactory by the University. By 1911 this number had grown to nearly three hundred standard ones! This remarkable growth in the number of high schools was due in no little measure to the influence of the University, not only in providing teachers, but in providing a positive leadership in the development of high schools.

Chancellor Marvin was one of the first to stress the need for a more adequate high school system. In his report for 1877 appear these words:

"What our young state now needs to unify its otherwise excellent plan of public education is the

108

academy, or the equivalent high school: not one, not five, on these eighty thousand square miles, but, in the more densely populated portions, one for each county, or central for at most a group of four counties. A day's drive could take the pupils to or from school. Visits from home would be practicable. Home supervision would not at once be removed, and a great reduction of cost over sending children to the University for preparatory training would be secured. The best result would be the better education of all the people."

Marvin had gone even further than this statement suggests, for in the spring of 1876, with the approval of the Board of Regents, he had circularized the high schools of the state proposing and outlining a uniform three-year course for all high schools, three years then being the standard high school term. In the event that a high school adopted the plan outlined, the proposal was made that its graduates be admitted to the freshman class of the University without examination. Four high schools agreed to the plan and were placed on the first accredited list of the University: Atchison, Emporia, Winchester, and Lawrence.[1] The number on the list grew more rapidly than the years, for within five years the accredited list contained the names of nineteen high schools. This increase in the number of satisfactory high schools had a reciprocal effect on the University; the preparatory work was gradually excluded from the curriculum, as has already been described.

The University's interest in the high schools of the state, however, did not cease with this new epoch in its career, and efforts to increase both the quality and quantity of high school work have continued to this day. To increase the quality of instruction, for example, sample examinations were given in the University catalogs of the early nineties, with the statement that in order to do the work of the freshman year, entering students should be able to pass such examinations. "Extract the square root of

$$x^4 - x^3 + 5\frac{x^2}{4} - \frac{x}{2} + \frac{1}{4}"$$

and "Give a brief description of each of the four principal invasions of Britain" were matters that all high school students entering the University were supposed to have at their tongue's or pencil's end in 1892.

To increase the quantity of preparatory work, University entrance requirements were gradually raised. Up to 1902, a student was admitted to the University with but three years of high school training. Beginning in that year, requirements were gradually increased from year to year until in 1906 graduation from an approved four-year high school[2]—the present standard—was necessary for entrance to the undergraduate schools of the University.

---

[1] Chancellor Marvin's son F. O. Marvin, later Dean Marvin of the School of Engineering, was at that time (1877) principal of the Lawrence High School.

[2] My statement does not imply that four-year high schools did not exist in the state prior to 1906. The larger high schools had been giving four-year courses since the eighties, at least. It should also be stated that the accrediting of high schools is no longer a function of the University but of the State Board of Education. By legislative enactment in 1915 all graduates of accredited high schools are admitted to the University.

54. Semicentennial

The committee appointed by the University Senate to report plans for the celebration of the semi-centennial of the opening of the University estimated the cost of the affair at $4,000.00 or more. Thereupon the Senate decided, in effect, that the state of the University's finances does not warrant the expenditure of so large a sum at the present time.—*Graduate Magazine*, May, 1916.

INCLUDED among the local items of the *Lawrence Tribune* for December 13, 1887, is the brief record, "The telephone at the University became out of order this morning. It is hoped that repairs can be made in a few days." Twenty years later (March, 1907) a private branch exchange of over a hundred phones was first installed for the University and nine years after this telephonic event, hundreds of University alumni, students, faculty, and friends took part in a long-distance telephone program that in-

cluded New York City, Lawrence, and San Francisco.

This program, held on April 8, 1916, marks the only event—because of the vicissitudes of the times—that even approaches a formal celebration of the fiftieth anniversary of the University. The rapid upswing in the enrollment begun ten years before was creating difficult problems in making legislative appropriations cover the needs of the growing University. Repairs on other buildings, upkeep on the newer buildings, the

Audience in Robinson Gymnasium, April 8, 1916. The Lawrence audience of the transcontinental alumni reunion is not engaged in prayer, but each member is listening to his own receiver. Chancellor Strong is delivering his address by phone at the speaker's table. The photograph was taken from the east gallery of the Gymnasium, the camera being pointed purposely—but unfortunately—toward the south to avoid the historic recording of the stage and setting for the student production, *The Passing Show of 1916.*

necessity of an increased teaching force, and attempts to raise the low salaries paid the faculty members strained the resources of the University to the utmost. However, a committee to arrange for a semicentennial celebration was appointed in the spring of 1916 but soon reported that it would be advisable to postpone the celebration "until next year" in the hope that in the meantime the Legislature would have granted funds to carry out a program. In the upheaval of University affairs following the entrance of the United States into World War I in the "next" year, the celebration plans were completely forgotten. The famous telephone "reunion," then, marked the only commemoration of the University's first fifty years.

The suggestion for the transcontinental reunion by wire came from New York alumni, some of whom took the matter up with officials of the American Telephone and Telegraph Company. The first trunk line across the country had been completed less than a year, and the chance for

securing publicity for their enterprise appealed to the officials of the company. As a result, a simultaneous program was arranged in each of the three cities, each member of all three audiences being provided with an individual receiver. In addition, a transmitter was placed at a central desk in each audience. Some 70 alumni and friends were in the New York group, 35 at San Francisco, and 500 in Robinson Gymnasium at Lawrence.

The 'phone company was busy some days prior to the event in Lawrence, making the necessary installation and connection of equipment; and when the program started, it went smoothly along its course for an hour.

The first words came from the west coast: "Hello, Central, W. H. Carruth at San Francisco talking. The K.U. alumni of the Golden Gate desire to speak to the K.U. alumni of New York, also to the alumni at Lawrence and Chancellor Frank Strong." New York and Lawrence joined in immediately and Chancellor Strong then gave a five-minute address. After reviewing the growth of the University in its first fifty years, Strong concluded with the words:

> The University of Kansas owes a large debt to the past, to the great English and French universities that have helped make the culture of Western civilization. It has even a more intimate connection with the great institutions that sank their roots deep into American soil during colonial times and have given to state universities a large proportion of their teachers and investigators. The University of Kansas owes much to the early pioneer days of Kansas when Kansans were in a mood to sacrifice largely for the upbuilding of sound education. It owes a great debt to the noble body of teachers who have served it so faithfully at a small recompense during its fifty years of service. It owes a great debt to its alumni who have fulfilled the promise they gave when on Mt. Oread and have lived sound and wholesome lives and upheld the best traditions of the American college. It owes its last and final debt to the great body of young people who in recent years have filled its halls to overflowing and have added from their own vigorous life to the intellectual and spiritual uplift of the University.

At the conclusion of this address, a resolution from the New York alumni to Governor Capper of Kansas was read urging greater state support for the University. Professor Carruth then gave a short talk from San Francisco; the K.U. Glee Club at Lawrence sang; members of the audiences were then called to the transmitter and exchanged greetings with friends across the country; and finally "The Crimson and the Blue" was sung, one stanza from each of the three cities.

The *Kansan* in commenting on the reunion in the next issue, headed its column "—And What Next?" and concluded with the prophecy, "The present generation is bound to see a great advance in the means and methods of accomplishing the world's work."

55. World War

The East, however, looks at the war from a different view point than the West. The great struggle assumes greater proportions in the Coast States than in the Middle Western States, and war is served for breakfast, dinner, supper and between dances. Nevertheless, the fact that the military spirit is not as strong here should not make the seriousness of the situation any less felt. What is finally done by the government will of necessity be done by the whole country, and we in the West are as interested as those in the East. The *Kansan* would like to hear student sentiment on the question of compulsory military training.
—*University Daily Kansan*, February 6, 1917.

IT IS difficult to believe, as one leafs through the pages of the *Kansan* from the fall of 1914 to February, 1917, that a war of the first magnitude began in 1914; for the war only remotely affected the campus during that time. True, occasional speakers on world affairs appeared, and their addresses were dutifully reported. Liberal funds were raised for Belgian relief in 1915 and for the Armenians in 1916; but these undertakings occupy a very minute fraction of the news space devoted to ordinary campus happenings. It is, of course, also true that the *Kansan* in those days made little effort to cover outside news, its primary object being "to picture the undergraduate life of the University accurately." The attitude, however, especially toward the happenings of the World War, was more or less typical of the entire West. The intensity of feeling against Germany, especially active along the Atlantic coast, only slowly penetrated westward. In Wilson's campaign for re-election the cry of "He kept us out of war" was to prove so popular west of the Mississippi in 1916, that it was the decisive factor in his campaign against Hughes.

It seems particularly necessary to point out these aspects of national history in a purely local history in order to appreciate best the contributions made and the profound changes occurring in University life during the two years beginning early in the spring of 1917. If the nation as a whole was unprepared for the gigantic effort, what could be expected of a small group of 3,500 souls living apart from the world on a hill 4,000 miles removed from the scene of conflict?

What did they do? A catalog of the contributions of the University during these years would alone take far more space than is available here, so that we can only suggest in broad strokes what was accomplished. There was, to be sure, much unnecessary marching up the Hill and marching

111

down again—both literally and figuratively—but so there was everywhere. The task of suddenly transforming a hundred million peaceful, industrious citizens into a vast war machine was nowhere done without great waste of time and effort—but it was done.

When early in February, 1917, the foreign situation became acute, students became suddenly interested. The merits of compulsory military training were argued pro and con by both students and faculty. Company M of the Kansas National Guard, which was composed of and officered by University men and which had only returned from Eagle Pass, Texas, late the preceding October after a summer spent on the Mexican border, was recruited to full strength. The faculty, feeling that it was their duty to take the lead in patriotic matters, wired President Wilson on March 2, assuring him of "their unqualified support in any measure taken to preserve the honor and integrity of the United States."

With the actual declaration of war on April 6, the campus became a scene of intense activity. Chancellor Strong and Dean Blackmar became members of Governor Capper's Kansas Council of Defense, an Emergency War Committee was appointed in the faculty to direct activities on the campus, military drill was started on April 10 with the organization of four student companies, over two hundred University women started work in Red Cross classes, research work relating to war supplies and the conservation of food was begun in the laboratories, plans were made to plant a part of the University campus to useful food products, and many of the boys of the University left school for farm and camp. In the first month after the declaration of war, 425 men withdrew from school, 185 of them to help on farms as suggested by the State Council of Defense, and the remainder to enlist in various branches of military service, many going to the first officers' training camp at Fort Riley.

Needless to say, during this month of feverish activity, regular school was almost forgotten, but by May 3, the *Kansan* was able to report: "Life in the University is more normal again since the excitement caused by the declaration of war has subsided somewhat. Most students are working

Upper: Barracks on the campus, east of Marvin Hall, 1918.
Lower: S.A.T.C. barracks on Mississippi Street, 1918; looking north.

Company M, Kansas National Guard. The photograph, taken about September 1, 1917, shows the University company encamped on the present lawn of Strong Hall. The view looks northwest from Robinson Gymnasium but does not include East Ad, which, if present in the picture, would be a little to the right of the right-hand margin. The picture gives a good idea of the extensive grading necessary to bring the lawn to its present level. Company M left the campus shortly after this photograph was taken; its members saw service overseas in the Thirty-fifth Division.

hard now to 'catch up' with their work. It is hoped that the professors will remember these weeks of excitement that have passed and give the students a fair chance to make good."

During the summer, work continued unabated although not on so large a scale as during the regular year. Special courses were given, and the campus had a more military aspect than ever, as Company M erected its tents on the site now occupied by the west wing of Strong Hall.

The fall of 1917 opened with a greatly decreased enrollment. The previous year it had reached a high water mark of over 3,400 students, but the following fall it was 600 smaller, with women outnumbering the men about three to one. Whereupon the *Kansan* remarked: "Gosh! Three women to one man at the University this year! The dance hall managers will look forward to only slight profits from their rental this season; the clothiers will get 'cold feet' on the size of the stock they should attempt to carry; and the restaurant folks will wonder who's going to buy the smooths and the cokes for the sweet young things all year." More than world war would be required to subdue the ever ebullient spirits of the young collegian.

The work of the University year, now that war was really under way and preliminary plans had given way to more permanent ones, ran more smoothly than the preceding year. There were many difficulties, of course. A considerable number of the faculty had been called into war work; the three full-time members of the Psychology Department were all taken by the Army, as were seven of the Engineering faculty and five of the Physical Education Department. The number of students enrolled in the French Department went up; in the German it went down. Red Cross and Liberty Loan drives were oversubscribed. Social activities of students diminished, the women of the University knitted and made bandages and the men drilled, and still others marched away to war.

Yes, the war had a profound effect on University life, but as Chancellor Strong pointed out when he unfurled the first service flag of the University containing nearly 2,000 white stars and eight gold ones at Commencement in 1918: "In this respect we are not different from other colleges and universities in our country. No more inspiring evidence of the loyalty of the young men of this country has even been seen than the stream of college men that has poured into the encampments in America and overseas, on to the fields of France."

Members of the S.A.T.C. lined up in front of Dyche Museum. Fall, 1918.

56. S.A.T.C.

Although a large force of carpenters is kept busy with the construction, working overtime and on Sunday, the finishing of the barracks by the first of next month depends largely upon the number of students who will work on them. "We can use between 200 and 250 students until they are finished," said Professor Williams. "Common laborers are to be paid thirty-five cents an hour, and carpenters sixty cents an hour with time-and-a-half for overtime and double time on Sunday."—*University Daily Kansan*, September 17, 1918.

IN AUGUST, 1918, the federal government decided on the plan of establishing the Student Army Training Corps at some 500 universities and colleges throughout the country. The University immediately made a contract with the government to maintain an S.A.T.C. unit of 2,000 men. The University was to superintend the erection of suitable barracks for the members of the unit and to provide instruction in certain new courses specified by Washington and in other courses selected from those already offered.

The size of the unit was later increased by the addition of 450 men who had already been in training on the campus during the summer for mechanical training of various kinds and by a naval unit of 200 students. The members of the S.A.T.C. received army uniforms, equipment, board, University tuition and fees, and, what was more important to a good many, the traditional thirty dollars a month from Uncle Sam. Registration took place on September 16, which gave the University scarcely more than a month to make the necessary preparations. If the entry of the United States into the war in April, 1917, produced turmoil on the campus for the faculty, the

condition following the announcement of the S.A.T.C. can only be characterized as bedlam. Housing had to be provided for 2,500 men, contracts for their feeding arranged, schedules prepared and new classes organized and instructors found. Some faculty members were sent out over the state to bring in carpenters, while others set to work drawing up plans for barracks and organization of classroom work. By September 16, some order had been restored and considerable progress made. Barracks were in the course of erection on Mississippi Street and east of Mc-Cook Field; others were being built on the Hill between Marvin and Haworth Halls; Professor Hodder had worked out a plan for fifty sections of one of the required courses, "War Aims," and had found instructors for them; and the University had decided to adopt the quarter system for the year rather than use the traditional semester plan.

Capt. B. T. Scher, assigned to the post of University commandant, arrived on the scene of action and was soon followed by eighteen commissioned officers. Enrollment day arrived, and by five o'clock in the morning a line of registrants extended from Green Hall, Army headquarters, through Fraser, out past Dyche Museum and down Oread Avenue as far as Brick's—so for several days "the Army" had its hands full. Enrollment was finally complete; some semblance of system was installed; and by October 1, all was ready for formal induction of the S.A.T.C. into its country's service. In the presence of Governor Capper, members of the faculty, and many townspeople, Captain Scher administered the oath of allegiance to some 2,500 men at McCook Field. "It was probably the most impressive ceremony the University of Kansas ever has seen," reports the *Kansan*. "Plain, simple, without pomp, void of the petty glare that a monarchy might have thrown about it, it was full of sincere, full-hearted patriotism and close-to-earth humanity. It existed but for one purpose, that the Hun may be more thoroughly and expeditiously licked."

No sooner was the work of the unit under way than its greatest crisis appeared. Influenza made its appearance and swept through the ranks, followed by a rapidly rising toll of death. Hundreds were sick at a time, and the Medical Corps, despite its most earnest efforts, could not cope with the situation. The University was closed for five weeks; medical students from Rosedale came up in a body; and the women of the faculty, town, and University labored day and night as nurses and dietitians, or scoured the town for sheets, towels, and pajamas. The barracks originally used as an infirmary proved woefully inadequate; four others were pressed into service; and a hos-

Interior of one of the barracks on Mississippi Street; looking west.

pital, Sunshine Hospital, was hurriedly erected at the south end of the main row of barracks to house the most serious cases. Fortunately the epidemic was not long sustained; and by Thanksgiving, Sunshine Hospital was closed.

In the meantime, the great news of the Armistice had been received and the members of the S.A.T.C. had hopes of immediate release from reveille and drill; but it was not until nearly Christmas that most members were mustered out, although some were unfortunate enough to be retained until January.

The work of the second quarter was started on a more normal schedule and by Commencement time there was little left that would indicate the remarkable events of the year. The barracks erected at a cost of $120,000 were sold for a salvage of $11,000 and disappeared in the spring of 1919 almost as rapidly as they had been put up.

57. The End of an Era

The dear old brothers and sisters kicked up an awful dust in front of the gym during the entire period of registration, toting rushees to and fro. Registration day showed not only the biggest registration of the University but the largest crop of automobiles that has yet been developed by the undergraduate body.
—*University Daily Kansan*, September 16, 1919.

TIME has been dated for the American public by wars. One war established the nation; another united it so thoroughly that for many years events were described as taking place "before the War" or "after the War." World War I was likewise another figure in the calendar of history, for life was never again the same after this war as before. Especially is this discontinuity apparent in the affairs of the University. The months succeeding the War mark the end of one era and the beginning of another.

Fortunately the War did not last long enough to determine whether the S.A.T.C. could be called a successful or an unsuccessful fusion of army and college life, but its effect on students can be realized in the attempt to establish a Reserve Officers' Training Corps. In the spring of 1919 it was announced that an R.O.T.C. would be formed the following fall, but when enrollment day arrived only fifty-two applicants volunteered. As a hundred men were necessary for the formation of the corps, the University was

Frank Strong Hall. Photograph made about 1920.

in danger of losing the unit. A special appeal was made for enlistments and finally the necessary quota was secured.

That the experiences of the S.A.T.C. had a very real part in the lack of interest in the new military organization is shown by the fact that the enrollment of students, especially of men, exceeded all previous records. Indeed, the effect of war is nowhere more noticeable than in the violent fluctuation of the number of students. The total enrollment of the University for the school year 1915-16 was practically 3,000. The changes during the World War period can best be seen in the following simple table.

	Enrollment	Change
1915-16	2,959	
1916-17	3,437	(+478)
1917-18	2,840	(—597)
1918-19	3,916	(+1,076)
1919-20	4,002	(+86)

The administrative ingenuity necessary to keep one jump ahead of these variations can only be faintly imagined, for the problem involved not only changes in faculty numbers and classroom space but in living quarters for students as well. The housing problem was particularly acute in the fall of 1919, for in the previous year barracks had been available for the men. "Rooms are absolutely impossible to find," reports the *Kansan*, "and it looks as if half the students will be forced to sleep in the streets if something isn't done to aid the situation." An appeal, which met a ready response, was made to Lawrence citizens to open their homes to students. Automobiles, too, appeared in unusual number with the students, and parking space was where you found it. One hardy soul even advocated the unheard-of plan of taxing the owner for a space in which to park his car, the size of the tax to be graduated

in accordance with the location of the space.

The student body was characterized, too, by other features in addition to number and automobiles. The men, on the average, were older than the girls, for many service men were back in school. To these, not only did many of the traditions of University life seem trivial, but the teaching did, too. Criticism of teachers and methods became outspoken and infected the student body especially in the spring of 1919.[1] One faculty member, however, had the inspiration to suggest a K.U. loyalty campaign which had no small part in the success of "the Million Dollar Drive" launched the following year. This redirection of student energies simply marks another turning point in the life of this period.

Even the faculty reacted to the times. The high cost of living, a gradually growing specter in pre-war days, took on the appearance of a very aggressive villain in post-war days. Salaries that had been meager in the good old days would scarcely buy the baby's shoes in the new dispensation; and this unfortunate condition prevailed despite a general prosperity. "I'll bet the outfit that girl is wearing," remarked one instructor as he enrolled freshmen in the Gymnasium, "cost more than the clothes my entire family wears when we are fixed up in our Sunday best." It was partly the professor's fault, however, as he had a family of six; but even for those who practiced economy in family size, times were bad enough—so bad, indeed, that the incredible hap-

---

[1] Don't misunderstand me. Service men were not responsible for this attitude, which was almost universal. In fact, judging from the *Kansan*, students were even more critical and restless in the spring of 1919—before the service men returned—than they were the following fall. As a matter of fact, I have it on good authority that much of the blame for this trying period should be charged to the faculty in their attempts to enforce outmoded rules.

pened. The faculty asked for increased salaries; not just any increase, but a 50 per cent increase!

It is little wonder, then, that confronted by the rapidly multiplying complexities of University life, Chancellor Strong decided that it was time for him to step aside, and let a younger man assume the burden of University direction in the new era; and on September 12, 1919, he announced his decision to resign the chancellorship at the following Commencement. "The great changes that have come over the world in the last five years in my judgment," wrote Dr. Strong, "require many new adjustments in American universities. These changes ought to be well considered and in my opinion it will require a considerable term of years to carry them out. . . . I regard it as important to the success of the University for the next eighteen years that the one who has to carry out the plans should be the one to make them." If Chancellor Strong was attempting prophecy he was good, as his successor served not eighteen but nineteen years.

58. A New Administration

A completed strip of white and beautiful concrete highway now extends to Topeka without a break. The last strip of slab was laid in July, and the road was formally opened to traffic on August 22 by a half-way picnic, with Lawrence and Topeka people extending the hand of fellowship. The drive to Topeka can now be made in an hour, and makes a pleasant trip for those who have motor cars. On the other side of Lawrence the road is completed as far as Tonganoxie, and makes another nice drive.
—*University Daily Kansan,* September 11, 1922.

ANNOUNCEMENT of Chancellor Strong's resignation brought on the usual flood of speculations concerning a successor. It soon became evident that Governor Allen and the Board of Administration would not consider any staff member of the University for the position; and all through the school year of 1919-20, numerous outside possibilities were discussed. At one time late in the spring, according to the press, the choice had narrowed down to three candidates. None of the three names was that of the man finally selected, but it is interesting to note that E. E. Slosson, of the class of 1890, was among them.

The Board's choice of the new University head was finally announced early in June, 1920, as Dr. Ernest H. Lindley, president of the University of Idaho. Like his predecessor, Dr. Lindley was extremely tall, with "a boyish face topped by a heavy mop of silvery gray hair . . . a fine figure of a man." Dr. Lindley arrived on the campus during the summer of 1920 and was then present for the opening of school the following fall. That fall did indeed mark a new era, for no longer was Uncle Jimmy Green a familiar figure on the campus. Dean Templin, too, had resigned his position in the College and had been succeeded by Joseph G. Brandt. The outlines of North College, long since known as "Old North," had disappeared also by 1920, the building having been dismantled the previous year because it was no longer considered safe.

Although the campus had expanded greatly during Dr. Strong's regime, and many new buildings had replaced Old North, the physical appearance of the campus still left much to be de-

Chancellor Lindley; a photograph made at the time of his election to the chancellorship in 1920.

The campus about 1920. Looking northeast toward Bailey Laboratory from Robinson Gymnasium. "Parking space was where you found it!"

sired when Dr. Lindley arrived. This was particularly true of the campus roads. Increasing numbers of students brought increasing traffic, which, coupled with the construction of Strong Hall, made the unpaved University drive, especially in wet weather, a sight to behold. "In crossing the campus on our former cinder highways," stated the *Kansan*, "a car traveled approximately two blocks forward and three blocks up and down and gave visitors a rugged and rocky impression of the University and the eminence upon which it is built." To relieve this situation the first paving of the road was undertaken (September, 1920); but work progressed slowly through the year because of the shortage of materials due to the national building boom. The first section of paved road, when completed, extended only from Spooner Library past the west end of Green Hall.

The student body that greeted Dr. Lindley was larger by several hundred than it had been the previous year. Evidence of change in the appearance of the students was also manifest. For one thing, the University was beginning to take on a more cosmopolitan air. Up to the end of the school year 1919-20, some 60,000 students had enrolled in the University; and of these, only 89

had come from foreign countries. In the fall of 1920 students were enrolled from China, Japan, the Philippines, Mexico, India, Russia; and, as a result, the Cosmopolitan Club was formed in this year.

In still another way, the student body was undergoing a change. Bobbed hair and short skirts made an occasional appearance. An accompanying phenomenon was the "shimmy," which, by 1920, was a dance as well as a garment—both odious, it must be said, to the eyes and ears of the proper. The "shimmy"—as a dance—was officially banned on the campus, and its companions in disgrace were the "camel-walk," the "toddle," and the "shuffle."

To relate still further the time to the happenings of the outside world, it could be observed that none other than Franklin D. Roosevelt, a candidate for Vice-President, appeared in Lawrence early in the school year and was heard by many townspeople and students. After raking Senator Harding and the Republican party vigorously over the coals, Roosevelt concluded with the sage observation that "the voters of Kansas have an independence of thought peculiar to that state alone"; an observation which time has made appear still more sage.

118

It is doubtful if Roosevelt's judgment on the nature of Kansas voters had any influence in determining the initial policy of Chancellor Lindley's administration, but Roosevelt's method of taking his cause directly to the people and depending on their independence of thought for a favorable result was exactly the one that Chancellor Lindley himself employed. Lindley soon recognized the task before him. Inadequate faculty salaries resulting in continual loss of personnel, and the need of additional teachers and of new equipment and buildings in order to accommodate the horde of students arriving on Mount Oread were placed foremost on his list of conditions requiring immediate and serious attention. Formulating a plan calling for a greatly expanded but definite budget, Chancellor Lindley started on his campaign. It was presented to the students, to the alumni, to the press, directly to the people of the state by innumerable speaking engagements, and to the Legislature itself not once but many, many times. Emphasizing his ideal plan that the University be the servant of the state, a potent force in building the life of the commonwealth, he urged all friends of the University to join him in his campaign.

The campaign brought an immediate and enthusiastic response from the students. Bubbling over with optimism, the *Kansan* states (October, 1920): "This University of ours has started on a new era of growth. We're going to make it the biggest and the best in the Middle West. And how? Why, by every single student in the school boosting all the time, doing everything he can to increase fellowship, to promote loyalty, to develop a sense of responsibility among students. . . and to raise scholastic standards." Although the last objective may have been added by the editor as a perfunctory afterthought, the enthusiasm generated was spontaneous and effective. It spread among the people of the state and finally and, most necessarily, it was caught by the Legislature.

The action of the Legislature when it met early in 1921 must have been extremely gratifying to

The campus, 1920. Looking south toward Blake from near Myers Hall; Spooner Library at the extreme left, Dyche Museum at the extreme right.

Chancellor Lindley, for it appropriated over three million dollars to the University for its work of the following two years. The meaning of this amount becomes apparent when it is recalled that it exceeded by over a million dollars any previous appropriation for the University. Increased salaries and maintenance were allowed, and, in addition, funds were provided for the construction of a new library, a new power plant, a girls' dormitory, a cafeteria, a new medical building, and a new engineering laboratory; and a quarter of a million dollars was allotted for the completion of the Administration Building.

Recognition of Chancellor Lindley's share in this major achievement was prompt in coming. At his inaugural in Robinson Gymnasium on June 7, 1921—a part of the Commencement program—Dr. Strong voiced the sentiments of many: "We are happy in the belief that our new chancellor has the vision, the training and experience, the administrative power, and the high noble purpose of making our University all that its dearest friends could desire."

119

First air view of the campus, September, 1921. Note the east side of the Stadium under construction and the Observatory (west of Haworth Hall), which had been on the campus two years when this photograph was made.

59. The Stadium

Nebraska is now in the midst of a stadium drive. Just as has been done at K.U., it is to be a Memorial Stadium, dedicated to the memory of Nebraska sons who made the supreme sacrifice in the Argonne as comrades of the Kansas boys in the 89th division. Nebraska intends that its drive shall succeed. Yet, after all, Kansas is the pacemaker, and I wish to give credit where credit is due.
—C. S. Sherman, sports writer, *Lincoln Star,* reprinted in the *Graduate Magazine,* November, 1922.

YEAR one of the fabulous twenties did not get away to a very good start in Kansas. The munificence of the Legislature meeting early in 1921 had been based on the preceding boom years; if it had met in the fall of that year, the University undoubtedly would have suffered severely, for the index number of all farm prices took a sickening lurch from 205 in 1920 to 116 in 1921. It was "Perhaps the most terrible toboggan slide in all American agricultural history," wrote Stuart Chase in 1927, although Mr. Chase was to live and learn about really low prices for farm products in a few short years.

The depression of 1921 was but little felt for the moment at the University[1] even if it did gravely affect the farms of the state. It did have the effect, however, of slowing up the Million Dollar Drive launched in the fall of 1920.

The Million Dollar Drive, a movement initiated by faculty, students, and alumni, had as its goal the raising of the fund indicated and the construction of a memorial for the men of the University who had died during the World War and for all others who had been in the service of their country.[2] Considerable discussion as to the nature of the memorial was carried on in the year following the close of the war. An auditorium, a health building, a student loan fund, and a tower and chimes were among the many suggestions.

It was finally decided, however, to construct a

[1] It did eventually catch up. The next Legislature (1923) was asked for four million dollars, a million more than was granted the University in 1921. Two and a half million dollars was the best the Legislature could do.

[2] The Million Dollar Drive also included as one of its objectives the erection of a memorial to Dean James W. Green. The "Uncle Jimmy" statue secured as a result of the drive was the work of a noted sculptor, Daniel Chester French. It was unveiled at Commencement, 1924.

120

stadium and a student union building as the memorials. The campaign for funds began on November 18 among the students and faculty, and within three days over $200,000 had been pledged, the major portion of which was eventually paid. The raising of this sum represented a genuine sacrifice to many students, but a sacrifice that sinks into insignificance when compared with that of those for whom the memorial was intended. Among the students alone, however, the average contribution was nearly sixty dollars, and many students working their way through school pledged even more than this amount. The campaign for funds was renewed at intervals for some years until nearly the entire sum originally set had been pledged. Sufficient funds from pledges were available by the spring of 1921 to warrant beginning the first of the memorial structures—the stadium.

Several possible sites for the new stadium had been discussed, but it was finally decided to erect it on McCook Field. Plans were made for removing the old stands, the stands before which Tommy Johnson, Pete Heil, Rock Crusher Ammons, Shorty Hammil, Scrubby Laslett, and a host of others had won their way to gridiron glory. No tears were shed, however, for removal of the stands was a matter of student rejoicing. Stadium Day was declared; the students were given a holiday; and faculty and students, arrayed in working clothes, went at the destruction of old McCook with a will. Over four thousand turned out for the event, which was "a grand and howling success. Every detail of work and entertainment was run off in schedule time, or better than schedule time. In only one hour and eighteen minutes after the work of devastation was fully under way, the stands had gone down, and students were piling the lumber in an assembling yard east of the field."

The four thousand were fed. Then a snake dance was staged for Pathé News, and the crowd, after listening to speakers, concluded the celebration by observing the event of the day: Chan-

Upper: Stadium Day, May 10, 1921. "One of the greatest events in the history of the school," reports the *Kansan*, Lower: The Missouri game in the new Stadium, Thanksgiving, 1921; looking north.

121

cellor Lindley, clad in overalls, plowed a straight furrow across McCook, breaking ground for the Stadium.

Active construction was begun in the fall, and by the time of the Aggie game on October 29, the first two sections were in use; by Thanksgiving four more sections had been added.

The formal dedication of the Stadium took place the following year, appropriately enough, on Armistice Day and just before the Kansas-Nebraska game, which, of course, was won by Nebraska. To the original six sections of the Stadium, two more were added in 1925. As the stadium era was still an expanding one, the horseshoe was added in 1927, giving the completed structure a seating capacity of 38,000.

60. The Commons

A very casual investigation shows that many of our students are spending between $5.50 and $7.00 a week for their meals and feel that they are well fed. So far we have not been able to find anyone who has averaged $1.00 a day for meals.—Rebecca Barnum, director, University Commons, November, 1921.

A PLACE to eat on the campus has not always been as readily available as it is today, and the University cafeteria through the years has seen more extremes of fortune than has the Gymnasium. Not until 1922 was the present cafeteria system able to conclude its first year of service to the students.

The first attempt to furnish meals on the campus was made by one George Falley in the fall of 1887. Falley was given the use of a basement room in Fraser, which, after being fitted up with a stove and lunch counter, began its business of feeding the students. The place seems to have been popular, but a helper employed by Falley nearly succeeded in burning down the building late one night. Whether it was this accident that caused the suspension of the new venture at the end of the school year there is no way of determining, but the lunchroom did not open for a second year. The University took no action for many years in securing a successor.

About 1899, however, another private venture was made, which, at this time, was located just off the campus. For twelve years it was a famous student institution. William (Billy) Reynolds, of the class of 1900, first opened the place as a lunch wagon on wheels but soon converted it into a more permanent structure and installed Mrs. H. L. Beatty as its operator. How much of a reputation it established can be seen from the following report in the *Kansan*, when it was closed in the fall of 1911: "No more chapel time breakfasts for the late risers, no more hamburgers, cream pie, and chocolates for the fusser and his lass, no more chicken pies and fruit salads for the between meals piecers. The Oread Cafe—Billie's—The Dog House—has quit. The little box that sits over on the east edge of the campus in front of Fraser has been one of the traditions of the University for the past twelve years. It was the official gossip house of the University. It was the beauty barometer of the Hill, for in years when the co-eds were pretty, business was always rushing for the host of Billie's. More dates have been made and 'cases' sealed over the counter at Billie's than at any other one place in Lawrence."

The closing of the Dog House apparently again directed the attention of University authori-

Chancellors Strong (left) and Lindley (second from right) on Stadium Day. At the right (face turned toward Chancellor Lindley) is Professor W. J. Baumgartner, whose energy and enthusiasm contributed in a large measure to the success of the Million Dollar Drive.

Campus view, about 1925. The Commons, built in 1921, appears in part at the extreme right; vine-covered Snow Hall, "Old Snow," is the building to the extreme left of the Commons; Fraser Hall in the background.

ties to the eating problem, for it was announced, shortly after "Billie's" closed, that a University cafeteria would be opened the following semester. Through the spring of 1912, a cafeteria operated by the Home Economics Department in the basement of Fraser gave satisfactory service. The following fall the rapidly growing department needed more room for its teaching activities; and, as no other rooms were available, the cafeteria was again abandoned.

The next event in our chronicle of gustatory establishments was an important one. Brick's was opened. For many years—for that matter, until World War II—Brick's place has played as important a part in the lives of students as did Billie's. The Oread Cafe, just off the campus on Oread Avenue, was acquired by E. C. Bricken in the spring of 1914 and soon became known as Brick's Place or, more shortly, as Brick's. Bricken, who had been headwaiter at Lee's, another popular eating house at the foot of Adams (Fourteenth) Street on Tennessee, ran the place for nine years, before he sold it; but so popular had Brick's become that it continued under its original nickname.

After the venture of 1912, the students had no eating place directly on the campus until the S.A.T.C. year, when the University, again through its Home Economics Department, conducted a cafeteria in Myers Hall. It was not opened, however, in the fall of 1919 because of lack of suitable rooms. The food problem became acute in 1920, when with the large enrollment and high prices (board was $7.50 a week in the fall of 1920), students were complaining bitterly about the situation. The budget presented to the Legislature that year asked an appropriation of $40,000 for the establishment of a cafeteria in Fowler Shops. Only $15,000 was granted in 1921, and with this sum a "temporary" frame building was constructed west of Old Snow. It was opened

Class Day exercises, June 8, 1909. This photograph, taken from an upper floor of Fraser Hall and looking east, is notable for two reasons. First, the small building in the background is "Billie's"; and second, the class of 1909 is grouped around the Totem Pole. First used by the class of 1893, the Totem Pole has had a checkered history. It has been "lost" several times—as it is at present.

123

A close-up of the Totem Pole. Commencement, Fraser Hall in the background, 1912.

for student use in October, 1921. The cafeteria continued to use this building until the completion of the Union Building, when service in its new quarters was begun in September, 1927.

The building deserted by the cafeteria was pressed into service as the offices for the Stenographic Bureau and the *Jayhawker,* and as a practice room for the University orchestra. In 1932, the "temporary" building was acquired by the Department of Anatomy, and for some years was known as the "Anatomy Building," where budding young M.D.'s first had a chance to sharpen and use their knives. Doubtless it would still be in use to the present day if it had not been almost completely consumed in a spectacular fire on March 3, 1943.

61. Corbin Hall

I have three women at my house, my wife, my daughter, and my mother, and I fail to see why they should not have as good a right to vote as myself. When the amendment to the Constitution comes up at the next election, I shall vote "yes," and I sincerely hope that the amendment will pass.
—Chancellor Frank Strong, after a chapel speech by Sylvia Pankhurst, the suffragette; quoted in the *University Kansan,* March 16, 1911.

QUESTIONS of student eating and living quarters have been perennial ones. The University cafeteria solved the first of these difficulties, but the first definite efforts to solve the second one came from the alumni of the University in 1911, when alumni, faculty, and students undertook to raise $75,000 for the construction of a girls' dormitory. The campaign was conducted with some vigor through the school year of 1911-12 and five or six thousand dollars was raised.

The original enthusiasm abated somewhat in

Corbin Hall. A photograph made in 1929.

North College Hall, 1951.

subsequent years, and the fund grew more and more slowly until finally the attempt was given up. The funds collected, however, were used to purchase four co-operative houses for the use of University women. After the completion of Corbin Hall, the houses were sold. In the meantime, suffrage had been voted the women of Kansas in 1912; and Kansas women, always a potent power in Kansas politics, were more than anxious to prove their interest in public affairs. In 1916, the Kansas Council of Women appointed a committee to undertake a legislative campaign to secure residence halls for women in all the state schools, although the State Federation of Women's Clubs had begun such a project as early as 1908. The plan was vigorously presented throughout the state, and bills were introduced into both houses of the Legislature in 1917; but not enough support was secured for enactment. Again in 1919, the women of the state attempted to secure action and again failed. The proverbial third time proved the charm, for upon presenting the case to the Legislature of 1921, Kansas women were rewarded by the passage of an act allotting half a million dollars to the state schools at Lawrence, Manhattan, Pittsburg, Emporia, and Hays

for the construction of women's dormitories. Realizing that the sum provided would be inadequate for the construction of all five buildings, the Kansas State College generously waived its rights in the hope that it would be provided for by the next Legislature.

The work of constructing the dormitory at the University was begun in July, 1922. After some thought, the committee selected as the site of the new building the eight-acre tract upon which North College had been built. Since the destruction of Old North in 1919, this ground had not been used. It was hoped in selecting the dormitory site that Corbin Hall would be the first of a group of buildings—possibly eight or ten—that could be erected for housing the women of the University. An addition to Corbin in 1951 was another step in the realization of this hope. By the fall of 1923, the original dormitory was ready for 120 women.

The leader in the state campaigns of 1919 and 1921 for a dormitory fund had been Dr. Alberta Corbin, of the class of 1893, professor of German at the University. Dr. Corbin had, in fact, been one of the leaders in the original dormitory movement in 1911; and the final success of the move-

125

ment can, in no small measure, be attributed to her persistent and thoughtful efforts. The decision of the Board of Administration in May, 1923, to name the new dormitory Corbin Hall, in spite of Dr. Corbin's protests, was altogether fitting and met with instant and popular approval. Dr. Corbin, in addition to her other duties, was also, from 1918 to 1921, adviser of women, an office first established in January, 1914, although as long ago as 1887 a "preceptress" had been appointed. The title "adviser of women" was changed in 1921 to "dean of women"; and the office of "dean of men" was established for the first time.

The occupants of these offices during the decade of the twenties had an unenviable task. The complexities of life that had increased so rapidly from 1900 to 1920 and to which adjustment was just being made, were thrown into new turmoil by the revolution in manners and morals of the 1920's. The deans of women and men, in their attempts to advise students, had to face problems of dress, drink, sex, deportment, and smoking to a degree unprecedented in collegiate history. Smoking, of course, had been the God-given right of men since the establishment of the American college; but when women, in the early twenties, wanted to enjoy its pleasures, their efforts were frowned down. "Cigarette smoking," said a prominent K.U. faculty woman in 1923,

"is injurious to women. It induces increased pulse rate, heightens blood pressure, and causes irritable hearts. Intemperate smoking causes nervousness and may lead to something worse. Women who use cigarettes cannot be temperate. At best it is a horrible weed and should be let alone. It fouls the breath and makes women unwomanly." In spite of such warnings, University women, both on the local campus and on others, continued, in growing numbers, to acquire the habit. By 1930, the *Kansan* was willing to admit that "the practice is not merely a temporary fad but an established habit."

Campaigning for woman suffrage, Lawrence, 1912. University women took an active part in the campaign, as can be seen from the fact that Mrs. Frank Strong is the middle figure (dark coat) in the back seat. The photograph was made on Vermont Street and looks toward Massachusetts.

62. Watson Library

The opening of Watson Hall Thursday should mark the beginning of a new attitude toward books at the University of Kansas. For several years even those who were most interested in reading and studying have found it difficult to get much pleasure from it in Spooner Library because of the crowded condition of both stacks and the reading room.—*Daily Kansan*, September 9, 1924.

IF SOCIAL conditions were disturbing in the early 1920's business conditions left little to be desired. The depression of 1921 soon passed, and a tidal wave of prosperity followed. At the University, the six years from 1921 through 1927 saw a reflection of this prosperity in the erection or completion of ten new buildings, in the improvement of the appearance of the campus, in an increase in enrollment from 4,200 students to over 5,200, and logically enough, in the establishment (1924) of another of the present schools of the University, the School of Business.

On the Lawrence campus, the completion of the Power Plant in 1922 and of Watson Library in 1924 involved the largest expenditures of

funds. The physical growth of the University had required a continual enlargement of its heating and power plant. One of the more interesting features of this series of enlargements, and certainly the most noticeable one, was the succession of smokestacks, of which there have been at least four. The last one was—and is—by far the tallest, towering over 250 feet above its base and making a conspicuous landmark.

The development of the Library, although not as noticeable to the casual visitor as the succession of smokestacks, was of far greater importance to the University. In the period of years elapsing since the completion of Spooner Library in 1894, the addition of books had caused, by 1923, an eightfold increase in its contents. In this period of years, the Library had literally grown into Spooner and out of it; for when the building was opened, its 20,000 volumes had looked meager on shelves providing space for five times that number. By 1915, however, its capacity was exceeded; and departmental libraries had sprung up over the campus, partly for convenience but more largely because there was no longer sufficient space in Spooner.

The library appropriation of $250,000 provided by the Legislature of 1921[1] was particularly welcome to the University, and plans for the new structure were undertaken. Construction was delayed because the original plans, providing for

[1] Increased by $60,000 in 1925.

Above: Watson Library with the "temporary" wooden entrance steps that remained for twelve years. Old Snow Hall is seen at the right. Photograph made about 1925.
Lower: Another view of Watson, made in 1936, showing the smokestack built in 1922 at the right.

The last of "Old Snow." Watson Library in the background. 1933.

a ten-year growth of the Library, could not be used with the money available.

A site for the new building, however, had been selected late in 1921. Its selection caused a good deal of discussion among students and faculty, as it was located behind Snow Hall, Old Snow, on the south side of the Hill. As the selection of the site contemplated the eventual razing of Snow, considerable objection was raised to the plan. Snow Hall, however, was beginning to show the effects of age, and as the new location of the Library was considerably more central on the campus of 1921 than was Spooner, objections gradually faded away.

The construction was begun early in the spring of 1923; and all through the spring, a high steam shovel worked on the excavation, attracting

crowds in exactly the same manner as does a similar event in any blasé city of the present. When the monster mechanism left in May, the *Kansan* records its departure with sorrow: "No more will the cheerful 'hiss' of escaping steam vie with professorial outburst of like character. No more will gaping crowds gather on the brink of the abyss to watch it greedily scoop up into its cavernous maw great rocks of limestone. . . . Alas, our excuse that we did not hear the assignment because the steam shovel made so much racket will be no longer effective, and we shall be forced to seek a new alibi."

The shell of the new building was nearly completed by the following January, but moving day from Spooner to the new building did not come until summer. The building was opened to student use on September 11, 1924. Students were greatly puzzled at first to find their way around in the new building, as the number of corridors, reading rooms, and special libraries was greatly increased. It was even reported on good authority that the habit of escorting "fair young damsels home from the scene of their evening's educational endeavors" was seriously interfered with, so difficult had it become for a pair of partners to find each other. The maze, however, was soon learned.

The name of the new building had been announced as Watson Library during Commence-

The campus, November, 1924. This photograph, looking east from the top of Marvin Hall, shows Watson Library (at the right of Fraser) just after completion; the paving in front of Strong Hall, too, was then less than a year old.

128

ment week, 1924. The Board of Administration at the request of many alumni had made this decision in order to honor Miss Carrie M. Watson, of the class of 1877, who from 1887 to 1921 had been the librarian of the University. Governor Jonathan M. Davis, a former student had himself written Chancellor Lindley, "I have a very warm place in my heart for this woman who disciplined us 'in silence' and inculcated in us a respect for good books."

As soon as Spooner Library had been vacated, it was decided to house in it the extensive art collection offered the University by Mrs. W. B. Thayer of Kansas City in 1917; and in the spring of 1926, Spooner Library was reopened as the Spooner-Thayer Art Museum.

63. The Board of Regents

Certainly our educational institutions should be removed entirely from politics and from even the suspicion of politics. This can best be accomplished by a board whose members serve because of the honor of this service to the youth of the state. In my opinion, the penal and charitable institutions should remain under the control of the State Board of Administration but the educational institutions should be under a separate government with a board whose members are nonsalaried and who are chosen because of their partisanship interest in education.—Governor Ben Paulen in his annual message to the Legislature, January 14, 1925.

GOVERNOR Jonathan M. Davis, as chairman of the State Board of Administration, announced on December 27, 1924—barely two weeks before his own retirement from office—that the chancellorship of Dr. Lindley had been terminated. Although newspapers had intimated for several days preceding the announcement that serious difficulties were developing, such drastic action came as a decided shock to the University, and to the citizens of Lawrence and the state. The differences between Governor Davis and Chancellor Lindley had, however, apparently been developing for some time. Among other charges, Governor Davis maintained incompetency and insubordination as the most important. The Chancellor, on the other hand, felt that the Board was attempting to make positions on the University staff a matter of political patronage. The complete history of the controversy has never been revealed—and may never be. There are two important aspects of the case, however, which deserve even the limited space we can give it here.

Campus view, January 5, 1925. The photograph shows students and faculty entering Robinson Gymnasium to hear Chancellor Lindley speak at an all-University convocation after being removed from office by Governor Davis.

129

The Board of Regents as reorganized in April, 1925. Back row (left to right), C. M. Harger, Abilene; C. W. Spencer, Sedan; Earle W. Evans, Wichita; W. J. Tod, Maplehill. Front row, C. B. Merriam, Topeka; Mrs. J. S. Patrick, Satanta; Chairman W. Y. Morgan, Hutchinson; B. C. Culp, Beloit. Former Governor George H. Hodges of Olathe was also a member of the Board but was not present when the photograph was taken. The precedent for a woman member of the Board had been set as early as 1881, when Mrs. Cora M. Downs had been appointed a University Regent.

In the first place, the reaction of the public was decidedly in Dr. Lindley's favor. Students, alumni, citizens, and state and national press joined in such a chorus of defense that the first action taken by Governor Ben Paulen, the successor of Governor Davis, was to call the State Board of Administration together and instruct them to reinstate Dr. Lindley. Such action was taken by the Board on January 13, 1925, the day after Governor Paulen's inauguration.

In the second place, the Supreme Court of Kansas had decided in the interval between Chancellor Lindley's dismissal and reinstatement that the Chancellor of the University held office only "at the pleasure" of the State Board and that they could dismiss him for any cause or without cause. In effect, this decision of the court made the chancellorship solely dependent on the action of a single man, the Governor of the state, for the Governor not only was the Chairman of the Board of Administration but also had sole appointive and removal power of its membership.

The Board of Administration was the successor of the Board of Regents, the original governing body of the University. The changes in these controlling boards can most conveniently and properly be outlined here. Certainly the boards deserve mention, for in their collective memberships they have included many notable names

in the state's history; and together they have contributed in no little measure to the development of the University.

The original charter of the University placed the government of the University in a Board of Regents of fifteen members, twelve of whom were to be appointed for a term of six years by the Governor of Kansas, subject to the approval of the state Senate. The State Superintendent of Public Instruction and the Secretary of State were to be members of the Board *ex officio*. These fourteen members were to elect a chancellor who, by provision of the charter, was to be the president of the Board of Regents. So strong was the influence of the clergy upon collegiate education of 1864 and so equally determined were the framers of the charter that sectarianism should not get a foothold in the young University that the charter provided "That not more than three of the Regents to be appointed shall be members of the same religious denomination." The passage of years was to see a shift in this requirement, however, from religious denomination to political denomination. With this directing organization, the University got under way. The first important change was made on December 4, 1867, when General Fraser was elected chancellor, the Board then deciding that the chancellor should not only be the president of the Board

130

but also, ex officio, the president of the faculty as well. The chancellorship was continued in this dual capacity for the next forty-six years.

By action of the Legislature of 1873, the number of regents was reduced to seven, including the chancellor. The other six members were still to be appointed by the Governor, subject to the consent of the Senate, but the term of office was reduced from six to four years. Uniform action was taken for all state educational institutions, each institution having its own Board of Regents.

Although all previous legislation affecting the University was repealed by the Legislature of 1889, new enactments perpetuated the original name University of Kansas and continued both the location of the University at Lawrence and a governing body of seven regents in the same manner as the act of 1873. The revision of the statutes made possible an internal reorganization of the University, which at that time was discontinuing its preparatory courses. With this legislative change, no further action was taken until 1913, when the Board of Regents was abolished and the State Board of Administration was organized.

The Board of Administration consisted of three paid members, appointed by the Governor and confirmed by the Senate, who were charged with the control of all educational institutions dependent upon the Legislature for their support. The principal reason for this change was a desire to eliminate unnecessary duplication of work in the state schools.

Its work unfortunately was not long continued, for the Legislature of 1917, in an attempt to consolidate and eliminate unnecessary boards, organized a second State Board of Administration. The new Board was charged with the control of all educational, charitable, correctional, and penal institutions of the state, numbering altogether some twenty-five organizations! Further, the Board comprised four members. The Governor of the state was, by virtue of his office, the Chairman of the Board, and he was authorized to appoint three additional members for four-year terms whom he could remove "when in his judgment the public service demands it." It was the Board as thus authorized by the Legislature, the representatives of the people, that removed Dr. Lindley from office and restored him to it.

The aftermath following Chancellor Lindley's reinstatement produced (1925) a new Board of Regents of nine members who were charged with the control of the five state educational institutions of higher learning only. As the new Regents were to be appointed by the Governor for a four-year term without approval of the Senate, and without the possibility of summary removal, it was the expressed hope at the time that the new Board would place the schools outside the field of politics—a hope that time did not altogether

Laying the cornerstone, Memorial Union Building, April 30, 1926. This view, looking north from Dyche Museum, shows not only the progress in the construction of the Union and the audience for the exercises, but the water tower (with class numerals) as well. The tower was nearing the end of its career when this photograph was taken.

131

Parade forming in front of Haworth Hall for the exercises at the cornerstone-laying, April 30, 1926. Note the tower of KFKU behind Marvin Hall. KFKU was a fairly recent addition to the campus when this photograph was made. Its first program was broadcast on December 15, 1924.

justify. Legislation affecting the Board was again enacted in 1939, when four additional educational institutions were placed under its jurisdiction; appointment to the Board was made subject to the confirmation of the Senate, and it was further provided "that at no time shall more than five members of said Board of Regents be members of the same political party."

64. The Memorial Union Building

The purpose of the new building as set forth by the Student Council is to furnish a place where all the students of the University can congregate. A large rotunda or central room will occupy the main part of the building. This rotunda will accommodate a large number of students and can be used for mass meetings. The Students' Union Building will centralize all activities around the campus. Visiting athletic teams will be entertained here. A commons, or dining hall, for the men will be found in the building.
—*University Kansan,* September 21, 1911.

THE desire for a student building, as the above statement shows, is an old one. The building described was to cost $100,000, and the sum was to be raised from that ever hopeful source, the alumni. The plans were not pressed with vigor at the time, but growing sentiment for a student center led to more positive results two and a half years later. After a campaign for funds among the men of the University for over a year, a house was rented and furnished at 1200 Tennessee Street and officially opened on March 5, 1914, as the Men's Student Union. Five hundred men attended an enthusiastic housewarming, making the building so dark with tobacco smoke that the pianist had difficulty in finding his instrument.

It was found, however; and after singing "There's a Girl in the Heart of Maryland" and other songs of the day, the five hundred concluded the ceremonies with the Rock Chalk. The Union unfortunately was far from the campus, the first enthusiasm dwindled with time, sufficient funds to pay the rent became more difficult to obtain; and after running a year, the Union was forced to close.

This disaster had the effect of dampening further efforts in this direction until after the War, when with the launching of the Million Dollar Drive, a student union was planned as one of the memorial units, the Stadium and the Uncle Jimmy Green statue being the other two. The

132

plans for the Union Building were slow in taking form. Money pledged in the drive came in slowly, and was first absorbed in the building of the Stadium. A site, the present one, was selected in 1924; and ground for the new structure was broken during Commencement of 1925. Although the cornerstone was laid on April 30, 1926, and the shell of the building was completed by the fall of that year, it was not opened until September, 1927, when the Commons began service. That sixteen years had wrought changes is seen by the fact that it was not "a commons or dining hall for the men" but a commons for all, both men and women. Two months after the Commons opened, the lounge on the main floor was put into use; the remainder of the building was completed as funds became available, one of the finishing touches being the Kansas Room, completed in 1939.

The Memorial Union Building, let us never forget, is a monument in brick and stone to the 129 men and women of the University who gave their lives for their country—for us—in World War I. The first of these to fall was Lieut. William Thomas Fitzsimmons, of the class of 1910, who was the first American officer to be killed in action during the World War. Lieut. Fitzsimmons has a special memorial of his own, the Fitzsimmons General Hospital at Denver, the largest

Upper—Hoch Auditorium under construction, winter, 1926-27. This photograph was made from approximately the same position as the one taken in April, 1926, before construction started. (See page 132.)
Lower—the completed Auditorium, 1928.

army hospital in the country and one of the largest hospitals in the world. But as one reads the record further—"killed at Belleau Wood," "killed

Air view, May, 1925. Notice cars parked on main drive—before parking regulations went into effect. Notice, too, the unfinished Stadium and the Mississippi Street approach (paved in 1922).

in action near Vierzy," "died in the Argonne For-
rest," "killed in action in the St. Mihiel drive
while leading his men"—and views the portraits
of those whose lives were all too brief, any memorial—no matter how extensive—seems piti-
fully inadequate—inadequate, not only because
no man-made memorial can replace a single human life, but because the hopes and aspirations of
the sacrificed could never be realized.

Such hopes, the hopes of those who marched
away and did not return, found expression among
their own number. The following verses, published in the *Kansan* at the end of the first year
of war, express in poignant words the ardor of one
American soldier. The three simple stanzas were
found among his possessions as he lay on a field
in France.

Ye who have faith to look with fearless eyes
Beyond the tragedy of a world at strife,
And know that of death and night shall rise
The dawn of ampler life,
Rejoice, whatever anguish rend the heart,
That God has given you a priceless power,
To live in these great times and have your
part
In Freedom's crowning hour.

That ye may tell your sons who see the light
High in the heavens—their heritage to
take—
"I saw the powers of darkness put to flight;
I saw the morning break!"

How sadly now we read those words and
wonder if these our dead have indeed died in
vain! The fault lies not with the dead but with
the living. We, each of us, became so engrossed
in our petty affairs that the achievements of blood
and toil faded from our minds as the years went
on. The developments of recent years should
cause each of us to recall anew the gifts of those
who gave "the last full measure of devotion"; each
of us should most fervently labor to the end that
these sacrifices have not been lost by the mistakes
of the intervening years.

* * *

Let us hope that those boys who cheerfully left
the campus in 1917, never to return, would have
been pleased with their memorial. It is a place
of activity, a place where people happily meet,
where they mingle together. If this spirit of in-
termingling, this spirit of fellowship could only
have become international!

65. Hoch Auditorium

University students have no more need for a car than a horse has for gasoline. There are few students
who live so far from their classrooms but that they can walk with benefit to themselves. Automobiles are
purely a luxury for most of those who own them, and without doubt they are a luxury for students. Much
pleasure can be had with a motor-car, it is true; in the same manner, much grief can be had from them, as
anyone who has even owned or driven a car can testify.—*University Daily Kansan*, September 13, 1922.

AN ex-collegiate Ford will serve to orient
University life with the life of the outside
world as school opened in the fall of 1927. Lying
in a ditch beside one of the approaches to the Hill,
its tires gone, its hood bent and rusted, and its
top a tattered remnant, it bore on its side the
legend, "I do not choose to run in 1928."

Although this particular car may not have
chosen to run, there were many that did—in
fact, too many, from the standpoint of the administration. The automobile problem had, however, changed considerably from that of the early
nineteen hundreds; for by the middle twenties it
was becoming more a question of mortality than
of morality.

Accounts of car accidents in the *Kansan* increase through the twenties because of an increasing use of cars by the students—a barometer of

the times—and an increase in the number of good
roads. The paved highway from Lawrence to
Topeka was opened to traffic in the summer of
1922, and in the same year speed limit signs appeared on the edge of the campus; but what is
more important, Chancellor Lindley began his
first annual campaign to reduce the number of
student cars. Despite his efforts, the number of
cars increased, and after the paving of the main
drive through the University was completed in
the summer of 1925, the problem became acute.
As a result, the licensing of cars on the campus
was begun in the spring of 1926 with the issuance
of the first K.U. license plates permitting cars
to be parked in restricted areas only and not on
the main drive. By the fall of 1927, then, the
campus drive had much the appearance that it has

today; and not as many cars were visible as there had been a few years earlier.

The rising barometer of prosperity was apparent in a number of other ways, however. Five new Greek-letter houses were under construction with sixty or seventy thousand dollars casually mentioned as their individual cost. Watkins Hall had been completed the previous year (1926); the Stadium was dedicated for the third or fourth time before the Wisconsin game on October 8, 1927; the Memorial Union was dedicated the same day; and a week later Hoch Auditorium was also dedicated.

The Legislature of 1925 had granted $250,000 for the erection of an auditorium, and shortly after the grant was made, the site between Haworth Hall and Marvin Hall was selected. The frame observatory used by the classes in astronomy, which has occupied a portion of the selected site since its erection in 1919, was moved west of Marvin Hall in the spring of 1926, so that excavation for the auditorium could begin.

In making plans for the new building, deliberate efforts were made in its design to provide for as many activities as possible. Although by 1926 the University possessed two auditoriums,[1] both were woefully inadequate in caring for the public exercises of the University; and Robinson Gymnasium, possessing a large floor space but otherwise unsuitable as an auditorium, had served to the best of its ability since 1907 in accommodating convocations, lectures, concerts, and commencements, in addition to its primary function.

The wave of greater public interest in athletics that followed in the wake of World War I brought increased attendance at football and basketball contests. The Stadium amply accommodated those interested in football; but Robinson Gymnasium held basketball crowds in the early twenties that literally hung from its rafters; and the attendance at the first home basketball game in 1899, be it recalled, had been "about 50."

To meet this popular interest in Dr. Naismith's game, the auditorium was designed to include two balconies and a level floor parallel

---

[1] Fraser Chapel and the one in Strong Hall.

Dedication of Hoch Auditorium, October 14, 1927.

to the stage but below it and sufficiently large to provide a basketball court. Movable seats were to be added to this space when the building was to be used for ordinary assembly purposes, its total seating capacity to be some 3,900.

The construction of the auditorium as thus planned was carried out, but its completion required a grant of another $100,000 by the Legislature of 1927. The dedication of the building was observed on October 14, 1927, Charles F. Scott, of the class of '81, and editor of the *Iola Register,* giving the principal address. In 1929, by legislative enactment, it was named Hoch Memorial Auditorium, in honor of former Governor E. W. Hoch, onetime member of the State Board of Administration.

66. New Snow Hall

Numerous improvements and changes will greet old students returning this fall. The completion of the athletic plant, the remodeling of Fraser Chapel,—[the building] of a new drive into Chancellor Lindley's residence,—[and] new paving at the rear entrance of the Administration building, extending along the drive for 100 feet each way from the entrance, and the drive all around is being covered with gravel.—Columns for the first floor of new Snow Hall facing the street are now being set, and the framework is going up rapidly.—*University Daily Kansan,* September 7, 1928.

IT HAD been found early in the construction of buildings on Mount Oread that it was necessary to rest the main walls on footings extending to solid rocks. Failure to carry out this precaution, coupled with attempts to secure more space by excavation after the completion of the building, had resulted in serious damage to Fraser Hall, and much time and money were expended in the eighties in repairing this error of construction. When plans were made for the erection of Snow Hall in 1885, it was distinctly stated in the building contract that all walls, interior as well as exterior, should rest upon bedrock. Twenty-seven years later (1912) the state architect upon examining the building reported to the Regents that rebuilding the foundation was necessary for its preservation; and in 1916 Chancellor Strong stated: "The University must expect to discontinue the use of Snow Hall before many years have passed. I am informed by officials of the University, competent to judge, that the original construction of the building was not of the best, that the foundations are inadequate, that the in-

Vine-Covered Old Snow Hall, shortly before dismantling began. The photograph, looking west, was taken in the summer of 1931; most of the work of dismantling took place slowly through 1933.

136

View from an upper floor of New Snow Hall, looking east, probably taken in the summer of 1930.

terior walls have sunk to a dangerous degree, and that the building is deteriorating very fast."

Dr. Strong expressed the hope that Snow Hall could be replaced within ten years after making this statement. Eleven years later the Legislature did appropriate $200,000 for this purpose. The need of a new building, however, was far from being solely a matter of physical deterioration of Old Snow. During the forty-four years of its service, an enormous growth had taken place in the extent of human knowledge and especially in the biological sciences.

When Professor Snow moved into Snow Hall in the fall of 1886, he, together with the help of his single assistant (L. L. Dyche), taught thirteen courses in fields of botany, entomology, zoology, geology, meteorology, physiology, and anatomy. Forty-four years later fifty-three instructors taught 151 courses in these same fields, together with an additional one which was virtually unknown in 1886—bacteriology.[1] Although the instructors and equipment for courses in anatomy, physiology, geology, and meteorology—among the courses originally taught by Professor Snow—had found other quarters when the ap-

propriation for a new biology building became available, the remaining work far overcrowded the capacity of Old Snow. A description of the interior of the building, shortly before it was vacated in 1929, reads more like a description of the

[1] The first course in bacteriology offered at the University is described in the catalog of 1890-91. It was taught by "Prof. Snow and Mr. Stevens." Marshall A. Barber was the first instructor whose title carried bacteriology in its description. In 1899, he became "associate professor of cryptogamic botany and bacteriology." The Department of Bacteriology was organized as a separate unit in September, 1914, having previously been a part of the Department of Botany.

New Snow Hall, 1930.

137

View from Marvin Hall, early fall, 1928. Note the changes of four years (see page 128). The pile of lumber at the extreme left was to be used in the construction of New Snow, which, at the time of this photograph, had just been started.

Hobo Day. The photographer who took this picture thought it was taken in 1924. Thomas Larrick, of the class of 1928, who saw the picture in the earlier edition of this book and identified himself as the gent in the frock coat (third from right in front row), is sure that it was taken the day before Kansas defeated Missouri 10 to 7 (with the aid of a place kick by Stony Wall) in 1925.

138

confusion that must have existed aboard Noah's Ark than the description of a University building.

When the funds for the new building became available, a site was selected, which, upon second thought, was re-selected. Plans were drawn up for a building to house the Departments of Zoology, Entomology, Botany, and Bacteriology, but as the appropriation was not sufficient, no provision was made in the plans for any future growth in these fields. Ground was broken for the new building in June, 1928; by the following summer it was under roof.

That other people besides college professors make mistakes became apparent when the interior finishing began. The plumber, on beginning his installation of pipes according to blueprints, found them going up in front of windows and through the center of rooms. The unfortunate error was traced to the fact that the State Architect in making the plans for heating and plumbing had not drawn them from the finally accepted master plan of the building but from a provisional plan quite different from the final one. As a result, all plumbing had to be installed by trial and error and the work of completion was seriously delayed.

The Department of Entomology, then located partly in Old Snow and partly in Dyche Museum, started moving into its new quarters in December, 1929, and was followed by the Departments of Botany and Zoology. First classes were held when the University reopened after the Christmas holidays on January 6, 1930. The Department of Bacteriology joined its colleagues at mid-semester.

Snow Hall—the question of name for the new building was never debated—was dedicated on June 8, 1930. One of the addresses on that occasion was delivered by Professor W. C. Stevens, of the class of 1885. Professor Stevens' concluding words are not only typical of the man who said them but representative of the sincere feeling of the many faculty members who have devoted long and efficient lives to the University: "The spirit of its founder lives on in the new Snow Hall—the spirit of progress, of fair and honest work, the spirit of concern for the welfare of the State in whose service it stands. All hail and farewell to the old Snow Hall; salutations and good will for the new."

It was, of course, unfortunate that the old building had to be razed—unfortunate for sentimental reasons, for many a graduate recalls Old Snow with nostalgic longing, housing as it did so many activites of the University in its formative years; unfortunate, too, for practical reasons, as its continuance on the campus, had it been possible, would have given a welcome addition in answer to the continual cry for space, more space.

67. Looking Back on the Nineteen Twenties

EVERY STUDENT GENERATION HAS HAD ITS CRITICS
Judge Thacher led Chapel exercises Monday morning after which the Chancellor made some remarks to the students in regard to a false statement published in a Topeka paper concerning the moral character of K.U. students. The Chancellor showed plainly that the morality of students had been on steady increase. Judge Thacher also spoke showing that the article in the Topeka paper was a base fabrication from beginning to end.
—The *University Courier*, May 3, 1894.

THE TEN years between 1920 and 1930 were for the University one of its most extraordinary decades. The changes which took place in this period were, of course, made possible by the prevailing economic and social orders and disorders of those days. The year 1930 saw the close of one of the greatest building decades in the history of the University, when a sum approaching five million dollars went into the structures erected. As a result, on the University campus alone the number of buildings was nearly doubled; off the campus, but still in Lawrence, twenty-four costly sorority and fraternity houses were built or remodeled; and at Rosedale, the new medical plant rapidly took its present form.

The changes were not confined, however, to buildings. The student enrollment increased from 4,226 (1920-21) to a high mark of 5,896 (1930-31).[1] To instruct the increasing number of students, the size of the faculty had been increased from 205 in 1920 to 263 in 1930. These figures on the size of the faculty do not include the entire teaching force. They have, purposely, been re-

[1] These figures include the two semesters and the summer session, and represent only unrepeated names. The greatest attendance at any time during this decade was reached on November 1, 1939, when 4,610 were present—4,342 on the Lawrence campus and 268 at the Kansas City division. The peak attendance at Lawrence was reached on November 1, 1936, when 4,372 were present, and at Kansas City on November 1, 1940, when 276 were present.

139

stricted to the number of instructors having the rank of assistant professor or above, for the reason that this group, it should be expected, would be the stable group, the faculty group in which the least change in the course of years would become apparent. Yet, if we consider the ten years elapsing between April, 1920, and April, 1930, out of the original 205, practically half were no longer teaching in the University at the latter date. Further, included in the changes were the entire administrative staff—the Chancellor and the dean of every school in the University. The changes were, of course, largely economic in their origin. Possibly ten were due to death or retirement, but most of the other changes were caused by those who followed the lure of higher salaries than the University could pay.[2]

Although faculty changes were among the most important University events of the 1920's, the changes in the appearance of the students were far more noticeable. If the dean of women in 1920 could have been suddenly transported to the campus of 1930 she doubtless would have caught her breath—and then gasped again. Although an occasional short skirt was seen on the campus in 1920, the prevailing mode, as can be seen by examining the *Jayhawker* for that year, was for a decidedly long skirt. But the trend upward was starting, to the vast discomfiture and

[2] The following decade also saw numerous changes among the same faculty group. The total number increased from 265 in 1930 to 277 in 1940; 77 of the 265 of 1930 were no longer among the full-time teaching members of the staff in 1940. Of the 77, however, some 30 changes had been caused by death or retirement.

Classroom scenes, thirty years apart. Upper, about 1899; lower, 1929.

alarm of many. Even one University president joined in the chorus of condemnation with ". . . the rolled hose and short skirts are born of the Devil and his angels and are carrying the present and future generations to chaos and destruction." By 1930, the short skirt was accepted without comment and if any dared to criticize, even the conservative press came boldly to its defense.

If short skirts were accepted for the women of the campus by 1930, bare legs were not. For bare legs in 1930 had the same status then as short skirts did ten years earlier. Although I have found no statement bearing on this subject from local authorities, the status of this new clothing problem can be seen from a ruling on another state university campus. "They shall not pass through the portals of our dining halls," declared one dean of women, "unless they are fully clad, including their hosiery."

Men of the campus, too, were noticeably different in appearance by 1930. Caps, which were the prevailing headgear of 1920, had completely disappeared by 1930, and although a considerable number wore hats, the majority of men went bareheaded. Men's collars, too, were noticeably lower and softer than they had been ten years earlier. These changes were but a forerunner of a decreased formality in everyday dress which became particularly noticeable by 1940 for both men and women.

The morals of flaming youth which startled their elders at the beginning of the twenties were becoming more stabilized again by the end of the decade. It is doubtful if youth ever flamed in Kansas as generally or as violently as it did in eastern or metropolitan centers. For one thing, the heritage of the state exerted a greater restraining influence in Kansas than elsewhere. The state, even in the late twenties, maintained conventions —either by usage or legislation—which prohibited the sale of cigarettes to all, which prohibited Sunday movies, which prevented the opening of the University Library on Sundays, which prohibited Sunday tennis, and which prevented the public playing of cards and of dancing on Sundays in all organized houses. Such conventions at least made modern youth keep his efforts to be modern under cover, if they did not actually restrain him.

There is, however, more positive evidence on this point. Even as late as 1927, if one can believe the *Kansan,* Jayhawkers were behind the times. Answering a charge of Bernarr Macfadden that colleges were hotbeds of vice and im-

The Commencement procession, 1931. Looking East, Green Hall on the left.

morality, its editor writes: "Kansas, true to tradition, seems to be far behind in its educational program. The schools that Mr. Macfadden loves to talk about make our beloved K.U. appear as innocent and pure and behind-the-times as little Susie Corntassel, who thought that spooning was a course in the home economics department designed to teach babies how to eat."

That a change in student behavior had taken place during the twenties is reported by a still more competent observer — Joe, the waiter at Brick's. Joe's remarks are particularly relevant, as the type of student with whom he came in contact would be the ones most likely found in the vanguard of a free and easy life, for it is doubtful if many Phi Beta Kappas made a practice of hanging around Brick's as regular and constant customers. Joe's testimony on the question reads: "Now [1927] the people in school are all such kids, every year the freshmen seem to get younger. And they all sit around with those at their own table, quiet like. Students now are all so sort of literary. Yes, the younger generation has sure settled down." His evidence is given greater weight by the admission that a few years earlier, conditions had been pretty bad—so bad that Brick's had to have the partitions between eating booths cut down so that the occupants were under public observation.

The twenties also saw the establishment of several notable student activities and traditions. Hobo Day, a day of student rallies for the events of the annual homecoming, and characterized by old clothes, red handkerchiefs, and burnt cork, made its appearance on the campus in the fall of 1923. It was not altogether successful, from a faculty point of view, but was celebrated annually, with one or two exceptions, until 1939. Another student enterprise was the *Dove,* "a jour-

Dedication of Watkins Memorial Hospital, June 5, 1932. Chancellor Lindley is speaking at the entrance of the Hospital; Blake Hall at the left.

nal of liberal opinion" which made its bow in 1924, but the most important student event of the 1920's was the establishment of the ceremony of student induction, which also began in 1924.

This impressive service in which the traditions of the University are explained and a pledge of loyalty invoked, has been a memorable day in the lives of many new students.

68. Watkins Memorial Hospital

The New University Hospital, located northwest of the Engineering Building, is a two-story frame structure surrounded by a small grove. For next year the upstairs, consisting of five rooms and one large hall, will be used as the hospital. The rooms have outer openings, make it possible to keep patients with contagious diseases.—The *Kansan*, May 12, 1908.

IN the spring of 1905, a University student developed a case of smallpox. There was no University hospital nor detention house; and to make matters worse, the city hospitals would not receive the patient. The Health Committee of the University—in existence since 1896—was sorely distressed. It was necessary that the case be isolated so that the danger of infecting other students would be diminished. Fortunately, the student was not seriously ill, nor the weather severe, so that the student was really isolated by placing him in a small cabin on an island in the Kaw River! Fellow students ferried food to him each day and left it on a tree stump near the shore of the island.

In time the student recovered, but the method

of treating him brought sharp criticism from the local and out-of-town press. As the result of this criticism, greater efforts were made to provide more adequate health protection for the students, especially when in the following year, an epidemic of typhoid fever developed. University funds from the state were not available for this purpose, however; and the efforts to improve the situation had to come almost entirely from the voluntary efforts of faculty and students.

In the fall of 1906, a Benefit Health Association with a fifty-cent fee was started to provide hospital insurance for students. Only forty-two joined, and but two students were able to secure any of the "benefits." At Lawrence, one of the men on the Medical School staff, Dr. S. C. Emley,

142

did give free consultation to students and free treatment to students earning their way through school.

The following fall, students were unusually healthy, with the natural result that the Benefit Health Association itself developed a precarious condition; but, after the holidays, diphtheria came to its rescue and the membership increased rapidly. Medical students were interested in the organization, and because of their efforts a campaign for a student hospital was undertaken. In May, 1908, the *Kansan* was able to announce that the Regents had approved the plan and the Spencer house,[1] "a quarter of a mile northwest of the Engineering building," was rented for a hospital. A voluntary health fee of two dollars from each student was also approved. The hospital plan nearly fell through in the fall of 1908, for only 400 students had paid the health fee up to October first, and 700 were needed in order to secure the necessary funds for its support. Disease again came to the rescue with the announcement of two cases of typhoid fever and the medical students—56 in number—were given a day's holiday to solicit memberships for the Hospital Association. By evening of their holiday, the necessary number of members had been obtained and the hospital was assured. The first year of the hospital was a success, for all bills were paid and a handsome balance was left over; in addition, over 250 patients were cared for during the year.

Some form of student health service has been in effect since the days of the first hospital in 1908-09. The student hospital has frequently changed its location, no less than five residences, erected originally in each case as private homes, being used for the purpose between 1908 and 1932. From 1908 to 1912, a private physician, Dr. H. L. Chambers, was employed as a part-time University physician. From 1912 to 1928, a number of other part-time physicians—usually University staff members—had charge of the student health service.

In 1928, the first full-time physician was employed to direct the work of the student hospital and health activities, and it was not long before his troubles began in earnest. Early in December it became apparent that an influenza epidemic of proportions approaching the disaster of 1917 was

on the way. The student dispensary, equipped to care for not more than seventy-two consultations a day, was forced to accept patients at an increasing rate, so that on December 11th, 237 cases had been handled by the wearied physicians. The normal 22 hospital beds had been increased to 38 by doubling beds in rooms and using the operating room; all were full, and many cases needing hospitalization were turned away.

At this juncture, a survey of the extent of the epidemic in all organized houses on the campus was ordered. A dozen interns were brought down from Bell Hospital at Rosedale to help the survey. The rumor spread over the campus that there was a possible closing of school in prospect if the cases found were excessively high in number. As a result, when the interns arrived at a house, practically everyone was in bed. By a careful check of pulse and thermometer readings, however, it was established that there were a large number of actual cases of influenza on the campus, and the University was ordered closed. The administration felt, judging from the rapidly rising rate of infection, that the University would be totally unable to give the cases adequate medical care. Students seriously ill, however, were taken care of locally, and the rest cautioned and advised. The epidemic proved, fortunately, to be of mild form and departed almost as rapidly as it had come, for when school was resumed three weeks later, on January 2, 1929, very few cases developed and no fatalities had resulted from the earlier ones.

The epidemic had shown, however, that the hospital facilities were woefully inadequate for a student body of four thousand students; and the tragic note in the situation was that little could be done about it by the state. It was with genuine satisfaction, then, that a year later all friends of the University read the announcement that Mrs. J. B. Watkins, the donor of Watkins Hall, had offered to build and equip a hospital for student use. The offer was accepted with rejoicing and careful plans were made for constructing the new addition to the campus. Ground was broken west of Blake Hall for the building in the spring of 1931, and on December 28, 1931, the first of its many patients was admitted for treatment.

The beautiful and modern building, erected at a cost of $175,000, was formally dedicated at Commencement, 1932.

[1] Later the home of former Chancellor Strong upon his retirement.

69. Lean Years

Any number of students who have formerly held summer jobs to help defray their college expenses were unable to get work during the past summer months. This makes it necessary to return to college with little or no funds and it has caused a new employment problem at the University here. One reason for the lack of jobs was that the organized houses which formerly employed outside help are trying to economize, and the work is now being done by the members of the fraternities and sororities.

—*University Daily Kansan,* September 23, 1930.

AFTER 1931, no new building appeared on the University campus until 1937—a marked contrast to the similar period ten years earlier when the University was experiencing the greatest building activity in its history. This span of years in the thirties, however, despite the lack of construction, was by no means a quiescent era. Economically and climatically, it saw violent changes.

The social historians have fixed on October 29, 1929, as the end of an era—the day the biggest crash in the New York stock market came. The day was scarcely noticed by most Kansans—save for the born gamblers who, it can be said, are still lamenting their sins. Even the Federal Reserve Bank of Kansas City, after the height of the crash, issued a report showing optimistic gains in every branch of trade and concluding with the statement that "the activities of the stock market which have affected conditions in every part of the country have apparently done little damage in this district."

Little damage was at first apparent. The athletic department used a photograph that fall in its football advertising campaign showing thirteen men; under the picture appeared the caption "University of Kansas Coaching Staff." As the football squad contained on its rolls but thirty-four men, it was apparent that prosperity was affording lavish training, to say the least. The *Kansan,* not to be outdone, joined the prosperity train with an elaborate twenty-two page—large ones, too—special issue for the homecoming game with Missouri. Missouri must have provided its players with a still more ample coaching staff and more vociferous and enthusiastic journalism, for it won, 7 to 0. The resulting defeat was for the moment far more important on the campus than the depression.

In fact, depression did not rear its ugly head on the Hill until the following fall, when it first became noticeable that the students who were working their way through school—always a very considerable number—were having difficulties in finding jobs. Special appeals were made by the Chancellor and the student employment agen-

cies to faculty and townspeople to provide work. To aid further, a campaign to increase the student loan fund was begun and a considerable measure of success was achieved.

By the fall of 1931, the depression was approaching a little closer to the University. Enrollment fell off by several hundred, and the operating budget was reduced by over a hundred thousand dollars, although faculty salaries were still unaffected for that school year. It was apparent to Governor Woodring and the Board of Regents by the spring of 1932 that still more drastic retrenchment was necessary; and for the school year of 1932-33, a 10 per cent reduction in faculty salaries was announced. Even this reduction was insufficient to keep expenditures within the bounds of the budget allowed by the Legislature of 1933; and the following fall saw salaries reduced from 15 to 25 per cent below the 1931-32 scale. The lean years had again arrived for the faculty.

If conditions appeared gloomy for the faculty, they were far worse for the students. Many, because of lack of funds and jobs, could not return to school. As a result, the enrollment decreased for the school year of 1932-33 by over a thousand from its high-time level of two years earlier. But what was still worse, many of those graduated at the Commencements of 1931, 1932, 1933, and even 1934 were unable to find work for which they had been trained. The more fortunate and pluckier ones took any jobs they could find, although a few years earlier the usual report before Commencement read, "Graduates have been refusing offers from big firms for six weeks." These graduates of the depression years were indeed "the lost generation"; the effects of these lean years will doubtless never be effaced from their memory, not only for the trials of the years succeeding graduation, but for the handicaps and difficulties under which they labored while in school.

To cite but a single instance of the tribulations of the lost generation, I know I shall be pardoned for describing a first-hand observation, especially as it reveals a side of college life too often overlooked, yet repeated with numberless variations even in more pleasant eras. One Saturday afternoon in the fall of 1933, I had occasion to see a professional man in a downtown office building. After concluding my business with him I left his office and came out into the corridor. Hearing a radio broadcast, punctuated by occasional suppressed cheers, I paused and listened further. Curiosity getting the better of me, I followed the sound to its source and came to an open door. Someone within caught sight of me and called out to me to come in. I entered a dark, unplastered room at the back end of the corridor. At my left, as I stepped in, were half a dozen University boys grouped about a battered radio listening with bated breath as a dramatic and greatly ex-

Some of many NYA activities are illustrated in these photographs of projects carried out between 1936 and 1939.

cited announcer described the drive of the Jayhawker football machine to within fourteen yards of the highly touted Notre Dame goal line. Being familiar with the past dozen years of football history, I was startled by this remarkable event, and for a while I followed the fortunes of the game to the exclusion of time and surroundings. As the drive bogged down, my interest waned; I began looking about me, and what I saw remains vividly in my mind to this day. To my right, in the two far corners of the room, were piles of straw spread out to form two beds. Thrown over the straw were several soiled and tattered blankets and comforts. Between the two beds was a box, holding the several remains of what had once been respectable suitcases. Another box, to my left in a third corner of the room, was used as a table upon which was placed a two-hole gas burner, one leg of which had given up the struggle and limped away to seclusion. A meal was in preparation, for upon the burner there was a gallon fruit can, emptied of its original contents and now serving its purpose as a cooking pot. It was nearly full of unpeeled potatoes bobbing up and down in the boiling water. Although I looked, I saw no other food. After circling the room my eyes came back to the group around the radio which occupied another box in the fourth corner. The boys, stretched out on the floor, were intent on the game, and as K.U. advanced the ball time and time again in a game the description of which is still exciting reading, yells and cheers of encouragement urged on the team hundreds of miles away. For some reason, I lost all interest and stumbled out of the room, mumbling thanks for the privilege of listening to the broadcast; but my thanks were wasted, for they fell on heedless ears.

As I walked down the hall, I met the owner of the building. "Good God," I said, as I asked the needless question, "do those boys live in that hole?" "Yes," he replied, "they were having a pretty hard time when they came here so I told them they could have the room if they would sweep the hall and keep the washroom clean." He paused. "The room's warm," he added as an afterthought.

This case, multiplied by many others of greater and less severity, was the cause of genuine concern to the administration and to the faculty as the depression reached its stride in Kansas. It was with a feeling of the greatest satisfaction, then, that Chancellor Lindley was able to announce in January, 1934, the decision of the federal govern-

Leaving convocation, Hoch Auditorium, on September 20, 1935. The view looks west; Marvin Hall is the second building on the left; Snow (New Snow) at the extreme right. Over the Chi Omega House (at end of drive) may be seen another distinguishing feature of the Hill skyline, an auxiliary water tower built in 1934.

146

ment to come to the aid of college students as part of its national relief policy. Chancellor Lindley had, in fact, been one of the first to present the matter to the national administration. Making a trip to Washington early in January of 1934, he urged some form of federal action to President Roosevelt, Relief Director H. L. Hopkins, and Dr. George F. Zook (of the class of '06), U. S. Commissioner of Education. The plan appealed strongly to these men, and the organization of the College Students' Employment Project (CSEP) followed shortly after Dr. Lindley's visit.

The plan as put into action at the University for the first time in February, 1934, provided for the part-time employment of 350 students, whose average stipend for specific tasks assigned by a University committee amounted to fifteen dollars a month. Necessary qualifications in securing CSEP positions included definite proof that paid work was necessary for the maintenance of the student and that he had the ability to maintain at least an average grade in classroom work. This measure, which benefited some 75,000 students throughout the country in its initial trial, was, like other relief projects, subjected to considerable criticism. The plan was continued from 1935 under the National Youth Administration until World War II was under way. Whatever its merit, the NYA was a godsend to thousands of students, especially during the years of greatest want.

70. Vagaries of Kansas Weather

More than 60,000 hours of work were performed for the University of Kansas in the spring semester, by 374 different persons, employed by the federal government under the College Student Employment Project. Sixty-nine persons did 11,507 hours of work as research assistants. . . . Additional stenographers numbered 36, and clerical assistants, 57. The Student Hospital, and the Medical Hospital at Kansas City were able to extend their service by student assistance, and the University Library was kept open an hour more daily.
—*Summer Session Kansan,* July 10, 1934.

NATIONAL economic conditions at the time of the organization of the CSEP were bad enough, but to make matters worse, the elements added their share to the general grief. Some Kansans were inclined to blame the Democrats for the weather, but others felt that a just retribution had at last caught up with them. For they remembered that in 1932 nearly a quarter of a million voters, in the hectic struggle for the governorship, had been lured from the narrow path of Republican and Democratic rectitude, by the siren song of "a lake in every county and a goat in every yard."

Whatever the cause, in the years 1932 and 1933, the rainfall in Kansas was considerably below its average value; and in 1934 it sank still lower. Not only was it dry; it was excessively hot, as students and faculty in the summer session of that year can testify. It was, in fact, the hottest summer on record. The University weather station reported fifty days when the temperatures were one hundred degrees and over, sixteen of the fifty days occurring in succession. As the summer session students were thankfully leaving in August, the thermometer soared to an all-time high of 114°. To illustrate the vagaries of Kansas weather, however, the September which followed this inferno was one of the coolest ever known in the state;

and the following month, according to the official weather report, was "one of the most pleasant Octobers on record in Kansas."

The long-continued dry weather brought another phenomenon in its train. Western Kansas and the adjoining territory, always semiarid, had during these years of dry weather, almost passed into the arid class. Conditions in the fields, aggravated by the excessive breaking of the cover sod during the booming days of high-priced wheat, allowed the dry topsoil to move with every vagrant breeze. When the high winds of March struck across this barren land, the dust was lifted higher and higher and moving eastward settled over many states. The worst of these dust storms reached Lawrence on March 20, 1935. In the morning of that day, the sky was hazy; but as the day progressed, it became darker, and by two o'clock street lights and automobile headlights were turned on. All the rest of the day darkness remained; but by the following morning the dust haze was gone, leaving a murky mantle in its train that had penetrated even closed doors and windows. University students from western Kansas, however, only grinned at the complaints about a dust storm, for they knew what real ones were like. When a return engagement of the dust appeared, a year later almost exactly to the day, even the most optimistic out-of-state member of the faculty began to wonder if he hadn't made a mistake in coming to Kansas.

Our tale of meterological woes is not yet complete, for the dust storms of 1935 had not much more than abated before the Kansas River went on one of its more or less periodic floods. Although the crest of the flood of June, 1935, was not as high as in 1903, the damage done was excessive, the flood waters covering thousands of acres of valuable farm land.

The many vicissitudes of the lean years had their compensation, however. For one thing, the coonskin coat as an emblem of collegiate life had disappeared during these unusual days. The jazz age likewise had gone the way of all flesh, as admitted by one of its severest critics, the Sage of Emporia, who stated that "the more homely

Dust storm of 1935; looking east from in front of Bailey Laboratory toward Fraser Hall. The decrease in visibility caused by the dust may be observed by comparing the upper with the lower photograph, taken from the same spot on a clear day. (Lower photograph made on February 10, 1941.)

148

things of life are the new order of the day." Students, too, became increasingly aware of problems outside their own immediate difficulties. Stimulated, no doubt, by their own quandaries, they began considering again those of others. The nature of the times brought first a flood of economists to the platform of the Auditorium, all explaining the causes of the depression and offering their own way of economic salvation. The seriousness of the foreign situation, too, suddenly dawned on all citizens of the Hill; and during the spring of 1934, the columns of the *Kansan* were filled with discussion of world affairs. The youth and peace movements of 1935 were the more or less logical consequences of this interest in the outside world.

It must not be thought by the reader of future years that the unusual problems and difficulties—economic, climatic, and foreign—of this half decade were the sole topics of consideration. University life as a whole went on in its usual routine fashion. Classes had to be met, taught, and prepared for by students and faculty as they had from time immemorial. As for youth, its exuberant spirit may have had its ardor dampened occasionally by the blasts from the cold, cruel world; but "As far as the spirit of fun and frivolity is concerned," reads the *Jayhawker* for 1934, "there is no depression apparent on the Hill. There are no flags at half-mast for the youth of the campus. And as for the wolf at door—the most popular tune on the Hill today is, 'Who's Afraid of the Big Bad Wolf?'"

Signs that the depression was lifting were becoming apparent by the fall of 1935. Faculty salaries had begun their tedious and painfully slow upward toil. The number on the staff was increased somewhat, and the enrollment started an upward swing that brought, the following fall, the greatest number of students on the campus up to that time—some 4,600. In the spring of 1936, when representatives of business concerns again appeared on the campus in considerable numbers to interview prospective employees, times became still more cheerful. To clinch the argument that times were improving we can be still more statistical. Take the matter of paper towels supplied to the University washrooms, for example. During the school year of 1932-33, in the effort to reduce the University budget, only 46 cases of towels, costing $212, were purchased. The following year 405 cases were bought and in 1934-35, $1,373 was spent for 456 cases of the necessary articles. These figures show conclusively that the tide of the depression was running its course and by 1935 there was no longer need of University students belonging to the great unwashed.

71. The Watkins and Summerfield Gifts

The old University is doing wonderfully well these days. Everybody is rejoicing over the gift a few days ago of a student hospital from Mrs. Watkins. That magnanimous woman knows how to spend her money effectively for others, doesn't she? The various university departments are working harmoniously, so far as we can learn and instructors report an eager group of students this fall. The Dean of Women says the incoming class is the most sophisticated she has seen.—*Graduate Magazine*, October, 1930.

FROM 1930 to 1940, no building was added to the campus at Lawrence as a result of appropriations from the Legislature. Yet during this decade, the University acquired seven additional buildings. All but one of these seven were the result of gifts to the University. The exception was the practice house of the Home Economics Department, built in 1930 from savings in fees collected by the department.

Miller Hall and the Watkins Home for Nurses were both completed in 1937, and both were gifts of Mrs. J. B. Watkins, who had already been most generous to the University in providing Watkins Hall and Watkins Memorial Hospital. Like Watkins Hall, Miller Hall was a dormitory erected east of Fraser to provide a home for girls working their way through school. Together, they accommodate seventy-eight students. The Watkins Home for Nurses gives excellent quarters for the nurses employed in the Hospital and is located on the hillside below it and to the south.

The munificence and generosity of Mrs. Watkins, a former student of the University, did not, however, cease with her donation of these four buildings. Upon her death on June 1, 1939, she bequeathed her residence on a site affording a wide view of the Wakarusa and Kansas valleys, to the University, to be used as a residence for the Chancellor. In addition to this bequest, endowments were provided for Watkins Memorial Hospital and for Watkins and Miller Halls, and thousands of acres of farm land were also willed

149

Mrs. Elizabeth M. Watkins, from a photograph made about 1930.

to the University. The total value of Mrs. Watkins' gifts is over two million dollars, making her the most generous private donor to the University.

Although gifts to the University from Mrs. Watkins and other sources are not large in comparison with those received by the heavily endowed private colleges of the East, or for that matter by some of the larger state universities, the actual value reaches a far from inconsiderable sum. What is more important, these gifts have come from many, many sources. Friends of the University, alumni, and students have been most generous, in many cases far more generous than their circumstances would apparently warrant. Such devotion is some measure of the esteem which the school has achieved during the years of its existence.

These pages have already recorded a number of these gifts: the original University building ("North College"), Spooner Library, Fowler Shops, and the Union Building, to mention but a few of the buildings thus provided. The most recent additions to the University's physical plant

in this same manner have been Templin Hall and Battenfeld Hall, dormitories for men. Templin Hall—named for Professor Olin Templin, Dean of the College from 1903 to 1920—was purchased by contributions from many alumni. Battenfeld Hall was erected by Mr. and Mrs. J. R. Battenfeld in memory of their son, John Battenfeld, a student of the University, killed in an automobile accident on December 16, 1939. Together with Carruth Hall[1]—the former Chancellor's Residence, also a gift to the University, it will be recalled—Templin and Battenfeld Halls provide accommodations for 120 men. They were first opened for occupancy in September, 1940.

But in addition to buildings, much of the present University campus has been acquired by gift. Governor Charles Robinson, Frank B. Lawrence, a nephew of Mrs. Robinson, and the city of Lawrence have been among these larger benefactors. The list of books, teaching equipment, objects of art and objects of historic interest and value which have enriched the University's holdings through the liberality of many persons would alone form a catalog of imposing proportions.

Notable also among the University's gifts are the many loan and scholarship funds begun with the establishment of a student loan fund by the class of 1894. One of these later gifts in particular should be mentioned because of its unique character and the important influence which it has had—and will continue to have—on the improvement of scholarship at the University. In 1929 it was announced that Solon E. Summerfield, of the class of 1899, would give the University a sum of money amounting to some $20,000 annually during his life, and an endowment to make available a like annual sum after his death. The gift was to provide an education at the University for a number of boys, graduates of Kansas high schools, chosen by competitive examinations. A provision of the Summerfield Scholarships states that the recipient shall be given only such financial assistance as is necessary "above his personal resources." Examinations were first given in the summer of 1929 to 174 applicants. Ten were chosen and received stipends, in accordance with the above provision, ranging from $300 to $500 annually. Since the examination was given each year, by the end of four years some forty Summerfield Scholars were part of the student body. The plan, now nearly twenty-five years in opera-

[1] Carruth Hall—as such—existed from 1940 until 1953 (see page 181).

150

tion, has brought many brilliant students to the University.

More recently, honor scholarships for women, awarded on a plan somewhat similar to the Summerfield stipends, have been established. The funds for these scholarships have likewise been gifts to the University and have come from several sources. The first qualifying examination was held in the spring of 1940. Although the women's scholarships are neither as numerous nor as valuable as those for men, it is hoped that eventually additional gifts from still other sources will equalize the present discrepancy between men and women.

The Summerfield Scholarships and many other gift funds to the University are administered by the University of Kansas Endowment Association, a privately chartered institution which accepts and administers any trust to be used for the benefit of the University. The Endowment Association was organized in 1893 as the result of a peculiar provision in the state Constitution. Through this provision, only the interest on a direct gift to the University may be utilized. To make matters worse, in actual practice any such interest is deducted from the legislative appropriation for the University. In effect, then, the state, and not the University, is the real beneficiary of *gifts to the University.*

72. The Development of the Medical School to 1941

No longer is our beloved University without the gentle heart to cheer and the trained hand to soothe the ills of human kind. Arising from the depths of obscurity with no light to guide, the first and most illustrious class ever to be graduated from the K.U. Training School [for Nurses] stands as a marvel of perfection. Never again will methyl salicylate and guaiacol be so well and so vigorously applied. Never again will the chief surgeon receive such valuable assistance and advice.—*Jayhawker,* 1909.

FEW students of the University, and few of the faculty for that matter, are familiar with those parts of the University campus not located at Lawrence. Yet the University campus includes at least two areas removed by many miles from its main site. Indeed, one addition to the campus may be found in another state, but we shall postpone its description for the moment.

The School of Medicine at Kansas City is, of course, the most important addition to the out-of-Lawrence campus. The years elapsing since 1907 had seen marvelous changes in its extent and

Watkins and Miller (right) Halls. The photograph (taken in July, 1937) looks east from Blake Hall.

151

character, with the greatest changes coming after 1924. How important was this transformation can be seen by the statement of its dean, in 1938, that the School of Medicine "has developed in the past fourteen years from one of the weakest to one of the best and most outstanding medical plants in the country."

The comparatively slow growth of the Medical School from 1905 to 1924 can be traced to several sources. In the first place, the original site at Rosedale was found to be small, hilly, and inaccessible, and it was not long before it was apparent that a new location would be necessary. This possibility again brought up the old question of division of University facilities, which was further complicated by suggestions that the hospital be removed to Topeka or Wichita. The problem was debated at some length in 1911, and more than eight hundred doctors of the state were asked to give their advice in the matter. Over 60 per cent were in favor of continuing the Medical School at Rosedale, but the question was only temporarily settled for that year by increasing somewhat the size of the Hospital; and the question continued to come up at intervals for many years. It was not until after the Legislature of

1927 met and appropriated $300,000 for the erection of medical buildings that the *Graduate Magazine* was able to state: "The appropriation for this use indicates that the state intends to build its Medical School at Kansas City, a policy that has been undecided for some time."

Events had earlier occurred that made this decision the logical one. Alumni and friends of the University, together with the city of Rosedale, purchased and presented to the state, in 1920, a new site of fifteen acres about a mile distant from the original Bell Memorial Hospital. The new location was level and very accessible to city transportation facilities. In addition, the Legislature of 1921 had granted $435,000 for the enlargement of the site and the construction of new buildings. With these funds there were constructed the new Bell Memorial Hospital, a power plant, and two temporary frame buildings which were ready for occupancy in 1924. The $300,000 appropriated in 1927 was used for the construction of the Nurses' Home and the Ward Building, the cost of which was completed by a legislative grant of $50,000 in 1929. After 1929, no great change in the medical campus—for the obvious reason—appeared until 1937. During the four succeeding

University of Kansas Hospitals, Kansas City, Kansas. An air photograph made in September, 1940.

years a number of important buildings were added, the expansion being particularly noticeable by 1938. Included in the additions were the Eaton Building, the Children's Pavilion, the Clinic Building, and the Hixon Laboratory for Medical Research, the entire plant for a time being officially designated as the University of Kansas Hospitals.

The cost of erecting these buildings has been borne by the state, the federal government (through PWA grants), the earnings of the Hospital, and lastly by several notable gifts from private sources. The appearance of the medical campus was also greatly improved through efforts of the WPA, over a quarter of a million dollars being expended for this purpose alone.

While this important growth in the physical plant of the School of Medicine had been unfolding since 1905, an equally important change had taken place in medical education. When the four-year medical course was begun in 1905, graduation from a four-year high school would permit a student to enter the Medical School. By September, 1909, entrance requirements had been raised to two years of approved college work; ten years later, a year of internship was added to the four years of medical training; and in 1939, three years of college work were necessary for entrance; after 1940, students were required to complete the work for the bachelor's degrees before they were admitted to the second year of the medical course.[1] The work of all medical schools, too, in this period of development had been subject to scrutiny and standardization by the American Medical Association, and schools that could not meet the necessary qualifications were dropped from the approved list. As a result of this examination and approval, the number of medical schools in this country was reduced by one-half between 1909 and 1924.

[1] The distribution of time in the four-year medical course proper was changed in 1911 so that a student spent the first year and a half at Lawrence and two and a half years at Kansas City; by 1952, one year in Lawrence, three in Kansas City.

73. End of a Long Administration

Communistic and Fascist activity, while present on the University campus, is to be found here in no greater amount than in other large universities, in the opinion of a special committee of the Board of Regents, which made public a summary report of its investigations Friday. The report of the investigation absolved the University faculty from any "red" tinge and stated the investigation had "entire cooperation from University authorities." "We have not found where any faculty member has exceeded his authority in teaching theories of government. Neither have we found any faculty member who is affiliated directly with any leftist group."—*University Daily Kansan*, November 13, 1938.

THE school year of 1938-39 opened amid wars and rumors of wars, but the international pulse slowed somewhat after the "peace" plan for the dismemberment of Czechoslovakia was signed late in September. On the campus nearly 4,600 students began the annual routine, some 1,600 of them looking for work to help them through school. As the year progressed the *Jayhawker* announced a bean-counting contest, with two winners to be given a week's free trip to Hollywood. Another student achieved a national reputation as a goldfish swallower, when, in the presence of a thousand wide-eyed students, he gulped fifty live goldfish in succession.

In addition to these student foibles, events of considerable importance occurred; but none caused greater surprise on the campus than the announcement of Dr. Lindley on December 1, 1938, that he had asked the Board of Regents to accept his resignation as Chancellor, effective the following June. Chancellor Lindley pointed out in making the announcement that while he would soon reach the retirement age of seventy, his resignation in June, 1939, would permit his successor to obtain a year's acquaintance with the problems of the University before the meeting of the Legislature in 1941. The Board, in accepting the resignation, granted Dr. Lindley a year's leave of absence, with the understanding that he would return to the University as professor of ethics. His untimely death at sea on August 21, 1940, was a matter of real sorrow to the University and to the state.

After an extensive canvass by the Board of Regents, Deane W. Malott was offered the chancellorship on April 10, 1939. Mr. Malott at the time of election was an associate professor of business at Harvard University and a former assistant dean of its Graduate School of Business Administration. A native Kansan, he was also a graduate of the University in 1921, and was thus the first of its graduates to become Chancellor of

Chancellor Lindley and Chancellor-elect Malott on the center steps of Strong Hall, April 11, 1939, the day after Mr. Malott's election by the Board of Regents.

the University of Kansas.[1] The inauguration of Mr. Malott on September 22, 1939, was marked by its simplicity, the ceremony consisting of the introduction of Mr. Malott by Fred M. Harris, Chairman of the Board of Regents, to a convocation audience of faculty, students, and citizens, followed by the inaugural address.

Chancellor Lindley, upon retirement, had completed an administration of nineteen years, the longest chancellorship in the history of the University. These pages have indicated some of the changes that took place during this period, so that it will not be necessary to recount them again; but attention might be directed to several interesting parallels between the Strong and the Lindley administrations, which together have included practically half the life of the University. In the first place there was the rather odd coincidence of height—to be repeated again in the case of Mr. Malott. Both were very tall men, so tall as

[1] Mr. W. C. Spangler, of the class of '83, was, however, twice the Acting Chancellor.

154

to be conspicuous for that reason. In the next place the term of office of each was nearly the same,—eighteen years' service for Dr. Strong and nineteen for Dr. Lindley. Both came to the University at the beginning of eras of great prosperity, and the first half of the administration of each was marked by large gains in the physical plant on the campus. The last half of each administration saw grave problems arise, World War I and its aftermath in the case of Dr. Strong and the world-wide depression of the thirties in the case of Dr. Lindley. Despite the rise and fall in the tide of fortune, great advances had been made in the University in the years between 1902 and 1939. Accompanying the tremendous growth in its physical plant there had been large increases in the legislative appropriations for the annual support of the University, rising—irregularly, to be sure—from somewhat over one hundred thousand dollars in 1902 to over a million dollars in 1939. The enrollment, too, had increased from 1,200 students to 5,550. In considering these changes it is well to keep in mind the fact that they were not dependent on changes in the population of the state, for the net change in state population was comparatively small, increasing from roughly a million and a half citizens in 1900 to some 300,000 more in 1940. Rather the growth of the University is more nearly in agreement with the growth of the wealth of the state during the same period of time.

Statistics, however, are of little use in tracing another development during this same period. With the growth of the University, the duties of the chancellorship have gradually undergone change. The earlier chancellors included teaching in their line of duty, the remainder of their time being given over to administering the funds of the University and presiding over the faculty. As state-service work developed, the chancellor became more and more a public figure and public servant. Chancellor Snow was the first to feel this effect, but with the succeeding chancellors, Dr. Strong and Dr. Lindley, both of whom emphasized greatly the state-wide functions of the University, this aspect of the chancellorship became possibly its outstanding one; and both were continually called upon to expound and to interpret the University to its citizens and, of course, to solicit aid for its continuance.

As they were thus placed increasingly in the public eye, it was but natural that the state as a whole should give all the credit for any gains achieved by the University to its incumbent chancellors. But if credit for its gains had been in part his recompense, the Chancellor has also had to bear the burden of any and all criticisms directed against the University. Ranging all the way from the trivial to the profound, these criticisms have forced on the Chancellor the additional role of being the University's chief defender. Any political, economic, or social heresy, real or rumored, engaged in by student or faculty, sooner or later would call for an explanation by the Chancellor.

A greater source of grief for the Chancellor than these difficulties has been charges that the football team was incompetent! Here, unfortunately for the Chancellor at least, there was evidence that the charge had some foundation in fact. Just what the critics expected the Chancellor to do about these situations was not clear—to anyone—but anyhow the Chancellor was to

blame! Even this difficulty has ancient origins. It plagued not only Dr. Strong and Dr. Lindley, but even Dr. Snow. Listen to this complaint from the *Florence Bulletin* of 1894: "Chancellor Snow is fooling away his time explaining why there are no snakes in Ireland. That won't satisfy the people of Kansas, Mr. Snow, and you might as well know it first as last. We want to know why the University football team got the stuffin' beat out of them every game last fall, and what you have done toward providing 'diseased' chigres for use next summer."[2]

[2] The first reference in the quotation is to a popular lecture of Dr. Snow's. The last, "diseased chigres," refers to a method announced by Dr. Snow for destroying chinch bugs by infecting them with a suitable culture. Incidentally, this instance is the first time I have ever seen a Kansan spell the lowly chigger as "chigre"—a form preferred by Webster for some years. At present, however, Webster has agreed that "chigger" is the preferred form.

Another important event of 1939 was the Dramatic Club production of *Emperor Jones* with a cast composed largely of colored students. The characters are (left to right): Rolla Knuckles, Alonzo Fox, Anderson Preyer, Lorenzo Fuller, Neil Holliday (kneeling), Ellis Harrison, Daniel Mitchell. In the past eighty-eight years colored students to the number of more than two thousand have attended the University in the state where John Brown first rose to fame. Although it would be senseless to deny that there are no race problems in the University, it is safe to say that there are few universities in the country where the color line is so indistinctly drawn and where the colored student more nearly enjoys all privileges of the white student.

155

74. The Campus in Colorado

I would most respectfully call your attention to that portion of the Territory lying in the region of the recent gold discoveries. A large number of our own citizens, and emigrants from other states, have already located there—. The county of Arapahoe already established and organized by my predecessor, Governor Denver, in September last, includes within its boundaries nearly, if not the whole of the gold field. I might here suggest that a Memorial to Congress for the establishment of a mail route from Fort Riley to some point within the gold field, might not be inappropriate, but of great importance.

—Governor Samuel Medary's Message to the Kansas Territorial Council, January 3, 1859.

KANSAS is a great state, as even its most modest citizen freely admits. Its resources are numerous and diverse, its climate so variable and invigorating that self-satisfied inaction does not have a chance to develop; its inhabitants, unique, although occasionally vociferous in their uniqueness; and its landscape beloved. To the outlander it is the landscape which is as surprising as any feature of the state. An Easterner making his first trip to Mount Oread is always profondly impressed. "Why—you have a hill in Kansas!" was the deep observation of a visiting celebrity as he viewed "the golden valley" on a recent autumn day. Yes, Kansas has several hills; the state is not one vast, flat, and level table, as seems to be the popular imagination of those who have never seen it. It varies from the often rough and rugged lands of eastern Kansas to the rising rounded bluffs of the Flint Hills, which form the backbone of the state, until finally there emerges the rolling grandeur of the High Plains.

Despite our affection for our varied landscape, most of us would admit that a first-class mountain chain would be a desirable addition to our geographic wonders. The unfortunate thing about this desire is the fact that it could have been granted for the asking. When the Territory of Kansas was organized in 1854, the westernmost boundary of Kansas was placed as "the summit of the Rocky Mountains," which designation, although vague, would include about two-thirds of the present state of Colorado. When Denver, for example, was settled in the Pike's Peak gold rush of 1858, mail for the embryo city was addressed "Denver, Kansas Territory." The western

boundary of Kansas, when it was admitted as a state in 1861, however, was placed considerably east of the Rockies; and thus we lost our possession of real mountains. Moreover we can't blame the Democrats for this loss, as an examination of the record shows that the Democrats were in favor of the original boundary when the State of Kansas was organized.

If our mountains have been lost to us we still retain a proprietary interest in them; and every summer, almost from the beginning of the University, a considerable colony of K.U. folk has been found among the Rockies. It is altogether fitting and proper, then, that part of our campus has been extended to their slopes. The Department of Geology, realizing the teaching value of the varied terrain on the east side of the Front Range, established a permanent camp some eleven miles from Canyon City, Colorado. A long-term lease was secured on a suitable site; and with the aid of funds given by alumni, modest residence and study halls were constructed and first put into use in the summer of 1940. As further funds are accumulated, the plans call for an extension of these facilities.

Closely associated with the Department of Geology has been the State Geological Survey. Indeed, through the Geological Survey and the Extension Department, the University first began its off-the-campus activities. Both were organized about the same time. A School of University Extension was formed in 1891, and regular courses of instruction by members of the University faculty were given at Olathe, Kansas City, Topeka, and Wichita. Over 350 students were

156

enrolled in these courses the first year. For several years this work was continued; but because of the increasing number of students on the campus, the burden of giving extension courses became too great, and such work was greatly diminished in volume. The service was re-organized in 1909 as the University Extension Division and in 1947 the official title was changed to University Extension.

Provision for the State Geological Survey was made in the reorganization of the University in 1889, but it was not formally created by the Board of Regents until 1895. Field work on the geology of Kansas had, to be sure, already been begun by two faculty members, S. W. Williston and Erasmus Haworth, who, like many of their colleagues, put in long hours at no pay during the summer months for the University and the state.

As a result of the work of Professor Haworth and his students, the first volume of a long series of publications dealing with the geology and mineral resources of Kansas was published in 1896. It would be difficult, if not impossible, to give a true estimate of the value of this knowledge to the enrichment and development of the state. Not only have these studies been of value in the location of minerals, and of gas and of oil, but also in that most priceless of all products of the ground—water itself. For in the dry years, when search for water was under way, valuable aid came from these fundamental studies. In the very early years of the Survey's history, irrigation also came within its province. Indeed, in one early report, the Survey is called the State Geological and Irrigation Survey.

The Colorado campus, 1940. The main building may be seen at the left, temporary student sleeping quarters in the center, and the staff house at the top of the slope at the right. Water is forced up from the valley below in the pipe line which nearly forms a diagonal in the picture. The picture on the preceding page, taken from a greater distance, shows better the neighboring terrain.

After seventy-five years. Snow Hall appears near the center of the photograph and West Ad at the right. Across the street may be seen Haworth Hall and Hoch Auditorium. The photograph was made April 17, 1941.

After seventy-five years. A typical classroom scene in the seventy-fifth year of the University. This photograph, taken April 18, 1941, shows the class in "Psychology I," sitting for its collective portrait. The psychological reaction of the young man at the extreme left (front row) is undoubtedly caused by the loss of time from class work occasioned by the taking of the photograph. For a comparison of student dress with that of earlier decades, turn to pages 66, 101, 140.

158

After seventy-five years. Looking east past Green Hall toward Spooner-Thayer Museum (April 21, 1941). The Laws still whistle, but not to themselves, as the girls pass by.

75. The Diamond Jubilee

I don't know in what form the dictator philosophy in the totalitarian state will meet you in your lives, dearly beloved. But it is out of bounds today. It stands just beyond our borders waiting. What your sacrifices will be, what hardships you may meet, what anguish you may know, I cannot prophesy. I only know unless that beast is chained upon the fields of France your lives will be marred and mangled by its claws.

—W. A. White, Alumni Address, June, 1940.

NEW ways of life were indeed being initiated as the University opened in the fall of 1940. On the 17th of October 1,083 University men registered in the Kansas Room of the Memorial Union Building for the first peace-time draft in the history of the nation. The *Dove*, liberal campus newspaper, was so stirred by the event that it came out from a two-year retirement to protest the "conscription bill." Events had transpired and were shortly to transpire to make the *Dove's* protest but faintly heard in the turmoil that was even then occurring. These events were immediately reflected in the University enrollment, which had remained at a high level for a number of years. Three hundred fewer students, chiefly men, were present on the campus in the fall; the R.O.T.C., however, had a record enrollment of 706, and the head of this military organization made a journey to Washington, where he proposed and had approved a Military Science Building to house the enlarged activities of his department. The building finally materialized, but was not officially opened until December 10, 1943. The three-year delay was the result, of course, of the travail of preparation for World War II.

The first University building to be erected by the state for over ten years had meanwhile taken form. An active campaign for a Mineral Indus-

159

The Kessler Plan for Campus Development, 1904. The long range of this plan is best realized when it is pointed out that only the buildings in the left third of the design had actually been built when the plan was conceived. To aid in orienting the reader, one may point out that Spooner Library is the building at the extreme left; across from the Library is Dyche Museum. Above and a little to the right of Dyche is Green Hall, which had not been started when the plan was drawn. Above Green Hall is Fraser. Around the curve (to the right) past Green Hall are Snow Hall and Bailey Chemical Laboratory, the latter then the westernmost building on the campus. A central Mall, leading past a stadium on the right and a gymnasium on the left, ascended the Hill to a "Grand Court" and the "main College Hall" with park areas on both sides. The buildings on the west ridge (at the right) were indicated on the plan as "Dormitories or other Buildings," "Homes of Faculty." The influence of the Columbian Fair of 1893 and the St. Louis Fair of 1904 are readily discernible in the plan. It doubtless is no exaggeration to state that if this plan, or any similar one employing a central approach to the campus, had been fol-lowed, we would easily have had today the most impressive campus in the country —even with our buildings of many architectural forms.

tries Building to house the Geology Department and the Geological Survey was begun in the fall of 1940 by the Alumni Association. That the campaign was effective is evidenced by the fact that the Legislature meeting in the spring of the following year appropriated over $400,000 for the new building. A government priority, one of the new facts of the new life beginning in 1941, was secured late in 1941 and construction was started. Despite priorities, the difficulties of securing materials was so great that the building was not ready for opening until the summer of 1943. The first occupants of the building, however, were not members of the Geology Department but were some 250 youngsters of the Army A-12 training program who arrived about August 1 and were housed in Lindley Hall. They were the first contingent of the A-12 program, eventually numbering 800 individuals, who made Lindley Hall their temporary home. Not until the spring of 1945 was Lindley Hall utilized for its original purpose.

Postponing for the time being, however, further consideration of the terrific impact that World War II had upon University life, let us return to late pre-war days.

The administration exploded a bombshell in the regular routine of student life by announcing in the fall of 1940 that "long and popular week ends are not helpful educational adjuncts" and that when the spring semester of 1941 arrived students would be expected to take more of their class work in the afternoons or on Saturdays. More space for offices and classrooms, as well

After seventy-five years. If one picture is more eloquent than ten thousand words, two pictures are better than twenty thousand. Compare this photograph, looking south on Massachusetts Street, and made on April 17, 1941, with the one shown on page 5, taken from almost exactly the same spot seventy-four years earlier, and I believe you will agree. The Eldridge Hotel, rebuilt between 1925 and 1929, is at the right.

161

After seventy-five years. Part of the University viewed from the south on April 15, 1941. This photograph should be compared with a similar one made in 1896 and shown on page 60. The towering smokestack rises behind the power-house that was new when the earlier photograph was made. Watson Library, to the right of the stack, and Watkins Hospital, between Blake and Fraser, have also materially altered the skyline in the intervening years.

Seventy-fifth Anniversary. One of the Anniversary hostesses, Dorothy Mae Nelson, opening the gates to the driveway at the Chancellor's Residence. June, 1941.

as the need for more helpful "educational adjuncts," was the reason advanced for such changes. A wholehearted howl of protest from students, especially when Saturday classes were mentioned, was, of course, the result to be expected. When the spring schedule of 1941, however, was announced it showed but 17 of the University's 775 offerings scheduled for Saturday classes—and students breathed again with freedom; although it is more probable that their breathing was never seriously altered by the situation.

As the school year of 1940-41 drew to a close, however, two events of importance occurred: Dyche Museum was opened to the public for the first time in eight years, and the University celebrated its seventy-fifth anniversary, its diamond jubilee.

Dyche Museum had been closed late in 1932 by order of the State Architect and State Fire

Marshal because of its poor condition. The depression years had followed, and sufficient funds were not available for some years to undertake the necessary work of rebuilding the interior.

By means of several legislative appropriations and the help of W.P.A., the interior remodeling was finally completed. On May 19, 1941, the Museum was again reopened to the public. The remodeling which had occurred was not only of structure but of exhibits as well. Numerous natural history dioramas skillfully modeled by Bernard Frazier, with natural background paintings by Walter Yost, were among the notable changes, but the spectacular panorama and background of North American animals on the main

The Student "Strike" of November 17, 1941. Marching down Seventh Street, downtown Lawrence.

From the top of Fraser Hall in 1899. When we compare this photograph with the one on the next page (the two were taken from almost the same position), we see the developments of forty-two years more clearly than any words could portray.

163

floor of the Museum was doubtless the cause of more praise and wonder than any of the other changes effected. Comanche, too, the sole survivor of the Seventh Cavalry in Custer's last stand, again came in for his share of attention. The natural history displays of Dyche are doubtless the object of more attention by visitors than any other spot on the campus.

The Diamond Jubilee, beginning on June 5, lasted for five days. Reunions, exhibits, costumes of bygone days, dinners, imported celebrities and pageant, and the return of many distinguished alumni marked the occasion. Possibly the most extraordinary feature of the event was the fact that students of every year of the University's seventy-five years of existence were present. How strange the campus of 1941 must have seemed to the lone student of 1866 who appeared for the event after many years' absence! But nothing more fitting than this appearance could serve to dramatize the fact that the life of the University —from a struggling pioneer academy to a great and complex institution—had been encompassed in the lifetime of an individual.

After seventy-five years. Even the paving was beginning to show its wrinkled age as we look from the top of Fraser Hall. Dyche Museum and the Kaw River appear in the left half of the photograph; the town of Lawrence and Spooner-Thayer Museum at the right. Photograph taken April 17, 1941.

164

After seventy-five years. Changing 11:30 classes on April 21, 1941 (the photograph on the opposite page was also made on this date). The view looks west, Bailey Laboratory on the right; Robinson Gymnasium at the left.

76. World War II Begins

In addition to all the special courses and lectures about the war—they [returning students] will find a contingent of the Navy quartered right in the middle of things, in Frank Strong Hall, the administration building. Also they will find the town of Lawrence teeming with workers of Sunflower Ordnance Works, a giant explosives factory located a dozen miles east of town. With their double deck beds moved into former classrooms for art, history, economics and the like and with the former physiology laboratories reformed into shower rooms, the white uniformed Navy boys have erected a set of clothes lines along the rest of the Hill north of Strong Hall. The clothes and their flopping loads make a freak sight on the campus.

—*Graduate Magazine,* September, 1942.

WITH wars and rumors of wars drawing ever closer, the University year began a nearly normal start in the fall of 1941. True, over 300 fewer men appeared on the campus than had been present the previous year, but most of the usual activities went on. Then, too, the football team defeated Kansas State on November 17. So unusual was a football victory that year that stu-dents immediately demanded a holiday. The re-fusal of their request led to a "sit-down" strike at convocation, students refusing to go to class. A parade through University buildings, campus and downtown streets, kept many students busy during the day. "Peace terms" by the adminis-tration and students were finally signed, with a promised vacation if the Missouri game, the

165

After seventy-five years the flags were flying high on Fraser Hall, the first building on the present campus. To the left of Old Glory may be seen the University flag, a fairly recent addition to the skyline. It was designed by Eleanor Grider, of the class of 1943, and was first flown from the north tower of Fraser on December 6, 1939. This view was taken from the steps of Robinson Gymnasium; Bailey Laboratory at the left.

homecoming game, was won. The Missourians had evidently heard of the proposal, for they settled the question decisively and in their own way. Dashed hopes, rain, and snow and a score of 45 to 6 made one reporter write, "It was indeed a dreary day."

Several weeks later many of the University community were seated at their Sunday dinner tables. The day had begun as a bright and peaceful one as far as Lawrence was concerned—but war for all was at hand. The fateful news of the attack on Pearl Harbor came by radio with shocking force. The full impact of war reached the University with still greater realization when there were shortly announced the deaths of Ensign Eddie Olson, '37, at Pearl Harbor on that terrible day of December 7, and of Lieut. Max Louk, a former student, in the Philippines, on the following day.

In retrospect, the four years that followed seem now incredible, so greatly changed did Univer-

sity and civilian life become. Chancellor Malott announced to the student body on January 16 some of the proposed changes that might be expected: the Easter vacation was eliminated; the summer session was made longer so that students, by continuous attendance, could be graduated in two and a half years; and many new courses designed to contribute directly to the war effort were announced for the spring semester. The Navy had announced about the same time a V-7 program, the first of the many special military programs to be started. It permitted junior and senior students in certain fields the opportunity of completing their work and then qualifying for a Navy commission. Possibly of all these changes, the one which caused most student "comment" was a course in "physical conditioning." It was announced at first that the course was offered for the benefit of "students and faculty." Apparently, as I now recall the bodily outlines of faculty members of those days, few of

166

the faculty took advantage of the benefits to be derived, but they were insistent that the course be required of all students, both men and women, graduate and undergraduates, except those excused as a result of physical examination. The course for men was a "toughener": ability to walk distances without fatigue, to jump into deep water and then swim thirty yards, to climb obstacles (a barrier "thirty feet tall" was one of the obstacles, a graduate student reported to me—but he was prejudiced before he started) were among the objectives set up. Another required course of the early days of the war for many students was a weekly lecture on "The World at War." That these lectures filled a real need is indicated by the fact that frequently the attendance was nearly twice the number enrolled and difficulty was encountered in providing a suitable meeting place for all who desired to attend.

The long list of rationed items which was to affect faculty and student life began early in January of 1942. "First full realization of the horrors of war," reported the *Kansan* for January 8, "was brought to University students last week —[in the] greatly restricted sales of automobile tires, making it impossible for University students to buy new tires . . . ." The manufacture of new cars had ceased by this time and, with the shortage of cars and rubber, bicycles that for many years had been stored away were brought out. After a few attempts to pedal up the Hill, even by the easiest approach, this form of transportation retired again to the limbo of forgotten things. Tire-rationing boards, however, were but the forerunners of more extensive forms of rationing. In May, all University students, no matter where they ate, had to register at the Union Building for twenty-eight sugar stamps—one year's supply—as well as a ration book which "may be used later for other products"—and it certainly was used for many other "products." Gasoline rationing came late in the fall and the days of free-and-easy travel—days greatly cherished by Americans—were over for three years.

The announcement late in March that a huge munitions plant was coming to the Kansas

Raising the colors in front of Frank Strong Hall. A daily campus occurrence during World War II. Photograph, about 1943.

prairies a dozen miles from Lawrence forecast another change in town and University life. Soon the town filled with construction workers. Every house, room, and spare building was brought into use and many students had great difficulty in finding quarters. Rent controls—new words in Kansas—came to have a familiar meaning. Training workers for the new Sunflower Ordnance plant and employment in the plant for students and even some faculty and staff members were still more direct impacts on University life.

The martial aspect of the campus was greatly augmented in the summer of 1942, when several hundred *sailors* took quarters in Strong Hall. The west wing of Strong and the top floor of the building were taken over as offices and sleeping quarters for the naval contingent, and storeroom and canteen were provided for the group by fencing off a portion of the basement. The offices and departments moved out of Strong were scattered and crowded in many places over the campus. The naval trainees were being prepared as machinists' mates at first, but during the later part of their stay, electricians' mates took over. The course was of four months' duration, so that many men in these programs were present on the campus during the war years (2,100 in 1942-43; 1,617 in 1943-44; and 409 in 1944). The University offered instruction in mathematics and shop work, and it was not long after the sailors' arrival until Fowler Shop was used continuously twenty-four hours a day. It was a weird

Physical conditioning for everyone—except the faculty. 1942-43.

167

Jayhawkers and former Jayhawkers celebrating Kansas Day, January 29, 1944, "Somewhere in Oahu."

sight on leaving the campus well past midnight to see the eerie glow of fluorescent lamps light all the windows of the Shops and see the students busily at work.

To provide an adequate teaching corps for this and other military groups on the campus, as well as for the civilian students, was a problem. Probably the Mathematics Department was as hard-pressed as any in finding a sufficient staff. The surrounding country was scoured for ex-teachers and retired teachers, teachers from junior colleges where the enrollment was low were brought in, and University teachers in other departments where the enrollment had fallen off, were transferred to the Mathematics Department. Teachers of English, of botany, of economics, of voice, among others, hurriedly reviewed their college algebra, had some of the rust of years removed by their more practiced colleagues—and went to work. Possibly as many as fifty senior engineers and others were drilled in the elementary mathematics required for the machinist's-mate and similar programs, and secured practice—and some cash—that they would not have otherwise acquired.

But even in those harrowing and busy days, all was not work and worry. The *Kansan* thanked God for Kansas State in a dismal football season; a co-ed complained because the Library was "a den of wolves"; students complained so vociferously and strenuously about a too short Christmas vacation that they were granted three days additional to the original six days; "Music Week" went on despite the war; and Commencement took place as always but nearly three weeks earlier than the accustomed time (on May 17, 1943), the earliest University Commencement on record.

77. Troublous Years

The first Lawrence collection of tin cans for war uses will be held Friday, it was announced at the city council meeting last night. Citizens are asked to leave their cans at the curb in containers, such as baskets and boxes, Thursday evening because the collection will start early Friday morning.
—Lawrence Daily Journal-World, January 26, 1943.

THE early Commencement of 1943 had been caused by the fact that the University had gone over to a trimester basis, trimesters of sixteen weeks each. A shortened semester began late in January of 1943 and the first of the sixteen-week periods began on July 1. They were continued until the conventional eighteen-week semester began again in the spring of 1945; but so complex had the University schedule become during the war years that it was not until well into 1946 that the "normal" routine was reestablished.

The men in uniforms steadily increased in number. Five hundred men in the Navy V-12

Review, winter, 1943-44.

The campus, November 11, 1943. Changing classes. Note that but two cars appear in the view.

program reported on the campus on July 1 and were housed in seven fraternity houses and a scholarship hall (Templin) and were fed in the Union Building. By the middle of August nearly 800 men in the Army Student Training Program were housed in Lindley Hall and eventually were fed there. Each of these units had its own schedule, sixteen-week terms being provided for the Navy and twelve-week terms for the Army, with special terms for groups who reported to the University at regular intervals. On October 1, 1943, for example, there was in progress a five-week term for civilians, a five-week term for the Navy, a twelve-week term for the Navy, and a twelve-week term for the Army. In each of these terms, all classes were separate even though the same course was being given. A member of the Department of Chemistry, for example, at the middle of August, 1943, was teaching classes in general chemistry to civilians, general chemistry to a V-12 group, and the same course (general chemistry) to an ASTP unit. Many of the teaching staff had left for military service or other war duties, replacements were impossible to obtain, and the University was virtually in continuous session the year around after May, 1943, with the result that, for the teachers remaining, the day

was long and the burden heavy. Those of us who remained on the campus all too frequently wished for the leisure most willingly reported by our colleagues in the service. According to such accounts most of the time of these faculty service men was spent sitting in swivel chairs awaiting orders or hurriedly making cross-country trips by train in search of units to which they had been assigned. If we are to believe them, they never were able to make connections.

But those of us that stayed at home had some pleasure. Every few months we had to line up for new ration books and saw friends in line that we hadn't seen in weeks. And some of us had faculty gardens. Indeed as I look back on these years, the brightest spots in my memory are the hours spent with my partner in our attempts to be farmers. In general, considering our ignorance our efforts were highly successful, although on one occasion they were successful in growing a crop which could not be utilized. Probably more salsify, for which we could find no consumers, was grown one year than has even been produced in Lawrence before or since.

Staff members who had early classes in the fall and winter of 1942-43 had indeed a day that seemed interminable. Daylight-saving time had

169

Electricians' Mates on the way to drill, 1944.

begun in February of 1942 and although the lengthened day was noticeable then, it came at a time when daylight hours were becoming longer. As the next year rolled around, beginning classes for the day were set at 7:30. Many a morning (as I have written elsewhere) I hurriedly and doggedly made the bus to the Hill in a darkness so black that it but added to the unreality of the situation. The bus reached the campus in time for its passengers to come to attention as the bugle sounded its call for the raising of the flag in front of Strong Hall.

Mount Oread was thus an armed camp, and the rhythmic tramp of soldiers and sailors going and coming to class or at drill was the most characteristic sound of the day. Civilian students were still present, of course, but they were largely women. On October 1 (1943), there were some 4,000 students on the Hill, of many categories and classifications. Half of these were in uniform, the remaining half civilians. Of the civilian half, less than 400 were men; women thus outnumbering the civilian men better than three to one. Not too many tears should be shed for the women, however, for there were times when the military were "released": many co-eds, too, found male company by serving as junior hostesses on Saturday nights at the Lawrence Community Building, where they entertained servicemen.

Probably military activities on the campus reached their apex late in the fall of 1943. Some 2,300 men in various organizations were present. Reports from our services at the front showed that the tide of battle had turned. The Solomon and Gilbert Islands had been invaded and won; the North African and Sicilian campaigns were over and Italy had been invaded; and the allied air offensive over Germany was reaching devastating proportions. The two-year handicap had been overcome but at a staggering cost of life, toil, and suffering.

The two years of war had further effects on campus life. Service ribbons from far-flung cam-

paigns appeared among the V-12 contingent as men with active war records were returned for officer training. Greater and greater need for manpower in the armed forces produced tighter draft regulations and the number of civilian men—both students and instructors—became fewer and fewer in number.

Most of the ASTP was withdrawn for combat duty in the spring of 1944 and by fall of that year the electricians' mates, who had succeeded the machinists' mates, disappeared from the campus. Strong Hall reverted to civilian use exclusively, the twenty-four hour day at Fowler Shops was discontinued, and after November 1 but 400 servicemen in uniform remained, chiefly V-12 men and the army and navy medics. "Rather than virtually resembling a military encampment, the school has assumed some of the college atmosphere which exists in normal times," reported the *Kansan* that fall, and continued, "—officials are calling meetings and holding long discussions over the problem of what to do for the returning veterans. Special programs are being planned and arrangements are being made to give soldiers credit for some of the work they have done in specialized training programs."

By the spring of 1945, seventy discharged veterans were back on the campus, and campus problems of unforeseen magnitude were arising. University administrators at this time predicted that the enrollment might go as high as 6,000 and that housing for veterans, since many were married, would be difficult to provide. The last prediction was certainly correct, but the deluge of students which was shortly to descend upon us was totally unexpected.

The collapse of Germany in May, 1945, was followed in August by the surrender of Japan. Heartfelt thanks on the campus followed each of these major events in the lives of us all. And what

Navy V-12, PT-3, 1943.

was the cost? No one can faintly estimate the cost. As far as the lives of University students were concerned, over 7,000 men and women who had at one time or another been University students played some part in the activities of our uniformed forces. They gave up an appreciable share of their lives, in some cases four years or longer, to the service of the country. And many University men and women gave their lives!

Doubtless the fact that war was actually over was really brought home to those of us on the campus by the announcement that the day after Japan surrendered, gasoline rationing had even ended; before the year was over, most rationing controls no longer hampered our activities.

One of the unusual sights on the campus during this period were the groups of German war prisoners, "farmed out" to the University to aid in the relief of a pressing labor problem.

The close of war in the summer of 1945 did not immediately produce any great increase in the number of students. As a matter of fact, when classes began in the fall of 1945, there were only some 3,000 students on the Lawrence campus; that is, the enrollment was nearly similar to that during a period thirty years earlier in the history of the University. Nearly 300 veterans were present, however, among these students, and the *Kansan* reported, for the information of women students, that only 180 of them were single.

78. The Tide Sweeps in

For the first time since before the war, the physical education requirement for both men and women has been dropped it was learned today. Enrollment in women's gym classes had dropped from 550 to 250, while only 65 men are enrolled in College physical education classes.—*Kansan*, September 27, 1945.

THE sudden decrease in gym classes was not the only change in the collegiate atmosphere of that fall. "Western Civilization," after a wordy and heated battle in faculty meetings, had been added to the work required of College freshman; so had "General Biology."

The fall semester of 1945 began on September 24 with its regular eighteen-week semester, but the presence of some remaining V-12 men on the campus again necessitated a sixteen-week term, beginning on November first, as well as a twelve-week term for veterans who arrived on the campus too late for September classes.

If schedules were still somewhat confused, a student walkout after another Kansas State defeat on November 17 showed that normalcy was beginning to return to campus affairs. Agitation, and eventually decision, for a student book store also marked the events of the semester. The need for a student store, urged for many years, became particularly acute as the result of a wholesale lack of textbooks; a lack that had its origin in wartime shortages and a growing student population. The student bookstore did not become an actuality until the opening of school in the fall of 1946.

By the spring semester of 1946 the release of men from the armed services made its effect felt on the campus. The enrollment at Lawrence went well beyond 5,200, the highest so far in its history. So men were housed in Thayer Museum, not as museum pieces, as an inquiring reporter pointed out, but because the housing shortage was becoming acute. Virtually all the living inhabitants of the Museum were GI's. Married GI's began finding apartments at Sunflower, thirteen miles away, and a bus schedule was arranged to bring students from Sunflower directly to the campus. Eighty new staff members were hurriedly added to the faculty as plans were made for further staff additions and housing to accommodate new faculty members; for a still larger student group was indicated by the spring rush.

During the spring of 1946, plans for a memorial to those of the University who died in service in World War II were discussed, a memorial drive on the north side of the campus and a bell-tower were decided upon, and a campaign to raise the necessary funds was started. Danforth Chapel, gift of the Danforth Foundation and other University friends, was formally dedicated, the first of its many weddings having occurred nearly two weeks before its dedication.

Commencement of 1946 was the first "normal" Commencement in five years. During the war years Commencement had been held two and three times a year. Even in 1945, Commencement had been restricted to a single day with baccalaureate service in the morning and graduation ceremony in the evening, and the out-of-town alumni who were present were greatly reduced in number by wartime restrictions of travel. But in

171

1946, alumni reunions and a three-day Commencement program were back again. School closed on a note of optimism: 7,000 students might be expected in the fall and there were prospects that the football team might do unusually well.

When the University opened in the fall, however, faculty and administration were dumfounded. Within two days after the opening of school over 8,500 students had enrolled and in two weeks the number had become almost 9,100! And this number on the Lawrence campus alone. Of this number, 5,600 were veterans. Nearly a thousand were housed in barracks at Sunflower; McCook Hall under the Stadium, another dormitory west of the Stadium to take care of 160 men, and Smith Hall (a downtown church building) for fifty men were completed as rapidly as possible to care for the deluge of students. Housing for the new members of the greatly and rapidly expanding faculty and for some graduate students was available in the Sunnyside addition on the south slope of the campus, a unit that eventually provided 186 homes.

Sleeping rooms in organized houses were so crowded as to draw the criticism of the county health officer; large Quonset huts, to be used as study halls, were brought to the campus; night classes, in order to take care of all students, became necessary, and parking space was totally inadequate for the multitude of cars. Peace was bringing nearly as many problems as war.

By this time (the fall of 1946) there was well under way a unique period in the annals of student life. Of the 9,000 students on the campus, 1,575 were husbands! In other years there had been an occasional married student, but husbands in such unprecedented numbers were a phase of college life quite different from the past. In a number of cases (135 was the count reported) both husbands and wives were in school, but usually the veteran—for most were veterans of World War II—was the student, and the wife stayed home and looked after the little dependents. For many, the problem of support was acute. The government allotment was $90 a month ($105 with little dependents; later increased to $108 and $120), and with a rapidly ris-

The student-housing shortage of 1946 according to Cartoonist Bibler in the *Graduate Magazine* of January, 1946.

ing price index, family problems became urgent. "Putting the little woman to work" was one method that helped in many instances, but all too often it was a case of a bare existence. When V.A. checks were late in arriving—a frequent circumstance in the early days of the Veterans Administration affairs—the moans of anguish were only too audible. There were pleasant aspects to this unusual situation, of course. Many of the veterans' families made up a more or less homogeneous group which found housing at Sunflower—such as it was—and living together, they shared each other's troubles and successes. A baby contest for K.U. veterans at Sunflower aroused considerable interest and brought an entry of 198 youngsters, a fact which produced some comment on the "falling" birth rate. Awards were given for the most attractive, the healthiest, the happiest, the most helpful, and the orneriest. Three faculty members bravely volunteered to serve as judges and lived to see another day.

The problem of the baby on the campus, too, occasioned comment as babies appeared in classes from time to time. Possibly the most extraordinary case was that of the harassed father, a freshman engineer, who left his ten-month-old youngster parked in the rear seat of a car behind Lindley and who "checked him" between classes, as he usually slept most of the time. After one class, however, the youngster awakened and howled so lustily that he attracted the attention of passing students who took him into the building. Here an extra diaper and a bottle of milk found with the boy easily quieted him, and he soon became the center of attention of a large group of admiring students. When the disturbed father finally found him he explained that the mother was in the hospital and that there was no one with whom the baby could be left. Such were the difficulties of a different student age.

The racial question, too, was another problem that provided difficulties during the year. The presence of a number of colored students who

The registration line, Strong Hall, February, 1947. Longer lines than this were formed in the "boom" years.

had served in the armed forces presented the advocates of equal rights a chance to advance their views on this ever-recurring question, and there was some advance in its solution.

Through the school year of 1946-47 efforts were continually being made, under the trying difficulties of shortage of materials, to enlarge the facilities of the University so that some measure of adequate space could be provided for the growing throng of students. Ten frame buildings were secured from army camps at Lake City, Missouri, and Coffeyville, Kansas, and during the summer of 1947 these "temporary" buildings were placed behind Strong Hall, Blake Hall, and Lindley Hall and on the south slope of the Hill. Additions to the Union Building and to the Library were also under way at the same time.

Commencement of 1947 reflected the large increase in students during the year. The graduating class numbered over 1,200, just a few under the all-time previous record set in 1939. Although the graduating class of 1947 was double that of 1946, the number who marched down the Hill was soon to become the equivalent of several regiments as the flood tide of students was reached.

79. Flood Tide

It Wasn't That Bad; It Just Seemed That Way

All previous attendance records at K.U. were broken for the third consecutive year when enrollment closed Saturday with a student body of 9,597. Fewer veterans are now attending the University. Veteran enrollment is 4,790, 646 less than last year's figure.—*Kansan*, September 20, 1948.

THE two years between 1947 and 1949 saw University enrollment reach its high water mark, the peak being established in the school year of 1948-49. The total enrollment for the first of these years was 10,891 and for the second year 11,199.[1] On the Lawrence campus 9,090 students were present at the end of the second week of

[1] These figures include Summer School enrollments.

school in the fall of 1948, and at the corresponding time the next fall there were 9,295. The school year of 1946-47 had been the hardest one as far as the University staff goes. As school opened in the fall of 1948, some dozen and a half emergency buildings had been provided for office, classroom, and laboratory space, and the teaching staff had been greatly augmented, so that a faculty of more than a thousand persons (including assistant instructors) were on hand to care for the large enrollment; the following year Chancellor Malott announced that the teaching staff numbered 1,200.

That the expansion of faculty was necessary almost goes without saying, but several specific cases will show the conditions under which we labored during the early post-war years. In the Mathematics Department, for example, whose teaching load had been heavy even during the war years, the "student-hours"[2] increased from around 3,000 in 1945-46 to well over 10,000 the following year. In the Chemistry Department, to cite an example still more familiar through personal experience, the end of the war found us with a staff of seven full-time teachers and five assistant instructors. Before the war the department had numbered ten full-time teachers and twenty assistants, but death, resignations, and draft had lowered our number. When the deluge reached us, our depleted staff, which was small even for peacetime, labored overtime and our number was augmented as rapidly as possible. By the fall of 1947, a full-time staff of 12 were present and assistant instructors to the number of 44 aided in caring for over 1,000 chemistry students. And so it went; English instructors were increased from 39 to 60; Fine Arts, Latin and Greek, and German Departments, among others, had to be increased greatly during post-war years; for the demand for training and knowledge was general and not restricted to special fields.

One of the most extraordinary developments of University life in this period, and another factor that sorely taxed the facilities of the University to keep pace with it, was the development of research, especially in medicine and the sciences. Although in pre-war years, fundamental research had been regarded as one of the primary objec-

tives of the University, after the war, its development flowered on an unprecedented scale. Grants for the support of investigations in many medical and scientific fields were literally showered on University departments. The donors were federal agencies (Army, Navy, Air Force, Public Health, Atomic Energy Commission, etc.) and many state and national organizations and private industry. The University of Kansas Research Foundation had been established in 1943 amidst the difficulties of war and employed at first eight persons working either full or part time, when it was financed by grants that totaled some $25,000. By early 1949, 156 persons were engaged in research projects in various capacities and were supported by grants that exceeded $400,000. Since 1945, grants awarded the University for these purposes total well above a million dollars and would doubtless have been even more extensive if facilities and personnel had been available for other projects. Although under considerable criticism at first from the fear that federal financing, which constituted the larger share of funds used for these purposes, would bring a paternalistic control over University affairs, the development of this side of University life has brought little realization of the original fears. On the other hand, it has stimulated research to an extent undreamed of in earlier times. From actual contact with this development, two outstanding criticisms may be made of post-war University research. The first criticism is that much of it has been applied research (as contrasted to fundamental research unrestricted in direction), and the second is that the utilization of large research grants has detracted from the quality of teaching by the junior staff. That is, stipends paid for research assistants have, in general, been considerably higher than those paid teaching assistants, with the natural result that competition has drained off superior students into research projects. A still more extraordinary development in this field has arisen within the last two years, the discussion of which we shall postpone to a later page.

The great demand for University teachers beginning in 1945 and 1946 also brought a result most pleasing to the older members of the University staff. For many years, in comparison with faculties of similar state institutions, the University staff was among the more poorly paid. Beginning in 1947, the salary scale was revised rapidly upward, until at present our salaries are such that the University of Kansas can compete more favorably for the services of faculty mem-

---

[2] A "student-hour," for the benefit of non-administrators, is a student enrolled for one hour. An enrollment in a five-hour mathematics class would therefore appear in the statistics as five student-hours. This explanation is made primarily for the benefit of my colleagues in English and other non-mathematical departments.

bers in comparable schools; a condition that should bring satisfaction to all Kansans—as well as faculty members—since Kansans have always prided themselves on their progressive character and the quality of their institutions.

The rapid increase in faculty salaries in 1947—it should be emphasized that the increases were only "relatively" large—were, of course, related directly to the prosperity of the state. In fact, so extensively had the prosperity of the state, especially the western half of it, been reported in the eastern newspapers, that *Life* sent a photographer to the campus in the fall of 1947 to picture the sleek convertibles driven by the sons and daughters of western wheat magnates. Even in succeeding years when the wheat crops didn't fill the elevators so successfully, eastern newspapers gleefully reported hard times in Kansas by referring to the poor wheat rancher who was forced to the necessity of washing his own Cadillac. The scale of student living in these years ranged all the way from that of the harassed father who left his son in the car between classes—note that he had a car—and that of the drivers of the Cadillacs.

By this time, too, six campus cops were necessary to regulate the traffic flooding University drives, two football championships had been tied for—unheard-of events—and the coach who led the assault, after being awarded a handsome new car for his efforts by downtown quarterbacks, resigned to see what improvement he could make in the Naval Academy team.

Ten hours of foreign language, the College faculty decided after some vehement expressions of opinion, would be required of its students; the Engineering faculty decided that its students should get more culture and reduced the number of technical courses required for graduation; only half the students were permitted to see basketball games at home; and Harry Truman, much to the astonishment of most inhabitants of the campus, was elected President. Undoubtedly Truman's election had some relation to University affairs, but to trace the relation would take more space than we have here. In the same election, however, Chancellor Malott received a number of votes for justice of the peace, as did the dean of men; the dean of the Law School did even better in securing votes in his silent campaign for constable. The election board who had to count and record these votes failed to see the collegiate humor involved, but they should have been prepared for the worst. Previous to the fall election of 1948 the state's Attorney-General had ruled that college students who claimed "their legal residence in the precinct where they now live may register and vote in the precinct." The older average age of students of post-war years, while it may have given them the vote, had not stilled their effervescent spirits.

80. "A Friendly Rustic Community"

"A Friendly Rustic Community"
"Welcome to K.U.," the sign said in bold black print as I reached the crest of the peak I was scaling. As I drew closer I was able to read the small print also. "Speed limit 20, No Parking without Permit, No Smoking, No Drinking, No Visitors after 3:00, No Radios after Midnight, No Unchaperoned Dates, No Singing, No Beer, and—No Fieldhouse." "Aha," I sighed to myself, "What a friendly rustic community."
—The *Jayhawker*, Midwinter, 1949.

OUR friendly rustic exterior hides an amazingly complex University interior. Any institution whose annual income exceeds $12,000,000 a year, as has ours for the past six years, and whose interests extend in so many diverse directions, is of necessity intricate in organization. In addition to teaching and administration, a bewildering variety of talents is needed in carrying out the plans and objectives of the institution. The service departments of the University provide, for example, the work of carpenters and cooks, typists and nurses, physicians and plant engineers, janitors and watchmen, plumbers and painters, accountants and photographers, mechanics and laundry workers, electricians and dietitians, to mention but a few. An almost interminable number of trades and professions are represented in the hundreds of men and women who serve the University in other capacities than the ones most infrequently recalled when the word "university" is spoken.

When it is realized that the number of individuals who are currently employed by the University at Lawrence and at the Medical Center in Kansas City in all capacities totals nearly 3,000, the necessity for a large income becomes appar-

University foreign students. Photographed in the Memorial Union Building, 1951.

ent. Our income, however, especially that from the Legislature, has of necessity been unusually large in recent years, for a variety of reasons. Inflation, which has sent all costs spiralling upward, and a continued large enrollment, despite the decrease which occurred after 1948-49, have contributed their share. Another major factor has been a continuation of the building program of the University. Construction of added facilities during the war years was virtually impossible, a situation which continued because of shortage of materials for several years after the war.

One of the first major additions to the Lawrence campus, when construction again became possible, was completed late in 1949 and had its formal opening on January 18, 1950. This contribution consisted of two wings added to the University Library. The expansion of this vital center of University activity had been needed for many years and the enlargement of research and service activities after the war made increased space a necessity, especially since several remarkable collections have been added to the Library in recent years. The Ellis Collection in the field of natural history (valued at $500,000) and more recently the Fitzpatrick Collection (chiefly botany) and the John Crerar Collection in the history and theory of economics, have swelled the Library holdings to a number which now exceeds 600,000 volumes. From the size and variety of its holdings, this branch of the University is

176

rapidly taking its place as one of the important libraries of the trans-Mississippi West. The professional libraries, too, have been enlarged, and on the Lawrence campus the new modern home of the library of the Law School was occupied in the fall of 1953. It is an addition to Green Hall and can house 100,000 volumes. At the Medical Center an important library gift of recent years has been the Clendening Collection in the history and philosophy of medicine.

The facilities of the University Libraries were, in effect, also greatly extended by the formation in 1949 of the Midwest Interlibrary Center in Chicago. This organization, of which the University was one of ten charter members, is a cooperative institution in which the member universities have contributed certain of their holdings. Housed in its own building, the Center loans to its members any of their holdings on request. The rapid development of the extensive scientific Linda Hall Library in Kansas City has likewise been of benefit to the University, as its holdings are now catalogued in the University Library. Teletype and rapid delivery service facilitate the ease with which all these materials can be obtained.

If library and books were provided in increasing size and numbers for the intellectual life of students and faculty, their physical comforts were not completely overlooked. Since an addition to the Union Building completed in 1948 was far from adequate, plans for a million-dollar addition to double its size were actively under way in the spring of 1950 and construction was started in the summer; the Faculty Club was in progress at this time, but shortage of materials was to delay its opening until May, 1951. Dormitories and scholarship halls to house students were also being provided, but not until 1951 and 1952 did they affect the problem of student living.

The problem of student clothing, however, was easily settled by students of 1950—for both men and women in increasing numbers wore blue jeans, though not without exciting comment. A woman wearing jeans, one observant male student wrote, "is one of the most unsightly and disgusting things I have yet had the dubious honor of viewing." A female defender of the jean—or is it jeans?—replied by stating, "It may be giving away a trade secret but they make a girl feel a little easier. None of this careful pattering around. With jeans, you can romp as steadily as the most playful male, but yet have no fear of creating a minor sensation." She went on to say that a long, gawky boy in tight jeans was no work of art and that the better-upholstered males when arrayed in this manner were no pictures of grace and manly beauty. When members of the faculty took to wearing jeans—yes, sir, I have seen them with my own eyes—the height of Western university informality in attire had been achieved.

Still another factor in student appearance which would have given a founding father of the University considerable pause if he could have suddenly been transported in time to the campus of 1949-50, was the presence of many foreign students, some of whom still retained their native dress. At one time nearly 200 such students from 46 nations were among those enrolled. International relations were further extended at the same time for both students and faculty, through the use of a considerable number of Fulbright grants.

But the boys of 1950 had more serious problems than those of blue jeans or the flaming robes of foreign students. As summer rolled around, the gradual involvements of the Korean War led again to anxieties and uncertainties in student plans. Draft calls were affecting more and more lives, and even veterans of World War II, especially those enlisted in reserve forces, felt the impact of the world situation. The first of the deferment tests under Selective Service was given in May of 1951, and greatly increased enrollment in officer-training programs on the campus was among the immediate results of troubled days.

Although the effects of the Korean War were doubtless of primary concern to the male students of 1951, two other events before the opening of school in the fall of 1951 were important in the lives of the University community: the flood of 1951 and the resignation of Chancellor Malott.

The flood of 1951 surpassed even the great flood of 1903 in magnitude. The increased development of nearly fifty years along the Kaw basin provided the opportunity for damage which greatly exceeded that caused in 1903. At its height in mid-July, a view from the top of Fraser Hall showed a country that was virtually surrounded by waters extending many miles in width. Although Lawrence was not completely shut off from the rest of the outside world, mail, rail service, freight, and supplies of all kinds were delayed in arrival for some days. University students and staff again were called to aid in battling flood waters and in rescue work.

Chancellor Malott had left before the flood, as his term of office ended on July 1. His resignation, to accept the presidency of Cornell University, had been announced late in January, 1951. The twelve years during which Mr. Malott had been the executive head of the University included a decade which, while not unique in University annals, saw violent extremes and singular measures. Although the decade which included World War I forecast some of the difficulties of the 1940's, the latter decade produced extremes of a different order of magnitude. The enrollment of this decade fluctuated from 3,800 in 1944-45 to a number virtually three times as large in 1948-49. Direct contribution to the war effort on a scale greatly in excess of the years 1917-19 was made and was followed eventually at the close of World War II by a building program involving an expenditure which exceeded by many millions of dollars the amount spent after World War I.

When Mr. Malott left the campus in 1951, there had been completed in the construction program begun after 1945, the addition to Watson Library, North College Hall, and New Fowler Shops. Under construction when he left were the field house for which the Legislature had appropriated over two and a half million dollars,[1] the massive Science Building (completed in the spring of 1954 at a cost of $3,225,-000), the additions to the Union Building, the

---

[1] Delayed in construction because of the steel shortage caused by the Korean War; return to construction was begun in the fall of 1953.

remodeling of the original Fowler Shops for the School of Journalism, as well as major changes at the Medical Center and a number of residence halls to be described in the pages which follow. The Campanile and the Memorial Drive—the World War II Memorial—were virtually complete, the dedication of the Campanile having occurred on May 21, 1951, shortly before Mr. Malott left the campus. Certainly another major change in the appearance of the campus during the Malott administration was the extensive landscaping carried out; efforts which added materially to the beauty of a university setting difficult, if not impossible, to surpass. One of the pleasantest spots on the campus resulting from this program of beautification is the picnic and recreation area overlooking Potter Lake, a gift of the class of 1943. Completed in the summer of 1946, it finds almost continuous use evening after evening during the warmer months. If one would find

relief from the cares of his own troubled world, let him sit here on some quiet summer evening as twilight comes on, the lights of the Campanile appear and are reflected in the still waters of the Lake below, and a soft breeze brings relief from the heat of the day.

This is not the place to make any assessment of the achievements and failures of this period in University history, but to my mind one of the unique and extraordinary accomplishments of Mr. Malott is indicated by a relatively small sum of $600,000 ($300,000 for each of the two years of the biennium) that appeared among the University appropriations for 1951, an appropriation that totaled over sixteen million dollars. Its unique character becomes apparent when its purpose is described. This sum was provided for "General Research." Although appropriations for specific research projects had been allowed in other years

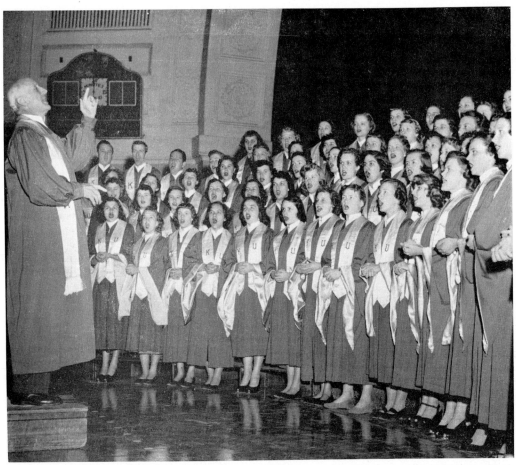

The famed A Cappella Choir, 1950. No organization on the Hill has contributed more to the cultural and emotional life of the University community than has the Choir in its nearly twenty years of existence.

178

—usually small in amount—this was the first time that a fund had been placed under the direction of the University for fundamental research in any direction. Thus, in addition to the sciences, which have profited extensively from outside grants, all fields within the University were eligible for carrying on investigation with the promise of some support. Researchers in philosophy, political science, English, Romance languages, sociology, design, among other fields, have been able to make studies that otherwise would have been impossible, and thus contributed to a primary purpose of the University. Certainly the provision and apportionment of this sum were one of the most enlightened and progressive advances ever made by the University and reflect credit on both Mr. Malott's administration which proposed the idea and the Legislature which made it possible.

81. Advances in Medical Education

It comes as a shocking surprise for many to know that in 1906 with a population of 1,544,968, Kansas had 2,732 physicians; in 1948, with an increase in population to more than 1,900,000, the number of physicians had fallen to about 1,900. To put it another way, with an increase of 20% in population, the number of physicians in Kansas not only has not increased proportionately but has actually fallen by 30%.
—Franklin D. Murphy in the *Graduate Magazine*, October, 1948.

THE health of Kansas citizens has long been a matter of major interest to the University and much effort, time, and ability have been expended in years past in both preventive and alleviative medicine. The years of World War II left little time for outside service by the Medical School as this division of the University, like all others, carried on a continuous year-around schedule in the efforts to keep up the supply of nurses and physicians against an ever increasing demand. After 1941 no building funds were available at the Medical School until 1947, when a legislative appropriation of some $50,000 was made for an addition to one of the ward buildings.[1]

The problem of public health, including medical education, was soon recognized as one of the major and most difficult problems of post-war years. Following the appointment of Franklin D. Murphy as dean of the Medical School on July 1, 1948, a co-ordinated effort by several agencies devised a three-part plan, whose realization would attempt an answer to the problems raised. To provide more physicians, nurses, and technicians for Kansas, extensive expansion of the Medical School facilities was proposed; an expansion that would raise the annual number of medical graduates from 80 to 100. To insure that the young M.D. should remain in Kansas, it was urged that Kansas communities, especially the smaller ones, should build and equip small hospitals or clinics. To keep the physicians of Kansas up-to-date on modern medical procedures, it was proposed that a variety of postgraduate courses be frequently given by the Medical School. Although this plan was sponsored by the University, the Kansas State Medical Society, and the State Board of Health, the burden of presenting it to Kansans fell largely on the shoulders of Dean Murphy. For some months Dean Murphy traveled over the state, discussing the plan in many communities and before many organizations. The approval and aid of the influential Kansas Farm Bureau were obtained, and the needs of the Medical School in carrying out the plan were presented to the Legislature of 1949. With the widespread approval of the citizens of the state, the Rural Health Bill was passed by the Legislature. An appropriation of nearly four million dollars was made available for use in extensive additions to the hospitals and the Medical School. The Kansas City facilities, which on June 13, 1947, had become the University of Kansas Medical Center by action of the Board of Regents, were enlarged between 1949 and 1954 by additions to the ward buildings and the nurses' home, by erection of the Basic Science Building, the Clinic Building, and the Service Building, and by special buildings for chest diseases and psychiatry. The generous support by the state brought welcome and substantial grants from the National Heart Association and the National Cancer Association, which aided in the construction and equipping of a number of these buildings. Private gifts also provided a Public Health Laboratory Building, as well as the most recently completed building on the medical campus, the Continuation Study-Student Union Center. The

---

[1] An exception to this statement was a legislative appropriation of $10,000 in 1943 for "equipment."

View of University of Kansas Medical Center from the air, 1953.

last building, completed early in 1954, at a cost of over half a million dollars, was the result of a great many contributions. Friends and associates of Dr. C. B. Francisco, for many years a member of the Medical School staff, were among the early contributors. Mrs. Edward H. Hashinger (the former Mrs. J. R. Battenfeld, Sr.), friends of the Medical Center in Greater Kansas City who more than matched a contribution of $150,000 given by the Kress Foundation of New York City, have made possible this beautiful and useful addition to the facilities of the University. The Kress Foundation also made grants totaling $50,000 a year for five years (beginning in 1951) to further the postgraduate study programs at the Center and to establish a pilot program in the education of practical nurses; grants that will be of direct aid in carrying out the program originally proposed in 1948.[1] Extensive gifts for medical research from Dixon Fagerburg, of Prescott, Arizona, and from the estate of Henry J. Haskell have also done their share in making the University of Kansas Medical Center one of the best-equipped and best-integrated institutions for medical education and research in the nation.

If the Medical Center was fortunate in having in recent years such a host of generous and liberal friends, the campus at Lawrence has also benefited from loyal friends. In addition to the gifts referred to in our preceding chapter, especial note should be made of the progress in University housing. The residence halls, Templin and Battenfeld, mentioned in section 71, became in the course of several post-war years the nucleus of a considerable group of dormitories. Pearson and Stevenson Halls for men and Sellards Hall for women were added to the group in 1951. Across Louisiana Street from this group, Carruth (the "old" Chancellor's residence) was razed in 1953, and there are now (early 1954) in the process of construction two women's dormitories, Douthart Hall and Grace Pearson Hall. Two men's residences had been added, Jolliffe Hall (east and south of the above group) in 1942 and Foster Hall (at 1200 Louisiana Street) in 1943. One of the most recent developments in student housing was the beginning, in the fall of 1953, of two connected dormitories for men, Carruth-O'Leary Halls. At the west end of the campus above Potter Lake they will provide together quarters for 200 men.

More than $600,000 toward the construction of these dormitories have been gifts from Mr. O. Jolliffe of Peabody, Kansas, from Lela Douthart, '99, and her sister Ava Douthart Chronister, '01, (supplemented by a gift from Mrs. Chronister's husband, Mr. Bert Chronister of Kansas City), and from Mr. J. R. Pearson and his wife Grace Sellards Pearson of the class of '01, of Corsicana, Texas. The Endowment Association has also contributed generously to this development in the life of the University. The remaining costs of construction and equipment will be provided by the issuance of bonds, authorized by law, which will be slowly retired from earnings.

Although progress has been made and is being made on the solution of the housing problem, it will be an ever continuing one. Over 2,500 students now live in private homes off the campus. It is estimated that in the next ten years, the University enrollment will reach 10,000 students and even with continued development of dormitory facilities in this period a greater number of students than is now the case, will be living in private homes.

In addition to these gifts to the University which are of so much aid in solving the housing problem, two other gifts should be mentioned. In 1945, friends of the late William Allen White by gifts which now total $100,000 established the William Allen White Foundation. The primary purpose of the Foundation is to further the cause of Kansas journalism by holding annual editorial conferences and lectures and by the creation of a historical center of American journalism, particularly the journalism of the Midwest. The Reid collection of newspaper cartoons, for example, is an important part of the material available in this historical center.

Communications between Kansans and their less fortunate fellow men—an activity in which Kansans have always taken particular delight—can be effected in more ways than one in this modern day. The facilities for another type of communication were greatly enlarged for the University in September, 1952, when KANU went on the air. KANU, an FM radio station, and the most powerful in Kansas, was a gift of Jack and Sid Harris, members of a family long known in Kansas journalism. As a matter of fact, the University now operates three radio stations, for, in addition to KANU, KFKU, the original station which went on the air in 1924, and KDGU find use. KFKU, an AM station, still

---

[1] Altogether, since the close of World War II, some seven million dollars for buildings and equipment have been expended at the Medical Center.

broadcasts after thirty years but on a restricted schedule, and KDGU is used solely for the instruction of students. The activities of the University in this field resulted on July 1, 1951, in the establishment of a division of radio and television. Although the University hopes to operate its own educational television station in the near future, a pioneering step in television for teaching in a medical school was initiated in September, 1949, at the Medical Center by the use of a closed-circuit television system. This initial step was followed on November 29, 1951, at the Center by the transmission of color television for instruction.

82. A Change of Administration

To be given the administrative responsibility of directing a great university, can, in most circumstances, be expected to stir deep currents of feeling in a man. But to one who spent his boyhood under the regional influence of this University, whose father was a member of its faculty, and who, himself, learned to love its beautiful campus as a student—to one so situated, an occasion like this is bound to create violent riptides of emotion, defying expression.

—From the inaugural address of Dr. Murphy, September 17, 1951.

THE appointment of a new administrative head is always an important event in the life of the University; second only, if we may judge by the volume of newspaper comment, to the appointment of a new football coach. The academic life of a football coach, however, is usually not long. The term of office, on the other hand, of the University chancellors has been, at least in recent years, of long duration. Furthermore, even most rabid sports followers would be willing to agree, if they could be stopped long enough to reflect, that the chancellorship is the most important single office in the University.

Following the resignation of Chancellor Malott, the Board of Regents began their search for his successor. The name of Franklin D. Murphy was early submitted and from the start of the Regents' canvass, his name was the most frequently discussed possibility. His extensive travels over the state during his three years of deanship of the Medical School had made him many friends, and his advocacy of the Rural Health Plan had brought him national recognition. Young, energetic, and friendly, he became the unanimous choice of the Board. His appointment was announced July 2, 1951, and Dr. Murphy assumed office the following September. Dean John H. Nelson of the Graduate School served as Acting Chancellor in the interim between Mr. Malott's resignation and Dr. Murphy's arrival on the campus.

The installation of Dr. Murphy as the ninth Chancellor of the University took place at an all-University convocation on September 17, 1951. After his installation by the chairman of the Board, Lester McCoy, Chancellor Murphy made his inaugural address. The youngest of the nine chancellors upon his acceptance of the office, Dr. Murphy, of the class of 1936, was thirty-five years old at the time of his inaugural.[1] Despite his youthfulness, he was—and is—understanding and considerate. His three years of public life as dean of the Medical School stood him in good stead and his appointment met with widespread approval. Some light will be thrown on his character by a personal story which may help to re-

Chancellor-elect Murphy (right) and Acting Chancellor Nelson, July 2, 1951.

[1] Dr. Whitney Griswold, president of Yale University, in the fall of 1951 told Dr. Murphy, who soon tired of being pointed to as the youngest president of a major university and who threatened to dye his hair gray: "Two more years at the job and your hair will *fall out*." After examining several portraits of Dr. Murphy in the intervening years, I am inclined to think Dr. Griswold is an inductive scientist of great acumen.

From the Picnic Ground above Potter Lake toward the Campanile. September, 1952.

lieve a bare recital of facts in these pages and which may therefore be warranted. Shortly after Dr. Murphy's appointment as dean of the Medical School he appeared and spoke on the Lawrence campus. At the conclusion of his talk I went up and introduced myself. "Why," he said, "I already know you. I was in your class in physical chemistry in 1935." A quicker-witted person would have replied, "To be sure. I recall you now. You were the bright boy on the front row who always asked such intelligent questions." Instead I blurted, "Well, you couldn't have been awfully poor or awfully good in class because I don't remember you." I did take the trouble to look him up in my roll book and found that my memory was really defective, as Franklin Murphy had made an excellent record in physical chemistry. One might think Dr. Murphy would have resented my ungracious reply but apparently he bears me no ill-will, for he speaks to me nearly every time he sees me and at times even smiles faintly.

Dr. Murphy had more important tasks, however, than recalling the behavior of former teachers at the University. The complex University budget had to be prepared for the Legislature of 1953, housing problems were pressing, and the achievements and needs of the University had to be presented time and time again to the people of the state.

That the Legislature recognized these achievements and needs, so well presented by the young Chancellor, is shown in the fact that nearly nineteen million dollars was appropriated for the use of the University at Lawrence and Kansas City for the two years 1953-55. How extraordinarily complex, extensive, and expensive the University had become by 1953 is shown again when it is realized that these appropriated funds represent slightly less than half the income of the University; gifts and fees of many kinds making up the remainder of the University income.

Although the University enrollment decreased with Dr. Murphy's arrival on the campus, a trend

183

"Do any of you remember where I was when my lecture was interrupted—I've given it so many times I wasn't listening."

"I'll continue now, if there are no further irrelevant questions."

College Humor of 1953. From the *Daily Kansan*, February 11 and March 23, 1953. Compare these cartoons with those on pages 20, 31, 33, 69, and 70, to see what students of earlier generations thought was funny.

that had already made itself apparent because of a decrease in veteran enrollment and the effects of the Korean War, the following year (the fall of 1952) showed an unexpected increase of some four hundred students, and a still larger enrollment resulted the following year.[2] The tide, apparently, is coming in again.

Certainly one of the most vividly remembered events attendant upon Dr. Murphy's initial year was the record of the basketball team. Big Seven champions—of course—the team went on to win regional play-offs, the national intercollegiate title and, in a final burst of glory, a place on the Olympic team of 1952. Each of these events brought enthusiastic celebrations at Lawrence—usually the celebration occurred after midnight—

until even the most rabid sports enthusiasts were exhausted with their efforts and thankful that there were no more crowns for the team to gain.

If the mention of basketball prowess seems of importance in a University history, far less spectacular but probably in the long view of greater importance are the advances of the University in its function as a repository of man's cultural knowledge. For example, although few basketball fans of the early 1950's ever noted the changes in the Museum of Art in this period, nevertheless significant changes were made. Completely reorganized and remodeled with a new organ installed and new collections acquired, the Museum celebrated an official reopening on February 2, 1951. In succeeding years, extended loans by the Metropolitan Museum of New York have made available for study and enjoyment to all interested, including no doubt some basketball enthusiasts, the work of many artists not previously available in the Midwest.

---

[2] The figures from the Registrar's office give a grand total (Lawrence and Kansas City) of 7,886 for 1951-52 and 8,235 for 1952-53. The figure for 1953-54 had not been compiled as this note goes to press, but the fall enrollment of 1953 was up a little better than 5 per cent over that of the previous fall.

184

83. After Eighty-seven Years

It goes without saying that the general level in Kansas is thought to be exceptionally high. Kansans do not regard themselves as mere Westerners, like Iowans or Nebraskans. Having passed through a superior heat, they are Westerners seven times refined. "It is the quality of piety in Kansas," says Mr. E. H. Abbott, "to thank God that you are not as other men are, beer-drinkers, shiftless, habitual lynchers, or even as these Missourians."—Carl Becker, *Kansas,* 1910.

WHEN the school year of 1952-53 closed, the University had completed its eighty-seventh year. Through its halls has flowed a never-ending stream of youth whose numbers have grown far more rapidly than the years. Over a hundred thousand students have come and gone and still the stream flows on. Those who have left Mount Oread have spread across the land, some to the far corners of the world. Many have finished their tasks, but through them and through those who remain, the influence of their alma mater has been carried afar. To many—and let us hope to most—of its living sons and daughters, the vision of the University on the Hill returns again and again to aid, to comfort, and to encourage them on their way.

During 1954, Kansas celebrates the one hundredth anniversary of its establishment as a territory in these United States of ours. For eighty-seven of these one hundred years, the University has played its part. This transformation of a wilderness to a great commonwealth, and as one of the facets of this growth, the transformation of a bare and treeless hill into a community of learning, is a change at which I never cease to marvel. This change is all the more remarkable when it is realized that there are persons still living in Kansas who encompass the entire life of the University. Not many months ago, for example, a man in an audience which I addressed was intro-duced to me, and he told me that he came as a youngster to Wyandotte County, Kansas Territory, in 1857.

This relative youth of the state and of the University also impresses many of our students and visitors from abroad where age—a venerable age of centuries—is usual, and an upstart stripling of a hundred years or less is merely at the beginning of its activities.

But what has been the culminative result of these years, few in history, but long in the life of a single individual?

To many, the University of Kansas is the embodiment of lofty spirit and high ideals and a recollection of the goodly company of faculty men and women who, shaping those ideals and creating that spirit, spent long lives in the service of Kansas youth. In the faith of these idealists, then, the University is an intangible spirit of service, a creator of passion for knowledge, beauty, and justice. Does this faith seem visionary and fantastic in a very real and practical world? Has the University lived up to any such idealistic creed?

Only the future can give the complete answer to these questions. We are yet too young to make any more than a fragmentary and imperfect judgment. What we now consider our successes, the future may disregard. It is with greatest temerity, then, that any judgment is passed. If any criticism is advanced—and it will be exceedingly mild—remember that it is advanced in the same spirit that actuates a loving wife, who "will do anything for her husband except to stop criticiz-

One of the more than 1,700 courses offered by the University. After assiduously reading the University catalog I have arrived at the conclusion that these serious young ladies are members of a class in "Interior Design." Photograph, December, 1952.

"New" Fowler Shops, April, 1953. The view looks northwest; that is, it was taken on the south side of the Hill.

Lindley Hall, April, 1953. The view looks southwest.

ing him," in the hope—usually in vain, I fear—that she will improve him. If our affection for the University is genuine, it should not blind us to its mistakes and shortcomings.

Viewed in the light of the students who have come under its influence, the University has achieved its greatest successes in its graduates who have been stimulated in their pursuit of knowledge; to a lesser extent in its students who have won some distinction in the accomplishment of justice; and to a still smaller degree in those students who have been the creators of beauty.

It must be admitted that if we are to claim credit for the achievements of our students, we shall also have to be judged by those of our graduates upon whom we have left little imprint. If, through some fault of the University, there be those among its graduates whose character has not yet been deepened and chastened, who have not received some intellectual and spiritual impetus, who have not developed into honorable, responsible, and intelligent citizens, to that extent the University has failed in its purpose.

We do not keep track of our failures as assiduously as we do of our successes; but if ever the account be drawn, we can rest assured that the thousands of students who have justified the promise of their youth and the expectations of their alma mater will far outnumber those upon whom we have left no mark. But to forget any of our mistakes, we point with pride to those of our students who, being blessed by greater talents or greater fortune, have achieved, vicariously for us, our greatest successes. It is with satisfaction that we claim, "Kansas ranked first among all state universities or colleges in the proportion of its graduates starred in *American Men of Science*" or the "University of Kansas has a higher percentage of its Engineering alumni

represented in *Who's Who in Engineering* than several of the most famous schools of engineering and leads all schools in the Middle West." With equal satisfaction we also call attention to those among the students of the University who have achieved success as liberal leaders and writers, apostles of social and economic justice. No other names than those of William E. Borah and William Allen White need be mentioned in this connection; but many others could be added to the list of men and women who have labored for the common good as long and as valiantly, if not as illustriously, as these two.

All of these representatives of the University have been concerned with the "practical" affairs of men or things. Many—possibly all—have been creative artists in their own fashion; but we usually look in vain, at least among the older students, for those who have achieved reputations as outstanding in the field more correctly called the creative arts. Artists, dramatists, composers, novelists, poets are represented by a very small number in our group of distinguished former students and graduates.[1] True, the total number is smaller, and the chances of success therefore are smaller, but the lack of both success and number traces back to the same source.

The natural inquiry concerning the cause of these differences is difficult to answer, as many factors enter in. During the latter part of the present life of the University, say from 1916 on, the twentieth century influence—the influence of the prosaic and blasé automobile and stadium age—may have been the predominating one. It is on the successes of our students in the earlier years, however, that our reputation has been largely established. Confining our attention solely to this earlier period, one might plausibly suggest that the preponderance of graduate successes in

[1] This statement does not mean that University representatives of the creative arts have made no contributions to our culture. They have; but I am here referring to the achievement of groups as measured by present standards; for example, the reputation of scientists as a group compared with that of artists as a group. It is difficult to name a University graduate who has achieved a national or international reputation as a professional novelist, dramatist, artist, or composer. Even as late as 1930, the Kansas Historical Society compiled a list of Kansas musicians, i.e., musicians who had ever lived in Kansas, been born in Kansas, or been trained in Kansas. Not one in the list who had been a student at the University had achieved sufficient national recognition to be listed in *Who's Who in America*. A similar list for artists, published in 1928, showed only one University student who had ever been included in *Who's Who*, Albert T. Reid; but even Reid is listed as "a publisher, writer, artist." Although one recognizes the inadequacy of a criterion involving inclusion in *Who's Who*, such comparisons are about the only ones available.

186

the sciences, in engineering and law, in journalism and business (in the practical as against what —for want of better word—I may call the idealistic professions) is the logical result of the environment of a frontier and agrarian state. Although the day of the frontier has passed, the children and grandchildren of the frontier were our older students. They were brought up in an era when the frontier influence was still the prevailing one; where the first law of nature took precedence over all others; where the practical aspect of life was the predominant one. It is amazing that any beauty should have been created under these conditions. Not that there was no beauty in the external world, for such lines as:

A haze on the far horizon,—
The infinite, tender sky,—
The ripe, rich tint of the corn-fields,
The wild geese sailing high,

show that there was and is; but the hands and voices to make this beauty articulate have been all too few and far between.

Postponing for the moment further analysis of the causes of this condition, one may point out that developments in recent years should, in time, rectify this situation. The growth of the School of Fine Arts, the establishment of the Department of Speech and Drama, and a greater emphasis on and realization of the possibilities of the past Kansas scene as source material for all the arts cannot fail to produce some fruit. The tragic days of territorial and Civil War Kansas,

the growing pains of the late sixties presenting kaleidoscopic views of civilian, army, and Indian life, the disasters of the seventies, the expansion into western Kansas in the eighties, the turbulent days of the Populists' nineties, to say nothing of the more recent adversities of the Dust Bowl era, are pregnant themes which all the arts may utilize in fusing the past with the present; a powerful aid in prepetuating the democratic life as the Kansan sees it. That the next dozen years—before the one hundredth birthday of the University is reached—will produce a far richer fruition in Kansas art, I do not doubt. Once the direction has been given and the possibilities revealed, the very fact that we are so recently descended from a state not greatly past its frontier days will, in itself, furnish the wellspring for the arts. Citizens of a western frontier state, I believe, had outstanding characteristics; they were an acquisitive but an independent and creative people; they transformed a wilderness into a new kind of civilization. It matters not what additional qualities—or lack of qualities—they possessed, they were creators. Is not this a plausible explanation of the fact that the sons and grandsons of these creators have distinguished themselves in the creative sciences? Possessing this creative quality, our gifted students were caused by their environment to put it to some immediate or practical use. Enthusiastic teachers in the persons of Snow, Blake, Marvin, Bailey, Haworth, and Williston doubtless furnished the di-

The massive character of the new physical science building which houses the Departments of Physics and of Chemistry and the School of Pharmacy, is seen from this photograph taken in the summer of 1954. The view looks north; that is, it is the rear of the building and its parking area that are portrayed. On November 5, 1954, the $3,250,000 building was named Malott Hall for former Chancellor Malott.

Sellards Hall, April, 1953, looking southwest. The white building which is seen at the left of Sellards Hall is now Jolliffe Hall.

rective influences which have been responsible for the greater success of our students in science and engineering.

If this creative quality, however, has been productive in the sciences, it will eventually flower in the creative arts—if the influences of the automobile age have not too greatly diluted this impelling force. As a matter of fact, in quite recent years, there are evidences that "the ultimate cradle of American creative expression will be located in the Middle West." The University is beginning to realize its part in this cultural growth.

But we must return briefly to the cause of our lack of success in the creative arts. We come from so many racial stocks that this past deficiency cannot be attributed to any lack of love of beauty. Rather, we must call attention to the lack of direction in these avenues and to a lack of training and appreciation. The two deficiencies are intimately related. Training itself involves direction—and expense. Since culture—to use the term as meaning the appreciation of and production in the creative arts—is expensive, a realistic frontier dictated its elimination,—if it considered culture at all. Bread came first, and the fancy trimmings of life could be acquired if and when money was available.

In the early years of the University, funds were available to give only the practical courses, and training in the arts—outside of music—was a very minor element in the offerings of the University. Even as late as 1902—when the University had reached nearly half its present age—out of a total enrollment of more than 1,200 students there were only forty-five regularly enrolled undergraduates in the School of Fine Arts, and doubtless most of those were in music. Only one teacher gave instruction in drawing and painting;

188

and the home of Fine Arts in this period,—well, the reader should turn back to page 55.

In fact, this lack of appreciation of the creative arts is nowhere more apparent than in the external features of the University. With a site scarcely equalled by any university in the country, there has been assembled on its crest a collection of buildings of many diverse forms; and placed, considering the magnificence of the location, with little architectural planning. At least fifteen types of architecture—including good examples of the neo-mongrel style—have been used in erecting the University buildings; and at least four distinct types of campus planning have been suggested,—and none followed with any degree of success. Not that we are without beautiful buildings, for we have a considerable number. Nor are we alone in the matter of lack of campus planning, for there are few universities in the country, especially state universities, that have followed any definite plan of development. Long ago, however, Thomas Jefferson had led the way in designing the campus of the University of Virginia. Anyone who has seen the Virginia campus will agree that the unity of design planned by Jefferson—but not even there completely utilized—adds to the impressiveness and dignity of the buildings. Order and unity, according to students of the arts, are roots of all beauty. Both are lacking in considerable measure on our campus. Fortunately, the beauty of distant valleys overshadows the lack of campus planning.[2]

One reason for this architectural deficiency comes back again directly to the matter of cost. Planning, and following definite plans, costs money. Money comes from the state, which has

[2] In case you are interested in this point, I have made a few additional observations in the notes to section 83.

The enlarged Memorial Union, April, 1953. Looking northwest. The wing at the left was formally opened in the spring of 1953.

to be convinced that artistic desirability is a practical necessity; a difficult task, to say the least.

Still another complicating factor in the architectural development of the campus, and for that matter, in all phases of University development, is the fact that the University is conducted by a biennial method. All plans must be made as if the University were to have a life of only two years beyond its last appropriation. It is little wonder, then, that expediency and emergency have played their part in wrecking any plans for campus development. An important step forward in this respect has been taken by the Legislature of 1941 in the enactment of a long-term plan, which will provide funds from a state-wide mill tax—a tax made possible by popular vote in 1918 but not enacted into working law until 1941—for the building needs of all state schools.

The University is seen differently through the eyes of each student, of each faculty member, of each visitor. Each observer has his own impressions, colored by his likes and dislikes, by his previous experiences, by his own background. In order that the impressions and judgments included in this brief history be not solely those of an ancient faculty member, I recently asked four students of today to tell me what were their impressions by asking them what they liked best about the University, what they found most objectionable, and what events they considered the most important of their years on the Hill. As they provided answers that were independent, I shall make a summary of their judgments here. All four thought the friendly attitude of Hill inhabitants one of the most striking features of University life. The beautiful campus was still another University asset greatly admired. As for

Student room, April, 1954, North College Hall. Compare this student room with the one sixty years earlier shown on page 51. The dolls and the textbooks (geology and Greek plays) show that our students are still in an "in-between" age.

important events of University life, the most important in the lives of these youngsters were the basketball victories of 1952. Objectionable features of University life included unfairness of some teachers, racial discrimination shown by townspeople, and, it seems to me a particularly acute observation, so great an emphasis on sports that other activities are virtually excluded: "—students are missing the point when they live for sports and forget about the other wonderful opportunities the University has to offer." Judging from the reaction of the public at large, sports continue, after graduation, to be the most important single feature of interest in University life.

The University as seen through the eyes of an observer from abroad was briefly summarized for me by the first Rose Morgan Visiting Professor, Dr. N. A. Faris of Beirut, who was on the campus during the school year of 1953-54. Dr. Faris wrote:

I was impressed by the friendliness of both the University and the community and by the vitality of academic life in general. I was amazed at the extent of the activities which the University undertakes throughout the State, but often wondered how many of these are really the function of a university. I was gratified at the truly enlightened and international outlook of the institution, but was equally shocked to note the persistence of some vestiges of provincialism which at an extreme seemed to exclude most of the world outside Douglas County.

But the general impression was one of throbbing life and growth. Maturity, not yet apparent, is sure to come, where life and

A ballroom can have more than one use, as this photograph shows. Conferences are held the year around in the modern air-conditioned Memorial Union Building. The photograph, taken January 28, 1953, shows a state-wide United Nations conference.

vigor abound and where men and ideas are in constant interaction. Though a state institution, I found the University a haven of freedom and an arena for free thought. May it always so remain.

If there is any institution that epitomizes the growth of democracy, it is the state university. One principle upon which democracy is based is the education of all its people through schools provided by the common purse, schools ranging from the kindergarten to the state university. That the common purse has largely been responsible for the physical growth of the University of Kansas, these pages have testified time and time again. I do not know how many times the words "the Legislature" have appeared between these covers; if not on every page, certainly on every other one. To the members of the Legislature, the representatives of the people, has fallen the duty of determining the appropriations for the support of the University. Through discussion and argument, these appropriations have been made; made by a truly democratic process.

Thus, at the end of eighty-seven years, the University of Kansas stands, a bulwark built by the people of the state; one bulwark against ignorance, injustice, and intolerance in an insane world. If one primary purpose of the University is to train its citizens in securing an honorable, decent, and important living, a second purpose of equal value, and one which cannot be measured in dollars and cents, is to inculcate as never before a spirit of service, a love of knowledge, of beauty, and of justice in the hearts and minds of its students.

Have you ever lifted your eyes toward Mount Oread at twilight? Listen, while Helen Jaka, of the class of '24, expresses what you may have felt:

Dusk falls, and now a star appears,
A single gem of light, above thy buildings
Etched against a sky
That breathes the coming night.
One window seeks to catch and hold
The last clear light of day,
And mirrors in its heart, the red
Against a field of gray.
The golden fingers of the sun
Reach down at noon to thee,
And, trembling, paint around thy walls
A gilded canopy.
But I would have thee standing there,
With one clear star on high,
While shadows lurk around thy walls,
And far-flown night-birds cry.

Do memories come rushing in, does longing for distant days overwhelm you? Remember that only by fulfilling the obligations of the present can any hope and promise of the future be assured.

Sources and Notes

SECTION 1

Several reviews of the early history of Mount Oread have been published. The most useful is one by Sydney Prentice, of the class of 1896; see the *Graduate Magazine*, v. 17, 1918-19, p. 102. The quotation used in the first section is credited to Charles Robinson in a small pamphlet published in 1854: *Nebraska and Kansas. Report of the Committee of the Massachusetts Emigrant Aid Co.* (Boston), p. 14. The words appear in a portion of Robinson's diary written when he was on his way to California in 1849 and dated May 11, 1849. It seems probable that Robinson's view of the surrounding territory which produced the quotation was on an elevation some miles east of Mount Oread and not from Mount Oread itself. For early contemporary information and description of Mount Oread see Sara T. L. Robinson, *Kansas, Its Interior and Exterior Life*, Boston, 1856, p. 37. Mrs. Robinson also (p. 11) describes the naming of Mount Oread; see also Andreas (below), pp. 308 and 313. A letter dated "Mount Oread, Kansas Territory, August 17, 1854" appeared in the *Boston Daily Commonwealth*, Sept. 4, 1854. It is the earliest contemporary mention of Mount Oread in the newspapers of the day that I have seen. For the original Mount Oread and the school on its summit (at Worcester, Massachusetts), see Martha B. Wright (editor), *History of the Oread Collegiate Institute*, New Haven, 1905, p. 2.

A portrait of Monchonsia will be found in Thomas L. McKenney, *History of Indian Tribes of North America*, Philadelphia (*ca.* 1836-38), Plates, v. 11. Other Kanza chieftains are portrayed and described in George Catlin's *North American Indians*, London, 1876, v. 2, p. 23. The dispossession of Indian tribes from Kansas Territory is described in *Indian Reservations in Kansas and the Extinguishment of Their Title* by Anna H. Abel, Master's Thesis, University of Kansas, 1900; reprinted in *Kansas Historical Collections*, 1904, v. 8, pp. 73 ff. The quotation "as long as the grass should grow and the water should run" is requoted from Miss Abel, p. 86 (*K.H.C.*). Actually Mount Oread and its surroundings prior to 1854 and back

to 1825 were part of the Shawnee Reservation. Originally, this region had been part of the Osage domain with Kanza territory just across the river; see Abel, cited above. The "Shining Mountains" was the original appellation of the Rockies; see R. G. Thwaites (editor), *Original Journals of Lewis and Clark Expedition*, New York, 1904, v. 2, p. 176.

For the location of the California Road, I am indebted to Professor James C. Malin, of the Department of History, who has examined the contemporary maps in the Land Office at Washington. Reference to the California (and Oregon) Road is made by Mrs. Robinson, cited above (p. 37); see also lithograph in the possession of the Kansas State Historical Society (Topeka), "View of Lawrence, Kansas, Looking South West, May, 1858." A ceremony dedicating an Oregon (California-Oregon) Trail Marker on the University campus was held April 17, 1954.

For reference to border wars in territorial days, see Mrs. Robinson, cited above; *Harper's Weekly*, v. 1, June 6, 1857, p. 356 (view of Mount Oread); A. T. Andreas, *History of the State of Kansas*, Chicago, 1883, pp. 81 *et seq.* The most exhaustive and scholarly treatment of any part of the Kansas territorial troubles will be found in James C. Malin's *John Brown and the Legend of Fifty-six*, Philadelphia, 1942, 794 pages. The flood of 1844 is also described in Andreas, p. 292.

From a topographic map furnished by Professor W. H. Schoewe, of the Department of Geology, the following facts were obtained:

North Hill, the original site of the University, is 150 feet above the floor of the valley; the site of Fraser Hall is some 70 feet higher.

It is 3/5 of a mile from North College to Fraser Hall and the same distance from North College to the nearest contact with the Kaw. Fraser Hall is 2/5 of a mile east of the California trail. Early maps show a sudden elevation in the Hill at about the present location of Twelfth Street.

SECTION 2

Speer's remarks will be found in the *Lawrence Daily Tribune*, Dec. 7, 1871, p. 1, c. 2.

The second quotation is from the *Third Annual Report of Superintendent of Public Instruction for the Year Ending December 31, 1863*, p. 53.

For charters granted collegiate institutions in early territorial days, see *Statutes of the Territory of Kansas Passed at the First Session*, 1855, pp. 789, 931, 936, 939; *Laws of the Territory of Kansas, Second Session of General Legislative Assembly*, 1857, pp. 112-122. The charter of the "University of Kansas Territory" will be found in the first citation, p. 931.

The *New York Tribune* account will be found in the issue for Jan. 10, 1857, p. 6, c. 5.

The copy of the Wyandotte constitution that I have used will be found in *General Statutes of Kansas*, 1889, v. 1, p. 50. Paragraphs 75 (p. 50), 141 (p. 73), and 183 (p. 86) deal with the University. The early history of the organization of the University is described in Wilson Sterling's *Quarter-Centennial History of the University of Kansas*, Topeka, 1891, pp. 65-77; see also my article in the *Kansas City Star*, Sept. 12, 1937, p. 1C.

The act organizing the University was first published in *The Laws of the State of Kansas, 1864*, Lawrence, 1864, pp. 195-199. The first meeting of the Board of Regents was held March 21, 1865; see *Journal of the Board of Regents of the Kansas State University*, v. 1 (MS), p. 4. This source of information is referred to hereafter as *Journal*.

A report of the Board of Regents in the *Lawrence Daily*

Tribune, Dec. 10, 1865, p. 2, states that the University building had been started and that the Legislature would be asked for $4,000 for professors' salaries and $3,000 for equipment. The *Journal*, p. 22, stated that work began on the building Oct. 1, 1865. The *Tribune* for Feb. 21, 1866, p. 2, reported the debate in the Senate on the original appropriation. The *Junction City Union* for July 7, 1866, p. 2, reported that the University building "is rapidly approaching completion and will be done in about a month"; the *Lawrence Daily Tribune*, July 19, 1866, p. 3, reported that the University building was "now nearly ready for occupancy."

Election of the first faculty was announced in the *Lawrence Daily Tribune*, July 21, 1866, p. 3; see also *Journal*, p. 27, and C. K. Hyder, *Snow of Kansas*, Lawrence, 1953, chap. VI. This source is hereafter referred to as "Hyder."

The view of Lawrence reproduced in this section has been dated (publication date) "1860 or shortly thereafter" in *American Historical Prints*, by I. N. P. Stokes and D. C. Haskell, New York, 1933, p. 125.

Charles Robinson, whose name appears several times in these pages, was the first governor of Kansas when it became a state in 1861. He was early identified with the educational interests of the territory and the state and from 1864 until his death in 1894—with the exception of a short interval—was a member of the University Board of Regents. The most inclusive biography of him is *The Life of Charles Robinson*, by F. W. Blackmar, Topeka, 1902.

SECTION 3

The *Junction City Union*, the *Lawrence Daily Tribune*, and the *Leavenworth Conservative* have all been examined for the years 1865 and 1866, and their contents is the basis of my general discussion in section 3; see also the first few letters of Bayard Taylor, *Colorado, a Summer Trip*, New York, 1867. The most important material dealing with the University and immediate locality of 1866 are Professor Snow's letters. They will be found in the *Graduate Magazine*, v. 3, 1904, p. 81; see also Hyder, chap. VI. For population of Kansas in the sixties see *New York Tribune*, Aug. 6, 1866, p. 6, c. 6; *Kansas Historical Collections*, v. 12, 1912, p. 44; Taft, *Kansas Historical Quarterly*, v. 3, 1934, p. 13, where information on the photographs reproduced in section 3 is also given.

For contemporary mention of early colleges in Kansas see *Leavenworth Conservative*, Oct. 17, 1865, p. 1. For the history of the Kansas colleges mentioned, I have consulted J. T. Willard, *History of Kansas State College*, Manhattan, 1940; Lyman B. Kellogg, "Founding of State Normal School" (Emporia), *Kansas Historical Collections*, v. 12, 1912, p. 88; for Baker University reference should be made to: *Lawrence Daily Tribune*, Jan. 17, 1873, p. 1, c. 2; *Catalog*, 1865-66; *Alumni Record of Baker University*, Baldwin, 1917;[1,2] for Highland College: *Catalog of Highland University*, 1870-71; *100th Anniversary of Founding of Presbyterian Mission at Highland, Kansas*, 1938 (?); for Ottawa University: *Lawrence Daily Tribune*, July 15, 1871, p. 2; *Catalog*, 1879-80; *Catalog*, 1890-91; for Lane University, *Otterbrelasen*, v. 1, 1900; v. 3, 1902;

[1]An interesting sidelight on the quality of collegiate instruction in Kansas in 1866 is found in a letter of Professor Snow's written Sept. 30, 1866; "A young lady presented herself the day before yesterday who had been through the Sophomore year at Baker University. She wanted to enter our Junior year, but we could not comply with her wishes, as according to our standards of scholarship she was not quite ready to enter our Freshman class." See *Graduate Magazine*, v. 3, 1904-5, p. 85.

[2] A recent history of Baker University should be added to the growing fund of information on Kansas collegiate institutions: H. K. Ebright, *The History of Baker University*, Baldwin, Kansas, 1951, 356 pages.

Catalog, 1899; *Topeka Capital*, Nov. 26, 1902; for Lincoln (Washburn) College: *Washburn College Bulletin*, April, 1932, p. 10; *Catalog*, 1867-68; for St. Mary's College: *St. Mary's College Bulletin*, v. 9, No. 2 (1913); *St. Mary's Star*, Oct. 22, 1931, p. 1; for St. Benedict's College: *St. Benedict's College Bulletin*, June, 1939, p. 14.

SECTION 4

For other mention or accounts of the original dedication see *Lawrence Daily Tribune*, Sept. 13, 1866, p. 2; Sept. 25, p. 2; Sept. 14, p. 2, c. 2, 3, 4, 5; the last citation contains Thacher's address.

The data on the opening of other state universities of the Plains states were secured from J. H. McCracken, *American Universities and Colleges*, 2nd edition, 1932; the information on coeducation comes from the same source, p. 11; see also the *Nation*, v. 11, 1870, p. 383, and *Annual Enc. for 1867*, New York, 1868, p. 282.

Copley's quotation on coeducation at the University will be found in his booklet *Kansas and the Country Beyond*, Philadelphia, 1867, p. 60.

SECTION 5

For the selection of the first faculty see Sterling's *Quarter-Centennial History*, p. 84; *Journal*, p. 27; Hyder, chap. VI; for reference to scarcity of collegiate teachers in this period see the *Annual Encyclopedia for 1867*, New York, 1868, p. 282.

Information on Rice will be found in the *Lawrence Daily Tribune*, July 8, 1866, p. 3, c. 1, when Rice visited Lawrence in search of a new location. Rice's poor health was referred to in the Snow letters of 1866, *Graduate Magazine*, v. 3, 1904-5, p. 90, where other reference to Rice will be found.

Rice has been referred to many times in University circles as "president pro-tem." but the available evidence indicates that he was actually president for a brief term. *The Minutes of the Executive Committee of the Board of Regents of the Kansas State University*, p. 23, under date of July 24, 1866, recorded, "Prof. E. J. Rice was by resolution appointed President of the Faculty." The Executive Committee of the Board had power to act between meetings of the entire Board. The date of the Committee meeting shows that Rice was appointed president five days after the election of the first faculty. When the entire Board met again on Dec. 5, 1866, the Board "modified" the action of their Executive Committee and specified that Rice was to be "Acting President of the University"; see *Journal*, p. 29. Rice was therefore in the interval from July 24 to Dec. 5 the President of the Faculty, which accounts for the confusion existing concerning Rice's actual position. In the interval during which he was president, advertising, the first University catalog, Rice's report in the *Sixth Annual Report of the Superintendent of Public Instruction*, 1866, p. 52, all bear Rice's title as "President of the Faculty." After Dec. 5 and until his resignation, he was "Acting President."

For the resignation of Rice see the Snow letters and Professor Robinson's report in the *Seventh Annual Report of the Superintendent of Public Instruction*, 1867, p. 22. For a short biographical sketch of Rice see the *Graduate Magazine*, v. 10, 1911-12, p. 281.

For information on Robinson, see the Snow letters; an obituary in the *Kansas University Weekly*, Sept. 6, 1895, p. 29; a biographical sketch in *Agora*, v. 5, 1895, p. 1; and recollections of students in the *Graduate Magazine*, v. 5, 1906-7, p. 275. Professor Robinson's own recollections of University life are also of interest. They will be found in Sterling, *Quarter-Centennial History*, p. 159.

For biographical data on Snow, see the Snow letters already referred to and the Snow memorials in the *Graduate Magazine*, v. 7, 1908-9, p. 121, as well as subsequent mention in this book. The chief source of information now (1954) available is, of course, the very

valuable biography by Professor Hyder, *Snow of Kansas,* already referred to in these notes.

The framing of the organic law of the University is described in Sterling's *Quarter-Centennial History,* p. 74. Rice in his report in the *Sixth Annual Report of the Superintendent of Public Instruction,* 1866, p. 52, refers to the fact that the University was modeled after the University of Michigan; see, also, *Lawrence Daily Tribune,* Dec. 1,1866, p. 3. For the original charter of Michigan see B. A. Hinsdale, *History of the University of Michigan,* Ann Arbor, 1906, pp. 17 and 26. For failure to elect a chancellor at Michigan, see Hinsdale, p. 37, and F. W. Shearman, *System of Public Instruction and Primary School Law of Michigan,* Lansing, 1852, pp. 185-187.

The duties of the original Chancellor of the University of Kansas are described in the *Journal,* p. 38, and reported in the *Lawrence Daily Tribune,* Dec. 16, 1866, pp. 2 and 3.

SECTION 6

Fraser's inaugural address was given June 17, 1868; see *Kansas Tribune,* June 13, 1868, p. 3, c. 2; June 18, 1868, p. 3, c. 2.

The two most important sources of information on Fraser's life are biographical sketches by S. A. Riggs, *Graduate Magazine,* v. 4, 1905-6, p. 117, and Hannah Oliver, *Graduate Magazine,* v. 6, 1907-8, p. 282; see also the Snow letters, *Graduate Magazine,* v. 3, pp. 96, 102, 103; *Annual Report of the Board of Regents,* Dec. 5, 1867; *Annual Report of the Board of Regents for 1868,* p. 6; the *Lawrence Daily Tribune,* June 13, 1868, p. 3, c. 2; June 18, 1868, p. 3, c. 2; May 12, 1869, p. 3, c. 2; Dec. 16, 1871, p. 2, c. 2; Jan. 14, 1872, p. 4, c. 1; June 12, 1872, p. 2, c. 1; Sterling's *Quarter-Centennial History,* p. 170. *Kansas Tribune,* May 12, 1869, p. 3, c. 2; Jan. 8, 1870, p. 2, c. 1; Aug. 24, 1871; Jan. 14, 1872, p. 4, c. 1; June 14, 1873, p. 4, c. 2; April 23, 1874, p. 4, c. 1.

For the controversy resulting in Fraser's resignation see, in addition, E. Miller, *Graduate Magazine,* v. 3, 1904-5, p. 123; letter (MS) of faculty members addressed to Fraser and dated Dec. 19, 1873 (now in the present Chancellor's office); "Outline of Defense" (MS) dated June 2, 1874, and written by Fraser, the original of which is in the Kansas State Historical Society; *Lawrence Daily Tribune,* June 14, 1873, p. 4, c. 2 (general harmony in the faculty); March 18, 1874, p. 4, c. 2; March 21, 1874, p. 4, c. 2; April 25, 1874, p. 4, c. 1; May 26, 1874, p. 2, c. 1; *Observer of Nature,* June 10, 1874, p. 4, c. 2. The Regents themselves adopted a resolution in which they stated their belief that the "present" high position

of the University with respect to the scheme of instruction and the plans and appointments of the new building were largely due to Fraser (*Journal,* April 15, 1874, p. 174).

For the naming of Fraser Hall, see the Oliver reference listed above and *Kansas University Weekly,* v. 4, 1897, p. 338, c. 2; v. 5, Oct. 23, 1897, p. 1, c. 2.

SECTION 7

For the early history of the campus, see Sterling's *Quarter-Centennial History* and W. C. Hoad, "A Historical Survey of the Campus," *Graduate Magazine,* v. 3, 1904-5, p. 281. Sterling speaks of the North College site as ten acres, but Hoad lists only eight acres. The Regents' minutes of Dec. 6, 1865 (*Journal,* p. 6) refer to the original campus as "ten acres or thereabouts." Chancellor Oliver's report to the Regents on July 18, 1866 (*Journal,* p. 13) stated that the Hon. Jas. H. Lane sold to him (Oliver, for the University) 2¾ acres at $100 per acre "to complete the square around the University."

For the early history of University Hall, see Sterling; the Regent' Reports for 1871, 1872, 1873, and *Lawrence Daily Tribune,* Jan. 8, 1870, p. 2, c. 1; Feb. 4, 1870, p. 2, c. 1; Sept. 8, 1870, p. 3, c. 3; Aug. 24, 1871, p. 2, c. 1; Dec. 7, 1871, p. 4, c. 2; Dec. 16, 1871, p. 2, c. 2; Jan. 14, 1872, p. 4, c. 1; March 28, 1872, p. 4, c. 4; June 12, 1872, p. 21, c. 12; Jan. 1, 1873, p. 4, c. 2. Early descriptions of the building can be found in the *Tribune,* March 31, 1872, p. 1, c. 2; Sept. 4, 1872, p. 4, c. 3; Dec. 4, 1872, p. 4, c. 3. The last citation contains a description of the opening exercises. For the naming of University Hall, see the *Tribune,* Nov. 23, 1877, p. 4 and *Regents' Reports* (1877-78), p. 2. If I read the minutes of the Regents' meeting aright, the Regents meant to name the assembly room of the new building "University Hall" (*Journal,* Nov. 22, 1877, p. 259). The name, however, was soon popularly and officially used for the building; see, for example, the *Regents' Report for 1881-82,* p. 6, where the valuation of "University Hall (new building)" is given as $150,000.

SECTION 8

Information concerning the first Commencement has been obtained by examining the first programs, on file in Watson Library; from the account in the *Hierophantes* (the first annual), 1874, p. 27, but chiefly from the *Lawrence Daily Tribune.* The *Tribune* citations include June 4, 1873, p. 4, c. 2; June 10, 1873, p. 2, c. 1; same date, p. 4, c.3; June 11, 1873, p. 4, c. 2, 3, 4; June 12, 1873, p. 4, c. 3; same date, p. 2, c. 1, 2, 3, 4, 5 (the Ingalls oration); June 13, 1873, p. 1, c. 3. For the appearance of the chapel in 1873, see *Superintendent of Public Instruction, 15th Annual Report,* 1875, pp. 133, 134; *Graduate Magazine,* v. 6, 1907-8, p. 42. The stage in the chapel was changed from south side to east side in 1874; *Observer of Nature,* May 26, 1874, p. 4, c. 2.

SECTION 9

The earliest criticism of students by a Lawrence citizen that I have found is in the *Lawrence Daily Tribune,* June 6, 1874, p. 4, c. 1.

Information on the beginning of a street railway system in Lawrence will be found in the *Tribune* from April to Nov., 1871. The opening of the system is described in the issue of Nov. 26, 1871, p. 4, c. 1 and 2.

Information bearing on Chancellor Carpenter's election and resignation will be found in Sterling's *Quarter-Centennial History,* p. 97; *Lawrence Daily Tribune,* July 16, 1874, p. 4, c. 2; Aug. 30, 1874, p. 4; the *Second Annual Report of the Board of Commissioners,* 1874, p. 31; *Western Home Journal* (Lawrence), July 23, 1874, p. 3, c. 4; Sept. 3, 1874, p. 3, c. 2; the Regents (*Journal,* v. 1, p. 182) appointed a committee of Messrs. McFarland and Emery to meet Carpenter "at Lawrence at his earliest convenience." Later (*Journal,* p. 183) Mr. McFarland "of the committee appointed to meet Dr. Carpenter" reported to the Regents that Carpenter had declined. Carpenter was in New York when elected to the chancellorship (*Wisconsin State Journal,* Madison, July 30, 1874) but the same *State Journal,* Aug. 27, 1874, p. 4, c. 1, reported: "Dr. S. H. Carpenter, recently elected President of the Kansas University, while he was spending a vacation in New York, has just returned from a visit to the institution he was asked to preside over. We are glad to learn that he will not accept the position offered. The loss to Kansas will be our gain." I am indebted to the Wisconsin State Historical Society for an examination of the *State Journal* for the summer of 1874. A biographical sketch of Carpenter, who died in 1878, is given in *Collections of State Historical Society of Wisconsin,* v. 8, 1879, p. 86. The grasshopper infestation began July 25, 1874, and soon covered the entire state. The month of July and most of August had very high temperatures. For the source of this information consult the *Third Annual Report of State Board of Agriculture,* Topeka, 1874, pp. 13 and 14; *Western Home Journal* (Lawrence), Aug. 6, 1874, p. 3, c. 2; Aug. 13, 1874, p. 3, c. 1; Aug. 20, 1874, p. 2, c. 1. I have reviewed these events in "The Grasshopper Year" reprinted from the *Transactions of the Kansas Academy of Science,* Dec., 1952.

For early reference to Chancellor Marvin see *Lawrence Daily Tribune,* July 19, 1874, p. 4, and *Kansas Collegiate,* March 21, 1877, p. 7. The denominational question was still an important factor in filling University posts. The Methodists had apparently brought Marvin to Lawrence and had presented his candidacy to the Regents before Carpenter's election but their first effort failed. Persistence won the day, however. See "The True Issue" in the *Lawrence Tribune,* Aug. 13, 1874, p. 4, and letter of A. W. Smith in the *Tribune,* Aug. 15, 1874, p. 4. The *Tribune* reports on Sept. 3, 1874, p. 4, that the Regents were still unprepared to elect a chancellor. A brief biographical sketch of Marvin will be found in *The History of the First Methodist Episcopal Church of Lawrence,* by Mary P. Clarke, Kansas City, 1915, p. 46. Marvin died in Lawrence on July 9, 1901 (*University of Kansas News Bulletin,* Aug. 1, 1901).

Section 10

For the improvement of University Hall and grounds see *Kansas Collegiate* (adv.), March 21, 1877, p. 8; Oct. 23, 1877, p. 7; Nov. 22, 1877, p. 6; March 29, 1879, p. 3; April 30, 1879, p. 9; Regents' Reports, 1876, p. 11; 1877-78, p. 9; 1879-80, pp. 6, 7; 1881-82, p. 26; *Kansas Review,* April, 1881, p. 204. Marvin's brief statement quoted on p. 19, will be found in Regents' Reports, 1875, p. 133.

The smokestack was erected in the spring of 1880; *Kansas Review,* June, 1880, p. 204. The east stone steps were started in the spring of 1880 and finished in the fall; *Kansas Review,* March, 1880, p. 127; June, 1880, p. 204; Oct., 1880, p. 45. Compton, *The Building of the University of Kansas,* 1932, p. 101, stated that the east portico was obtained from the insane asylum.

The visit of Hayes is described in *Lawrence Daily Tribune,* Sept. 29, 1879, p. 4; and of Grant in the *Tribune* for April 26, 1873, p. 4, c. 3.

The concluding quotation is from *Lawrence Daily Tribune,* Aug. 10, 1871, p. 2, c. 1.

Marvin Grove was not officially named until 1906; see *Graduate Magazine,* v. 5, p. 31 (1906-7).

Section 11

For the part early played by fraternities and sororities, see A. G. Canfield in Sterling's *Quarter-Centennial History,* p. 134. For the beginning of downtown fraternity apartments, see *Kansas Collegiate,* March 21, 1877, p. 7. That the "Opera House block" was the scene of loud and festive activity at times, is seen in the two-column account of "A Jolly Time" in the *Courier,* Dec. 17, 1888,

p. 2, c. 2. The photograph used in this section is identified in the *Graduate Magazine,* Sept., 1926, p. 22, and Oct., 1926, p. 21. Contemporary mention will be found in *Kansas Review,* April, 1880, p. 151. For the first chapter houses, see *Courier,* April 4, 1894, p. 2, c. 2; *Student's Journal,* April 6, 1894, p. 1, c. 3; *University Weekly,* Sept. 20, 1895, p. 51. Previous to the organization of chapter houses, fraternities had clubs at special boarding houses; see *University Kansan,* Sept. 13, 1889, p. 1, c. 3; Sept. 20, 1889, p. 1, c. 2.

For some of the arguments on the fraternity question after the turn of the century see the *Graduate Magazine,* v. 5, 1906-7, p. 265; *Kansan,* Oct. 28, 1909, p. 1, c. 5; Feb. 8, 1910, p. 1, c. 3; Feb. 26, 1910, p. 1, c. 5; March 19, 1910, p. 1, c. 1; *Graduate Magazine,* Oct. and Nov., v. 12, 1913-14.

For statement on a later-day proportion of fraternity members in the University, see *Kansan,* Nov. 4, 1937, p. 1, c. 6; that the proportion of fraternity members ran much higher in earlier days can be seen from the fact that 118 out of 170 college students of 1884-85 belonged to fraternities; *Courier,* Aug. 1, 1885, p. 4, c. 5, and *Catalog,* 1884-85.

Section 12

For the beginning of the chemistry building, see *Courier,* March 6, 1883, p. 14; April 23, 1883, p. 13, May 6, 1883, p. 14, June 6, 1883, p. 5; *Courier,* v. 2, p. 110, 1883-84; *Regents' Reports,* 1879-80, p. 38; 1883-84, p. 14.

The effect of the frontier on college education in general is discussed in R. F. Butts, *The College Charts Its Course,* New York, 1939, chaps. 7 and 8; information on the local aspect has been taken from the University catalogs, from 1866 on; in addition, see especially *Annual Report of the Board of Regents for 1870,* p. 2, and an address by George T. Anthony at the University Commencement of 1874. The address appears in *University of Kansas Commencement Programs,* University Library, 1933; see also *Daily Lawrence Tribune,* June 11, 1874, p. 4, c. 1; June 12, 1874, p. 4, c. 3. The last citation is editorial comment on the Anthony oration, which is headed, "Was He a Success, or Did He Mistake the Proprieties of the Occasion and Offend Good Taste?" Even twenty years after the erection of Chemistry Hall, Chancellor Strong was to report, "The demand from the state as a whole is very strong for practical work" (*Report of the Board of Regents for Biennium Ending June 30, 1904,* p. 8).

For mention of first faculty of Kansas State see Willard, *History of Kansas State College,* p. 19.

Section 13

Accounts of the Dodge City bullfight will be found in the *Kansas City Times,* July 5, 1884, p. 2, the *Kansas Herald* (Lawrence), July 7, 1884, p. 1, and in Robert M. Wright's famous book *Dodge City the Cowboy Capital,* chap. XIII. The Robinson matter is reported in the *Herald* in the issues of June 30, 1884, p. 3 ("A Bad Example"); July 3, 1884, p. 3; July 7, 1884, p. 2. Robinson may not have gone to the bullfight despite all the newspaper publicity, as it is reported in "A Bad Example" that he denied that this was his purpose in going West. No public denial after all the publicity appeared, however, and the matter is not mentioned in the second Lawrence paper (the *Gazette*) nor is any reference made to it in the University papers when school began in the fall.

For history of Haskell Institute see W. P. Ames, *Highlights of Haskell Institute,* 1936 (MS in University Library). Marvin was the first superintendent of Haskell but held the position for only a year. Lippincott assumed office as Chancellor in September, 1883 (*Courier,* Sept. 10, 1883, p. 3, c. 1).

The early history of University journalism will be found in the *University Review,* June, 1884, p. 22; a most extensive review of the subject was made by M. W. Sterling, *Graduate Magazine*, v. 4, 1905-6, pp. 197, 233, 283; v. 5, 1906-7, p. 195. I have, of course, supplemented my reading of Sterling's articles with an examination (page by page) of all University newspapers available in Watson Library.

For a discussion of "Kansas history and newspapers" see *Graduate Magazine*, v. 4, 1905-6, p. 315; and especially Herbert Flint's *Journalism in Territorial Kansas*, Master's Thesis, University of Kansas, 1916.

SECTION 14

The discussion of the growth of University cabinets is based on the catalogs for the period involved and on the biographical sketches of Snow, *Graduate Magazine*, v. 7, 1908-9, pp. 122-143, and especially Hyder, chap. VIII.

For the building of Old Snow Hall see *Courier*, Oct. 17, 1884, p. 2; Dec. 12, 1884, p. 4; March 13, 1885, p. 2; April 10, 1885, p. 2; May 22, 1885, p. 4; July 1, 1885, p. 4; Oct. 2, 1885, p. 1; Oct. 16, 1885, p. 1; Oct. 23, 1885, p. 2; Nov. 20, 1885, p. 2; Aug. 26, 1886, p. 2; *University Catalog*, 1885-86, p. 82; *Lawrence Daily Tribune*, Nov. 16, 1886, p. 3, c. 2, and 3 (describes dedication); *Courier*, Nov. 19, 1886, pp. 2 and 3.

For mention of deterioration of Snow Hall see *Graduate Magazine*, v. 11, 1912-13, p. 157. The *Kansan* on Sept. 19, 1933, p. 1, c. 5, reported that only part of the basement walls remained and then on Sept. 6, 1934, p. 1, c. 3, it announced that the grading of the site formerly occupied by Old Snow had been completed.

SECTION 15

The expressed desire for a college yell will be found in the *Courier*, Feb. 26, 1886, p. 3, c. 1; March 12, 1886, p. 4, c. 1. The quotation from the *Topeka Capital* is reprinted in the *Courier*, March 19, 1886, p. 4, c. 1. Mention of the Science Club yell will be found in the *Courier*, Feb. 11, 1887, p. 1, c. 2; Feb. 18, 1887, p. 2, c. 3. The first published version of the Rock Chalk that I have found (it is given in the text) is in the *Courier*, Feb. 4, 1887, p. 2, c. 4; the second reference is in the *Courier*, Nov. 4, 1887, p. 2, c. 3. For subsequent early references see *University Review*, v. 9, 1888, pp. 166 and 198; *Courier*, Oct. 19, 1888,

p. 2, c. 5; Feb. 1, 1889, p. 1, c. 5; Sept. 18, 1891, p. 3, c. 2. The *Jayhawker*, 1917, p. 10, and the *University Review*, April, 1890, p. 225, contain brief accounts of the origin of the yell.

In the *Graduate Magazine*, v. 24, Feb., 1925-26, p. 5, there is a version of the history of the "Rock Chalk," credited to the research of Professor F. E. Melvin of the Department of History, which states that Professor A. R. Marsh was responsible for the addition of the words "Rock Chalk." Professor Melvin stated to me that he was misquoted on this point and that he believed that Marsh was *not* responsible for the introduction of "Rock Chalk."

For the origin of "Jayhawker" see *Kansas Historical Collections*, v. 8, 1903-4, p. 17; v. 14, 1915-18, pp. 203-207; *Western Home Journal* (Lawrence), Dec. 9, 1875, p. 3, c. 4; *Kansas City Times*, Feb. 5, 1890, p. 8; further information on the Jayhawkers of '49 will be found in William L. Manly, *The Jayhawkers' Oath and Other Sketches*, Los Angeles, 1949. That the term has had varied uses is further borne out by the signature "Jayhawk" in a letter written from Minnesota Territory in 1854; see the *New York Herald*, April 3, 1854, p. 8, c. 3, 4. That the word "Jayhawker," as a term of opprobrium, was in use in Kansas territorial days can be seen from the fact that a "novelized" history of southern Kansas ran serially in the *Herald of Freedom* (Lawrence) from March 26, 1859, to June 4, 1859, under the title "The Jay-Hawker."

SECTION 16

The early history of the Law Department may be found in the Regents' *Journal*, Nov. 16, 1876, p. 226, and especially Aug. 20, 1878, p. 279, where it is reported that action for the establishment of a law department had been taken, the first term to extend from Nov., 1878, to March, 1879, and fees of students to be compensation for the instructor; *Catalog*, 1878-79, p. 44; 1879-80, p. 47; Regents' Reports (*Second Biennial Report*), pp. 23 and 50 (where Green signs himself as "Dean" on Sept. 8, 1880; he is also so called in the above *Catalog*, p. 47); the *Graduate Magazine*, v. 4, 1905-6, pp. 45 and 60. The opening date of the Law Department is variously given as November 4, November 6, and "the second Tuesday of October," 1878. Actually the first dean appointed by the University Regents was J. A. Sewall on June 14, 1876. His title was "Dean of the Normal Department." Sewall apparently declined, because P. J. Williams became the dean of this department in September, 1876 (Regents' *Journal*, v. 1, pp. 218 and 220). The Normal Department, with a dean, was discontinued in 1885 but was followed by the "Department of Elementary Instruction" which had no dean at its head. This department is last listed in the *23rd Annual Catalogue of the University of Kansas 1888-89*.

SECTION 17

The account of the early conflict of Laws and Engineers may be found in the *University Weekly*, May 5, 1900, p. 1, c. 2. The first actual fight to which I have found reference is described in the *Weekly* for March 7, 1903, p. 2, c. 1; March 14, 1903, p. 4, c. 4.

Early history of the Engineering courses and faculty have been taken directly from the University catalogs on dates specified in text. The announcement of the electrical engineering course was made in the *Lawrence Daily Tribune* for July 12, 1887, p. 3, c. 2, and the beginning is described by Professor Blake in the *Sixth Biennial Report of the Regents*, 1887-88, p. 68.

The formation of the Engineering School is described in the *Courier*, April 10, 1891, p. 1, c. 1; April 17, 1891, p. 3, c. 2; Aug. 1, 1891, p. 3, c. 2; and by Chancellor Snow in the *Eighth Biennial Report of the Regents*, 1891-92, p. 11; the announcement of Marvin as dean appears in the *Courier*, Jan. 13, 1893, p. 3, c. 2.

The building of Blake Hall may be followed in the

Student's Journal, April 27, 1893, p. 1, c. 3; Nov. 17, 1893, p. 2, c. 1; Dec. (Holiday issue), 1893, p. 8; *Catalog,* 1894-95, p. 13; *Ninth Biennial Report of Regents,* 1893-94, p. 20; *University Weekly,* Dec. 6, 1895, p. 251. The quotation from the *Hutchinson News* is requoted from the *University Weekly,* Nov. 29, 1895, p. 228, c. 2. The naming of Blake Hall is mentioned in the *University Weekly,* April 23, 1898, p. 2, c. 4. For Blake's credit in securing Blake Hall, see *Courier,* March 16, 1893, p. 87, c. 2; *Kansas Engineer* No. 5, 1918-19, p. 57, v. 7, 1921, p. 12; *Graduate Magazine,* v. 30, Feb., 1932, p. 3.

For mention of summer camps, see *Student's Journal,* May 25, 1894, p. 3, c. 2. The quotation concerning "Engineering students taking draughting" will be found in the *Student's Journal,* April 20, 1893, p. 1, c. 2.

Information on early electric lighting on the campus will be found in the *Sixth Biennial Report of Regents,* 1887-88, p. 68; *Courier,* Oct. 16, 1891, p. 1, c. 5; March 18, 1892, p. 1, c. 1; May 27, 1892, p. 1, c. 2; *Student's Journal,* Nov. 10, 1892, p. 1, c. 3. The year 1887 also must have marked the beginning of electric lights in the town of Lawrence, for the *Lawrence Tribune,* July 13, 1887, p. 3, c. 2, reports: "Prof. Marvin was making a survey of the business houses on Massachusetts Street yesterday for Pierson Brothers to be used by them in wiring for their electric plant."

The brief mention of engineering education in general is based on R. F. Butts, *The College Charts Its Course,* New York, 1939. In the state, the University was the leader in engineering education; Kansas State did not offer a definite engineering curriculum until 1897-98 (J. T. Willard, *History of Kansas State College,* 1940, p. 111).

Section 18

The quotation on the location of the University was made by Isaac T. Goodnow, Superintendent of Public Instruction, *Third Annual Report,* 1863, p. 39.

The *Courier* advice on climbing the hill will be found in the issue for Sept. 18, 1891, p. 1, c. 2.

The *Tribune* account will be found in the *Lawrence Evening Tribune,* July 19, 1887, p. 3, c. 3.

For the new heating plant see *Sixth Biennial Report of Regents 1887-88,* p. 70. The *Lawrence Daily Tribune* reported on Sept. 28, 1887, p. 4, c. 3, that the new smokestack was only half completed; see also the *Courier,* Sept. 30, 1887, p. 2, c. 3; Oct. 21, 1887, p. 1, c. 4. The closing quotation is from the *Courier,* Sept. 30, 1887, p. 1, c. 3.

Section 19

For the organization of the Y.M.C.A. see the *Courier,* v. 1, Dec. 6, 1882, p. 11; *Kansas Review,* v. 4, 1882-83, p. 67; *Cyclone,* 1883, p. 68; *University Kansan,* Dec. 20, 1889, p. 6, c. 3. A review of the early history of the Y.M.C.A. will be found in the *Weekly Kansan,* April 9, 1904, p. 7.

The publication of the first handbook is recorded in the *Courier,* Sept. 11, 1891, p. 2, c. 3. For the first paid secretary and the first annual banquet, see the *University Weekly,* April 8, 1899, p. 4, c. 1; April 14, 1900, p. 1, c. 2; the *Jayhawker,* 1901, Y.W.C.A. page.

According to the Y.M.C.A. *Yearbook,* 1927, the Estes Park conference was first organized in 1907.

Section 20

For Marvin's statement see *Third Biennial Report of Regents,* 1881-82, p. 25. A history of early Kansas baseball by Harold Evans will be found in the *Kansas Historical Quarterly,* v. 9, 1940, pp. 175-192. The Evans material I have supplemented with references to the Frontiers, *Leavenworth Conservative,* July 22, 1866, p. 2; Nov. 6, 1866, p. 4; to the Hopes, *Conservative,* Oct. 21, 1866, p. 4; to the Wyandottes, *Conservative,* Oct. 26, 1866, p. 4; to the Antelopes, *Conservative,* Nov. 4, 1866, p. 4.

The description of the first University baseball game

will be found in the *Lawrence Daily Tribune,* Nov. 29, 1866, p. 3; Dec. 1, 1866, p. 3. For the 1867 games see *Topeka Leader,* Sept. 5, 1867, p. 3, c. 2, and F. H. Snow's letter, *Graduate Magazine,* v. 3, 1904-5, pp. 92, 94.

For baseball in the seventies, see *Observer of Nature,* April 1, 1874, p. 4, c. 2; *Graduate Magazine,* v. 22, Dec., 1923, p. 22.

Records of baseball games in the eighties will be found in *Athletics at the University of Kansas,* 1894, p. 7; a review of other early University athletics will also be found in this booklet.

The information concerning the Massachusetts Street baseball field was given me by the late Professor E. M. Hopkins; see also *Courier,* Sept. 18, 1891, p. 3, c. 2, and the bibliography in sections 21 and 24.

Section 21

Football in the eighties is also mentioned in the *Courier,* 1882, v. 1, p. 4; the *Cicala,* 1884, p. 74; the *Courier,* Oct. 24, 1884, p. 1; Oct. 31, 1884, p. 1, c. 1; Jan. 9, 1885, p. 4; see also *Athletics at the University of Kansas,* 1894.

The season of 1890 can be followed in the *Lawrence Journal-Tribune,* Oct. 29, 1890, p. 4, c. 5; Nov. 24, 1890, p. 4, c. 5; Nov. 27, 1890, p. 4, c. 6; Nov. 28, 1890, p. 4, c. 4; Dec. 9, 1890, p. 4, c. 4. For Carruth's comment on the game many years later see *Graduate Magazine,* v. 22, Nov., 1923, p. 12. For the organization of the intercollegiate association see the pamphlet, *Athletics at the University of Kansas,* 1894. Some pleasant reminiscences of University athletics, and other activities, will be found in *Some Memory Recitals after 50 Years of Things Athletic and Otherwise,* '91 to '96, of the "Gay 90's" by W. H. H. Piatt (1946?).

The home season of 1891 was also played on the Massachusetts Street grounds; see *Courier,* Sept. 25, 1891, p. 3, c. 2. The story of the first K.U. special train to Kansas City in 1891 will be found in the *Courier,* Oct. 30, 1891, p. 1, c. 1; Nov. 6, 1891, pp. 1 and 2; *Graduate Magazine,* v. 15, 1916-17, p. 38.

A review of college football in Kansas, by Harold Evans, will be found in the *Kansas Historical Quarterly,* v. 9, 1940, p. 285.

Section 22

For contemporary notice of the first glee club see the *Courier,* Sept. 26, 1890, p. 1, c. 4; Oct. 31, 1890, p. 3, c. 1; Nov. 7, 1890, p. 2, c. 1; Dec. 5, 1890, p. 4, c. 1; Dec. 19, 1890, p. 5, c. 2; May 8, 1891, p. 1, c. 5. Contemporary material on the second season will be found in the *Courier,* Nov. 6, 1891, p. 3, c. 1; March 4, 1892, p. 2, c. 4; March 25, 1892, p. 3, c. 2; April 15, 1892, p. 3, c. 2; Feb. 1, 1893, p. 1. A good review of early years in the glee club by John A. Rush will be found in the *Graduate Magazine,* v. 29, Dec., 1930, p. 13. According to the *Kansan,* the girls' glee club did not get under way until 1905; see *Kansan,* Feb. 23, 1905, p. 1, c. 4. Description of musical organizations preceding the original glee club will be found in the *Graduate Magazine,* v. 24, Jan. 1926, p. 12, and in the bibliography of section 27.

The *Courier,* Feb. 1, 1893, p. 1, reproduces the program of the glee club for the 1892-93 season; the concluding number on this program is listed as "*Carmen U. of K. . . Penny.*" This title, I believe, is the earliest positive reference to the Alma Mater,[1] for in the years succeeding, printed versions of the song appear variously as "Carmen of K.U.," "Crimson and the Blue (Carmen)," etc. ("Car-

[1] The late Professor Melvin called my attention to the fact that the *University Review,* v. 13, April, 1892, p. 228, referred, in an account of the glee club, to "the song of the yellow and the blue." This reference is undoubtedly to the Alma Mater, as the *Quivera* version is entitled the "Yellow and the Blue."

men" is technically used in music for a tune or song; see *History and Encyclopedia of Music*, edited by W. L. Hubbard, Irving Square, 1908, p. 90). For such reference, see *Quivera*, 1893, p. 98, and the program of the annual dinner for the *Thirtieth Annual Commencement*, 1902; *University Weekly*, March 16, 1901, p. 11; *Program*, Dedication Banquet, Robinson Gymnasium, Feb. 25, 1910.

I have seen at least three versions of the Alma Mater. The original one contained the chorus (as the University color was crimson in 1892; see section 25):

Hail to thee our Alma Mater,
Hail to K.S.U.,
Lift the chorus ever onward,
For the crimson hue.

This version is that given in *Quivera*, 1893, p. 98, which also states that the last line could be replaced by "The yellow and the blue," for the explanation of which, see section 25.

The chorus was rearranged by 1899 to read:

Lift the chorus ever onward
For the crimson hue;[2]
Hail to thee our Alma Mater
Hail to K.S.U.

These versions may be found in the program referred to above. The *Quivera* version of the Alma Mater also contains a verse now lacking. The additional verse reads:

From Mount Oread's heights she gazes,
Far beyond the Kaw
Blessing all her sons and daughters
Who have gone before.

One of the students who participated in the origin of the Alma Mater credits the words to Penny and confirms the initial date of 1892; see the *Graduate Magazine*, v. 10, 1911-12, p. 131. It should be stated that Penny is credited with the song (after Cornell) in the *Quivera* version.

According to Kate Stephens (*Graduate Magazine*, v. 14, 1915-16, p. 39) the music of both the Cornell and K.U. song is taken from an English folk song "Annie

—————
[2]Or "The yellow and the blue."

Lisle." I have had "Annie Lisle" played for me, and while the music of the two songs is not identical, there is not a great deal of difference.

Section 23

The reference made by the *Courier*, in the opening quotation in the text of section 23, to President Eliot is in error. Actually it was President Angell of the University of Michigan who stated that Kansas had made more progress in twenty-five years than Harvard in two centuries; see *Quarter-Centennial History of the University of Kansas*, 1891, p. 11.

The photograph shown in this section was probably taken in Feb., 1893; see the *Student's Journal*, Feb. 23, 1893, p. 1, c. 2.

For the discontinuance of preparatory work see *Fourth Biennial Report of Regents*, 1883-84, pp. 5 and 12; *Fifth Biennial Report*, 1885-86, p. 11; *Seventh Biennial Report*, 1889-90, p. 39; *Eighth Biennial Report*, 1891-92, p. 17. The quotation from Chancellor Lippincott's comments will be found in the *Sixth Biennial Report*, 1887-88, p. 17.

For the reorganization of the University, consult the catalogs from 1889-92; the *Courier*, June 10, 1891, p. 2, c. 2. The election of Snow to the chancellorship is discussed at some length by Hyder (chap. IX). It is interesting to note that Charles F. Thwing, later to become head of Western Reserve University, was offered the chancellorship prior to Snow's appointment but declined; see *Kansas City Times*, March 15, 1890, p. 3.

The activities of the faculty of the early nineties are described briefly in the *Seventh Biennial Report of Regents*, 1889-90, p. 37; *Eighth Biennial Report*, 1891-92, p. 5; see also a review of the scholarly activities of this faculty group by E. B. Stouffer prepared for the fiftieth anniversary of the local chapters of Phi Beta Kappa and Sigma Xi, *Graduate Magazine*, v. 39, Jan., 1941, p. 6. For the organization of the two honor societies, see *The Fiftieth Anniversary of Phi Beta Kappa and Sigma Xi*, University of Kansas, 1940, pp. 18 and 47.

Faculty stories have been told me in past years by many of the older members of the faculty. I have talked directly in my years on the campus with individuals who lived their lives in every year of University history from 1866 until the present.

Section 24

For contemporary reference to the beginnings of McCook Field see *University Kansan*, Sept. 19, 1890, p. 3, c. 2; *Courier*, March 20, 1891, p. 1, c. 4; March 27, 1891, p. 1, c. 3, p. 2, c. 3; May 1, 1891, p. 1, c. 3; March 18, 1892, p. 2, c. 2; April 1, 1892, p. 2; May 13, 1892, p. 3, c. 2; Aug. 1, 1892, p. 1; Nov. 4, 1892, p. 2, c. 3; *Student's Journal*, Nov. 3, 1892, p. 3, c. 2; *Seventh Biennial Report of Regents*, 1889-90, p. 39; *Eighth Biennial Report*, 1891-92, p. 13; *Quivera*, 1893, p. 141. The first reference that I have seen in print to the name "McCook Field" is in the *Courier*, March 18, 1892, p. 2, c. 2.

Section 25

The picture in this section has been dated from information in the *Student's Journal*, Nov. 3, 1892, p. 1, c. 2 (football sweaters white with crimson K); and the same *Journal*, March 2, 1893, p. 1, c. 1; March 9, 1893, p. 3, c. 2; *Courier*, Feb. 15, 1893, p. 22, c. 2.

The agitation for a change in colors may be followed in the *Courier*, Oct. 16, 1891, p. 2, c. 2, Oct. 23, 1891, p. 1, c. 2, and p. 2, c. 2 (where the adoption of crimson as the athletic color is first announced. The announcement is confirmed by a statement in *Athletics at the University of Kansas*, 1894, p. 5, where it is stated that crimson was officially adopted by the Athletic Association on Oct. 19, 1891); Oct. 30, 1891, p. 2, c. 1; Nov. 6, 1891, p. 2, c. 1 (advantage of crimson settled); Nov. 28, 1891, p. 2, c. 3 (letter from former student stating that he had worn yellow and blue as University colors "ten years ago"); Dec. 4, 1891, p. 2, c. 4 (advantages of crimson); April 8, 1892, p. 2, c. 5 (crimson is the University color).

The change from crimson to crimson and blue may be followed in the *University Weekly*, Feb. 7, 1896, p. 3, c. 2 (sky blue, corn yellow, and crimson, all mentioned as University colors); Feb. 14, 1896, p. 20, c. 1 (reception of athletic colors not favorably received in East. McCook suggests crimson and black or crimson and blue); Feb. 21, 1896, p. 36, c. 2 ("We owe nothing to Harvard"); May 1, 1896, p. 259, c. 1; May 29, 1896, p. 353, c. 1 (Athletic Board adopts crimson and blue); and p. 362, c. 1 (brown and yellow suggested); Oct. 10, 1896, p. 81 ("Let us adopt new colors gracefully"); Oct. 17, 1896, p. 109 (criticism of crimson and blue); October 31, 1896, p. 161, c. 1 (crimson and blue applied to football team); Nov. 14, 1896, p. 201, c. 1 (crimson and blue in use; see also the advertisement of Innes, same issue, p. 202, c. 1).

I have found no contemporary mention of the colors of the first graduating class. The second class to graduate (1874) had as its colors light blue alone (*Hierophantes*, 1874, p. 13).

Section 26

For the prank of 1873, see Sterling's *Quarter-Centennial History*, p. 175; contemporary mention of the event will be found in *Hierophantes*, 1874, p. 27. The hoax of 1880 is described in the *Lawrence Daily Tribune*, Jan. 15, 1880, p. 4; Jan. 16, 1880, p. 4. The perpetrators of the hoax were Wm. Thacher and E. C. Meservey. For Meservey's appearance in chapel many years later see *Graduate Magazine*, v. 9, 1910-11, p. 125.

W. Y. Morgan described the western experiences of the new faculty member of 1882 in the *Jayhawker*, 1912, p. 400. I have found no direct contemporary mention of this incident. The *Courier*, v. 1, No. 1, 1882, p. 9, however, reports, "Professor Thompson of Hamilton, N. Y., has been appointed instructor, vice-Prof. J. W. Gleed, resigned." A month later the *Courier* stated (Oct. 6, 1882, p. 12) that Gleed had just assumed teaching duties, which would indicate a hitch in the plans. As Thompson's name does not appear in the *Catalog* for 1882-83, these incidents have considerable significance, I feel, in the light of Morgan's subsequent story.

For student life in the 70's, 80's, and 90's, see the Canfield and Robinson accounts in Sterling's *Quarter-Centennial History*; *Graduate Magazine*, v. 6, 1907-8, pp. 41, 81, 195, 240; v. 29, June, 1931, p. 10; v. 37, Sept., 1938, p. 6; *The Galaxy*, 1900, p. 94; the *Courier*, v. 2, 1883-84, p. 109.

Boarding clubs can be traced in the *Courier*, Nov. 6, 1882, p. 12, c. 2; Sept. 11, 1885, p. 2, c. 3; *University Kansan*, Sept. 20, 1889, p. 1, c. 2; *Student's Journal*, Oct. 13, 1893, p. 2, c. 2; *Graduate Magazine*, v. 4, 1905-6, p. 210.

The anarchist, the evolutionist, and the free-trader are described by E. E. Slosson in the *Graduate Magazine*, v. 24, Oct., 1925, p. 17; see also the discussion of Canfield and free trade in the *Weekly University Courier*, Jan. 9, 1885, p. 2, and "Communism in the University," *Weekly University Courier*, March 13, 1885, p. 2.

The concluding quotation will be found in the *Courier* for Jan. 29, 1892, p. 2, c. 3, where it is reprinted from the *Kansas City Journal*. Although it cannot be proved with certainty that the author of these lines was W. A. White I am confident that White wrote them. The paragraph has White's unmistakable flavor and during the period in question he was an editorial writer for the *Journal*; see *The Autobiography of William Allen White*, chaps. XXIX and XXX. The file of volume 10 of the *Courier* in Watson Library contains two issues of Jan. 22, 1891 (both No. 18); not only is the year wrong, but the second issue should be dated Jan. 29, 1892, No. 19. It is this issue that contains the above-cited quotation.

Section 27

For the history of Music Hall, see *Eighth Biennial Report of Regents*, 1891-92, p. 10; *Ninth Biennial Report*, 1893-94, p. 21; the University *Catalog*, 1897-98, p. 14. For the use of North College as the home of Fine Arts see the *Courier*, May 6, 1892, p. 4, c. 1; *University Weekly*, Oct. 8, 1898, p. 1, c. 4; Old North is last listed in the University *Catalog* of 1916-17, section 5, p. 233, as in use; the *Catalog*, 1917-18, section 5, p. 241, states that temporary quarters of the Department of Music were located at 1406 Tennessee Street.

References in the text to the early history of music and other arts are taken directly from the catalogs for the year specified; see also *Report of Regents for 1873*, p. 38. A review of the early history of music in the University will be found in the *Graduate Magazine*, v. 10, 1911-12, pp. 86, 90, 91, 93, 125, 127, 128. An extensive history of Fine Arts at the University will be found in the Master's Thesis, *The History of Fine Arts School at the University of Kansas*, by Janet Coulson, 1940. This fine piece of work would have been greatly improved by more extensive documentation.

Reference to Mary Lease and Jerry Simpson will be found in *Collections of the Kansas State Historical Society*, v. 16, 1923-25, pp. 414 and 415; to music at Harvard in S. E. Morison, *Three Centuries at Harvard*, Cambridge, 1936, p. 352; and to Ben Franklin's maxim (requoted) in R. F. Butts, *The College Charts Its Course*, New York, 1939, p. 69.

Section 28

"Each in His Own Tongue" first appeared in the *New England Magazine*, v. 13, n.s., Nov., 1895, p. 322; it was reprinted, without comment, two months later in the *Kansas University Weekly*, v. 1, Jan. 10, 1896, p. 297. The *Weekly* for Nov. 19, 1898, p. 4, c. 1, has an account of the poem but says little about its original composition. The origin of the poem is told in Carruth's own words in the *Silhouette*, San Francisco, v. 2, No. 4, 1918, p. 90, and the *Kansan*, Dec. 17, 1924, p. 2, c. 1. Later mention may be found in the *Graduate Magazine*, v. 24, Nov., 1925, p. 33, and April, 1926, p. 27.

Confidence may be placed in the *Silhouette* account of the origin of the poem, as it evidently had Professor Carruth's approval. This account was furnished me by Professor John A. Hess (of the class of 1908) to whom Professor Carruth had sent a copy of the *Silhouette* in response to a query concerning the origin of "Each in His Own Tongue."

The volume *Each in His Own Tongue* was published by G. P. Putnam's Sons, New York, in 1908 and 1914. For reviews, see the *Independent*, v. 66, 1909, p. 638; the *Dial*, v. 46, 1909, p. 50; the *Nation*, v. 89, 1909, p. 55.

Mention of Carruth's political "career" will be found in the *University Weekly*, v. 2, 1896, p. 127, in the University Scrapbook (KB/El/Un L2/C61), p. 197; and in the *Clippings* described below.

For a biographical account of Carruth see *William Herbert Carruth Clippings* in Watson Library. The closing quotation is by J. Willis Gleed in a reprint of an address on Carruth given by Mr. Gleed on Sept. 30, 1926. The reprint will be found in the above *Clippings*.

Section 29

The photograph described in the text is mentioned in the *University Weekly*, Oct. 31, 1896, p. 149. The illustration reproduced in the *Weekly* is not identical with the one shown here but it is obviously a contemporary of it—possibly another exposure made at the same time; see also the frontispiece in the *Catalog*, 1896-97.

The appropriation for Blake was announced in the *Courier* for March 16, 1893, p. 83, c. 2. The Spooner legacy is described in the *Kansas Review*, Jan., 1881, p. 124; *Eighth Biennial Report of the Regents*, 1891-92, p.

19; the *Courier,* Oct. 16, 1891, p. 1, c. 3; Jan. 15, 1892, p. 2, c. 4. Construction of Spooner Library may be followed in the *Student's Journal,* Sept. 15, 1893, p. 2, c. 1; Oct. 13, 1893, p. 1, c. 4; Dec. (Holiday issue), 1893, p. 8; Oct. 12, 1894, p. 1. The quotation from *Harper's Weekly* is in v. 38, Nov. 10, 1894, pp. 1071 and 1077.

Construction of the Chancellor's residence is described in the *Student's Journal,* Sept. 15, 1893, p. 2, c. 1; Dec. (Holiday issue), 1893, pp. 8 and 10.

The erection of Blake is documented in section 17.

The quotation from the *Topeka Mail* will be found in the issue of Oct. 25, 1895, p. 2.

SECTION 30

The departure of Company H from Lawrence is described in the *University Weekly,* May 7, 1898, p. 1, c. 4; of the University contingent, in the issue for May 14, 1898, p. 4, c. 4.

Mention of the Rock Chalk in the Philippines will be found in the *Weekly,* Nov. 18, 1899, p. 1, c. 2, and *The Fighting Twentieth,* Topeka, Kansas, 1899. A list of University men in the war will be found in the University *Catalog,* 1898-99, p. 133.

The death of Alford is reported in the *Weekly,* Feb. 11, 1899, p. 1. A memorial tablet for Lt. Alford was placed on the south wall of Fraser Chapel on Decoration Day, 1900 *(Jayhawker,* 1901, p. 160). It was removed to the Memorial Union Building in 1929; *Kansan,* Sept. 27, 1929, p. 1, c. 3.

The photograph used in the text was originally reproduced in P. F. Rocket, *Our Boys in the Philippines,* San Francisco, 1899, 44th page of illustrations.

SECTION 31

The destruction of the power and heating plant and the ensuing vacation are described in the *University Weekly,* April 9, 1898, p. 1, c. 2. Fowler's original gift was announced in the *Weekly,* April 23, 1898, p. 1, c. 4; see also *Eleventh Biennial Report of Regents,* 1897-98, p. 14. The comment of Fowler's additional gift (in lieu of the Commencement address) will be found in the *Kansan,* Feb. 6, 1907, p. 1, c. 1; see also clipping (probably *Kansas City Star,* Feb. 11, 1900) in *Buildings of the University of Kansas* (scrapbook), p. 12, in Watson Library.

For the location, building, and opening of Fowler Shops see the *Weekly,* April 30, 1898, p. 4, c. 4; May 21, 1898, p. 4, c. 2; Sept. 24, 1898, p. 3, c. 3; Oct. 1, 1898, p. 1, c. 2; Oct. 29, 1898, p. 3, c. 3; Feb. 4, 1899, p. 1, c. 3.

The effect of the new shops on the growth of the University is commented on in the *Weekly,* Oct. 22, 1898, p. 2, c. 1; see the *Graduate Magazine,* v. 5, 1906-7, p. 117, for actual figures in this period.

The two fires in Fowler shops are described in the *Kansan,* May 10, 1918, p. 1, and *Summer Session Kansan,* July 19, 1932, p. 1, c. 5. For the comment on the architecture of Fowler, see J. H. Compton, *The Building of the University of Kansas,* Master's Thesis, 1932, p. 126.

The Department of Journalism became the William Allen White School of Journalism by action of the Board of Regents in June, 1944; see the *Kansan,* June 9, 1944. Classes in the School as such did not begin until the fall of 1948 *(Annual Catalogue of the University of Kansas— General Information,* Aug., 1951, p. 139). The dedication of remodeled Fowler Shops as the William Allen White School of Journalism is described at some length in the *Kansan,* Feb. 22, 1952.

The Journalism Press became the Bureau of Printing in the fall of 1940. In the summer of 1941 correspondence between Chancellor Malott and T. C. Ryther led to the adoption of the name the University of Kansas Press on September 1. In 1946 the Publishing Division was organized, bearing the same name as the Printing Division— that is, the University of Kansas Press. Dean John H. Nelson, on whose initiative the Publishing Division was or-

J. H. Compton

ganized, was appointed Chairman of the Press Committee, which supervises the Publishing Division of the University of Kansas Press.

Construction on the "new" Fowler Shops began March 15, 1948, and was completed by March, 1949. The building was first opened to the public on April 22, 1949 *(Graduate Magazine,* Sept., 1949, p. 8; May, 1949, p. 12).

SECTION 32

The first mention of basketball found in University papers is in the *University Weekly* for Feb. 14, 1896, p. 21, where a description of the game is made and its introduction advocated. The introduction of the game and the first season may be followed in the *Weekly,* Oct. 29, 1898, p. 1, c. 3; Feb. 4, 1899, p. 1, c. 4 (first game); Feb. 11, 1899, p. 4, c. 1 (first home game); Feb. 25, 1899, p. 1, c. 5; March 4, 1899, p. 1, c. 2; March 25, 1899, p. 1, c. 3 (rink burns); April 8, 1899, p. 1, c. 4 (first intercollegiate game); the *Oread,* 1899, p. 98. The game with Nebraska the following year is described in the *Weekly,* March 10, 1900, p. 4, c. 1. An extensive account of the first season appears in the *Kansan,* March 9, 1924, p. 3, c. 2.

For Naismith's account of the origin of the game, see *University Weekly,* Dec. 10, 1898, p. 1, c. 4; the *Kansan,* March 14, 1913, p. 7, c. 3; *Encyclopedia Britannica,* v. 3, p. 181, 14th ed., 1937 (an article signed by Naismith); and an obituary of Naismith in the *Graduate Magazine,* v. 38, Dec., 1939, p. 4.

SECTION 33

The first May-scrap is described in the *Courier,* May 8, 1891, p. 1, c. 4; p. 2, c. 2; (the second one) May 6, 1892, p. 1, c. 3; p. 2, c. 5. An injury in a class fight at the beginning of the year was reported in the *Weekly,* May 2, 1903, p. 2, c. 2, and in the *Kansan,* Sept. 24, 1904, p. 1, c. 4.

Opposition to the May fight is stated in the *Weekly,* April 12, 1902, p. 2, c. 1; April 30, 1904, p. 2, c. 1; May 7, 1904, p. 2, c. 1. The abandonment of class fights is discussed in the *Kansan,* May 4, 1905, p. 1, and p. 2, c. 1; Sept. 23, 1905, p. 1, c. 2 and 4. Strong thought the abandonment of sufficient importance to include it in the *Report of the Board of Regents,* June 30, 1906, p. 23.

The *Kansan,* Nov. 12, 1908, p. 3, c. 2, states that Herbert Hadley, of the class of '92, was the moving spirit in introducing the Maypole scrap in 1891.

For information on the water tower shown in one of the photographs of this section, see *University Review,* v.

8, Jan., 1887, p. 117; *Lawrence Journal-World*, April 8, 1931, p. 1.

SECTION 34

The section has been based on a page-by-page examination of all the University annuals; we are indeed fortunate that Watson Library possesses a complete file. Reviews of *Jayhawker* history will be found in the *Graduate Magazine*, v. 17, 1918-19, pp. 5 and 38, and the *Jayhawker*, v. 50, 1937-38, pp. 344 and 404. The statement that the magazine form of the *Jayhawker* was based on *Vanity Fair* and the *New Yorker* will be found in the *Kansan*, Sept. 16, 1933, p. 1, c. 1.

The number of issues of the *Jayhawker* was cut from five to four following the volume for 1941-42. The *Jayhawker* for the school year 1943-44, for an obvious reason, had only three issues. Since then there have been four issues per year.

On the editorial board of the famous *Quivera*, mentioned in the text, were Alberta Corbin and R. D. O'Leary. Both were devoted faculty members for many years. Dr. Corbin's work is mentioned, in brief, in section 61 and its notes. Professor O'Leary, of the Department of English, served on the University faculty from 1895 to 1936. Biographical information will be found in the O'Leary book in Watson Library.

Maloy's part in the creation of the pictured *Jayhawker* is described in the *Graduate Magazine*, v. 35, Nov., 1936, p. 7; see also letter by Maloy in *Kansan*, Nov. 12, 1951, p. 8.

SECTION 35

For Bailey's first request for a new building see the *Sixth Biennial Report of Regents*, 1887-88, p. 54. Snow's appeal of 1896 is found in the *Tenth Biennial Report of Regents*, 1895-96, p. 22; see also *Student's Journal*, Jan. 25, 1895, p. 5.

The construction of Bailey Laboratory may be followed in the *University Weekly*, March 11, 1899, p. 1, c. 4; March 25, 1899, p. 1, c. 3; May 6, 1899, p. 2; May 20, 1899, p. 1, c. 4; Oct. 7, 1899, p. 1, c. 2; Sept. 22, 1900, p. 3, c. 4.

The description of the building by the student reporter will be found in the *Jayhawker*, 1904, p. 60. Other details in the history of the Chemistry Department will be found in *History of the Chemistry Department, University of Kansas*, 1925; Franklin, p. 28, Duncan, p. 32; see also my account, *Fifty Years in Bailey Chemical Laboratory*, 47 pp., April 28, 1950.

For the naming of Bailey Laboratory, see the *Graduate Magazine*, v. 36, March, 1938, p. 2.

SECTION 36

For biographical data on Dyche, see the Dyche scrapbooks in Watson Library and the *Graduate Magazine*, v. 13, 1914-15, p. 143.

The Columbian exhibit is described in the *Eighth Biennial Report of the Regents*, 1891-92, p. 16; see also the *Twelfth Biennial Report*, 1899-1900, p. 16; *Scientific American*, July 15, 1893, p. 41. The item quoted from the *Topeka Capital* will be found in the Dyche Scrapbook, v. 1, p. 4. For information on Comanche see *Student's Journal*, Oct. 7, 1892, p. 1, c. 2; *Scientific American*, Oct. 7, 1893, pp. 234, 235; *Kansan*, Oct. 28, 1921, p. 4, c. 1; Oct. 21, 1923, p. 3, c. 1.

SECTION 37

The resignation of Chancellor Snow was announced June 2, 1901 (*Topeka Capital*, June 3, 1901); the resignation went into effect Sept. 1 (*University Weekly*, Sept. 28, 1901, p. 3, c. 3).

The Regents held very extended discussions on the election of a chancellor; see, for example, *University Weekly*, March 15, 1902, p. 1, c. 5.

For the election of Strong see the *University Weekly*, April 26, 1902, p. 1, c. 4; May 3, 1902, p. 2, c. 3. The inauguration of Chancellor Strong is described, and his address published in the *Graduate Magazine*, v. 1, 1902-3, pp. 19 and 33; see also the very extensive newspaper clippings in the *University of Kansas Scrap Book, 1876-1910*; *University Weekly*, Sept. 12, 1902, p. 4, c. 1; Oct. 18, 1902, p. 1, c. 4. Strong's review of his administration will be found in the *Graduate Magazine*, v. 18, 1919-20, p. 5.

SECTION 38

My information on the flood is based on accounts in the *Lawrence Journal* and the *Lawrence World* for the issues of May 28, 29, 30, 31, June 1 to 10, 1903.

For information on the Commencement of 1903 see the *Lawrence Journal*, June 10, 1903, p. 1, c. 2; *Graduate Magazine*, v. 1, 1902-3, p. 349.

The first Summer School is described in the *Graduate Magazine*, v. 1, 1902-3, p. 359, and v. 2, 1903-4, p. 14. It should be pointed out that, even in the eighties, members of the University faculty conducted their own private summer schools; see the advertisement "Summer school of languages" in the *Courier*, May 29, 1885, p. 3, c. 3.

SECTION 39

The changes in college courses and "The College" were taken from the University catalogs, 1866-1909.

The complaint of the ministerial student will be found in the *Courier*, Feb. 13, 1885, p. 3, c. 1.

One of the unusual requirements for graduation from the College in more recent years was the passing of an English proficiency examination. The requirement was first applied to those who received their degrees in June, 1940; see *Annual Catalog of the University for 1936-37*, Jan. 1, 1937, p. 58.

SECTION 40

The *University Weekly*, v. 2, p. 286, 1896, remarks, "We are not yet ready for a University daily." Extensive discussion preceded the establishment of the *Daily Kansan* in 1912; see the *Kansan*, Oct. 7, 1911, p. 1, c. 1; Dec. 7, 1911, p. 1, c. 1; Dec. 16, 1911, p. 1, c. 1 (No. 38) and 3 (No. 39). For a history of the *Kansan* see the issue for Dec. 20, 1911, p. 3, c. 1. The material in the text, of course, has been based on direct examination of the titles as given. The new courses mentioned in the text are stated in the *Catalog* for 1903-4 and in *Report of Board of Regents for Biennium Ending June 30, 1904*, p. 4.

That the *Kansan* and journalism classes had an office together is so stated in the *Kansan*, Oct. 1, 1904, p. 3, c. 1. Plans for reorganizing the management of the *Kansan* are described in the issues of Jan. 14, 1905, p. 1, c. 3, and Feb. 2, 1905, p. 1, c. 1. That the *Kansan* was printed off the campus prior to 1905 is so stated in the issue of Feb. 4, 1905, p. 2, c. 2; publication by the press of the Alumni printing plant in the basement of Fraser is so stated in the issue of Sept. 14, 1906, p. 3, c. 2.

The early history of the journalism courses may be followed in the *Graduate Magazine*, v. 2, 1903-4, pp. 43, 46, 187, 305; v. 3, 1904-5, p. 148. For the quotation of Howe see *University Weekly*, Jan. 9, 1904, p. 1, c. 2. Chancellor Strong and Professor Hopkins are given credit for originating the work in journalism by the *Kansan*, Oct. 1, 1904, p. 2, c. 2. Harger's appearance on the campus is stated in the *Kansan*, Sept. 8, 1905, p. 5, and Sept. 20, 1905, p. 1, c. 1. Journalism courses were established as a separate department according to the *Graduate Magazine*, v. 8, 1909-10, p. 107.

The move of the Journalism Department to Medical Hall is described in the first issue of the *Daily Kansan;* see facsimile in text, column 6. The *Jayhawker*, 1913, calls the building "Journalism" in its caption (4th page of building illustrations). The *Graduate Magazine*, v. 16, 1917-18, pp. 40 and 111, implies that journalism classes occupied *all* of Medical Hall; so does the *Kansan*, Sept. 13, 1921, p. 1, c. 1, and again on Oct. 3, 1923, p. 1, c. 5.

For a review of graduates in journalism see the *Graduate Magazine*, v. 35, June, 1937, p. 9; v. 36, Nov., 1937, p. 10; Dec., 1937, p. 11. An account of the change from the Department of Journalism to the William Allen White School of Journalism will be found in the notes of section 31.

Section 41

The story of the Law-Engineer squabble is told in the *University Weekly*, March 7, 1903, p. 2, c. 1, and March 14, 1903, p. 4, c. 4. The proposed use of the new building as a combined gymnasium, auditorium, and law school is described in the *Weekly*, Feb. 28, 1903, p. 4, c. 3; see also March 7, 1903, p. 1, c. 2.

Work on Green Hall was started in July, 1904 (*Kansan*, Sept. 24, 1904, p. 1, c. 1).

The completion and dedication of Green Hall will be found in the *Kansan*, Sept. 8, 1905, p. 2, c. 4; Sept. 16, 1905, p. 2, c. 1; Sept. 27, 1905, p. 1, c. 1; Sept. 30, 1905, p. 3, c. 3; Nov. 4, 1905, p. 1; *Graduate Magazine*, v. 4, 1905-6, pp. 33, 37, and 68.

The changing requirements for entrance to the Law School and for the course itself may be found in the *Kansas Lawyer*, Oct., 1901, p. 7; *Graduate Magazine*, v. 4, 1905-6, p. 45; v. 5, 1906-7, p. 31; *Kansan*, March 18, 1905, p. 4, c. 3; March 22, 1910, p. 1, c. 1; and of course, the University catalogs.

The statement concerning the farcical character of bar examinations will be found in the *Kansas University Lawyer*, v. 1, 1895, p. 3.

The suggested requirement of "good voice" appears in the *University Weekly*, March 17, 1900, p. 3, c. 5.

Section 42

The early history of the gymnasium may be followed in the *Courier*, Nov. 6, 1882, p. 12; April 14, 1884, p. 296; Feb. 27, 1891, p. 4, c. 1; *Eighth Biennial Report of Regents* (1891-92), p. 13; *Ninth Biennial Report* (1893-94), p. 10; *University Weekly*, March 6, 1896, p. 87; Nov. 12, 1898, p. 3, c. 3; March 18, 1899, p. 3, c. 4; *Graduate Magazine*, v. 1, 1902-3, p. 323; *Kansan*, Oct. 27, 1904, p. 1, c. 2. See also reviews in the *Jayhawker*, 1901, p. 132, and *Graduate Magazine*, v. 22, 1923, Oct., p. 11, Nov., p. 15, Dec., p. 23.

The construction of Robinson Gymnasium may be followed in *Report of Board of Regents for Biennium Ending June 30, 1904*, p. 9; *Graduate Magazine*, v. 3, 1904-5, p. 234; v. 4, 1905-6, pp. 34, 181, 260; *Kansan*, March 9, 1905, p. 1, c. 1; March 18, 1905, p. 2, c. 1; April 29, 1905, p. 1, c. 4; Sept. 16, 1905, p. 1, c. 4; Jan. 13, 1906, p. 1, c. 3 and 4; March 24, 1906, p. 1, c. 4; Dec. 20, 1906, p. 1, c. 3; May 15, 1907, p. 1, c. 3; May 17, 1907, p. 1, c. 3; May 29, 1907, p. 1, c. 3. The Gymnasium was dedicated at Commencement, 1908; see the *Graduate Magazine*, v. 6, 1907-8, pp. 297 and 353.

The growth of the campus may be followed in the *Kansan*, Dec. 15, 1904, p. 3, c. 2; and especially in the *Graduate Magazine*, 1904-5, v. 3, p. 281; v. 24, Oct., 1925, p. 11; v. 27, May, 1929, p. 8; see also the *Kansan*, March 30, 1924, p. 1, c. 7.

The requirements in physical education have been obtained by examination of the University catalogs; see also *Kansan*, Sept. 19, 1932, p. 1, c. 1; May 17, 1933, p. 1, c. 6.

Although the swimming requirement first appears in the *Catalog* for 1923-24, it had, in effect, been a requirement since (probably) 1901 as part of the curriculum in physical education; see the *Kansan*, Feb. 21, 1912, p. 4, c. 3; April 29, 1914, p. 1, c. 2; April 6, 1923, p. 2, c. 1; Sept. 24, 1924, p. 1, c. 2.

Section 43

The Medical Society of 1884 is described in the *Courier*, v. 2, 1883-84, p. 259; the *Cicala*, 1884, p. 64; see also the *Graduate Magazine*, v. 7, 1908-9, p. 262.

The Bell gift was first reported by Chancellor Snow in the *Ninth Biennial Report of Regents*, 1893-94, p. 23; see also *University Weekly*, May 28, 1898, p. 2, c. 1 and 3; *Kansan*, Feb. 25, 1905, p. 1, c. 3; Nov. 25, 1905, p. 1, c. 4.

Lippincott's statement, quoted in the text, appears in the *Sixth Biennial Report of Regents*, 1887-88, p. 19; see also *Seventh Biennial Report*, 1889-90, pp. 28 and 41; *Ninth Biennial Report*, 1893-94, p. 23. The establishment of the first Medical School is reported by Snow, *Twelfth Biennial Report*, 1899-1900, p. 14.

The merger of the Kansas City medical schools is described in the *Kansan*, April 8, 1905, p. 1, c. 3, and in Chancellor Strong's account, *Report of Board of Regents for Biennium Ending June 30, 1906*, p. 17, and *Graduate Magazine*, v. 18, 1919-20, p. 10.

The opening of the Medical School in Kansas City and the construction of the first two units of the plant are discussed in the *Kansan*, Sept. 13, 1905, p. 4, c. 1; Oct. 18, 1905, p. 4, c. 3; Nov. 25, 1905, p. 1, c. 4; Sept. 29, 1906, p. 4, c. 3; *Graduate Magazine*, v. 4, 1905-6, pp. 35 and 70; v. 6, 1907-8, p. 153.

The establishment of the nurses' training school is stated in the *Graduate Magazine*, v. 4, 1905-6, p. 183; see also the *Jayhawker*, 1909, p. 143. S. E. Morison, *Three Centuries of Harvard*, Cambridge, 1936, p. 393, cites 1892 as the date of establishment of the four-year medical course at Harvard.

Dr. Crumbine was secretary of the State Board of Health from 1904 to 1923; dean of the Medical School from 1911 to 1919. His own account of his life's work will be found in *Frontier Doctor*, Philadelphia, 1948. Marshall A. Barber's account of his world-wide experiences as an epidemiologist will be found in his *A Malariologist in Many Lands*, University of Kansas Press, 1946. Also of interest is Dr. Barber's autobiographical account of a country school district in southeastern Kansas in the 70's and early 80's, *The Schoolhouse at Prairie View*, University of Kansas Press, 1953. Dr. Barber was a graduate of the University in the class of 1891.

Section 44

The appropriations for 1907 are described in the *Kansan*, March 2, 1907, p. 1, c. 1; March 6, 1907, p. 2, c. 1; *Graduate Magazine*, v. 5, 1906-7, p. 220.

The construction of Marvin and Haworth may be followed in the *Graduate Magazine*, v. 6, 1907-8, p. 23; *Kansan*, March 21, 1908, p. 4, c. 1; April 18, 1908, p. 2, c. 3; May 7, 1908, p. 3, c. 2; May 5, 1908, p. 3, c. 3; Oct. 3, 1908, p. 3, c. 4; Oct. 8, 1908, p. 6, c. 2; Oct. 17, 1908, p. 3, c. 2; Nov. 3, 1908, p. 2, c. 3; Dec. 15, 1908, p. 10; Oct. 5, 1909, p. 1, c. 5; Nov. 16, 1909, p. 1, c. 3. For the naming and dedication of these buildings see *Graduate Magazine*, v. 8, March, 1910.

The first Engineers' Day is described in the *Kansan*, March 2, 1911, p. 3, c. 1; April 1, 1911, p. 1, c. 1, p. 2, c. 1; the *Jayhawker*, 1911, p. 297. For the Engineers' parade of 1913 see the *Kansan*, April 16, 1913, p. 1, c. 6; April 17, 1913, p. 2, c. 1.

SECTION 45

The early history of the May Fete is described by Professor Lynn in the *Graduate Magazine*, v. 9, 1910-11, p. 332. Criticism of the event will be found in the *Graduate Magazine*, v. 9, 1910-11, p. 138; see also p. 342 of this same volume. Chancellor Strong's statement on the abolishment of the May scrap will be found in the *Graduate Magazine*, v. 9, 1910-11, p. 10.

A description of the May Fete of 1908 is given in the *Kansan*, May 21, 1908, p. 1, c. 3; May 23, 1908, p. 1, c. 3; *Lawrence Journal*, May 19, 1908, p. 1, c. 8; May 25, 1908, p. 4, c. 3.

The automobile "endurance" run of 1908 is described in the *Lawrence Journal*, May 16, 1908, p. 1, c. 2, and May 18, 1908, p. 4, c. 2.

The *Kansan* for May 23, 1923, p. 1, c. 3, describes the May Fete of that year, but I find no description of a similar event for May, 1924.

SECTION 46

For the early history of student government see the *Kansan*, March 28, 1908, pp. 1 and 2; Jan. 7, 1909, p. 2, c. 1; April 20, 1909, p. 1, c. 1; April 29, 1909, p. 1, c. 1; May 4, 1909, p. 1, c. 1; May 8, 1909, p. 1, c. 1; May 13, 1909, p. 1, c. 4; May 18, 1909, p. 1, c. 3; May 20, 1909, p. 1, c. 3 and 4; Oct. 5, 1909, p. 1, c. 1; Oct. 26, 1909, p. 3, c. 2.

A few of the ups and downs of student government are mentioned in the *Kansan*, April 23, 1914, p. 1, c. 6; March 5, 1919, p. 1, c. 6; May 21, 1931, p. 1, c. 6; May 22, 1931, p. 2, c. 1; Nov. 5, 1931, p. 1, c. 4. For reviews of student government see the *Kansan*, March 8, 1910, p. 2, c. 1; May 28, 1939, section C, p. 1, c. 7; the *Jayhawker*, 1939-40, p. 280.

Student government has had a stormy career during its existence at the University. I have attempted no detailed history of its more modern aspects, but Diane Foltz, secretary of the Student Council, has prepared a brief review of the form of student government in practice today (1954). It is included here not only for its interest as contrasted to earlier years but possibly it may be of interest to some student of 2054. Miss Foltz's account reads:

STUDENT GOVERNMENT

The organization is called the Associated Students of the University of Kansas, and its purpose as stated in Article II of the constitution reads: "The purpose of this association shall be (a) to unite in a single self-governing body the students of the University of Kansas and to promote and regulate their extra-curricular activities (b) to coordinate student activities with the programs of the faculty and administrative governing bodies (c) by so doing to promote the highest interests of the University of Kansas and to cultivate loyalty to the University among its students."

The governing body is divided into two houses, a bicameral system, having a Senate and a House of Representatives. The Senate members are elected from their school district. There are ten school districts: Journalism, Fine Arts, Pharmacy, College, Engineering, Graduate, Education, Law, Medicine, and Business. Representation is according to the proportional representation—i.e., there is one representative for each 150 votes cast in that district. The larger school districts as the College, Fine Arts, and Graduate School are again subdivided into men's and women's divisions—again there is one representative per 150

votes. The House of Representatives members are elected from living districts. There are seven living districts: sororities, fraternities, independent organized men, independent organized women, co-ops and professional fraternities, freshman women's dormitories, and students in unorganized houses. There is one representative elected for each 150 votes cast out of the individual district.

Officers of the council are a President, who presides over the Senate; Vice-president, who is presiding officer of the House of Representatives; a Secretary elected from each house; and a Treasurer elected from the Senate. The President pro tempore of the Senate is the defeated presidential candidate. The President pro tempore of the House is the defeated vice-presidential candidate.

Both houses meet separately but usually on the same day. The purpose of a bicameral system on this campus is to divide the responsibility; to give a better representation of the student body; and to facilitate a more thorough consideration of matters brought before the council. Under a one-house system it was felt that individual thinking was influenced too much and decisions were not always thoroughly considered. With two houses before which all legislation matters must pass, a check is provided.

The responsibilities of the Senate are primarily of an executive nature, finances included among these. While the House is concerned with administrative duties as labor committees, smoking, etc., committees necessary to carry out the responsibility of student government on the campus.

The committee system is basically broken down into groups: standing committees, department of publications, department of student welfare, and department of student activities. These branches carry out the work of student government.

The judicial branch of student government is the student court. The Chief Justice of the student council is appointed by the Dean of the Law School in consultation with the Chancellor of the University. The prosecutor and justices are appointed by the President of the All Student Council with a ⅔ Senate approval. This body acts as a check over the legislative branch.

The view of the University Administration toward the All Student Council is a very liberal one on this campus. Although the student government is ultimately under the auspices of the Chancellor little intervention takes place. All legislation must be signed by the Chancellor, the final check on student government. A committee of faculty advisers is appointed by the President of the All Student Council subject to ⅔ approval of the Senate. These members sit in on council meetings and some committee meetings. The purpose is to give advice when needed and again, "Their view is to let the students do it."

Finances of All Student Council.—Each year the council receives a certain proportion of the student activity fee paid by each student. This money is used for operating the council. The council also makes appropriations to petitioning student organizations each year for their support.

For the "new" All Student Council of recent years, see *Kansan*, May 6, 1953.

The matter of class headgear may be followed in the *Kikkabe*, 1884, p. 14; *Graduate Magazine*, v. 6, 1907-8, p. 84; *University Weekly*, Oct. 21, 1899, p. 2, c. 2; *Courier*, Dec. 2, 1887, p. 2, c. 3; *Kansan*, Oct. 3, 1908, p. 4, c. 2; Oct. 13, 1908, p. 1, c. 3; Oct. 27, 1908, p. 1, c. 4; Sept. 21, 1909, p. 3, c. 1; Oct. 12, 1909, p. 1, c. 5; Oct. 14, 1909, p. 1, c. 1; March 8, 1910, p. 2, c. 1; Oct. 15, 1910, p. 2, c. 1; April 4, 1911, p. 1, c. 4; Sept. 27, 1912, p. 1, c. 2.

In 1944, the All Student Council voted that all freshmen were to wear caps, but K Club men were not to paddle any violators of the rule (*Graduate Magazine*, Oct., 1944, p. 6). The K Club had ruled the same year that freshmen, with the exception of veterans of World War II, were to wear caps and walk on the south side of the street between classes! This effort was apparently the last on the forced wearing of caps. Since 1944, Ku Kus, Jay Janes, and cheerleaders have sold them to aid in buying equipment for the pep clubs and cheerleaders (*Kansan*, Sept. 12, 1951). A post-war phenomenon has been the wearing of caps by girls as well as boys (*Graduate Magazine*, Oct., 1949, p. 10).

For the beginning of the nightshirt parade see the *Kansan*, Sept. 23, 1905, p. 1, c. 2; see also the issue of Oct. 6, 1908, p. 3, c. 1.

Fraternity difficulties are discussed in the *Kansan*, Oct. 28, 1909, p. 1, c. 5; Feb. 8, 1910, p. 1, c. 3; Feb. 26, 1910, p. 1, c. 5; March 19, 1910, p. 1, c. 1; Sept. 20, 1910, p. 1, c. 3. Theta Nu Epsilon (TNE) has been a recurrent problem; see *University Weekly*, March 19, 1898, p. 3, c. 2; *Graduate Magazine*, v. 8, 1909-10, p. 264; *Kansan*, Feb. 23, 1923, p. 2, c. 1. For TNE in recent years, see *Kansan*, Sept. 22, 1952.

The football situation in 1910 may be followed in the *Kansan*, Jan. 29, 1910, p. 1, c. 1; March 31, 1910, p. 1, c. 1; April 2, 1910, p. 1, c. 3; April 14, 1910, p. 1, c. 3; April 19, 1910, p. 1, c. 3; May 17, 1910, p. 4, c. 1; *Graduate Magazine*, v. 8, 1909-10, p. 183. For the death of a University football player see *University Weekly*, v. 3, 1896-97, pp. 210, 217, 221; see also *Kansan*, Feb. 10, 1910, p. 2, c. 1.

The University had a band as early as 1887; *Courier*, Dec. 2, 1887, p. 1, c. 3; see also *Courier*, April 27, 1893, p. 184, c. 1. The uniforming of the band can be followed in the *Kansan*, Oct. 17, 1906, p. 1, c. 2; Nov. 14, 1906, p. 1, c. 2; Nov. 13, 1907, p. 1, c. 1. The arrival of McCanles is reported in the *Kansan*, Sept 25, 1907, p. 1, c. 3; *Graduate Magazine*, v. 6, 1907-8, p. 19.

Section 47

In addition to the University catalogs, the following material on chapel has been used: *Courier*, Nov. 20, 1882, p. 14; March 20, 1883, p. 7; Nov. 6, 1885, p. 1, c. 1; Sept. 23, 1892, p. 3, c. 2. The increase in attendance after Chancellor Strong arrived is reported in *University Weekly*, Feb. 14, 1903, p. 2, c. 1; *Report of the Board of Regents for the Biennium Ending June 30, 1904*, p. 2.

Section 48

Early reference to electric cars will be found in the *Student's Journal*, March 16, 1893, p. 1, c. 1; *University*

Weekly, Oct. 8, 1898, p. 1, c. 4; the *Kansan*, Oct. 31, 1908, p. 1, c. 2; Nov. 7, 1908, p. 4, c. 1.

The actual construction of the line may be followed in the *Kansan*, Oct. 7, 1909, p. 1, c. 1; Oct. 12, 1909, p. 3, c. 1; Jan. 4, 1910, p. 3, c. 1; April 9, 1910, p. 4, c. 3 (first car on Hill); May 7, 1910, p. 3, c. 2. For the discontinuance of streetcars, see *Graduate Magazine*, v. 32, Nov., 1933, p. 18. Although not mentioned in the text, the first appearance of the Kansas City interurban is recorded in the *Kansan*, May 31, 1916, p. 1, c. 1.

Strong's statement on sewage disposal will be found in the *Report of the Regents for the Biennium Ending June 30, 1906*, p. 15.

Construction of tunnels is reported in the *Ninth Biennial Report of Regents*, 1893-94, p. 25; *Kansan*, Sept. 11, 1909, p. 1, c. 5; Sept. 13, 1916, p. 1, c. 1; Oct. 15, 1919, p. 1, c. 6; Nov. 28, 1927, p. 4, c. 2.

The construction of the tunnels and sewage system was only one of many factors in the eradication of typhoid. In 1910 a number of cases were reported; *Kansan*, Oct. 18, 1910, p. 1, c. 3; Oct. 20, 1910, p. 1, c. 1 and 5; Oct. 22, 1910, p. 1, c. 3, and p. 3, c. 1; Oct. 27, 1910, p. 1, c. 3. Cases were reported as late as 1916; *Kansan*, Oct. 6, 1916, p. 1, c. 4; Oct. 26, 1916, p. 1, c. 3.

Section 49

For the building of Potter Lake see *Kansan*, Oct. 1, 1910, p. 4, c. 1; Nov. 1, 1910, p. 2, c. 3; Nov. 8, 1910, p. 1, c. 1; Jan. 10, 1911, p. 3, c. 4; March 4, 1911, p. 4, c. 3; *Graduate Magazine*, v. 9, 1910-11, pp. 40, 109, and 345.

Tragedies in Potter Lake are recorded in the *Kansan*, May 27, 1911, p. 1, c. 3; May 8, 1912, p. 1, c. 6; May 23, 1921, p. 1, c. 4. Improvements for summer use are described in the *Kansan*, May 21, 1923, p. 2, c. 1; May 20, 1924, p. 1, c. 3; May 18, 1925, p. 3, c. 4. The opening of the public swimming pool is described in the *Kansan*, April 13, 1927, p. 1, c. 6; May 26, 1927, p. 4. For the discontinuance of swimming in Potter, see *Kansan*, May 28, 1928, p. 6, c. 1.

Section 50

The building of East Ad may be followed in the *Kansan*, March 9, 1909, p. 1, c. 1; Oct. 28, 1909, p. 4, c. 1; Dec. 9, 1909, p. 3, c. 1; Dec. 11, 1909, p. 3, c. 1; March 1, 1910, p. 1 (with cut of proposed building); *Graduate Magazine*, v. 9, 1910-11, p. 31; *Kansan*, Nov. 5, 1910, p. 3, c. 1; Jan. 7, 1911, p. 3, c. 3; Sept. 12, 1911, p. 3, c. 1; Sept. 21, 1911, p. 2, c. 2; Oct. 3, 1911, p. 3, c. 2; Oct. 31, 1911, p. 3, c. 1 (first use); Jan. 29, 1913, p. 1, c. 5.

The foundations for Central Ad were complete by Oct., 1913; *Regents' Report for Biennial Period Ending June, 30, 1912*, p. 21; *Kansan*, March 3, 1913, p. 2, c. 2; *Graduate Magazine*, v. 11, 1912-13, p. 58; v. 12, 1913-14, p. 9.

The construction of West Ad began in Sept., 1917; *Kansan*, Sept. 25, 1917, p. 1, c. 1; Feb. 21, 1918, p. 1, c. 3; April 16, 1918, p. 1, c. 3; May 7, 1918, p. 3, c. 1 (construction of West and Central Ad in full swing); Sept. 30, 1918, p. 4, c. 1; *Graduate Magazine*, v. 16, 1917-18, p. 84; *Kansan*, Nov. 19, 1918, p. 1, c. 2; Dec. 17, 1918, p. 1, c. 3; April 14, 1919, p. 1, c. 2. *Graduate Magazine*, v. 17, 1918-19, p. 263; *Kansan*, Sept. 18, 1919, p. 1 (first use).

The final completion of Strong Hall may be followed in the *Kansan*, Sept. 13, 1922, p. 1, c. 4; Jan. 31, 1923, p. 1, c. 7; Sept. 18, 1923, p. 3, c. 1; Dec. 9, 1923, p. 1, c. 7; *Graduate Magazine*, v. 22, Jan., 1924, p. 3. Grading of the grounds in front of Strong was carried out in the summer and fall of 1922; *Graduate Magazine*, v. 21, Oct., 1922, p. 7. The naming of Strong Hall was announced in the *Graduate Magazine*, v. 36, March, 1938, p. 2.

The adoption of the present examination system was announced in the *Kansan*, April 13, 1911, p. 1, c. 1; in 1909, enrollment took place in the "offices of advisers," *Kansan*, Jan. 11, 1910, p. 1, c. 2. The "new" enrollment system is described in the *Kansan*, Jan. 21, 1911, p. 1, c. 5; Feb. 4, 1911, p. 3, c. 1; Sept. 17, 1912, p. 1, c. 6.

The University whistle was used for the curfew according to the *University Weekly*, Dec. 9, 1899, p. 1, c. 3; and as the "alarm" at 7:45 in the *Kansan*, Jan. 29, 1910, p. 2, c. 1. Bells were in use to indicate the end of the class hours; *University Weekly*, Jan. 27, 1900, p. 1, c. 5; *Kansan*, Oct. 16, 1909, p. 3, c. 3. The present whistle system is indicated in the *Kansan*, Feb. 26, 1912, p. 1, c. 1; Feb. 29, 1912, p. 2, c. 3; March 13, 1912, p. 1, c. 3; March 19, 1912, p. 1, c. 1; March 25, 1912, p. 1, c. 1. The "old" whistle was replaced by a new one according to the *Kansan*, Jan. 2, 1923, p. 1, c. 6, and, in 1929, was automatically controlled according to the *Kansan*, Oct. 21, 1929, p. 1, c. 3.

Section 51

Some reminiscences of the period 1910-1914 will be found in "The Old Chambray Dress" by Helen Rhoda Hoopes, *Graduate Magazine*, Sept., 1948, p. 9.

The "new" Commencement is described in the *Graduate Magazine*, v. 6, 1907-8, p. 352; see also *Kansan*, June 2, 1908, p. 1, c. 2. At least in one year, each school of the University had separate Commencement exercises; see the *Courier*, May 25, 1893, p. 247; June 1, 1893, p. 262.

Reference to the matter of faculty caps and gowns is made in the *Kansan*, April 12, 1915, p. 1, c. 4; May 12, 1919, p. 2, c. 1; April 28, 1921, p. 1, c. 7; April 27, 1923, p. 2, c. 1; Dec. 9, 1924, p. 1, c. 3; Dec. 18, 1924, p. 2, c. 1; March 17, 1925, p. 2, c. 2; March 24, 1925, p. 1, c. 5; April 24, 1925, p. 2, c. 2 (Senate voted not to wear caps and gowns); May 2, 1926, p. 1, c. 6; *Graduate Magazine*, v. 24, June, 1926, p. 3 ("Faculty wore caps and gowns this year"). The faculty wore caps and gowns at Chancellor Lindley's inaugural in 1921 (*Graduate Magazine*, v. 19, May, 1921, p. 2), but not until 1926 did it become an unquestioned custom to wear faculty caps and gowns at Commencement exercises.

The Commencement of 1923 is described in the *Graduate Magazine*, v. 21, June, 1923, p. 3. The change of place to the Stadium was first announced in the *Graduate Magazine*, v. 22, Feb., 1924, p. 3; see also v. 22, May, 1924, p. 5, and June, 1924, p. 18. The first evening Commencement was announced in the *Kansan*, May 21, 1925, p. 2, c. 1.

For a history of Commencement dinners see the *Kansan*, May 22, 1912, p. 4, c. 1. The change of place for the dinner to the Union Building is mentioned in the *Graduate Magazine*, v. 27, June, 1929, p. 8.

Section 52

Even the Bowersock Theatre had a predecessor. It was called Liberty Hall. Miss Agnes Emery of Lawrence has in preparation a history of Liberty Hall. For the building of the Bowersock, see the *Courier*, Sept. 22, 1882, p. 10, c. 1. The Bowersock was destroyed by fire in 1911 and rebuilt; *Kansan*, Feb. 18, 1911, p. 1, c. 5. The theatre was remodeled in 1926 (*Kansan*, Nov. 9, 1926, p. 1, c. 4). For the introduction of talkies, see the *Kansan*, March 17, 1929, p. 3; March 19, 1929, p. 3, c. 1. I have seen advertisements in the *Kansan* of road shows at the Bowersock as late as Jan. 18, 1927 (p. 2, c. 3), but none after that date. For the changing names of the Bowersock, see advertisements in the *Kansan*, Sept. 17, 1929, p. 3, and *S. S. Kansan*, July 30, 1940, p. 4, c. 5 (adv.).

Clair Patee's account of the beginnings of the Patee Theatre will be found in *Lawrence, Kansas, 1870-1934, Clippings*, v. 1, pp. 2 and 58, Watson Library. For the early history of the motion picture theatre see Lewis Jacobs, *The Rise of the American Film*, New York, 1939.

The first senior play is described in the *Courier*, June 8, 1892, p. 4, c. 5. At least one University dramatic enterprise had preceded the first senior play; the Athletic Association gave *Midsummer Night's Dream* at the Bowersock

in the spring of 1891 (*Courier*, April 10, 1891, p. 1, c. 3; April 24, 1891, p. 1, c. 3).

The Bohemian Girl was given in 1891 as part of the Quarter Centennial of the University; see "Programme Quarter Centennial 1866-1891."

Additional history of University dramatics may be found in the *University Weekly*, Nov. 12, 1898, p. 2, c. 2; Nov. 19, 1898, p. 1, c. 4; *Jayhawker*, 1906, p. 212; *Graduate Magazine*, v. 11, 1912-13, p. 73; *Kansan*, Oct. 5, 1915, p. 2, c. 1; *University Catalog*, 1914-15, p. 161.

Section 53

The early history of Oread Training School may be followed in the *Kansan*, Sept. 19, 1911, p. 2, c. 3; Oct. 29, 1914, p. 1, c. 1; April 16, 1915, p. 1, c. 2; May 19, 1915, p. 1, c. 1; Sept. 13, 1915, p. 1, c. 2. The change of name from Oread to University High School is reported in the *Kansan*, Sept. 16, 1941, p. 3; see "It's Closing," *Graduate Magazine*, Feb., 1950, p. 5. An account of the opening of the remodeled building as the Faculty Club will be found in the *Kansan*, May 18, 1951.

The discussion of the relation of the University with the high schools of the state is based on an examination of the University catalogs, 1876 to 1907; see also *Annual Report of Regents for 1873*, p. 15; *Regents' Report*, 1876, p. 14; 1877-78, p. 7 (which includes the Marvin quotation); 1879-80, p. 27; *Third Biennial Report of Regents*, 1881-82, p. 28; *Eighth Biennial Report*, 1891-92, p. 19; *Courier*, June 10, 1891, p. 2, c. 2; *Tenth Biennial Report*, 1895-96, p. 8; *University of Kansas Programs, Important Letters and Records*, 1887-1914, p. 15; *Catalog*, 1914-15, pp. 47 and 107 (any graduate of accredited high school admitted to the University).

Section 54

Apparently the University had its first telephone in the school year of 1881-82, as an appropriation for the instrument appears for the first time in the Regents' *Journal* (vol. 1, Nov. 21, 1881, p. 365), and the *University Review* v. 3, 1881, p. 63, stated that the telephone "will be placed in the office next week." There is some question whether in the several years after 1881 the telephone was of much use. In the *Fifth Biennial Report of the Regents*, 1885-86, p. 26, there is record of telephone rental actually being *paid*. Further items on the history of the telephone at the University appear in the *Lawrence Daily Tribune*, Dec. 13, 1887, p. 3, c. 4; *Kansan*, Nov. 21, 1906, p. 1, c. 3; March 6, 1907, p. 4, c. 1; March 17, 1913, p. 4, c. 1; Oct. 4, 1951, p. 4.

The telephone convocation of 1916 is described in the *Graduate Magazine*, v. 14, 1915-16, p. 207; *Kansan*, April 6, 1916, p. 1, c. 1; April 7, 1916, p. 1, c. 1; April 10, 1916, p. 1, c. 3, p. 2, c. 1.

Regarding plans for a semicentennial celebration see *Kansan*, May 10, 1916, p. 1, c. 2; Sept. 21, 1916, p. 3, c. 2.

Section 55

The material included in this section is based very largely on a day-by-day examination of the *Kansan*, especially for the period Jan. to June, 1917; see especially *Kansan*, Feb. 2, 1917, p. 3, c. 1; Feb. 6, 1917, p. 2, c. 1 and 2; March 2, 1917, p. 1, c. 1; May 3, 1917, p. 2, c. 1; May 22, 1917, p. 2, c. 1; Oct. 26, 1917, p. 1, c. 1. Reviews on the University and the war will be found in the *Kansan*, May 10, 1917, p. 1, c. 3; April 5, 1918, p. 1, c. 1; *Graduate Magazine*, v. 15, 1916-17, p. 235; *Jayhawker*, 1918, p. 103. After my conclusion on the early effect of World War I had been written, I ran across a statement of Professor Morison's that shows the Kansas attitude was more or less general. Morison (S. E.), in *Three Centuries of Harvard*, Cambridge, 1936, p. 450, writes, "At the western university where I was teaching when the war broke in Europe, it seemed to the average student as unreal as the

War of the Roses; returning to Harvard early in 1915, one was on the outskirts of battle."

A chronological history of the activities of Company M in the World War will be found in the *Kansan*, May 8, 1919, p. 1, c. 1; for its original organization see the *Kansan*, May 7, 1910, p. 1, c. 5; for its service on the Mexican border, the *Kansan*, Sept. 11, 1916, p. 2, c. 1; Oct. 23, 1916, p. 1, c. 3.

SECTION 56

The erection and removal of the S. A. T. C. Barracks is described in the *Kansan*, Sept. 23, 1918, p. 3, c. 1; Nov. 29, 1918, p. 1, c. 1, p. 3, c. 4; Jan. 20, 1919, p. 1, c. 1; Jan. 23, 1919, p. 1, c. 5; March 27, 1919 p. 1, c. 1; Sept. 22, 1919, p. 4, c. 3; Dec. 6, 1927, p. 3, c. 2.

For the organization of the S. A. T. C. see the *Kansan*, Sept. 16, 1918, p. 1, c. 2; Oct. 2, 1918, p. 1, c. 1; Nov. 7, 1918, p. 1, c. 3; Dec. 12, 1918, p. 1, c. 6 (beginning of demobilization); Jan. 2, 1919, p. 1, c. 4. Reviews of the S. A. T. C. year will be found in the *Graduate Magazine*, v. 17, Oct., 1918, p. 16; Dec., 1918, p. 79; *Jayhawker*, 1919, p. 244.

The influenza epidemic is described in the *Graduate Magazine*, v. 17, 1918-19, p. 45; *Kansan*, Oct. 8, 1918, p. 1, c. 6, also extra edition, same date; Nov. 4, 1918, p. 2, c. 1; Nov. 25, 1918, p. 1, c. 4; *Jayhawker*, 1919, p. 246.

SECTION 57

The establishment of the R. O. T. C. may be followed in the *Kansan*, Feb. 19, 1919, p. 2, c. 1, p. 3, c. 1; March 26, 1919, p. 1, c. 6; Sept. 16, 1919, p. 6, c. 1; Sept. 22, 1919, p. 1, c. 3; Sept. 24, 1919, p. 1, c. 1. The original offices of the R. O. T. C. were in Robinson Gymnasium. They were removed to Fowler Shops in 1923; *Kansan*, Sept. 17, 1923, p. 1, c. 7.

For reaction between faculty and students in 1919 see the *Graduate Magazine*, v. 18, 1919-20, p. 226; *Kansan*, Feb. 18, 1919, p. 1, c. 3; Feb. 19, 1919, p. 1, c. 6; March 12, 1919, p. 1; March 13, 1919, p. 1; June 6, 1919, p. 1, c. 6.

The Strong resignation was announced in the *Kansan*, Sept. 15, 1919, p. 1, c. 6 and 7, p. 2, c. 1; see also *Kansan*, Sept. 16, 1919, p. 5, c. 1; *Graduate Magazine*, 1919-20, v. 18, p. 5.

SECTION 58

Speculations on the probable Chancellor will be found in the Kansan, March 15, 1920, p. 1, c. 5; March 22, 1920, p. 1, c. 3; April 16, 1920, p. 1, c. 3; April 19, 1920, p. 1, c. 5. Announcement of Dr. Lindley's election may be found in the *Graduate Magazine*, v. 18, 1919-20, pp. 252, 261.

For the changes noted in the school year 1919-20 see the *Kansan*, Sept. 15, 1919, p. 1, c. 4 (resignation of Templin); Nov. 4, 1919, p. 1 (death of Green); Sept. 13, 1920, p. 8, c. 1 (appointment of Brandt); *Graduate Magazine*, v. 17, 1918-19, p. 242 (disappearance of Old North).

The condition of the roads and progress of paving may be followed in the *Kansan*, Sept. 13, 1920, p. 2, c. 2; Sept. 23, 1920, p. 1, c. 2; Oct. 13, 1920, p. 1, c. 2; *Graduate Magazine*, v. 21, 1922-23, p. 7; *Kansan*, Sept. 12, 1922, p. 1, c. 6; Sept. 27, 1922, p. 1, c. 5; Oct. 18, 1922, p. 1, c. 1; May 4, 1923, p. 3, c. 3; Oct. 13, 1924, p. 3, c. 3; May 21, 1925, p. 1, c. 1; Sept. 7, 1925, p. 4, c. 1.

For foreign students and the organization of the Cosmopolitan Club see the *Kansan*, April 27, 1920, p. 2, c. 3; Oct. 11, 1920, p. 1, c. 4; *Jayhawker*, 1921, p. 227; *Kansan*, Sept. 11, 1922, p. 3, c. 2.

Short skirts are first reported by the *Kansan*, Dec. 7, 1920, p. 3, c. 1; an editorial on Nov. 23, 1924, p. 2, c. 1, called them indecent. Bobbed hair is reported in the *Kansan*, April 15, 1921, p. 1, c. 6. For the dances tabulated in the text see the *Kansan*, Feb. 25, 1919, p. 1, c. 3; Feb. 4, 1921, p. 1, c. 4; Feb. 7, 1921, p. 1, c. 7.

The appearance of F. D. R. at South Park is recorded in the *Kansan*, Oct. 5, 1920, p. 1, c. 7. That the voters of Kansas justified Mr. Roosevelt's judgment of "independence of thought" is seen by the fact that they failed to give him their votes in the election of 1920 but in 1932 and again in 1936 they strongly supported him. In 1940, Kansans again changed their collective minds and voted for Mr. Roosevelt's opponent. The campaign of Lindley may be followed in the *Kansan*, Sept. 13, 1920, p. 2, c. 1; Oct. 6, 1920, p. 2, c. 1; Oct. 12, 1920, p. 1, c. 3; and the *Graduate Magazine*, v. 19, Oct.-April, 1920-21. For the inaugural of Lindley on June 7, 1921, see the *Graduate Magazine*, v. 19, June, 1921, p. 3.

SECTION 59

The Million Dollar Drive was announced in the *Kansan*, Dec. 11, 1919, p. 1. For its progress, see the *Kansan*, Nov. 15, 1920, p. 1; *Kansan Supplement*, Nov. 23, 1920; *Graduate Magazine*, v. 19, Dec., 1920, p. 5; *Kansan*, Feb. 13, 1922, p. 1, c. 7; March 6, 1923, p. 1, c. 5; April 23, 1928, p. 1; Jan. 3, 1934, p. 1, c. 1.

A stadium had been planned south of the Hill as early as 1910 (*Kansan*, Dec. 14, 1910, p. 5). For the discussion on the site in 1920 see the *Kansan*, May 21, p. 1, c. 7; May 24, 1920, p. 1, c. 7.

Stadium Day is described in the *Kansan*, May 6, 1921, p. 1, c. 5 and 7; May 11, 1921, p. 1.

For the construction of the Stadium, see the *Kansan*, Sept. 12, 1921, p. 1, c. 1; Sept. 27, 1921, p. 1, c. 1; Oct. 26, 1921, p. 1, c. 6; Oct. 28, 1921, p. 1, c. 7; Nov. 18, 1921, p. 4, c. 3; Nov. 11, 1922, p. 1; *Graduate Magazine*, v. 24, Nov., 1925, p. 34; *Kansan*, Jan. 3, 1927, p. 1, c. 3; Oct. 5, 1927, p. 1, c. 2; Oct. 9, 1927, p. 1, c. 6; *Graduate Magazine*, v. 26, Oct., 1927, p. 15; Dec., 1927, p. 13.

For the unveiling of the Green Statue see the *Graduate Magazine*, v. 22, June, 1924, pp. 14 and 18.

SECTION 60

Information on the Totem Pole may be found in the program of Class Day, 1893, *Potlatch*, June 6, 1893, p. 2, where its origin is described; see also the *Kansan*, March 14, 1908, p. 2, c. 3; May 27, 1909, p. 4, c. 2; May 29, 1910, p. 1, c. 1; May 26, 1916, p. 1, c. 6; *Graduate Magazine*, v. 31, May, 1933, p. 8; *S. S. Kansan*, July 3, 1934, p. 1, c. 3.

Falley's eating place is mentioned in *Lawrence Daily Tribune*, Sept. 2, 1887, p. 4, c. 2; *Courier*, Sept. 16, 1887, p. 3, c. 2; Oct. 7, 1887, p. 1, c. 4. Other early ventures in eating places on the campus and off will be found in the *Kansan,* Nov. 29, 1911, p. 1, c. 4 (Billie's); Jan. 22, 1912, p. 1, c. 1; Feb. 14, 1912, p. 2, c. 1; Feb. 28, 1912, p. 2, c. 2; April 24, 1912, p. 1, c. 2; Dec. 11, 1912, p. 1, c. 2; Dec. 10, 1918, p. 3, c. 3; May 28, 1919, p. 1, c. 4; Sept. 17, 1919, p. 1, c. 4. The Commons of 1921 is reported in the *Kansan,* Sept. 12, 1921, p. 1, c. 5; Sept. 20, 1921, p. 1, c. 1; Oct. 10, 1921, p. 1, c. 5; *Graduate Magazine,* v. 27, Oct., 1928, p. 4; *Kansan,* Dec. 1, 1932, p. 1, c. 1. The opening of the cafeteria in the Union Building is reported in the *Graduate Magazine,* v. 26, Oct., 1927, p. 14. Reviews of University eating places will be found in the *Graduate Magazine,* v. 20, Jan., 1922, p. 10; *Kansan,* Feb. 14, 1937, p. 18.

Mention of "Brick's" will be found in the *Kansan,* March 23, 1914, p. 4, c. 4; April 17, 1923, p. 1, c. 4; March 23, 1926, p. 1, c. 3; April 12, 1927, p. 1, c. 2. "Lee's" was at the corner of Adams (Fourteenth) and Tennessee Streets; *Kansan,* Sept. 14, 1914, p. 3 (adv.).

SECTION 61

The early history of the dormitory movement may be followed in the *Kansan,* Oct. 24, 1908, p. 1, c. 1; Oct. 27, 1908, p. 2, c. 1; Sept. 12, 1911, p. 1, c. 5; Oct. 7, 1911, p. 1, c. 5; April 12, 1912, p. 1, c. 3; April 16, 1912, p. 3, c. 1; Oct. 8, 1919, p. 1, c. 1; *Graduate Magazine,* v. 19, March, 1921, p. 5; J. T. Willard, *History of Kansas State College,* Manhattan, 1940, p. 422. Although the Agricultural College hoped to secure funds for a women's dormitory in 1923, it was not until the Legislature of 1925 met that an appropriation of $200,000 was made for this purpose.

For the construction of Corbin Hall see the *Kansan,* Sept. 13, 1922, p. 3, c. 3; Oct. 31, 1922, p. 4, c. 2; Nov. 10, 1922, p. 3, c. 2; *Graduate Magazine,* v. 21, Dec., 1922, p. 9; *Kansan,* March 16, 1923, p. 3, c. 1; March 27, 1923, p. 4, c. 3; *Graduate Magazine,* v. 22, Nov., 1923, p. 16; Dec., 1923, p. 5. For the naming of Corbin Hall see the *Kansan,* May 1, 1923, p. 1, c. 5; Oct. 9, 1923, p. 2, c. 1.

The addition to Corbin, North College Hall, was ready for occupancy by the spring of 1951; see the *Kansan,* Sept. 22, 1950, and the *Alumni Magazine,* Oct., 1950, p. 5.

The death of Dr. Corbin occurred on March 18, 1941, after the section on Corbin Hall had been written originally. Professor Olin Templin's funeral address on Miss

WATKINS MEMORIAL HOSPITAL

Corbin's life will be found in the *Graduate Magazine,* v. 39, March-April, 1941.

SECTION 62

The changes indicated in the first paragraph will be found recorded in the University catalogs, 1920-28.

The building of the new power plant and smokestack is reported in the *Kansan,* Nov. 17, 1921, p. 1, c. 4; Jan. 3, 1922, p. 1, c. 7; Feb. 28, 1922, p. 1, c. 3 (letting of smokestack contract); April 12, 1922, p. 1, c. 1; Sept. 11, 1922, p. 1, c. 6 (smokestack completed).

The discussion concerning the site of the Watson Library may be followed in the *Kansan,* Nov. 22, 1921, p. 3, c. 2; Nov. 30, 1921, p. 1, c. 5; Jan. 3, 1922, p. 1, c. 7; Jan. 9, 1922, p. 2, c. 1; Jan. 11, 1922, p. 2, c. 2.

The construction of Watson is reported in the *Kansan,* Jan. 3, 1923, p. 1, c. 3; Jan. 15, 1923, p. 1, c. 7; Feb. 14, 1923, p. 4, c. 4; March 5, 1923, p. 1, c. 5; March 8, 1923, p. 3, c. 2; *Graduate Magazine,* v. 21, April, 1923, p. 5; *Kansan,* May 3, 1923, p. 3, c. 3 (source of quotation); Sept. 18, 1923, p. 3, c. 1; Jan. 23, 1924, p. 1, c. 4; Sept. 10, 1924, p. 5, c. 1 (first use); Sept. 28, 1924, p. 3, c. 1. The entrance steps to Watson were the cause of *Kansan* discussion for many years; a few items only are given: *Kansan,* March 22, 1934, p. 1, c. 6; Dec. 8, 1935, p. 1, c. 7; Dec. 18, 1935, p. 1, c. 2; Sept. 4, 1936, p. 8, c. 4. The naming of Watson and the quotation from Governor Davis will be found in clippings in *The Library of the University of Kansas,* 1933, p. 26.

The changes in Spooner Library subsequent to the completion of Watson are reported in the *Kansan,* Oct. 24, 1924, p. 4, c. 1; April 5, 1925, p. 1, c. 7; Sept. 11, 1925, p. 1, c. 2; Jan. 27, 1926, p. 1, c. 7; March 21, 1926, p. 1, c. 1; Feb. 5, 1928, p. 3, c. 3; May 1, 1928, p. 1, c. 7; p. 3, c. 2.

SECTION 63

The dismissal and reinstatement of Chancellor Lindley were discussed extensively in the press. The *Kansan* of Jan. 5, 1925, and Jan. 14, 1925, and the *Graduate Magazine,* v. 23, Jan., 1925, are of special importance. The most extensive list of reasons leading to the difficulty is that given by Dean Dyer in the *Kansan,* Jan. 5, 1925, p. 1, c. 5.

For changes in the governing body of the University see *Laws of the State of Kansas,* Lawrence, 1864, p. 195; *Catalog,* 1876-77, p. 43; *Catalog,* 1888-89, p. 5; *General Statutes of Kansas,* Topeka, 1889, vol. 2, p. 1982; *Catalog,* 1913-14, p. 31; *Catalog,* 1917-18, p. 37; *Kansan,* Feb. 18, 1925, p. 1, c. 1; March 3, 1925, p. 1, c. 5; *Kansan,* March 19, 1939, p. 1, c. 3; March 28, 1939, p. 1, c. 2; May 9, 1939, p. 1, c. 7. For reviews, see *Graduate Magazine,* v. 22, March, 1924, p. 10; J. T. Willard, *History of Kansas State College,* Manhattan, 1940, pp. 232 *et seq.*

SECTION 64

Early mention of a student building will be found in the *Kansan,* Sept. 21, 1911, p. 4, c. 3; *Jayhawker,* 1912, p. 20; *Kansan,* June 5, 1913, p. 1, c. 5; Sept. 16, 1913, p. 1, c. 1; Jan. 29, 1914, p. 2, c. 1; Jan. 30, 1914, p. 1, c. 6; Feb. 10, 1914, p. 1; March 5, 1914, p. 1, c. 1; Jan. 15, 1915, p. 1, c. 1.

The construction of the present Union building may be followed in the *Kansan,* Oct. 6, 1924, p. 1, c. 1, p. 6; *Graduate Magazine,* v. 23, June, 1925, p. 5; *Kansan,* Sept. 7, 1925, p. 4, c. 1; Oct. 29, 1925, p. 1, c. 1; April 30, 1926, p. 1, c. 7; *Graduate Magazine,* v. 24, May, 1926, pp. 23 and 25; *Kansan,* Sept. 13, 1926, p. 5, c. 1; Feb. 16, 1927, p. 1, c. 3; Sept. 10, 1927, p. 1, c. 4; Sept. 14, 1927, p. 6, c. 2 (adv. first use); Oct. 9, 1927, p. 1, c. 5, p. 2, c. 1 (dedication); Nov. 8, 1927, p. 1, c. 2; Nov. 30, 1927, p. 2, c. 1; *Graduate Magazine,* v. 38, Feb., 1940, p. 4; *Kansan,* May 24, 1940, p. 1.

The verse quoted in the text will be found on the front page of the *Kansan*, May 24, 1918. I am indebted to Capt. A. F. Uhl of the Fitzsimmons General Hospital for the information concerning Lt. Fitzsimmons and the Hospital which bears his name. Capt. Uhl wrote me from Denver under date of Jan. 18, 1941.

SECTION 65

The Ford that did not choose to run was reported in the *Kansan*, Sept. 15, 1927, p. 2, c. 2. Coolidge made his famous statement Aug. 2, 1927. The automobile problem, beginning in the twenties, is reported, in part, in the *Kansan*, April 8, 1919, p. 2, c. 1; Oct. 3, 1919, p. 2, c. 2; April 20, 1920, p. 2, c. 3; Jan. 11, 1922, p. 2, c. 1; Sept. 12, 1922, p. 1, c. 4; Sept. 27, 1922, p. 2, c. 2; *Graduate Magazine*, v. 24, April, 1926, p. 22; *Kansan*, March 31, 1926, p. 1, c. 5; Sept. 19, 1926, p. 1, c. 4; May 15, 1931, p. 1, c. 7; Sept. 25, 1936, p. 1, c. 3. The opening of Highway 40 is reported in the *Kansan*, Sept. 11, 1922, p. 2, c. 2.

The construction of Hoch Auditorium may be followed in the *Kansan*, March 16, 1925, p. 1, c. 7; May 13, 1925, p. 1, c. 5; Dec. 13, 1925, p. 1, c. 1; March 10, 1926, p. 3, c. 1; April 21, 1926, p. 1, c. 1; May 4, 1926, p. 1, c. 5 (excavation started); Sept. 14, 1926, p. 4, c. 2; Sept. 16, 1925, p. 4, c. 1; Sept. 26, 1927, p. 1, c. 2; *Graduate Magazine*, v. 25, March, 1927, p. 7 (additional appropriation); *Graduate Magazine*, v. 26, Nov., 1926, p. 21; Dec., 1926, pp. 5-7; *Graduate Magazine*, v. 36, March, 1938, p. 2 (naming).

SECTION 66

I have been told, on good authority, that part of the deterioration of Old Snow (and of Fraser as well) was due, not only to insecure footings, but to excavations under the footings in the attempt to secure more space. Reports on the condition of Old Snow will be found in the *Graduate Magazine*, v. 11, 1912-13, p. 157; *Second Biennial Report of State Board of Adm.*, 1916, p. 49.

Information on the changing courses in biology has been secured by an examination of the University catalogs, 1886-87 and 1929-30. For the Department of Bacteriology see the *Twelfth Biennial Report of Regents*, 1900, p. 10; *First Biennial Report of State Board of Adm.*, 1914, p. 44. A brief history of the department will be found in the *Graduate Magazine*, v. 25, Oct., 1926, p. 18.

The construction of new Snow may be followed in the *Kansan*, March 18, 1927, p. 1, c. 7; April 5, 1927, p. 1, c. 1; May 13, 1927, p. 1, c. 4; Sept. 14, 1927, p. 1, c. 5; Sept. 25, 1927, p. 1, c. 3; Nov. 2, 1927, p. 1, c. 6; Feb. 8, 1928, p. 1; Sept. 18, 1928, p. 3, c. 5 (ground broken, June 15); March 25, 1929, p. 1, c. 5; May 12, 1929, p. 1, c. 2; Sept., 1929, No. 1, p. 1, c. 3; Dec. 16, 1929, p. 1, c. 7; Jan. 6, 1930, p. 4, c. 1; June 8, 1930, p. 2, c. 4; *Graduate Magazine*, v. 28, March, 1930, p. 7.

SECTION 67

A review of ten years' building at the University will be found in the *Graduate Magazine*, v. 28, March, 1930. The changes of the nineteen twenties as a national phenomenon are discussed in Frederick Lewis Allen's *Only Yesterday*, New York, 1931.

In addition to the issues of the *Jayhawker*, see the following items for student dress in the twenties: *Kansan*, Dec. 7, 1928, p. 4, c. 2; Nov. 22, 1929, p. 1, c. 2; March 14, 1930, p. 4, c. 4; March 22, 1931, p. 2, c. 2 (comments on girls who wore *pajamas* to Roby's). Sundays on the campus and allied topics will be found in the *Kansan*, April 1, 1925, p. 2, c. 1 (cigarettes); March 10, 1927, p. 2, c. 1; March 13, 1927, p. 2, c. 1; March 17, 1927, p. 2, c. 2; Jan. 21, 1929, p. 1, c. 6 (Library); April 12, 1931, p. 2, c. 3 (movies).

The editorial of the *Kansan* quoted in the text is from the issue of May 5, 1927, p. 2, c. 1; Joe's statement will be found in the *Kansan*, Oct. 19, 1927, p. 3, c. 2; see also

Kansan, March 1, 1927, p. 2, c. 1; April 22, 1932, p. 1, c. 2.

The *Kansan*, Nov. 27, 1923, p. 3, c. 1, and the *Jayhawker*, 1924, pp. 141 and 142, describe the first Hobo Day. For its abolishment see the *Kansan*, Oct. 29, 1939, p. 1, c. 5. The establishment of the *Dove* in 1924 is described by the *Kansan*, Sept. 13, 1925, p. 2, c. 1. For the student induction see the *Kansan*, Sept. 17, 1924, p. 1, c. 5. The form of the exercise was changed somewhat in the first three years of its observance.

SECTION 68

The story of the segregation of the smallpox case was told me as a personal experience by Professor W. J. Baumgartner who was one of the persons that took care of the "case" on the island in the Kaw River. "We did all we could," stated Professor Baumgartner, "to make his stay on the island comfortable and visited with him—at a distance—to relieve his lonesomeness." I might add that such methods of segregation were common fifty years or so ago. I can remember from my own experience a similar situation in the spring of 1914 as an undergraduate student at a small Nebraska college, Grand Island College. Several boys became ill with smallpox and they were taken from the dormitory to an abandoned house over a mile from the college. A number of us took their meals from the dormitory to the confinement house and left the dishes out in the yard. They were then picked up by the least ill of the inmates, who waited on the other students.

The early history of student health service may be followed in the *Kansan*, Oct. 3, 1906, p. 1, c. 3; Oct. 6, 1906, pp. 2 and 3; Oct. 20, 1906, p. 1, c. 4; Nov. 10, 1906, p. 2, c. 3; May 7, 1908, p. 4, c. 3; Sept. 18, 1908, p. 3, c. 1; Oct. 15, 1908, p. 1, c. 5; Nov. 3, 1908, p. 1, c. 4; Nov. 2, 1909, p. 1, c. 5; Sept. 21, 1911, p. 1, c. 2. Reviews may be found in the *Kansan*, Nov. 24, 1931, p. 1, c. 5; *Graduate Magazine*, v. 30, Feb., 1932, p. 8. The epidemic of 1928 is described in the *Kansan*, Dec. 9, 1928, p. 1, c. 7; Dec. 11, 1928, p. 1, c. 5; Dec. 12, 1928, p. 1, c. 4 and 7; Jan. 3, 1929, p. 1, c. 5.

The building of Watkins Hospital is reported in the *Kansan*, Oct. 10, 1930, p. 1, c. 7; Oct. 24, 1930, p. 1, c. 2; Jan. 9, 1931, p. 1, c. 4; April 13, 1931, p. 1, c. 5; May 6, 1931, p. 1, c. 7; Oct. 4, 1931, p. 1, c. 6; Jan. 4, 1932, p. 1, c. 7; Jan. 5, 1932, p. 1, c. 6.

SECTION 69

For the beginning of the depression see the *Kansan*, Oct. 22, 1929, p. 2, c. 4; Nov. 22, 1929 (the 22-page issue) Sept. 23, 1930, p. 1, c. 5; Sept. 12, 1931, p. 6, c. 1; Nov. 2, 1931, p. 1, c. 3; Jan. 11, 1932, p. 2, c. 1 (W. A. White); Feb. 9, 1932, p. 1, c. 5; Feb. 17, 1932, p. 2, c. 1. Reduction of the University budget is noted in the *Kansan*, Sept. 29, 1931, p. 1, c. 7; Jan. 8, 1932, p. 1, c. 5; Feb. 24, 1932, p. 1, c. 7; March 16, 1932, p. 1, c. 7; April 17, 1932, p. 1, c. 1; May 9, 1933, p. 1, c. 5; circular letter, E. H. Lindley, July 7, 1933. The Notre Dame game is reported in the *Kansan*, Oct. 8, 1933, p. 1. For evidence that the living quarters of some students lacked perfection as late as 1940 see the *Kansan*, June 5, 1940, p. 1, c. 1.

The history of the C. S. E. P. may be followed in the *Kansan*, Jan. 16, 1934, p. 1, c. 1, and p. 2, c. 1; Jan. 17, 1934, p. 1, c. 3; Feb. 7, 1934, p. 1, c. 6; Feb. 16, 1934, p. 1, c. 5; March 6, 1934, p. 1, c. 5; *Literary Digest*, May 26, 1934, p. 9; *Kansan*, Sept. 12, 1936, p. 1, c. 3; Sept. 11, 1937, p. 1, c. 4. Brief reviews of the C.S.E.P. are given in the *Jayhawker*, v. 47, 1935, p. 10, and the *Kansan*, Nov. 3, 1939, p. 2, c. 1. With the advent of World War II, the N. Y. A. was terminated; see the *Kansan*, Nov. 22, 1942.

The year 1934 also marked the death of Frank Strong, for eighteen years the Chancellor of the University. His death occurred on August 6, 1934. Reviews of his life and service to the University will be found in the *Graduate Magazine*, v. 33, October, 1934, pp. 2 and 3.

Section 70

An unofficial report a few days after election stated the vote in the 1932 race: Landon, 271,000 votes; Woodring, 267,000; and Brinkley, the goat-gland specialist, 240,000 (*Kansan*, Nov. 10, 1932, p. 1, c. 4).

The meteorological records for 1934-36 may be found: (a) (heat) in the *Lawrence Journal-World*, Sept. 13, 1934, p. 1; *Climatological Data*, Kansas Section, U. S. Dept. of Agriculture, v. 48, 1934, pp. 41, 49, 57, 65, 73; (b) (dust storms) *Kansan*, March 21, 1935, p. 1, c. 3; March 22, 1935, p. 1, c. 3; *Lawrence Journal-World*, March 20, 1935, p. 1; *Kansan*, March 24, 1936, p. 1, c. 3; (c) (flood) *Douglas County Republican*, June 6, 1935, p. 1.

Interest in foreign affairs and the peace strike are reported in the *Kansan*, Feb. 25, 1934, p. 2, c. 1; March 4, 1934, p. 1, c. 4; p. 2, c. 1; Feb. 13, 1935, p. 2, c. 1; April 12, 1935, p. 2, c. 1.

The beginning of recovery is indicated in the *Kansan*, Sept. 6, 1935, p. 1, c. 2; Sept. 22, 1935, p. 1, c. 7; Jan. 21, 1936, p. 1, c. 3; April 3, 1936, p. 1, c. 5; April 16, 1936, p. 2, c. 3; Sept. 20, 1936, p. 1, c. 7.

Section 71

For the erection of Watkins Hall see the *Kansan*, Feb. 8, 1926, p. 1, c. 3; Sept. 14, 1926, p. 3, c. 1; for the home economics practice house see the *Kansan*, Oct. 3, 1929, p. 1, c. 2; Jan. 6, 1930, p. 1, c. 2; for Watkins Home for Nurses, the *Kansan*, Nov. 2, 1937, p. 2, c. 3; Feb. 2, 1938, p. 1, c. 2; for Miller Hall, the *Kansan*, Sept. 17, 1936, p. 1, c. 6; Oct. 21, 1936, p. 1, c. 3; Sept. 13, 1937, p. 4, c. 1.

The death of Mrs. Watkins and her bequests are described at length in the clippings to be found in *Watkins Gifts to Lawrence, Kansas and the University of Kansas*, 1939, v. 2 (in Watson Library). I am also indebted to Professor Templin for information included in this section. Reviews of some of the gifts to the University will be found in the *Graduate Magazine*, v. 27, May, 1929, and in the volume of clippings *Gifts to the University of Kansas*, 1935, in Watson Library. Templin, Carruth, and Battenfeld Halls are described in the *Graduate Magazine*, v. 38, March-April, 1940, p. 9; v. 39, Sept., 1940, p. 9.

For contemporary reference to the original Summerfield scholarships see *Graduate Magazine*, v. 27, June, 1929, p. 12; v. 28, Dec., 1929, p. 9; *Kansan*, Sept. 25, 1929, p. 3, c. 2. For the beginning of the women's scholarships mentioned in the text, see the *Kansan*, Feb. 7, 1940, p. 3, c. 1.

The Endowment Association was organized Oct. 31, 1891, and chartered on Jan. 11, 1893; *Graduate Magazine*, v. 3, 1904-5, p. 67; v. 28, Oct., 1929, p. 7.

Section 72

History of the Medical School from 1905 to 1927 can be followed in the *Kansan*, Dec. 14, 1910, p. 1, c. 3; Jan. 5, 1911, p. 1, c. 5; Jan. 14, 1911, p. 2, c. 1; Feb. 25, 1919, p. 1, c. 4; Nov. 1, 1923, p. 1, c. 5; *Graduate Magazine*, v. 25, March, 1927, p. 7, c. 2. For reviews of the Medical School in this period see the *Graduate Magazine*, v. 18, 1919-20, p. 9; v. 25, Oct., 1926, p. 5. The change of name to University of Kansas Hospitals was reported in the *Kansan*, Jan. 8, 1936, p. 1, c. 3. More recent history of the Medical School can be found in the *Graduate Magazine*, v. 27, May, 1929, p. 15; *Kansan*, Sept. 29, 1938, p. 1, c. 4; *Graduate Magazine*, v. 37, Oct., 1938, p. 4.

The changing requirements in medical education appear in *Report of Board of Regents for Biennium Ending June 30, 1906*, p. 17; catalogs, 1907-8, p. 352; 1918-19, p. 311; 1938-39, pp. 131 and 132; see also *Kansan*, March 4, 1924, p. 3, c. 1.

Section 73

The bean-counting contest is reported in the *Kansan*, Jan. 4, 1939, p. 1, c. 5, and the goldfish-swallower in the issue of April 2, 1939, p. 1, c. 5.

For the resignation of Chancellor Lindley see the *Kansan*, Dec. 2, 1938 (extra), p. 1; his death and memorial service (on Oct. 13, 1940) are reported in the *Graduate Magazine*, v. 39, Sept., 1940, p. 14; Oct., 1940, p. 6; see also the Lindley book in Watson Library.

The election of Mr. Malott was announced in an extra edition of the *Kansan*, April 11, 1939, p. 1. For his inaugural, see the *Kansan*, Sept. 22, 1939 (extra), p. 1, and the *Graduate Magazine*, v. 38, Oct., 1939, p. 5.

Snow was the last chancellor to teach during his incumbency of office and then, not regularly; see the *University Weekly*, Sept. 18, 1897, p. 1, c. 2. The quotation concerning Chancellor Snow and football was reprinted in the *Courier*, April 12, 1894, p. 42, c. 2.

Emperor Jones is reported in the *Kansan*, Oct. 3, 1939, p. 1, c. 5; Oct. 31, 1939, p. 1, c. 2. The history of the colored students at the University has been reviewed by L. M. Peace in the *Graduate Magazine*, v. 7, 1908-9, p. 293. Judge Thacher in his speech at the opening of the University on Sept. 12, 1866, specifically pointed out the "equal privilege of colored students" in the new University; see the reference in section 4. Snow relates the first application of a colored student for admission in 1867; *Graduate Magazine*, v. 3, 1904-5, p. 100. Total enrollment figures (1870-1940) on colored students have been furnished me by the Registrar's office.

Section 74

The history of the boundary lines of Kansas is the subject of a most interesting paper by Geo. W. Martin, one-time editor of the *Junction City Union* and later secretary of the State Historical Society, in *Kansas Historical Collections*, v. 11, 1909-10, p. 53; see also *The Birth of Kansas*, by G. R. Gaeddert, Lawrence, 1940, pp. 58 *et seq.*

Almost from the first issue of the University newspapers there has been mention of summer trips to Colorado. Prof. Snow and a party of five students went there in the summer of 1876 on a collecting expedition (*Kansas Collegiate*, Feb. 14, 1877, p. 4, c. 1). The *Courier* had many interesting accounts of trips to Colorado by faculty and student groups in the eighties; see, for example, the *Courier*, Oct. 1, 1886, p. 2, c. 4; Dec. 3, 1886, p. 3, c. 1; see also the *University Kansan*, Sept. 13, 1889, p. 3, c. 1, for a description of such a trip to Estes Park.

The information concerning the permanent University Camp has been secured from the members of the Department of Geology.

The early history of the State Geological Survey is found in the *University Geological Survey of Kansas*, v. 1, by Erasmus Haworth, Topeka, 1896, p. 1; see also the *Courier*, April 17, 1891, p. 3, c. 1; *Seventh Biennial Report of Regents*, 1889-90, p. 40; *Eighth Biennial Report*, 1891-92, p. 25; *Ninth Biennial Report*, 1893-94, p. 22; *Kansan*, March 5, 1917, p. 1, c. 1 (a review by Haworth).

For the Extension Division see the University *Catalog*, 1891-92, pp. 37 and 113; *Courier*, Sept. 25, 1891, p. 3, c. 3; *Catalog*, 1909-10, p. 36; *Kansan*, Nov. 2, 1909, p. 3, c. 1; see also Frank T. Stockton, *Forty Years of Correspondence Study at the University of Kansas*, 1909-1949, Lawrence, 1951. Professor Stockton has (1954) in preparation a review of the early history of the extension service. It will soon be published under the title *The Pioneer Years of University Extension at the University of Kansas: 1867-1909*.

State services of the University of the present day are described in detail in the *Thirty-eighth Biennial Report of the Chancellor*, Dec. 15, 1940, pp. 26 *et seq.*

Section 75

For the draft registration at the University see the *Kansan*, Oct. 17, 1940. The progress of the Military Science Building may be followed in the *Kansan*, Jan. 10, 1941; Feb. 11, 1941; Dec. 13, 1943; the *Graduate Magazine*, Feb., 1941. For the mineral industries building,

Lindley Hall, see the *Kansan*, Oct. 13, 1940; April 6, 1941; Nov. 7, 1941; Dec. 11, 1941; Sept. 22, 1942; Jan. 21, 1943; Feb. 28, 1943. For enrollment in the R.O.T.C. of this period, see the *Kansan*, April 27, 1941, p. 5.

For the arrival of A-12 on the campus see the *Summer Session Kansan*, July 30, Aug. 3, Aug. 6, and Aug. 10, 1943; *Kansan*, Sept. 27, 1943. Lindley Hall reverted to normal University use after Nov. 1, 1944 (*Kansan*, Oct. 4, 1944), but Dr. John Frye tells me that the Geological Survey and Geology Department moved in piecemeal for some months after the building was released and that it was not until well into 1945 that anything like normal use of Lindley was being made.

The Saturday class "scare" is reported in the *Kansan*, Nov. 19 and 20, 1940, and Jan. 19, 1941.

For the changes in Dyche, 1932-41, see *Thirty-fifth Biennial Report of the University*, 1934, p. 17; *Thirty-sixth Biennial Report*, p. 22; and the *Kansan*, May 20, 1941. The large background painting of the main panorama in Dyche was made by S. T. Dickenson. For Comanche, see book of clippings in the University Library, *Comanche*, 1928. Comanche came to the University upon his death at Fort Riley in 1891 because L. L. Dyche asked for him. Dyche mounted Comanche immediately after his death and he was first put on display at the Chicago World's Fair in 1893.

For the Diamond Jubilee see the *Graduate Magazine*, June, 1941, and the *Kansan*, June 5, 1941.

SECTION 76

For the enrollment in the fall of 1941, see the *Kansan*, Sept. 23, 1941. The "sit-down" strike and its aftermath are described in the *Kansan*, Nov. 11, 1941; the *Graduate Magazine*, Dec., 1941, pp. 67 and 68. Comment on local reaction to Pearl Harbor Day can be found in the *Lawrence Journal-World*, Dec. 8, 1941, "Sunday's Calm is Broken by Clash." The death of Ensign Olson is reported in the *Kansan*, Dec. 21, 1941, and of Lt. Louk in the *Lawrence Journal-World*, March 10, 1942. For Mr. Malott's war message, see the *Kansan*, Jan. 16, 1942. For the announcement of the V-7 program, see the *Kansan*, Jan. 7, 1942. For the physical conditioning course, see the Kansan, Feb. 4, 1942, Sept. 17, 1942, and Oct. 4, 1942; *Summer Session Kansan*, July 28, 1942. "The World at War" was announced by Mr. Malott's message of Jan. 16; for subsequent mention, see the *Kansan*, Jan. 25, 1942, Feb. 10, 1942.

For the beginning of tire rationing see *Topeka Capital*, Dec. 24, 1941; *Kansas City Times*, Dec. 30, 1941; *Lawrence Journal-World*, Feb. 19, 1942. For sugar coupons and ration books, the *Kansan*, April 30, 1942; *Lawrence Journal-World*, May 4, 1942; for gasoline rationing, *Kansas City Times*, June 4, 1942; Oct. 18, 1943. Gasoline rationing began Dec. 1, 1942; see the *Lawrence Journal-World*, Nov. 10, 1942, and Dec. 31, 1942.

Restrictions on the distribution of weather information by the Federal Weather Bureau began Dec. 15, 1941, and were relaxed Oct. 30, 1943. Some modification of the restriction was made Jan. 19, 1942 (information from the Kansas City Weather Bureau by letter of Aug. 24, 1953).

For the Sunflower Ordnance Plant see the *Lawrence Journal-World*, March 26, 1942, June 23, 1942, July 11, 1942, March 19, 1943.

For rent controls see *Lawrence Journal-World*, April 4, 1942, May 4, 1942. Training for employees of S. O. W. and other services is reported in the *Kansan*, Nov. 12, 1942, and Dec. 22, 1942. University Extension classes for the training of war workers over the entire state should also be mentioned. It was estimated in the summer of 1942 that 16,000 persons had been enrolled in such classes (*Summer Session Kansan*, July 21, 1942).

For the Navy Machinists' Mates' School at the University, see the *Lawrence Journal-World*, May 21, 1942; *Summer Session Kansan*, July 10, July 14, 1942; *Kansan*, Sept. 22,

Oct. 8, 1942; April 27, 1943; May 31, 1944, Sept. 15, 1944. Electricians' mates replaced the machinists' mates before Strong Hall was evacuated by the Navy. The first class from the Navy School was graduated Oct. 31, 1942 (*Lawrence Journal-World*, Oct. 29, 1942). For the enrollment figures of this program (given in the text) I am indebted to Miss Mae Rublee, Assistant Registrar. Enrollment in other special programs, not elsewhere discussed, are tabulated below:

	1942-43	1943-44	1944-45
C.A.A. Flight Training	268	463	31
Aeronautical technicians and foremen	66	295	80
Signal Corps Trainees	108	30	—
Special aeronautical trainees	—	30	19

For the Mathematics Department's difficulties of this period I am indebted to information from Dean E. B. Stouffer; see also *Lawrence Journal-World*, Jan. 22, 1943. A photograph of the Mathematics Department for the year 1942-43 appears as the frontispiece in "Kansas University—Items in Its History," Vol. 8, Watson Library, 1946, which shows members from other departments than Mathematics.

For the various activities listed in the concluding paragraph, see the *Kansan*, Oct. 20, 1942, p. 4; Oct. 25, 1942; *Summer Session Kansan*, Aug. 20, 1943; *Kansan*, Dec. 18, 20, 21, 22, 1942; April 30, 1943; May 6, 1943.

SECTION 77

The *Fortieth Biennial Report* (1944), p. 5, states that the trimester plan began July 1, 1943. Actually, however, the first shortened term of 1943 began on Jan. 19 and extended to May 14 (*Kansan*, Jan. 10, 1943; *Graduate Magazine*, May-June, 1943). For the return of school to a normal schedule, see *Kansan*, Dec. 21, 1944, p. 2; Feb. 15, 1945, p. 2; *Summer Session Kansan*, Aug. 17, 1945. Twelve- and sixteen-week terms were still being used in Nov., 1945, according to the *Kansan* of Nov. 8, 1945.

For the appearance of V-12 men on the campus and their housing see the *Summer Session Kansan*, June 29 and July 2, 1943; *Kansan*, Dec. 5, 1945, Dec. 10, 1945, Dec. 14, 1945, p. 4, Jan. 7, 1946.

For ASTP see the *Summer Session Kansan*, July 30, Aug. 10, Aug. 13, Aug. 31, 1943. Types of uniforms on the campus are identified in the *Kansan*, Oct. 1, 1943; the Marine Corps as well as Army and Navy were represented (*Kansan*, Feb. 2, 1943).

For daylight-saving time (Feb. 9, 1942-Sept. 30, 1945), see the *Kansan*, Nov. 13, 1942, p. 6; Sept. 28, 1945.

For ration books, see the *Kansan*, Feb. 12, Feb. 19, and Oct. 5, 1943; faculty gardens are described in the *Kansan*,

March 4, 1943; March 28, 1943; p. 7; April 3, 1944. My partner for two years in a faculty garden south of the Hill was T. C. Ryther.

The figure of 2,300 in military organizations is reported in the *Kansan*, Oct. 20, 1943.

For service ribbons on the campus, see the *Kansan*, April 26, 1944. For tightening draft regulations and its effects see the *Kansan*, Nov. 13, 1942, April 10, 1944, June 5, 1944.

Many of the ASTP left April 23 (*Kansan*, April 23, 1944); see also *Kansan*, March 21, 22, 23, 1944; it was apparently discontinued completely Nov. 1 (*Kansan*, Oct. 4, 1944).

For the enrollment for Oct., 1943, see the *Kansan*, Oct. 1, 1943. For the service of co-eds at the Community Building, see the *Kansan*, Dec. 3, 1942.

For replacement of machinists' mates by electricians' mates, see the *Kansan*, Dec. 6, 1943; for their departure from the campus, *Kansan*, Sept. 15 and Oct. 4, 1944. For the reoccupation of Strong Hall, see the *Kansan*, Sept. 15, 1944, and Jan. 26, 1945, p. 3. For the semester beginning Nov. 1, 1944, there were 432 Navy men and 127 Army men, not all of whom were in uniform (*Kansan*, Jan. 22, 1945). The quotation given in the text is from the *Kansan*, Sept. 15, 1944. p. 6.

For the predicted enrollment of 6,000, see the *Kansan*, May 17, 1945. The end of rationing for various classes of goods can be followed, if any one is interested, in the *New York Times* for the following dates: (gasoline), Aug. 16, 1945; (blue-point canned goods), Aug. 16, 1945; (shoe rationing), Oct. 31, 1945; (red-point goods and meats), Nov. 24, 1945; (tires, ended Jan. 1, 1946), Dec. 21, 1945. Sugar rationing was not discontinued until June, 1947 (*New York Times*, June 12, 1947).

The number of University students in the armed forces was reported by the alumni secretary; see the *Kansan*, May 17, 1945.

For German POW, see the *Kansan*, June 6, 1945; *Summer Session Kansan*, Aug. 3, 1945.

Section 78

For the requirements of Western Civilization and General Biology see the *Kansan*, Dec. 20, 1944, March 7, 1945, Sept. 26, 1945. For 12-, 16-, and 18-week terms see the *Kansan*, Sept. 24, 1945, and Nov. 8, 1945.

For the student walkout of 1945, see the *Kansan*, Nov. 19, 1945. For the Student Book Store, see the *Kansan*, Nov. 8, 1945, p. 2; Nov. 30, 1945, p. 4; Jan. 22, 1946; March 15, 1946; *Summer Session Kansan*, July 9, 1946; Sept. 23, 1946, p. 7 (adv.).

For the spring enrollment in 1946 see the *Kansan*, Feb. 13, 1946; Feb. 18, 1946, p. 4. The housing in Thayer Museum is reported in the *Kansan*, Feb. 11, 1946, p. 8; the bus schedule from Sunflower in the *Kansan*, Feb. 15, 1946. Sunflower, Kansas, it might be stated, is a village that developed during the construction and initial use of nearby Sunflower Ordnance Works. The addition of new staff members, many of whom were assistant instructors, is reported in the *Kansan*, Feb. 21, 1946, p. 2.

For the World War II memorial see *Kansan*, March 29, 1946, p. 2; Report, *Supplement to the Kansan*, April 9, 1946. For the dedication of Danforth Chapel, see the *Kansan*, March 29, April 1, and April 2, 1946. The first wedding in Danforth is reported in the *Kansan*, March 20, 1946.

Plans for housing are discussed in the *Kansan*, Jan. 11, 1946; May 22, 1946.

Plans for Commencement in 1946 are reported in the *Kansan*, June 4, 1946; for Commencement, 1945, see the *Kansan*, June 15, 1945; the *Graduate Magazine*, May-June, 1945, p. 5. For better football prospects in the fall of 1946, see the *Kansan*, June 4, 1946, p. 6; for the prediction of 7,000 students, the *Kansan*, June 5, 1946. June of 1946 also marked the end of the V-12 program on the campus; see the *Kansan*, June 4, 1946, p. 2; June 5, 1946.

For the enrollment of 1946 see the *Kansan*, Oct. 3, 1946; Feb. 14, 1947. The official enrollment at Lawrence, two weeks after the beginning of the semester, according to Miss Mae Rublee, Assistant Registrar, was 9,090; Miss Rublee's figure for the total enrollment for the school year 1946-47 was 10,439.

For housing difficulties see the *Kansan*, Sept. 23, 1946 (which reports 1,100 men in the barracks at Sunflower) and Sept. 30, 1946, p. 2, a report of Irvin Youngberg, housing director. For the Sunnyside housing addition see the *Kansan*, Oct. 15, 1946; Dec. 9, 1946; Jan. 24, 1947; *Summer Session Kansan*, Aug. 1, 1947.

The criticism of crowded quarters in organized houses is in the *Kansan*, Oct. 10, 1946; the addition of Quonset huts to the campus is reported in the *Kansan*, Sept. 20, 1946; Oct. 3, 1946; night classes, in the *Kansan*, Sept. 27, 1946; saturation of parking space, in the *Kansan*, Oct. 8, 1946.

For the married student on the campus see the *Kansan*, Nov. 20, 1946, p. 8 (where the figures 1,575 and 135 are reported); *Summer Session Kansan*, Aug. 8, 1947, p. 8. The baby contest at Sunflower is reported in the *Kansan*, Dec. 4, 1946, and Dec. 6, 1946. Delay of veterans' checks was a matter of frequent comments; see, for example, the *Kansan*, Nov. 18 and 21, 1946, and April 30, 1947. Single veterans had then a government allotment of $65 a month (later increased to $75). The affair of the baby parked behind Lindley is reported in the *Kansan*, Dec. 13, 1946, p. 8, and Dec. 16, 1946.

The magnitude of federal support for veterans on the campus during the school year 1946-47 is shown by the fact that $2,283,000, it was estimated, was paid by the government that year for students on the K.U. campus; see *Summer Session Kansan*, July 3, 1947.

For discussion on the racial problem see the *Kansan*, March 28, 1947; May 20, 1947; *Summer Session Kansan*, July 25 and July 29, 1947; May 16, May 20, 1952, p. 2; Dec. 9, 1952, p. 2.

For additions to University facilities see the *Kansan*, Dec. 10 and 12, 1946; Jan. 9, 1947; *Summer Session Kansan*, July 1 and 15, 1947; Aug. 5 and 15, 1947. The first addition to the Union building is reported in the *Kansan*, Jan. 14, 1947; May 12, 1947; *Summer Session Kansan*, July 18, 1947. The awarding of the contract for the enlargement of the University Library is reported in the *Summer Session Kansan*, Aug. 15, 1947.

The Commencements of 1946 and 1947 are reported in the *Graduate Magazine*, May-June, 1946, p. 4; May-June, 1947, p. 4.

Section 79

The enrollment figures reported were furnished by Miss Mae Rublee. The largest Summer School enrollment was reached in 1948 with students totaling 3,558. During the summer of 1949, 3,467 were enrolled (*Summer Session Kansan*, June 17 and 24, 1949).

Chancellor Malott's report on the size of the teaching staff in 1948 and 1949 will be found in the *Kansan*, Sept. 17, 1947, and *Summer Session Kansan*, July 1, 1949.

For "emergency" buildings added in post-war years, see the *Kansan*, Sept. 12, 1947, p. 7; Sept. 17, 1947; Oct. 23, 1947, p. 8; Nov. 21, 1947, p. 9. The enrollment in mathematics courses is summarized for the period 1920-1948 on pp. 32-34 of "Proposed Research Projects for the Dept. of Mathematics of the University of Kansas," Nov. 22, 1948 (MS). I am indebted to Prof. G. B. Price for the privilege of examining this manuscript. For Chemistry enrollment and staff see my *Fifty Years in Bailey Chemical Laboratory*. Other reports bearing on the rapid increase in the University teaching staff in the period 1947-1948 may be found in *Summer Session Kansan*, June 27, July 29, 1947; Sept. 23, 1947, p. 2; Oct. 23, 1947, p. 8; Nov. 21, 1947, p. 7; May 25, 1948, and Oct. 5, 1948, p. 8.

For the growth in research at the University see *Forty-second Biennial Report of the Chancellor*, p. 8; *Kansan*, Nov. 11, 1948; March 10, 1949; *Summer Session Kansan*, June 17, 1949, p. 12.

For the University salaries, see comment by Chancellor Malott in *Forty-first Biennial Report* (1947), p. 15: "The faculty [salary] scale is among the lowest in midwestern state universities"; *Forty-second Biennial Report* (1949), p. 23; *Forty-third Biennial Report* (1951), p. 7. Personal experiences both of myself and of departmental colleagues have also been recalled.

For Cadillacs and similar conveyances on the campus, see the *Kansan*, Oct. 17, 1947; Nov. 10, 1947; *Life*, Nov. 10, 1947.

Mention of six campus policemen is made in the *Kansan*, Feb. 24, 1948, p. 8. The football co-championships are reported in the *Kansan*, Dec. 2, 1946, and Nov. 24, 1947. For the resignation of the football coach, see the *Kansan*, Feb. 2, 1948. Chancellor Malott in the *Forty-first Biennial Report* (1947), p. 6, commented: "The athletic program of the University has been completely revamped looking forward to improved intercollegiate and intramural athletics. The result of this reorganization is already in evidence." This statement plus another one made by Mr. Malott in the *Kansan*, March 4, 1947, indicated that the problem of athlete subsidization was at least emerging into a matter of public discussion.

The foreign-language requirement in the College was reported in the *Kansan*, Feb. 25, 1948; the decrease in number of technical courses for the Engineering School in the *Kansan*, Sept. 15, 1947, p. 2; the curtailed attendance at basketball games was made necessary, of course, by the large student body and the limited seating capacity of Hoch Auditorium; see the *Kansan*, Oct. 13, 1947, p. 6, and Nov. 14, 1947, p. 1.

For the results of the election of 1948 see the *Lawrence Journal-World*, Nov. 4 and 6, 1948; the *Kansan*, Nov. 5, 1948, p. 9. The ruling of the Attorney-General will be found in the *Kansan*, Oct. 5, 1948.

Section 80

The income of the University is published in the Biennial Reports of the Chancellor. As had been pointed out previously, the income of the University is derived from appropriations of the Legislature, from student fees and from other sources. The appropriations of the Legislature for the last three biennia run, in round numbers, $18,-400,000 (1949-51); $16,400,000 (1951-53); $18,600,-000 (1953-55). I am indebted to Mr. Raymond Nichols for these data. None of the figures reported in the text or here in the notes include gifts to the University, which, in recent years, have amounted to well over a million dollars a year.

The Forty-first Biennial Report of the Chancellor (1947) on pp. 32-62 lists the employees of the University by trades and professions. Over seventy trades and professions are represented in the "classified service" alone.

The appropriations (which totaled $390,000 altogether) for the addition to the University Library was first made by the Legislature of 1945 (*Forty-first Biennial Report of the Chancellor*, 1947, p. 14; see also *Forty-second Biennial Report*, 1949, p. 22). The opening of the new Library additions are reported in the *Kansan*, Jan. 18, 1950, and Jan. 30, 1950, p. 2. The Ellis Collection was willed to the University upon the death of the owner Ralph Ellis in 1945. A legal contest of some length developed and the University did not acquire title to the collection until 1949; see the *Kansan*, Oct. 10, 1949.

Mr. Robert Vosper, the University Librarian, kindly supplied me with information concerning the present status of the Library. As of August, 1953, the holdings of the Library comprised 580,000 volumes, but this figure did not include the many volumes of the Fitzpatrick Collection and 30,000 volumes of the Crerar Collection, both at that time uncatalogued. For the library of the Law School see *Forty-third Biennial Report of the Chancellor*, 1950, p. 8; *Forty-fourth Report*, 1952, p. 15. For the Clendening Collection see the *Forty-first Biennial Report of the Chancellor*, 1947, p. 12; *Forty-second Biennial Report*, 1949, p. 19.

For information on the Midwest Interlibrary Center I am indebted to Dean J. H. Nelson, the University's first representative of the Center, who took an active part in its formation; see also the *Summer Session Kansan*, July 1, 1949.

For the problem and planning of dormitories see the *Kansan*, Dec. 21, 1949, p. 20; Jan. 10, 1950, p. 8 (North Hall); *Summer Session Kansan* (four scholarship halls), July 3, 1950; *Kansan*, Sept. 22, 1950 (North Hall ready by Nov. 1); March 6, 1951, p. 2 (furnishings for North Hall have arrived); Nov. 30, 1951, p. 6c (North Hall in use). For the first addition to the Union Building, see the *Kansan*, Jan. 14, 1947; May 12, 1947 (work begun); *Summer Session Kansan*, July 18, 1947; *Kansan*, May 21, 1948, p. 1. For the plans for the million-dollar addition see the *Kansan*, May 16, 1950, p. 8; Nov. 20, 1950 (bids opened); Jan. 17, 1951, p. 12 ("now under construction").

The progress of the Faculty Club is reported in the *Kansan*, May 24, 1950; *Summer Session Kansan*, July 28, 1950, p. 7; *Kansan*, May 16, 1951.

For the criticisms of jeans see the *Summer Session Kansan*, July 25, 1950, p. 6; Aug. 1, 1950, p. 10.

For the foreign student on the campus, see the *Jayhawker*, fall, 1948, p. 76; the *Kansan*, Oct. 10, 1950. For information on the Fulbright and other similar programs, I am indebted to Professor J. A. Burzle. For the past three years, the University has also served during the summer months as one of the orientation centers in the United States to introduce foreign students who were enrolling in American universities to American customs and ways; see the *Summer Session Kansan*, July 27, 1951; see also *Kansan*, Nov. 10, 1950, p. 2; May 17, 1951; May 22, 1951; *Summer Session Kansan*, June 12, 1951, p. 8.

For the impact of the Korean War on the campus, see the *Summer Session Kansan*, June 27, 1950, p. 6;

July 3, 1950, p. 4; Sept. 13, 1950; Sept. 19, p. 2; Dec. 4, 1950, p. 6 (student editorial); Dec. 13, 1950; Jan. 8, 1951; April 4, 1951; May 9, 1951; May 23, 1951; *Summer Session Kansan*, June 15, 1951; June 19, 1951; June 22, 1951, p. 5.

The flood of 1951, actually two floods following each other in fairly rapid succession, is only briefly reported in the *Summer Session Kansan;* see issues of June 26, 1951, July 17, 1951. The crest was reached at Lawrence on July 14; more extensive information on the flood of 1951 will be found in the *Lawrence Journal-World* for June and July, 1951.

Chancellor Malott's resignation was announced by an extra issue of the *Kansan*, Jan. 27, 1951. Discussion on the possibility of the event will be found in earlier issues. Brief reviews and appreciations of Mr. Malott's administration will be found in the *Summer Session Kansan*, July 1, 1949 (for a ten-year period); in the *Kansan*, May 22, 1951, pp. 6 and 7; and the *Alumni Magazine*, Oct., 1949, p. 12 (by Dolph Simons; for enrollment figures cf. p. 5); Feb., 1951, pp. 7 and 8 (by Roy Roberts).

The buildings completed during the latter part of Mr. Malott's administration are described elsewhere in these pages.

The original appropriation for the Field House was made in 1949 as was that for the New Science Building; see *Forty-third Biennial Report of the Chancellor*, 1951, p. 21; supplementary appropriations for both buildings were made in 1951, *Forty-fourth Biennial Report*, 1951, p. 15. Work for the Field House and Science Building were both started in the spring of 1951; *Kansan*, May 2, 1951, p. 8. Priorities for steel were secured for the Science Building but not the Field House; as a result the Science Building is now (summer, 1954) rapidly nearing completion.

For the Campanile and Memorial Drive see *Graduate Magazine*, Nov., 1945; *Graduate Magazine*, May, 1949, p. 5; June, 1951, p. 11; *Kansan*, Dec. 4, 1951 (opening of Memorial Drive). For landscaping and improvement of campus, see the *Graduate Magazine*, December, 1945, p. 3; *Kansan*, May 16, 1950 (resurfacing of campus streets). For the picnic and recreation area see the *Kansan*, Oct. 2, 1945, p. 2; *Graduate Magazine*, September, 1946, p. 14.

Other class gifts, including those that have aided in beautifying the campus, will be found in a review in the *Alumni Magazine*, May, 1952, p. 5.

The General Research Fund is described in Mr. Malott's request to the Legislature in the *Forty-third Biennial Report of the Chancellor* (1951), p. 23.

As I was greatly interested in the origin of the General Research Fund, I wrote Mr. Malott concerning it. He replied by letter of September 3, 1953. Evidently the real significance and importance of this venture was not realized by Mr. Malott as he replied that he could not tell me how it originated. Upon talking with Dean Nelson and Executive Secretary Nichols, I have come to the conclusion that the Fund had its origin in a suggestion by Mr. Nichols. It was pressed so vigorously by Dean Nelson and Mr. Nichols that Mr. Malott agreed to add it to the Budget then being prepared. Mr. Malott then saw that its successful passage by the Legislature and the Governor was insured with the remainder of the 1951 Budget.

SECTION 81

For the material in the text bearing on the development of the Medical School in post-war years, I have depended very largely on the extensive newspaper and magazine clippings assembled in *Franklin D. Murphy, M.D.*, in the University of Kansas Library. In the early pages of this scrapbook will be found much material. Virtually all the items are identified as to source and date—bearing on the development of the "Three-Point

Plan" and the passage of the Rural Health Bill by the Legislature of 1949. National recognition of the Rural Health program—and of Dr. Murphy—will be found in the *Saturday Evening Post*, May 26, 1951. Mr. Raymond Nichols and Dr. Glen R. Shepherd have furnished me with extensive data on the use of funds in the development of the Medical Center in recent years. Other sources of information on these matters will be found in the *Forty-fourth Biennial Report of the Chancellor*, Dec. 1, 1952, and the issues of *Kansas University School of Medicine and Medical Center Bulletin*, v. 1, 1949, to the present. The dedication of the Medical Student Center is described in *Daily Kansan*, April 12, 1954, p. 1.

For recent University residence halls and dormitories see *Daily Kansan*, Feb. 15, 1952, p. 8 (Stephenson Hall); *Summer Session Kansan*, July 11 and 18, 1952 (Sellards, Pearson, Battenfeld, Jolliffe and Stephenson Halls); *Daily Kansan*, Oct. 17, Nov. 14, 1952, p. 1 (dormitory plan); *Summer Session Kansan*, June 16, 1953, p. 3 (razing of Carruth Hall, the old Chancellor's residence); Irvin Youngberg, "Student housing, K.U.'s No. 1 Problem," *Alumni Magazine*, May, 1954 (the most recent developments in housing).

For the William Allen White Foundation, see Minutes of Meeting of Wm. Allen White Memorial Foundation, Nov. 20, 1944, where the articles of incorporation of Wm. Allen White Foundation, Inc., were first approved; see also *"Organization and Objectives" of the William Allen White Foundation*, 1950.

A brief review of the radio and television division of the University will be found in *Annual Catalogue of the University of Kansas* (General Information), Aug. 1, 1953, p. 129. For colored television in Medical School instruction at K.U. see the *New York Times*, Nov. 25, 1951, section 1, p. 66.

SECTION 82

For the appointment and inauguration of Chancellor Murphy, see *Summer Session Kansan*, July 2, and 3, 1951; *Daily Kansan*, Sept. 12, 1951, p. 8a, Sept. 17, 1951, p. 1; *Alumni Magazine*, Sept., 1951. The text of Dr. Murphy's inaugural address will be found in the scrapbook in the University Library, *Franklin David Murphy, M.D. Chancellor of the University of Kansas*, v. 1, p. 44. A review of Malott's administration will be found in the *Summer Session Kansan*, July 3, 1951, p. 8.

For Dr. Murphy's report on the first year of his activities, see *Biennial Report of the Chancellor for the Biennium Ending June 30, 1952*. The total legislative appropriation for the University at Lawrence and Kansas City for all uses—maintenance, salaries, building, etc.—totaled $18,602,415 for the biennium 1953-1955; for 1951-1953, the total was $16,359,563. According to a report of Chancellor Murphy early in 1954, 52 per cent of the University expense is earned through fees of many types, the remaining 48 per cent represents the appropriation; see *Lawrence Journal-World*, April 10, 1954, p. 1.

The enrollment figures, of course, given in the text come directly from the Registrar's office; the surprising increase in college enrollments for the fall of 1952 is reported in the *Daily Kansan*, Oct. 6, 1952, p. 1, and for forty-two Kansas colleges in *Transactions of the Kansas Academy of Science*, v. 55, 1952, p. 391.

For the basketball victories of the spring of 1952, see the *Daily Kansan*, March 11, March 28, March 31, April 1, 1952. The following year, the University basketball team were finalists in the N. C. A. A. competition, losing to the University of Indiana by a single point; see the *Daily Kansan*, March 19, 1953.

For information on the remodeling and reorganization of Spooner Hall, see the *University of Kansas Newsletter*, May 5, 1951, and May 24, 1952; the *Daily Kansan*, Feb. 27, 1953, p. 1. The organ in Spooner Hall was the gift of Arthur Weaver, '15, and Charles McManus, '36. Many other friends have contributed generously to the development of the Museum of Art in recent years.

SECTION 83

I am indebted to J. B. Priestley for the analogy of the criticizing wife. It will be found in *Rain upon Godshill*, New York, 1939, chap. 13. Incidentally this book and a previous one by Mr. Priestley, *Midnight on the Desert*, 1937, present some intelligent criticisms and appreciations of American life in general and western life in particular.

For the claim of distinguished graduates in the sciences, see *The University and the State*, Bulletin of the University of Kansas, Lawrence, Jan. 15, 1939, p. 24; *American Men of Science*, v. 1 to 6.

An interesting review by H. E. Zabel, "The Contribution of Kansas to *American Men of Science*, 7th Ed." will be found in *Transactions, Kansas Academy of Science*, v. 48, pp. 409-421 (1946). In the 1950-51 edition *Who's Who in America*, 231 University alumni were listed, putting Kansas 24th in numbers among the universities of the country and 12th among state universities; see *Kansan*, Nov. 20, 1951, p. 7; March 26, 1952, p. 6.

In recent years, the achievements of alumni have been the subject of much review. The pages of the *Graduate Magazine* are, of course, the logical place to look for such records; see especially, however, *Graduate Magazine*, v. 33, June, 1935, p. 11; v. 34, June, 1936, p. 10; v. 35, June, 1937, p. 9; v. 36, Nov., 1937, p. 10; Dec., 1937, p. 11; June, 1938, p. 11; v. 37, June, 1939, p. 15. There are also in Watson Library a number of volumes of clippings dealing with the accomplishments of former students. One does not ordinarily think of a state university as a developing ground for foreign missionaries, but they are referred to in one of the citations given above; and the *Kansan*, on Sept. 12, 1921, p. 1, c. 4, listed eighty-three living graduates in this field. When we mention University students who have played prominent parts in the life of the state we should not, of course, forget its governors. Alfred M. Landon, of the class of 1908, and Walter A. Huxman, of the class of 1914, both have achieved this enviable distinction. Landon, as all Kansans know, was the Republican presidential candidate in 1936. In addition to these two men, Gov. Jonathan M. Davis and Gov. Ben Paulen, were also one-time students at the University.

Reviews of the West and its effect on culture, or vice versa, are few and far between. The nearest approaches to the subject will be found in W. P. Webb's *The Great Plains*, Ginn and Company, 1931, chaps. X and XI; Everett Dick's *The Sod House Frontier*, New York, 1937, chaps. 24, 26, 35, and D. E. Clark's *The West in American History*, New York, 1937, chap. 26; see also the first two chapters in William Allen White's *The Changing West*, New York, 1939. White has also commented directly on the failure of Kansas and the University to produce many notables in the arts; see *Daily Kansan*, April 9, 1924, p. 1, c. 5. I have seen no study on Kansas, although Floyd Benjamin Streeter, one of the class of 1911, in his book *The Kaw*, New York, 1941, chap. 23, does review Kansas writers. Of the writers selected by Streeter for discussion, only one, W. A. White, was a University student. Other reviews, which include Kansas writers, will be found in Mae Reardon, *A Glance at the Kansas Novel*, Master's Thesis, University of Kansas, 1915; James P. Callahan, *Kansas in the American Novel and Short Story*, Master's Thesis, University of Kansas, 1926 (reprinted in *Kansas Historical Collections*, v. 17, 1926-28, pp. 139 ff.); Myra E. Hull, *Kansas Prose Writers*, University of Kansas, 1936; Elizabeth B. Culver, *A Collection of Writings by Kansas Authors*, Master's Thesis, University of Kansas, 1937.

The list of Kansas musicians referred to in the text will be found in Edna Reinbach's *Music and Musicians in Kansas*, Topeka, 1930. It might be added as a matter of University interest that of the three best-known Kansas composers (not native Kansans, however, or products of the University) in Miss Reinbach's list, two, Carl Preyer and Charles S. Skilton, were for many years members of the faculty of the University of Kansas. In the recent death of Professor Skilton (March 12, 1941), the University has lost one of its most creative figures. The third Kansas musician referred to above was Thurlow Lieurance, of the faculty of Wichita University.

The review of Kansas artists (also by Miss Reinbach) will be found in the *Collections of Kansas Historical Society*, v. 17, 1926-28, p. 571. As supplementing the argument on the effect of the frontier environment on culture, it might be pointed out that only three native Kansans appear on Miss Reinbach's list who have achieved recognition as painters in *Who's Who in America*: John Noble, Henry Salem Hubbell, and Van Dearing Perrine. Of these three, one was self-taught; the other two were trained outside the state. I might add that, in recent years, I have made an extensive study of genre artists in the region lying between the Mississippi River and the Pacific Coast states. Hundreds of biographies and accounts have been examined. I have concluded that indigenous artists in this region are few in number and almost unknown. Up to 1910, only two, George Bingham of Missouri, and Charles Russell, a Montanan, had received national recognition. Two Kansas artists, George M. Stone and Henry Worrall, belong to the small group of indigenous artists. Although Stone had a local reputation far beyond that of Worrall, yet Worrall was probably known to a far larger national audience than Stone. I doubt, however, if there are a half dozen Kansans living today who have ever heard of Worrall or know anything about his work. This same western region had, however, been visited by many celebrities in the painting world who came in search of material: Albert Bierstadt, Sanford R. Gifford, Thomas Moran, Gilbert Gaul, William J. Hays, R. A. Blakelock, and Frederic Remington—a resident of Kansas in the early eighties—to mention but a few; see my book *Artists and Illustrators of the Old West*, New York, 1953.

As far as I have been able to learn, the University has no graduate who achieved national recognition as a dramatist, although Brock Pemberton, of the class of 1908, is listed in the last edition of *Who's Who* as a theatrical producer. For the formation of the Department of Dramatics, see section 52. The single teacher of art in 1902, referred to in the text, created an important influence in the early development of art courses and of art appreciation which has persisted to this day. His name, as many older students of the University will recall, was Professor W. A. Griffith, a native Kansan. He was, in a large measure, responsible for securing the notable Thayer art collection for the University. Discussions of his work will be found in the Griffith book of clippings in Watson Library. The expansion of training in fine arts began in the early 1920's; see, for example, the *Kansan*, Sept. 12, 1921, p. 1, c. 4.

The quotation concerning the Middle West as the ultimate cradle of creative expression will be found in an article by Bernard Frazier, of the class of 1929, a young sculptor of whom the University may well be proud. The article was published in the *Kansan*, April 28, 1940, p. 6, c. 3. Frazier reviews briefly the recent contributions of Midwesterners, including Kansans, to art. Also pertinent is the appearance of W. L. White's novel *What People Said*, New York, 1938. White's work, based on the recent Kansas scene, won the approval of many critics. Any credit that the University may claim in Mr. White will have to be shared, however, with Harvard.

The architecture of the buildings on the campus is discussed in J. H. Compton, *The Building of the University of Kansas*, Master's Thesis, K.U., 1932; see also the interview with Goldwin Goldsmith in the *Kansan*, Sept.

11, 1916, p. 6, c. 1. Compton, Professor J. M. Kellogg, and Dean Rexford Newcomb, a former student of the University and now Dean of the College of Fine and Applied Arts of the University of Illinois, all have expressed a preference for Fowler Shops (especially as it was before the fire of 1918) as the best building, architecturally, on the campus; Compton in his thesis, Kellogg by an interview, and Newcomb in a recent letter to me. Other friends to whom I have talked about the matter prefer Fraser Hall as the most pleasing building on the campus. Such preference is probably based on its construction from native stone, and its massive size and splendid proportions; there is something about the shape of its roof, however, that doesn't seem quite right—a flaw that an architect probably notices at once. It would have been far better, from the standpoint of architectural unity, I believe, to have followed the pattern set by Fraser, as it was the first building on the present campus. Endless variations and improvements in the style could have been effected with the passing of years in subsequently built additions to the campus. I have heard it stated, however, that construction of University buildings of native stone was not possible after 1910 because of a lack of a sufficient number of suitably trained masons. Goldsmith criticizes Fraser on the ground that it is a composite of too many styles, an example of my "neo-mongrel" style. It is more typically Kansan, however, to my way of thinking, than any other building on the campus.

It is not surprising that the first well thought-out campus planning came from Professor F. O. Marvin. A discussion of this plan, for the original forty-acre campus, will be found in the *University Weekly*, Nov. 13, 1897, p. 1, c. 5. It should also be pointed out that it is not surprising that earlier plans of campus planning were not suggested. Although Jefferson had early led the way (see H. B. Adams, *Thomas Jefferson and the University of Virginia*, Washington, 1888), state universities in general, like Topsy, just "growed." It was not until the most important figure in American landscape architecture, Frederick Law Olmsted, planned the grounds for the Columbian Exposition in 1893, that the science of city and institution planning became well recognized; Olmsted had, however, by the late eighties laid out the design for Leland Stanford University (see

Dictionary of American Biography, New York, 1934, v. 14, p. 24).

Later plans for University development will be found in the *Graduate Magazine*, v. 3, 1904-5, p. 111; *Catalog*, 1904-5, opp. p. 33; *Kansas Engineer*, No. 1, 1914-15, p. 3; *S. S. Kansan*, July 11, 1919, p. 3, c. 1; *Kansan*, March 22, 1922, p. 1, c. 5. It should be mentioned that still another important factor in the diverse character of the buildings on the campus has been the architectural preferences of the incumbent Chancellors. Judging by the buildings erected during their terms of office, Snow preferred the Romanesque; Strong a more classical style (inferred from the two most important buildings, architecturally, erected during his term of office, Green Hall and Strong Hall); Lindley, the Gothic. Of course, it also might be observed that the Chancellors were probably reflecting the prevailing architectural fashions of their time.

It should be noted that legislative appropriations now constitute only about half the income of the University. Receipts from student fees, service departments, etc., form the remainder; see *The University and the State*, Jan. 15, 1939, p. 9.

A ten-year building program was proposed in 1952 by Chancellor Murphy; see *Kansan*, Sept. 29, 1952.

For the mill tax see the *Kansan*, Nov. 7, 1918, p. 1, c. 6; Jan. 17, 1941, p. 1, c. 1; March 18, 1941, p. 1, c. 5. The R. O. T. C. building is reported in the *Kansan*, Jan. 10, 1941, p. 1, c. 1; March 13, 1941, p. 1, c. 5. For the mineral resources building, see the *Kansan*, Oct. 22, 1940, p. 3; April 6, 1941, pp. 1 and 3; April 25, 1941, p. 1, c. 1. The mineral resources of the state are briefly described in the booklet, *Resource-Full Kansas*, by Kenneth K. Landes and Oren R. Bingham, Lawrence, 1940. The data on wheat production in Kansas were secured from *Agricultural Statistics 1940*, U. S. Dept. of Agriculture, Washington, 1940, p. 13. The four students of 1954 who gave me their judgment on the University were Carolyn Husted, Nancy Alexander, Joyce White, and Joan Carter.

The poem by Helen Jaka will be found in the *Jayhawker*, 1923, p. 474. I have taken the liberty of adding one word to the second line and changing one word in the thirteenth line of the poem. I trust if the changes ever come to the eye of Miss Jaka that my sin will be forgiven.

The air photograph reproduced on the end sheets of *The Years on Mount Oread* was made for me by Roger H. Johnson on November 11, 1954.

Index

Notes, illustrations, and captions for illustrations, as well as the text, have been indexed. Titles of sections appear in capitals, with extra space above and below. The second number after a section title refers to the notes for that section.

215

218

219

220